Teaching What You're Not

Teaching What You're Not

Identity Politics in Higher Education

EDITED BY

Katherine J. Mayberry

New York University Press

NEW YORK AND LONDON

NEW YORK UNIVERSITY PRESS
New York and London

Library of Congress Cataloging-in-Publication Data

Teaching what you're not : identity politics in higher education /
edited by Katherine J. Mayberry
   p. cm.
Includes bibliographical references.
ISBN 0-8147-5531-3 (cl : alk. paper).—ISBN 0-8147-5547-X (pbk. : alk.
paper)
   1. College teaching—United States. 2. Education, Higher—political aspects—United States. 3. Multicultural education—
United States. 4. Identity (Psychology) I. Mayberry, Katherine
J., 1950– .
LB2331.T427 1996
378.1'25—dc20 96-9939   CIP

New York University Press books are printed on acid-free paper,
and their binding materials are chosen for strength and durability.

Manufactured in the United States of America

10 9 8 7 6 5 4 3 2 1

Contents

Acknowledgments   *ix*

1   *Introduction: Identity Politics in the College Classroom, or Whose Issue Is This, Anyway?*   *1*
     KATHERINE J. MAYBERRY

PART I   *Multiculturalist Pedagogies*

2   *Redefining America: Literature, Multiculturalism, Pedagogy*   *23*
     NANCY J. PETERSON

3   *Straight Teacher/Queer Classroom: Teaching as an Ally*   *47*
     BARBARA SCOTT WINKLER

4   *The Outsider's Gaze*   *70*
     JANET M. POWERS

5   *No Middle Ground? Men Teaching Feminism*   *85*
     J. SCOTT JOHNSON, JENNIFER
     KELLEN, GREG SEIBERT, AND
     CELIA SHAUGHNESSY

PART II   *The Class Roster*

6   *The Discipline of History and the Demands of Identity Politics*   *107*
     CHRISTIE FARNHAM

7   *Teaching What I'm Not: An Able-Bodied Woman*
    Teaches Literature by Women with Disabilities   *131*
    BARBARA DIBERNARD

8   *Theory, Practice, and the Battered (Woman) Teacher*   *155*
    CELESTE M. CONDIT

PART III   *Professorial Identities*

9   *Teaching What the Truth Compels You to Teach:*
    A Historian's View   *177*
    JACQUELINE JONES

10 *Pro/(Con)fessing Otherness: Trans(cending)national*
    Identities in the English Classroom   *195*
    LAVINA DHINGRA SHANKAR

11 *Caliban in the Classroom*   *215*
    INDIRA KARAMCHETI

12 *A Paradox of Silence: Reflections of a Man Who*
    Teaches Women's Studies   *228*
    CRAIG W. HELLER

PART IV   *The Texts and Contexts of Teaching What You're Not*

13 *Teaching in the Multiracial Classroom:*
    Reconsidering "Benito Cereno"   *241*
    ROBERT S. LEVINE

14 *"Young Man, Tell Our Stories of How We Made*
    It Over": Beyond the Politics of Identity   *259*
    GARY L. LEMONS

15 *Disciplines and Their Discomforts: The Challenges*
    of Study and Service Abroad   *285*
    GERARD ACHING

16 *Scratching Heads: The Importance of Sensitivity in*
    an Analysis of "Others"   *308*
    DONNA J. WATSON

17 *Who Holds the Mirror? Creating "the Consciousness*
    of Others"   *315*
    MARY ELIZABETH LANSER

18 Daughters of the Dust, *the White Woman*
    Viewer, and the Unborn Child   *335*
    RENÉE R. CURRY

    Contributors   *357*

    Index   *363*

Acknowledgments

A project such as this is obviously the product of a number of individuals—not only those whose names appear in the table of contents, but many who worked behind the scenes. While it is difficult to rank the credit owed, certainly a major share of the responsibility for this collection lies with Niko Pfund, editor in chief of New York University Press. Niko had the foresight and the expertise to recognize the timeliness of such an anthology as well as the energy and confidence to encourage me to take the project on.

I am deeply indebted as well to the contributors to the volume, all of whom demonstrated courage and honesty in shedding the protective covering of the scholarly persona in order to take on some hard and contentious questions. I was also fortunate in their remarkable degree of professionalism and cooperation. It is not an easy job to coordinate the efforts of eighteen overextended faculty members, but these eighteen made the job considerably easier than it might have been.

To those less visible supporters of *Teaching What You're Not*, I am immeasurably grateful. I thank Wade Robison, colleague and partner, who patiently listened to the series of struggles informing the composition of this book; Michele Burr and Judy Offen for helping me with the daunting volume of correspondence associated with a project like this; and, as always, my daughters, Carrie and Megan—my contexts in all things.

1

Introduction: Identity Politics in the College Classroom, or Whose Issue Is This, Anyway?

KATHERINE J. MAYBERRY

This collection is poised between a revolution and a counterrevolution. It emerges at a critical moment in American higher education—when the momentum of liberalization that transformed higher education in the second half of this century is decelerating in the face of conservative forces seeking their own brand of transformation by the opening of the next century. The story of the revolution begins fifty years ago, with VJ Day and the return of hundreds of thousands of GIs eager to receive their due and enter the elitist club of American higher education. Their example was followed in the 1950s, 1960s, and 1970s by veterans of Korea and Vietnam. Throughout this period, the dramatic growth of public institutions helped convert higher education from a privilege available to a few to a right accessible to all. With the victories of the civil rights movement of the 1960s and 1970s, including affirmative action legislation, the growing student population became increasingly diverse. In 1993, which may turn out to have been the watershed of university diversity, minority enrollment accounted for 26 percent of the total college and university undergraduate enrollment.[1]

Wooed and welcomed into institutions where they nevertheless remained distinctly marginal, African Americans and other minorities banded into campus communities whose badge of membership was a particular marker of "otherness"—color, accent, physical characteristics, and so forth. During this period, the term "identity" underwent a telling reconceptualization, evolving from its 1960s association with self-absorbed individualism à la Holden Caulfield to a signifier of group affiliation. Identity was no longer a personal, individuating matter, but a function of those phenomenological characteristics one shared with others. As their numbers grew on campus, minority identity groups began to articulate identity-based interests and submit identity-based demands that were, in many cases, met by administrations often unprepared to negotiate such delicate matters. The speed and effectiveness of the revolution was indeed remarkable: in the space of a generation, minority students saw those same identity markers that had always guaranteed their powerlessness and underrepresentation develop into sources of considerable influence and control. With the formation of the first black studies program in 1969 at San Francisco State University, "identity politics"—the negotiation of and for power derived from minority group affiliation—had become an operating reality within American academia.

The opening of the university to minority groups clearly set the stage for the phenomenon of identity politics. Less clear is the nature of the relationship between the rise of identity politics and the contemporaneous development of poststructuralist thought. Whether connected through causality or mere coincidence, the two movements have a good deal in common: both live, move, and have their being in the "deconstructability" of received truths, including, of course, the canon of white Western knowledge. While there are also crucial theoretical differences between the two, it is worth noting that the iconoclastic operation of identity politics found friendly soil in the irreverence of poststructuralist theory. Certainly, the simultaneous development of both projects contributed to the creation of a university climate in which knowledge, authority, and relationships are routinely exploded, politicized, or, to use a popular neologism of the 1990s, problematized.

In a setting where little was safe from interrogation, where ideologies were discovered behind every brick and ivy leaf, it was only a matter of time before white faculty—guardians of the now thoroughly problematized trinity of knowledge, authority, and tradition—were challenged. The most provocative of these challenges revolved around the issue of identity: within the last few years, minority constituencies on campus have begun to scrutinize the relationship between professors' identities (again, as determined by race, sex, ethnicity, etc.) and their claims to professional authority and expertise. This debate over identity-based credibility (teaching what you are versus teaching what you're not) is currently the most visible expression of identity politics in higher education.

Until fairly recently, there were few grounds on which a professor's authority could be impeached. Students might complain about a course's workload or a professor's teaching style, or in egregious cases about his or her professionalism (which more often involves inappropriate behavior than questionable expertise); fellow scholars might question the validity of a professor's scholarship; but for the most part, charges of pedagogical malpractice were unthinkable. The recent demographic changes in student and faculty populations, the radical revisions of canons and curricula, and the politicization of identity, knowledge, and authority have changed all this, introducing an identity-based definition of *credibility* as an entirely new precondition of professional authority.

As understood by the challengers, credibility goes beyond disciplinary expertise to include affiliational and experiential components; one is a credible professor/scholar in a particular minority studies field if one can claim origin and experience within that minority culture. The recent challenges to credibility are voiced by minority students and professors alike, and they identify a variety of pedagogical and scholarly offenses conceivable only within a context of politicized identity. Those being challenged are for the most part white men and women in the humanities and social sciences who teach and/or write about identity groups that are not only different from their own, but also historically oppressed by their own—for example, men teaching women's studies, whites teaching black studies, heterosexuals teaching queer studies, and so on.

At a time when faculty are being accused of willfully ignoring external challenges to what they do and how they do it, these internal demands for credibility have commanded their full attention. As the essays in this anthology demonstrate, faculty are not dismissing the credibility issue as an outrageous academic fad; on the contrary, they are taking it very seriously, formulating a variety of positions on the issue with fairness, intelligence, and probity. *Teaching What You're Not: Identity, Politics in Higher Education* is a collection of these positions, composed by individuals at all levels of the professoriate: prize-winning researchers, senior scholars, untenured professors, and graduate students. Written from a wide variety of identity perspectives, and in some cases impelled by firsthand experience with credibility challenges, the essays in this collection are a testament to the seriousness with which we take our teaching and the courage with which we examine and learn from critiques of our performance.

The debate over credibility and identity that this volume documents is taking place at a time when those demographic and ideological forces that have transformed American higher education in the last few decades are themselves meeting powerful challenges. With the ink barely dry on new curricula, expanded canons, and minority club charters, an educationally conservative political right is deploying its supplies of Wite-Out wherever possible. The momentum of the multicultural revolution is being counteracted by a conservative counterrevolution with a formidable momentum of its own, in large part driven by conservative lawmakers. To borrow the title of a recent book on the subject, higher education is under fire.[2]

The challenges aimed at higher education constitute a familiar litany: tuitions are too high; faculty are lazy, arrogant, unaccountable, and averse to undergraduate teaching; knowledge and truth have become the handservants of political correctness; identity is replacing expertise as a primary requirement for faculty appointments, and so on. Many of the detractors of higher education have the political, financial, and ideological wherewithal to act on these complaints: the dramatic changes in state and national legislatures resulting from the 1992 elections have placed a fiscal ax in the hands of the detractors. In perhaps the most staggering example, Republican governor George Pataki of New York proposed a $290 million reduction (31.5 percent) in the budget of the state university system (ultimately reduced by the legislature to $185.6 million).[3] At the federal level, the vote in the House of Representatives to discontinue the national endowments for the arts and humanities is only one of many sobering symptoms of the country's bad mood about higher education. The defeat of affirmative action in California demonstrates the vulnerability of the entire multicultural movement, as does the ease with which educational conservatives were able to parody the principles of multiculturalism in the political correctness debate.

In short, the American university system is on the defensive, and the current debate about identity politics is up for grabs as a weapon in the struggle. On the one hand, university critics are perfectly capable of turning it, like multiculturalism, into a caricature of itself—ludicrous measure of just how removed faculty have become from the job of educating. On the other hand, those faculty involved in the debate—and this includes those on both sides of the issue—could use it as a means of demonstrating just how seriously faculties and their universities take the job of teaching a highly heterogeneous student population. Every contributor to this volume has put the issue of identity politics to good use, in each case using it as a springboard for examining his or her own motives, qualifications, and goals as teachers and as scholars. The image of the professoriate that emerges from these essays powerfully belies the negative image currently circulated by its critics.

One might expect a certain degree of defensiveness on the part of those faculty whose credibility has been challenged. Surely for many "majority" faculty, the charges electrifying the air of "minority" studies touch a nerve much more sensitive than that of *professional* credibility. For those of us whose liberal political consciousness developed during the same period that incubated multiculturalism and identity politics, it is discomfiting to find ourselves identified as "them" in an "us versus them" scenario. The dissonance between our self-image as committed, card-carrying intellectual liberals and the challengers' view of us as underqualified cultural colonizers begs for resolution. In part, our responses to these challenges become the processes through which we resolve this clamoring dissonance.

But the essays in this volume are about far more than self-justification and conscience stroking: the issue—in some cases realized in painful personal confrontations—has driven all the contributors, and many more besides, to step back from their podium and ponder the teaching role, to reconsider and in some cases redefine the goals, methods, and informing ideological assumptions of undergraduate teaching. If for no other reason, the current debate over identity politics is momentous because it has elicited this attention to the business of teaching.

While identity politics may seem an unlikely catalyst for pedagogical review, it becomes quickly apparent to anyone interested in entering the debate that all responsible arguments must work from a clear identification of what one hopes to achieve through teaching and what methods are most likely to effect these goals. These do not sound like revolutionary questions, yet too few of us—trained as disciplinary scholars rather than educators—have seriously entertained them. Higher education is fortunate in its rich resource of dedicated professors, yet many of the most dedicated have neglected to subject their teaching to the same interrogations that have so dramatically altered what they teach and to whom. To reiterate a crucial point: the current challenges to credibility are important to all of us because they contain those interrogations and require us to review our personal missions as educators.

The essays in this anthology are written from a wide variety of identity interfaces: an African American man teaching feminist theory; white men teaching women's studies; a straight woman teaching lesbigay material; white women teaching and writing about African American history; an able-bodied woman teaching literature by women with disabilities. The positions, strategies, and arguments communicated in the essays are equally varied, as well as enormously rich and comprehensive. As the anthology editor, I am grateful for this richness, but it does make the job of organizing the essays a challenging one and any principle of organization inevitably arbitrary. A reasonable model of classification is implied in the grammar of the anthology's title—*Teaching What You're Not.* The phrase implies at least four questions: (1) what does *teaching* consist of? (2) *who* is doing the teaching? (3) *what* is being taught? and (4) *who* is being taught? Virtually all the essays address all these questions in some way, but with varying emphases; it is according to the emphases that the essays are grouped.

The essays in the volume's first part, "Multiculturalist Pedagogies," report a variety of pedagogical strategies developed by professors teaching a multicultural canon in a multicultural classroom. These essays allow us to observe how and to what end a progressive (or to use bell hooks's phrase, "transgressive"[4]) pedagogy emerges from classrooms in which identities are mixed in some way. They demonstrate as well how the multicultural classroom and canon have expanded not only the objects of intellectual inquiry but also the skills and methods taught in traditional liberal arts courses. Indeed, for each writer, the subject matter of the course is as much a means as an end—a tool through which certain widely applicable skills and perspectives can be developed. For Nancy J. Peterson, teaching American literature means more than teaching a particular set of literary texts and a particular critical idiom; it must aim as well to develop in students a multicultural perspective from which they can cooperate across divisive identity lines to effect social justice. Like most of the contributors to this volume, Peterson unblinkingly accepts the inevitable entanglement of teaching and advocacy. She teaches the skills of literary analysis not merely as tools for unpacking some transcendent textual meaning, but as methods of interrogation revealing the ideological foundation of representation—literary and otherwise. As Peterson's experience teaching a Toni Morrison course demonstrates, students are most likely to develop this perspective and these skills within a classroom that is a "learning community," where dialogue replaces monologue.

Working within a very different disciplinary and identity context, Barbara Scott Winkler is also concerned with building classroom community as a means of achieving a "transformation of consciousness" within her students. Winkler reports the strategies and methodologies she uses when teaching classes with a significant lesbigay component, both in content and in student population. Importing the feminist activist concepts of "coalition and alliance building" into her teaching practice, Winkler demonstrates a pedagogical resourcefulness that is necessary to any teacher faced with the challenges of identity politics; Winkler's essay is the first of many in this volume to demonstrate how the unprecedented circumstances of the contemporary college classroom are requiring faculty to look to unfamiliar disciplines and practices for suggestions about negotiating its complexities.

This resourcefulness is demonstrated as well by Janet M. Powers, who borrows methodologies far removed from literary study to help her maneuver in multicultural literature classes. Uncertain about her own motives for teaching what she is not, Powers is disturbed by the likelihood that her students will be influenced by her mode of "gazing at skin, language, habits of conversation, music, ways of relating that are different from my own." By resorting to ethnographic theory and practice in her classes, Powers believes she has at least partially mitigated the polarization of identities inevitable in multicultural classes.

The fourth essay in part 1 is a joint project written by a male professor of political science and three of his students (two women and a man) in a feminist political theory course. Challenged by students and colleagues alike for teaching a feminist theory course, J. Scott Johnson argues that professorial identity is no more or less an issue in feminist courses than in any other course. The purpose of his political theory course was not to enable a particular perspective capable of drawing certain political conclusions, but rather to model a set of skills that would allow his students to make reasoned judgments about the strengths and weaknesses of feminism in general and of specific feminist theories in particular. That Johnson achieved this goal is enviably demonstrated by one student's statement that "by the end of the semester, I understood and could defend exactly what I believed in." Like theater director Tyrone Guthrie, Johnson sees his teaching role as that of an "audience of one" who reflects student input in order to encourage students to evaluate and refine their own thinking. The student contributions to the essay, which describe Johnson's teaching method and reflect the independent thinking it fostered, are a testament to just how thoroughly the cooperative method succeeded—developing not only the skills of critical thinking, but also defusing the initially troubling issue of professorial identity.

The essays grouped within part 2, "The Class Roster," identify a consideration that is crucial to the current debate surrounding identity and teaching: a reasonable, defensible argument for or against teaching what you're not must take into account the question of *who* is being taught. These essays remind us of the numerous differences that exist in student populations—both within a particular class and, more generally, from institution to institution. These differences are definable not only in terms of color, culture, and gender, but also in terms of aptitude, education, class, values, political sophistication, and so forth. To assume a monolithic student body is to risk a useless because absolutist resolution to the debate. Put another way, pedagogical strategies that might work perfectly well in one classroom or one institution could be utter failures in a different class or institution.

Christie Farnham relates a hair-raising instance of classroom identity collision set in motion by the strong political and religious views of some of her students. Farnham's teaching of an African American history course at Iowa State University was repeatedly challenged by black students calling for a more Afrocentrist perspective. Convinced that Afrocentric history does not always meet historiographical standards, Farnham was unwilling to represent it as historical fact in her classes, despite aggressive student demands for its inclusion. In a situation that quickly escalated into an example of identity politics at their most extreme, Farnham's teaching was publicly excoriated by her detractors as alternately racist and incompetent. What Farnham's experience demonstrates is that "not all problems arising out of teaching what you are not—in this case, being a white woman teaching black history—can be reduced to pedagogy or personalities." Farnham's insistence on conforming to the standards of her academic discipline when determining what and what not to teach raises some provocative questions about the origins and functions of disciplinary authority. Her position also constitutes an interesting counterpoint to the broader-based pedagogical practices represented in some of the preceding essays.

Barbara DiBernard, an English professor and director of a women's studies program, has had striking evidence of just how variable the most seemingly homogeneous student populations can be. She opens her essay with an account of an epiphanic experience in a women's literature class that can serve as a cautionary tale for all faculty about the complex identities of every one of our students. Like many essayists in this anthology, her practical classroom experience makes her wary of the essentialist assumptions implicit in identity politics. In her teaching of literature by disabled women, she has become acutely aware of the arbitrariness of most identity markers; yet at the same time she realizes that in order to be a "political ally" of disabled women, she must agree to inhabit the position of "able-bodied" and to think in terms of polarized identities.

Celeste M. Condit's essay reminds us of yet another way a given student population can complicate a professor's teaching practice. In her discussion of teaching communication courses to undergraduates at the University of Georgia, Condit inserts a sobering reality check into the conversation about enabling, student-centered pedagogy. For Condit, whose communication classes consist of significant numbers of white Southern men, the problems of teaching *who* she is not are not mitigated by the application of progressive teaching styles. To cede authority completely by becoming a participant-observer or audience of one would put her hopelessly at the mercy of students who, in her experience, "are not sheep that we decide to teach 'actively' or 'passively.' . . . [but] highly motivated, highly skilled, and enormously self-interested people who . . . intend to minimize the pain we cause them, and sometimes to maximize the pain they inflict on us." Condit's experience of classroom politics may, as she observes, be a function of the differences between a professor's goals in teaching a course and those of her students in taking it. More fundamentally, her unhappy experience at the University of Georgia is an instance of a gender politics in which the woman—even if she is the professor—will always be the loser.

Part 3, "Professorial Identities," reflects a variety of perspectives on the issue of the relationship between a *professor's* identity and the material that he or she teaches.

Accustomed to having her scholarship challenged on the basis of

her racial identity, Jacqueline Jones, noted historian in the area of
African American women's history, takes the uncompromising position that the single most important qualification for any professor in
any field is expertise: "Whenever anyone expresses doubts about my
work as a white woman writing African American history, I reply . . .
'Let's begin the discussion with my footnotes, and go on from
there.' " Jones goes on to point out the political risks of assigning or
selecting scholarly and teaching specialties on the basis of narrowly
defined identity, pointing to the decidedly negative consequences of
the tradition in history of "white men of property and privilege . . .
writing about . . . white men of property and privilege."

The next two essays pick up Jones's point about the practical and
ideological consequences of identity-determined teaching and scholarship from a very different vantage point. Lavina Dhingra Shankar,
after persuasively arguing the enormous complexities of personal
identity, speaks to the professional straitjacket that many "minority"
faculty are forced to wear in a multicultural university. Despite her
decidedly Western(ized) education, Shankar's "postcolonial identity"
has dictated her curricular affiliation as much as, if not more than,
her professional interests and training. As Shankar puts it, "some are
born with identities, others have identities thrust on them."

Indira Karamcheti, English professor at Wesleyan University, is
also concerned about the commodification of identity in the multicultural university. As a member of a non-American ethnic group teaching primarily white American students, Karamcheti has always been
different from the students she teaches. As with many of the white
faculty contributing to this volume, the challenges that have been
posed to Karamcheti's professional authority are a function of the
phenomenological mismatch between her and her students; yet in her
case, the grounds for those challenges have more to do with old-
fashioned racism than contemporary identity politics. Karamcheti includes a number of passages from student papers that demonstrate
the double bind of "non-Caucasian" teachers, who must contend

with, on the one hand, students' low expectations of their ability to teach authoritatively, and on the other, students' equally reflexive tendency to abandon all reasonable standards of judgment once they recognize that these teachers are not "handicapped" by their ethnicity. Both Shankar's and Karamcheti's careers have provided ample evidence of the limitations that the American academy places on the pedagogical strategies and scholarly preferences of the minority teacher.

The final essay in part 3 returns us to the site of a women's studies class taught by a white male professor. Craig W. Heller's essay is concerned with the excess of authority automatically conferred by his positions as white male and professor. "How contradictory is it," Heller asks, "that I may be convincing students of the viability of a feminist message by, at least in some part, fulfilling the patriarchal expectations that many students have of male teachers?" Heller's hope is that the tension between his positionality and his pedagogical goals can be resolved by a pedagogical strategy of silence, absence, and invisibility, but he also recognizes that his "hands-off" approach is capable of sabotaging his goals every bit as much as a more authoritative style.

Part 4, "The Texts and Contexts of Teaching What You're Not," focuses very directly on the "what" of teaching what you're not. Each of these essays presents in considerable detail the use to which a particular text or disciplinary context can be put in classrooms where identity is an issue. In their concentration on specific contexts, some of these essays offer a case study approach to the issue that reflects in each instance significant learning on the part of the professor as well as the students. Robert S. Levine, professor of English at the University of Maryland, opens this part with a career-long overview of his teaching of Herman Melville's novella "Benito Cereno" to shifting student populations. Levine's essay is as good a defense of faculty seriousness about teaching as any of us could wish for; his account of a twenty-year struggle with "a recalcitrant text (and students)" provides not only a "concrete account of the implications of the curricular, pedagogical, and demographic changes" in the academy, but also a testament to the willingness of faculty to adjust to these sweeping changes.

Gary L. Lemons contextualizes his teaching strategies in a course called Redefining Womanhood: (Re)writing the Black Female Self within a short story by Audre Lorde called "Tar Beach." Lemons's course is explicitly political in its aim, which is to teach students "how to interrogate and critically oppose the capitalist, racist, sexist exploitation of women." Since his own intersecting positionalities as black, male, feminist, and professor can complicate or undermine the achievement of this goal, he has developed a pedagogy and a reading list intended to be liberating for both student and professor. By concentrating on Lorde's erotic story of lesbian union, Lemons seeks to destabilize certain limiting and generalized constructs of race, gender, and sexuality—a destabilization that not only enriches the class's view of womanhood, but also challenges their suspicions about their black, male professor self-identifying as feminist. In this course, Lemons manages to convert what might begin as the liabilities of his own identities into vehicles for achieving his liberatory aim. His essay and his courses are not about teaching what he is not, but, as he puts it *"teaching what I am*—an advocate of a feminist movement in which women *and men* . . . struggle to end sexual oppression."

The third essay in part 4, written by Gerard Aching, a member of a Spanish and Portuguese department, combines a theoretical argument for the substitution of *practice* for identity as the defining component of credibility, with a contextualization of this new definition. Aching agrees that the "identity-based definition of credibility can be misleading and essentialist in a debilitating and counterproductive manner" and proposes that credibility be understood as "an area and range of competitive practices or strategies," not as a function of race, gender, or ethnicity. The potential productiveness of transgressing identity lines and disciplinary specializations is demonstrated within his account of student experiences in a study and service abroad program.

Donna J. Watson's essay offers the perspective, not of teacher, scholar, or student, but of black woman writer whose texts might become the object of "alien" scrutiny in a classroom or professional conference. Watson's essay is not an argument for or against teaching or criticizing what you're not; rather, it is a powerful representation of what writing and written texts signify within the black female culture. Her contextualization of black women's writing within a history of silence, oppression, fear, and paralysis reflects the importance of black women's texts to black women writers and readers. Watson does not subscribe to the ownership school of literary studies, but she does recommend that any academic writer (or, by implication, teacher) remember and be sensitive to the context within which black women's writing is created and read.

Mary Elizabeth Lanser's essay also contextualizes a resolution to the identity/credibility debate—not by citing a discussion of her teaching within a certain text, but rather by inserting the historical and political context of black studies into the discussion. Lanser insists that "it is virtually impossible to comprehend the territoriality that has developed among black scholars in black studies" without understanding "the roots of black studies as both an intellectual pursuit *and a way of life*" (emphasis added). The context Lanser provides is critical to a full understanding of the exclusionary position held by some minority scholars. In Lanser's case, this context does not weaken her career-long commitment to teaching black studies, but it does put into relief the passions, energies, and principles that drive this commitment.

The text under review in Renée R. Curry's essay is Julie Dash's influential film *Daughters of the Dust* (1992). Curry uses her viewing of this film by an African American woman about African American women as a way of demonstrating the disadvantages a white woman brings to reading or viewing material emerging from a culture not her own. She recognizes that her own deafness to the historical, cultural, and semiotic resonances impoverish her viewing of the film. Yet she does not conclude that for this reason black texts should be the province of black women. Instead, she invites white scholars to use the reading (viewing) of texts by others to "undertake a spiritual as well as an intellectual and emotional transformation," which must involve their naming, witnessing, and accounting for their whiteness in the same way that they account for other politicized identities. Curry concludes that such meetings between white viewer and black text must continue so that all of us can grow "older, wiser, and stronger through our interconnected pasts, presents, and futures."

As members of the higher education community engage in the debate about identity and credibility, it is important that we remember the uneasy context within which this debate is taking place. The university is unquestionably under examination by those who, while perhaps lacking sound judgment, have a plentiful supply of political muscle and public support with which to act on these judgments. Axiomatic to any discussion of the future of higher education is the certainty that whether propelled from within or without, fundamental changes are going to be made to the enterprise of higher education—and sooner rather than later. Clearly, a target for change, if not extinction, is the entire multicultural project, which is threatened by economic exigencies as well as ideological disapproval. On the one hand, increasing tuition rates at private and public institutions and decreasing availability of state and federal aid are threatening to push access to a college education out of the reach of low- and even middle-income students. On the other, by caricaturing the curricular and canonical revisions of multiculturalism, conservative forces both on and off campus are moving the university ever closer to its earlier mission of teaching the dominant class all about itself and its sustaining ideology. Given this context, it is important to foresee any implications of the identity/credibility debate that could be used as canon fodder by those whom Bob Levine refers to as "the monocultural polemicists." In closing this introduction, I would like to identify three of those possible implications.

The first of these involves the issue of essentialism. A number of essays in this volume address the identity-based challenges to faculty credibility by complicating the concept of identity, demonstrating convincingly that identity consists of uncountable characteristics, not simply phenomenological markers. The point is indisputable, yet we should be wary of the direction in which it might ultimately be taken. If identity is finally vastly more complicated than one's race or sexual preference or gender, then those very markers that have commanded for underrepresented groups the attention and support of the modern university could be deemed irrelevant. The gains that have been achieved through the multiculturalist project depend on a broadly generalized definition of identity, which must at some level be perpetuated if these gains are to continue. We cannot afford to problematize identity out of existence until these gains include a completely equitable society.

A second concern both implied and stated within this volume is the question of professional expertise. Minority studies (which include, for example, women's studies, African American studies, postcolonial studies, lesbigay studies, etc.) are comparatively young interdisciplinary fields—indeed, younger than many university faculty. When we add to this that graduate programs in them are few and far between, we begin to understand why so many faculty gravitate toward these fields after their formal training is completed. In order for these departments to be accorded the institutional support necessary to their survival and growth, they must operate with the same intellectual rigor common in more traditional departments. There are many, many reasons why a white scholar should become interested in African American studies, for example, but none of those reasons constitutes a qualification. These fields have developed the reputation of "anybody-can-play pick-up game[s]," to use Ann duCille's rather chilling phrase,[5] which will have the effect of undermining the fields themselves as well as *all* the faculty who teach them—both qualified and unqualified. If credibility is the issue here, then we must understand that whatever else it may signify, credibility always assumes doing your homework, however variously that homework may be defined from specialization to specialization.

A final concern is the absence of essays that emphatically defend an identity-based definition of credibility. The "call for papers" soliciting submissions invited essays representing both sides of the debate. Having had my own credibility challenged at a major conference, I was well aware that there are many voices in the academy capable of voicing compelling arguments in support of "teaching what you are." Surprisingly (at least to me), while this volume received a flood of submissions, very few of them advanced such arguments. Those who are particularly defensive about having their credibility impugned might use this fact as an indication that, finally, when the chips are down, there is no reasoned, defensible support of a position that is often expressed spontaneously and emotionally (as in my conference experience), or naively by undergraduates who lack the intellectual sophistication to see its full implications. But I would raise a more troubling possibility, which is that the arguments are there, but those faculty, many of whom are members of minority groups and hold junior, untenured positions, do not feel safe publicly advancing what are unquestionably unpopular views. When, in response to my experience at the women's studies conference, I wrote a piece for the *Chronicle of Higher Education*[6] that called for greater understanding and sensitivity on the part of white scholars working in African American studies, the responses (which were numerous) were both surprising and disturbing. They were evenly divided between those who disagreed with my conciliatory stance (some quite vigorously) and those who supported my attempt to understand the position of my challengers. Those in the former camp were almost exclusively white, those in the latter, African American. Most interesting (and troubling), the disagreements took the form of published letters to the *Chronicle*; the agreements (and there were many over a period of six weeks or so) were communicated to me privately by telephone and letter. One hopes that this striking segregation of response is not evidence of how effectively a still hierarchical academic system can silence minority views, of how impotent identity politics finally are.

NOTES

1. *Chronicle of Higher Education,* almanac issue, 1 Sept. 1995, 14. "Minorities" include American Indian, Asian, black, Hispanic, and foreign students.
2. Michael Bérubé and Cary Nelson, eds., *Higher Education under Fire: Politics, Economics, and the Crisis of the Humanities* (New York: Routledge, 1995).
3. *Chronicle of Higher Education,* almanac issue, 1 Sept. 1995, 80.
4. bell hooks, *Teaching to Transgress: Education as the Practice of Freedom* (New York: Routledge, 1994).
5. Ann duCille, "The Occult of True Black Womanhood: Critical Demeanor and Black Feminist Studies," *Signs: Journal of Women in Culture and Society* 19 (spring 1994): 603.
6. Katherine J. Mayberry, "White Feminists Who Study Black Writers," *Chronicle of Higher Education,* 12 Oct. 1994, A48.

BIBLIOGRAPHY

Bérubé, Michael, and Cary Nelson, eds. *Higher Education under Fire: Politics, Economics, and the Crisis of the Humanities.* New York: Routledge, 1995.
Chronicle of Higher Education, almanac issue, 1 Sept. 1995.
duCille, Ann. "The Occult of True Black Womanhood: Critical Demeanor and Black Feminist Studies." *Signs: Journal of Women in Culture and Society* 19 (spring 1994): 591–629.
hooks, bell. *Teaching to Transgress: Education as the Practice of Freedom.* New York: Routledge, 1994.
Mayberry, Katherine J. "White Feminists Who Study Black Writers." *Chronicle of Higher Education,* 12 Oct. 1994, A48.

I

Multiculturalist Pedagogies

2

Redefining America: Literature, Multiculturalism, Pedagogy

NANCY J. PETERSON

In *Teaching to Transgress* (1994), bell hooks tries to stake out some middle ground on the issue of whether or not a teacher's identity ideally ought to correspond to the "identity" of a given subject or text. She writes,

> Though opposed to any essentialist practice that constructs identity in a monolithic, exclusionary way, I do not want to relinquish the power of experience as a standpoint on which to base analysis or formulate theory. For example, I am disturbed when all the courses on black history or literature at some colleges and universities are taught solely by white people, not because I think that they cannot know these realities but that they know them differently. Truthfully, if I had been given the opportunity to study African American critical thought from a progressive black professor instead of the progressive white woman with whom I studied as a first-year student, I would have chosen the black person. Although I learned a great deal from this white woman professor, I sincerely believe that I would have learned even more from a progressive black professor, because this individual would have brought to the class that unique mixture of experiential and analytical ways of knowing—that is, a privileged standpoint. It cannot be acquired through books or even distanced observation and study of a particular reality. To me this privileged standpoint does not emerge from the "authority of experience" but rather from the passion of experience, the passion of remembrance.[1]

I have quoted this passage at length because hooks is very careful here to explain her position: she acknowledges that white professors can successfully teach black history or literature if they do their homework (through books, observation, study), but she also asserts that the ideal situation is for black professors to teach black history and literature to black students. I think most of us would agree with hooks that the position of white scholars and black scholars regarding this subject matter is necessarily different: most black scholars probably do have a kind of engagement, a personal passion for the subject matter that would give them the "privileged standpoint" that hooks speaks of.

Looking more closely at hooks's wording here, though, I think it is important to note some significant qualifications in her remarks. First of all, she describes the ideal teacher as "a *progressive* black professor" (emphasis added), subtly recognizing that racial identity does not ensure that an individual black professor will be politically progressive.[2] The question might arise, then, of how to judge between a conservative black professor and a progressive white professor: who would be the ideal teacher in this pairing? Also, hooks's argument hinges on who would be the ideal teacher for black students, such as herself, which raises related questions: if all or most of the students are white, is the ideal teacher still someone who is black? Or what should be the case if the students and teacher are black but the subject matter is literature written by whites? Furthermore, hooks's remarks assume that in most universities there is only one person who specializes in black literature or history, which means that the identity and engagement of the professor teaching the subject matter become even more crucial. But an even more ideal situation, to my mind at least, is a university setting that allows for more than one professor to be invested in black literature or history so that white and black students could be exposed to analyses of race (gender, class, and so on) from more than one perspective, so that race does not come to be seen as the responsibility of blacks alone.

The separatism that seems inevitably inherent in the arguments for identity politics troubles me. While I agree with hooks that every university ought to have black faculty members who work on black sociology, history, literature, and so forth, and I remain adamantly committed to the need for institutional safeguards concerning the hiring, retention, and promotion of minority faculty,[3] I am also suspicious of recent policing strategies designed to discourage white scholars from teaching or publishing on African American literature.[4] The concern of black feminists regarding the co-optation of black women's literature is understandable and necessary. hooks argues for working toward a space of sisterhood between white and black women, while also noting that "[i]t seems at times as though white feminists working in the academy have appropriated discussions of race and racism." Specifically, hooks finds objectionable the fact that a focus on race almost always means a focus on *blackness* and not a focus on *whiteness:*

> Curiously, most white women writing feminist theory that looks at "difference" and "diversity" do not make white women's lives, works, and experiences the subject of their analysis of "race," but rather focus on black women or women of color. White women who have yet to get a critical handle on the meaning of "whiteness" in their lives, the representation of whiteness in their literature or the white supremacy that shapes their social status are now explicating blackness without critically questioning whether their work emerges from an aware anti-racist standpoint. Drawing on the work of black women, work that they once dismissed as irrelevant, they now reproduce the servant-served paradigms in their scholarship.[5]

It is no small irony that the intensive interest of white feminists such as myself in issues of race and racism was sparked by the brave black feminists of the 1970s and 1980s who spoke out about racism in the women's movement, who made us aware of how much it was a white middle-class women's movement. Because of the important 1982 collection on black women's studies edited by Gloria Hull, Patricia Bell-Scott, and Barbara Smith, as well as the work of writers like Audre Lorde and Alice Walker, to name just two, white feminists were forced to do some searing soul-searching.[6] One bittersweet measure of the success of these black feminists is the situation we have today in the 1990s, where black feminist scholars feel uneasy about the number of white women focusing on African American literature. I want to underscore hooks's judicious stance on this issue: even as she suggests that white women ought to focus on the meanings of whiteness, hooks also sees the potential for white women to produce work "from an aware antiracist standpoint."[7]

Extremely significant scholarship that crosses identity lines is already being produced. One of the most profound analyses of whiteness in literature, for instance, is Toni Morrison's *Playing in the Dark: Whiteness and the Literary Imagination.*[8] Morrison breaks the mold for previous analyses of black characters in literary texts authored by whites: rather than seeing black characters as mere decoration or offensive stereotype in such texts, Morrison argues that these characters reflect significant anxieties, desires, and dilemmas that white American culture cannot articulate directly. What I find inspiring about Morrison's book is that she avoids racial separatism: first, by being a black woman writing about whiteness, and second, by arguing that issues of black and white American identity are inextricably intertwined. At the same time, Morrison's approach does not allow white Americans who displace their own anxieties onto African Americans off the hook. *Playing in the Dark* is an exemplary model of scholarship that articulates a painful relationship in such a way that racial divides can be crossed.

Another work that has been particularly influential is Gloria Anzaldúa's *Borderlands/La Frontera: The New Mestiza.* Examining her own identity in this mixed-genre text (encompassing autobiography, theory, essays, and poems), Anzaldúa realizes she must create a new model for herself, a model that can allow all her multiple allegiances to come to voice: being Chicana in an Anglo-controlled country; being feminist in a male-dominated world; being lesbian in a homophobic society; being a poet in an economy that devalues such labor; being a Spanish, Spanglish, Tex-Mex speaker in an English-first culture; and

so on. In articulating these identities, Anzaldúa's text powerfully requires readers to move beyond fixed, simplistic concepts of identity
politics. Furthermore, although Anzaldúa acknowledges the incredi-
ble traumas of being marginalized in these various ways, she ends up
turning this situation into an empowering position in her concepts of
la mestiza and the borderlands. She describes and enacts this situation
of being at the crossroads of various identities and cultures in a poem
called "To live in the Borderlands means you," where the title leads
directly into the first lines:

> are neither *hispana india negra española ni gabacha, eres mestiza,*
> *mulata,*
> half-breed caught in the crossfire between camps while carrying
> all five races
> on your back not knowing which side to turn to, run from.[9]

A poem a few pages later develops the positive aspects of this
ambiguous multiplicity. Addressed to her niece, Missy Anzaldúa,
"Don't Give in *Chicanita*" is a poem of encouragement, which ends
with a look at the future for *mestizas:*

> Perhaps we'll be dying of hunger as usual
> but we'll be members of a new species
> skin tone between black and bronze
> second eyelid under the first
> with the power to look at the sun through naked
>   eyes.
> And alive *m'ijita,* very much alive.
>
> Yes, in a few years or centuries
> la Raza will rise up, tongue intact
> carrying the best of all the cultures.[10]

But in Anzaldúa's view, it is not only Chicanos or women of color
who will be able to evolve into this new species. Elsewhere she argues
that "[l]umping the males who deviate from the general norm with

man, the oppressor, is a gross injustice," and she asserts that "we [people of color] need to allow whites to be our allies."[11] Using texts such as Anzaldúa's as a guide, progressive people can learn to build bridges across racial—and other—divides.

Learning to build bridges is the principle that has guided my approach to teaching American literature from a multicultural standpoint. I teach American literature at a state university in the Midwest whose student body is predominantly white and generally conservative. We offer courses in African American literature specifically, as well as more general courses in American literature. One of my goals for teaching American literature to undergraduates has been to give them the sense that American literature has been and continues to be written by a fascinating range of authors (for example, I always include African American and Native American literature in the typical undergraduate American literature survey course, and I also attend to considerations of gender, class, and sexual difference).[12] Sometimes I have a class composed of undergraduates who are afraid that they will know nothing about the "canon" if they take my course, so on the first day I point out the various "great" authors on the syllabus and then "sell" students on the fact that in my section they will also read some remarkable texts that scholars have recently (re)discovered. By presenting the syllabus in this way, I introduce the idea of fluid and shifting definitions of "American" and "literature." This is strategic, because I consider the representation of American literature on my syllabus to be one significant way I can influence my students' ideas of what an American is and what kind of country America might be. As Mario T. Garcia has written, "We have always possessed a multiracial, multiethnic, and multicultural society," and I try to enable my students to recognize this alternative vision of America.[13] Moreover, I hope that my syllabus and class will challenge my students' often narrow visions of normativity along the lines that African American historian Elsa Barkley Brown has described:

How do our students overcome years of notions of what is normative? While trying to think about these issues in my teaching, I have come to understand that this is not merely an intellectual process. It is not merely a question of whether or not we have learned to analyze in particular kinds of ways, or whether people are able to intellectualize about a variety of experiences. It is also about coming to believe in the possibility of a variety of experiences, a variety of ways of understanding the world, a variety of frameworks of operation, without imposing consciously or unconsciously a notion of the norm. What I have tried to do in my own teaching is to address both the conscious level, through the material, and the unconscious level, through the very structure of the course, thus, perhaps, allowing my students, in Bettina Apthekar's words, to "pivot the center," to center in another experience.[14]

Trying to teach the literature of a multicultural America places me in the problematic position of speaking about experiences I have not had: I speak about Native America, for instance, when I teach Zitkala-Sa's autobiographical essays, and I speak about black America when I teach Langston Hughes. I also speak about white America when I teach *As I Lay Dying*, and I speak about lesbians when I teach Adrienne Rich's poetry. In the debates about who is entitled to publish articles about and teach African American literature I have been struck by the fact that these identity-centered arguments have not been applied more broadly to all texts. Why does no one question my ability to teach Faulkner, even though I have never been to Mississippi and am certainly not a white male? Should I be allowed to teach any literary text that does not reflect my own (white/feminist/middle-class/heterosexual) background and experience? What an impossible situation we would work ourselves into if we took the identity argument to its logical conclusion.

And yet I do not want to dismiss the problem of speaking about and speaking for. Although most progressive white feminists would claim to speak *about* rather than for experiences of people of color that we have not had, I am skeptical about the usefulness of this distinction. In some part, the distinction offers us a palliative, becomes a sign that we have interrogated our own privilege and have now arrived at a nonimperialist position regarding such material. But feminist philosopher Linda Alcoff compellingly deconstructs this distinction, arguing that

> when one is speaking for others one may be describing their situation and thus also speaking about them. In fact, it may be impossible to speak for others without simultaneously conferring information about them. Similarly, when one is speaking about others, or simply trying to describe their situation or some aspect of it, one may also be speaking in place of them, that is, speaking for them. One may be speaking about others as an advocate or a messenger if the persons cannot speak for themselves. Thus I would maintain that if the practice of speaking for others is problematic, so too must be the practice of speaking about others, since it is difficult to distinguish speaking about from speaking for in all cases.[15]

Alcoff's analysis moves us to a position where we must acknowledge that even speaking about experiences we have not had is a potentially dangerous situation fraught with the possibility of committing what Alcoff terms "discursive imperialism" or "discursive violence." In the face of these dangers, progressive white feminists might decide that silence is the only ethical stance to take. But even as she underscores the necessity of considering this option, Alcoff calls it into question: the retreat into silence, first of all, "significantly undercuts the possibility of political effectivity" because it "allows the continued dominance of current discourses and acts by omission to reinforce their dominance."[16] Furthermore, Alcoff points out that a retreat into silence may be a kind of cop-out, "motivated by a desire to find a method or practice immune from criticism" or motivated by "a desire for personal mastery, to establish a privileged discursive position wherein one cannot be undermined or challenged and thus is master of the situation."[17] Clearly, then, silence as a strategy is not necessarily politically efficacious or morally defensible.

Alcoff goes on to propose a double strategy to address the problems of speaking for/about and not speaking at all. Influenced by Gayatri

Spivak's work on the subaltern, Alcoff advocates first of all that we "strive to create wherever possible the conditions for dialogue and the practice of speaking with and to rather than speaking for others."[18] Following such a principle, as I see it, might entail reshaping teaching assignments so that classes in race, gender, and sexuality could be team-taught by professors of different positionality. Or it might mean following hooks's example of enacting an ethic of dialogue in conversational essays; she crosses differences and builds bridges between them in her dialogues with Cornel West, Mary Childers, and Ron Scapp.[19] The possibilities of speaking with and to have as yet been undeveloped, so Alcoff pragmatically addresses ways to lessen the dangers of speaking for: first, "the impetus to speak must be carefully analyzed and, in many cases (certainly for academics!), fought against."[20] Alcoff's point here is not to advocate a retreat into the silence that she deconstructs earlier in her essay, but to allow the time and space for a critical interrogation of our location, the context of our speaking, our openness to constructive criticism. The most significant thing to consider, however, is the effects of speaking for: "will it enable the empowerment of oppressed peoples?" is the question Alcoff formulates.[21] Although syntactically simple, this question introduces a complex framework by which progressive white feminists can consider seriously when our desire to speak for less privileged people might be appropriate and politically effective.

Part of my investment in teaching what I am not is to motivate students to be interested in the many parts of America that may not have any direct relation to their own lives. One of the reasons I continue to be passionately engaged in teaching American literature is that books allow us access to aspects of experience and history that might otherwise be unavailable to us. In my American literature classes, I try to use the texts to engage students with conflicting and competing ideas of Americanness and to envision an America in which it is possible to dialogue across differences. I have to admit that I cannot answer Alcoff's challenging question with a resounding yes concerning my American literature courses, but I would claim that if my courses help explode my students' concepts of normativity, then they might create the conditions under which students could begin to see themselves as willing to engage in practices that would undermine systems of inequality and privilege.[22]

I have found in my own classroom, in fact, that it is sometimes very productive for me not to be the same identity as a given text. I teach Adrienne Rich's work in both American literature and women's literature classes. The American literature undergraduate survey attracts mostly white, middle-class students from a wide range of backgrounds; many of them are disconcerted by class discussions that veer from analyzing technique, character development, patterns of imagery, foreshadowing, and so on. Introducing a productive discussion of lesbianism into such a context can be risky. I have found that students have even a great deal of difficulty saying the word "lesbian" in our discussions of Rich—often using the less-forbidden term "feminist" instead. As I do when I teach American Indian texts or African American literature, I have tried to be self-conscious regarding my own difference in positionality when I prepare to teach Rich. In fact, I used to focus on trying to foresee the ways my heterosexuality inevitably distorted Rich's ideas and words. I don't dwell solely on my negative qualifications anymore, though, because of a fortuitous accident. I taught Rich's work one semester when I was in the last trimester of pregnancy; for the first time, more than half my class at the end of the semester pointed to Rich as the one author who should definitely remain on the syllabus, and almost all the students could at least write—if not speak—the word "lesbian" by the end of the semester. As I have since analyzed this situation, I have concluded that my visible pregnancy signified to my undergraduates that I was not a lesbian; maybe even some of them typed me as a "family values" kind of person just like "normal" Americans.[23] On the one hand, someone might argue that I inevitably neutralized the subject matter by being heterosexual, that in order to teach such a radical challenge to what Rich calls "compulsory heterosexuality," I too must be outside the system of heterosexuality. On the other hand, because I was teaching material that the students did not identify me with, I was able to model for them what all of us—not just lesbians—might learn from reading Rich and her critical views of heterosexism. They, I hope, began the work of confronting their own homophobia by first allowing that "normal" people such as myself resist it.

By taking this position, I am not suggesting in any way that I can teach lesbian and gay literature better than or from the same point of engaged experience as a lesbian or gay scholar; what I am claiming is the possibility of *joining* in the struggle against heterosexism. I find Rich's widely debated idea of the "lesbian continuum," introduced in her influential essay "Compulsory Heterosexuality and Lesbian Existence" (1980), helpful in making a space for such an alliance. In this essay, Rich distinguishes between "lesbian existence"—identified with women who desire "genital sexual experience with another woman"—and the "lesbian continuum"—which includes "a range . . . of woman-identified experience." Rich eloquently explains why she insists on such a broad view: by

> embrac[ing] many more forms of primary intensity between and among women, including the sharing of a rich inner life, the bonding against male tyranny, the giving and receiving of practical and political support . . . we begin to grasp breadths of female history and psychology which have lain out of reach as a consequence of limited, mostly clinical, definitions of *lesbianism*.[24]

Rather than totally conflating lesbians and feminists or totally separating them, Rich establishes a middle ground on which lesbians and feminists join together in a common struggle. Hers is a model that does not erase difference but also does not allow difference to be unbridgeable.[25]

In the classroom, we have to work diligently to create those bridges—not only between our own positionality and the text at hand, but also between the diverse kinds of students we have in class.

Recently I taught a semester-long class on Toni Morrison to upper-level undergraduates. Five out of the thirty-five students in the classroom were black women; the remaining students were white, a majority of them women. For most of the white undergraduates, this was perhaps the most racially mixed classroom they had ever been in at my institution; they were uncomfortable at first even bringing up issues of race and racism—not because they weren't aware of them, but because they didn't have the language (or perhaps the courage) to discuss the issues. The first few weeks of the semester were too silent; the white students in particular wanted me to be the authority and initiate the discussion of the tough issues. I gently refused to be put in the position of speaking for them and instead began a discussion of our class dynamics. This discussion was halting at first, but eventually led to a mostly productive classroom. I also found that I had to assume a very complex role in this class: I had to try to discern instantaneously when to speak up from an ethical oppositional stance and when to let the discussion play out among students. I intuitively adopted what Chela Sandoval has described as "tactical subjectivity," the ability "to choose tactical positions ... to self-consciously break and reform ties to ideology, activities which are imperative for the psychological and political practices that permit the achievement of coalition across differences."[26] In other words, I had to adopt different subjectivities based on the differing needs of my students: the black students certainly didn't need me to make them more aware of race and racism; instead, I tried to make spaces for them to amplify Morrison's novels with their own experiences or to take issue with Morrison's ideas and my interpretations of blackness. The white students, however, needed me to show them how it was possible to speak about their/our areas of ignorance concerning texts that presented unfamiliar experiences. I found Morrison's novels to be especially useful in challenging both black students and whites, for they are directed so explicitly to a black audience and centered so earnestly in the black community that white readers are powerfully immersed in a worldview that contradicts many of the assumptions they take for granted; and yet the novels also present extremes of black experience (Sethe killing her baby girl rather than allowing her to be returned to slavery, Eva Peace burning Plum to "save" him, Pilate's birthing herself so that she has no navel), so that my black students found some of the content unfamiliar and challenging too. By using Morrison's texts as our common ground, I tried to avoid creating a classroom where "a comfortable set of oppositions" could be maintained, which Chandra Mohanty has described as a situation where people of color are "the central voices and the bearers of all knowledge in class" and white people are "'observers,' with no responsibility to contribute and/or with nothing valuable to contribute." [27]

I have no doubt that if bell hooks had been the teacher of this class, many of my students—black and white—would have been immeasurably enriched by her presence, wisdom, and engagement. But I have also come to recognize that there is important work in such a classroom for white feminists and white progressive professors to perform too. White professors who are willing to examine and question their own standpoint of privileged whiteness (to extend hooks's idea of standpoint) can help engage white students in similar kinds of critical analyses as well as demonstrate to black students that allies can be found to fight the war against racism. Again, I do not mean to suggest that white feminists exclusively ought to be teaching Toni Morrison; neither do I think that black faculty exclusively ought to teach her works. We need to be able to engage the issues of race, class, gender, and cultural difference from a variety of perspectives; we need to allow for multiple strategies of resistance to oppression. Those of us who find ourselves "teaching to transgress," to quote hooks's provocative title, need to forge alliances with one another even as our individual positionalities and transgressive strategies may differ.

This belief in multiple ways of engagement and resistance has transformed my pedagogy. Undergraduates in my Morrison class spent the first half of the semester doing various short writing assign-

ments requiring them to do some extracurricular reading: one assignment asked them to read, summarize, and evaluate a scholarly article
on *The Bluest Eye*; another invited them to adopt Morrison's voice
explaining to an interviewer some ways in which Ralph Ellison's *The
Invisible Man* influenced one of her novels; I also asked them to follow
a current news story about race or gender and relate it to some aspect
of Morrison (an especially timely assignment, since the KKK held a
public rally in our community that semester and the O. J. Simpson
case was constantly in the news); another assignment asked students
to explore contextual material—they chose one text from a list encompassing black women's history (Paula Giddings, Jacqueline Jones),
philosophy (Cornel West), feminism (hooks, Patricia Hill-Collins), and
so on, which they read, summarized, and evaluated, and then related
to Morrison. Through these kinds of assignments, I tried to show
white students how to be responsible participants by doing their
homework (like I do) so they could speak from an informed perspective.[28]

In addition, the skills these assignments called for—close reading,
critical thinking, making connections, pinpointing issues—were important in giving all students a new respect for intellectual activity,
and I hoped black students in particular would feel empowered in an
American literature classroom because the work of key black intellectuals was placed at the center. Henry Giroux argues that a responsible
and ethical progressive pedagogy necessarily involves a discussion of
the politics of representation: "cultural workers" must work against
"pedagogical practices which support a voyeuristic reception of texts
by providing students with a variety of critical methodologies and
approaches to understand how issues regarding audience, address,
and reception configure within cultural circuits of power to produce
particular subject positions and secure specific forms of authority."[29] I
tried to create the conditions for such recognition through the multiple
vantage points offered by the short papers. One effect of these assignments was to deconstruct monolithic concepts of blackness, to enable

students to see that we were not dealing with racial essences but various, sometimes conflicting ideas of blackness. The assignment calling for them to analyze the representation of blacks in a current news story, at the very least, enabled many of them to comprehend something about representational politics.

During the second half of the semester, my students focused on one longer project of their own design: they could write a traditional literary analysis if they thought doing so would best get them to engage in the aesthetic and political issues we had discussed, but they were also allowed to propose a creative project that responded in some way to the issues of our course. If they chose to do a creative project, students were asked to turn in a three- to four-page statement explaining what their project was, why they chose to do this particular project, and how it related to the works we had read during the semester. Two-thirds of the students in the Morrison class chose to work on creative projects, and most told me at the end of the semester that it was the most meaningful, exciting assignment they had worked on in their undergraduate careers.

Like Paulo Freire, I wanted to motivate students to begin to relinquish their belief and dependence on the banking system of education, where the professor is the authority who deposits knowledge into students. Instead, I hoped that I could act less as an authority and more as what Kenneth Mostern calls "a critical pedagogue":

> someone who teaches from where the student is at, rather than from where the teacher is at. This does not mean that the teacher denies his or her pedagogical intentions or specific expertise, but merely that s/he respects the myriad expertise of the students that s/he does not share. Second, the critical pedagogue works for social justice, and, living in a world of injustice, not only attempts to enact change in his or her classroom, but develops the strategies and confidence of students to work for social change beyond the classroom.[30]

The projects my students chose embraced a wide range of approaches, and outlining a few of them will, I hope, illustrate the beneficial effects of such a transformed pedagogy. One (white female) student, influenced by *Beloved,* researched slave ships and slave captains and used this information to create a watercolor rendering of African souls escaping the torment of the ship holds and flying back to Africa. Another (white male) student wrote a short story based on a family conflict about race, and in his statement, he not only gave credit to Morrison for enabling him to analyze the dynamics of this situation, but also self-consciously reflected on the meaning of his own privileged whiteness. A creative writing major wrote a story trying out Morrison's lyrical prose and sharp eye for contradiction and disparity; a white male, he found that a black woman writer offered him the most inspiring example of the kind of fiction he would like to be able to write. A (black female) student, gripped by *Sula,* chose to analyze the sometimes liberatory, sometimes threatening meanings attached to black women's sexuality in Morrison, Cornel West, and Spike Lee. A white woman studying English education used her project to plan a syllabus for teaching images of race, class, and gender in works by Mark Twain, William Faulkner, and Toni Morrison, specifically targeted for white rural high school students; motivated by two examples of progressive white female teachers from rural Indiana whose contracts had been terminated (implicitly) for bringing "radical" texts into the classroom, she was careful to design a syllabus that gradually offered more significant challenges to her students' preconceptions.

This last project brings up an important consideration that I think has gone unnoticed in the debates about who is entitled to teach and do scholarly work on particular kinds of texts: it may be the case that we are unfortunately abetting conservative defenders of the traditional American literature canon (and Western cultural hegemony, more generally) by focusing too concertedly on identity politics. When the call for black teachers exclusively to teach black subject matter, American Indians exclusively to teach American Indian texts, and so on coincides with arguments against multiculturalism as "political correctness," the stakes become almost too high for progressive white professors who want to engage in such issues. I am not suggesting here that racism even among progressive white professors ought to go without criticism; nor do I mean to dismiss the criticisms of a vapid classroom (or Bennetton) multiculturalism that allows our students to "celebrate difference" without interrogating the painful conflicts and power inequities that attend a deeper understanding of cultural and racial difference.[31] What I am calling for is an acknowledgment of an important role progressive white scholars can play in redefining America so that race, class, gender, and sexuality become personalized and politicized for everyone and are not always displaced "over there" onto "minorities."

Michele Wallace has similar thoughts on this controversy. Although she readily acknowledges various problems with "current left cultural and art world versions of multiculturalism," she also believes that "the link that multiculturalism is trying to establish between discourses on feminism, sexual preference, and ethnicity could be more usefully viewed as a pragmatic political coalition: the cultural left version of Jesse Jackson's Rainbow Coalition against the rising tide of the conservative Right." In fact, Wallace, almost anticipating the controversy associated with such a position, goes on to spell out her reasoning in a full paragraph:

> While multiculturalism's inclination toward unrestricted inclusiveness as opposed to hierarchical exclusiveness doesn't automatically lead to significant structural changes in existing aesthetic and critical priorities and institutional discourses of power, it could and thus far has offered more opportunities for critical discussion outside the dominant discourse, and dissent and debate within, than its present aesthetic and critical alternatives. These alternatives I see as 1) a "color-blind" cultural homogeneity which originates in liberal humanist ideology; 2) separatist aesthetics and politics such as "Afrocentrism"; and 3) racist/sexist aesthetics, which range from the cultural fascism of a Hilton Kramer in the New Criterion to the gangs that attacked Yusef Hawkins in Bensonhurst and the female jogger in Central Park. Thus, despite my reservations about multiculturalism, I have become a reluctant supporter of it. At the

same time it is crucial to its usefulness that we view multiculturalism not as an obdurate and unchanging ideological position, but as an opportunity for ongoing critical debate.[32]

I hope that we will take up this debate, learning to begin a dialogue and work together. For if we do not, if we remain distracted or if we keep silent, we will lose our chance to speak out against critics of multiculturalism who talk about "a cult of ethnicity" and see "the melting pot" of America "giv[ing] way to the Tower of Babel,"[33] or who unfairly characterize multiculturalism as an "ethnic separatism" that "fosters sensitivities, resentments, and suspicions, setting one group against another."[34] These are sentiments that would prove offensive not only to many African Americans, Native Americans, and other minorities, but to many white Americans as well. We must not concede to cultural conservatives the discussion of what a real American is or what an ideal America is. Moreover, we should not allow our internal debates to draw our attention away from conservatives' increasingly successful challenges to affirmative action policies and curricular revisions in universities across the nation.[35] Joan W. Scott has argued that now is the time for progressive university professors to begin "the reconceptualization of community in the age of diversity."[36] By joining together across race and other boundaries as critical pedagogues, by using diverse strategies to accomplish similar goals in our classrooms, we can help bring into being a multicultural America where critical debate and dialogue thrive.

NOTES

I am grateful to Aparajita Sagar, Marcia Stephenson, and Patrick O'Donnell for their comments on earlier versions of this essay.

1. bell hooks, *Teaching to Transgress: Education as the Practice of Freedom* (New York: Routledge, 1994), 90.

2. Elsewhere hooks has argued against assumptions of a monolithic black identity. See especially the essays "Postmodern Blackness" and "An Aesthetic of Blackness," in *Yearning: Race, Gender, and Cultural Politics* (Boston: South End Press, 1990).

3. The recent decision of the University of California Board of Regents to dismantle affirmative action programs is the most visible attack on such safeguards and is extremely disturbing in its suggestion that a level playing field exists today in America and in the American academy.

4. It has become an unfortunate occurrence at some literature conferences, most recently at some sessions of the Toni Morrison conference held in April 1995 at Bellarmine College, that black feminists leave a session when they see that white feminists will be talking about African American texts. See also Katherine Mayberry's column in *Chronicle of Higher Education,* 12 Oct. 1994, A48, and Malin LaVon Walther's letter in response (26 Oct. 1994, B3).

5. hooks, *Teaching to Transgress,* 103–4. Hooks includes a particularly pointed comment from one black woman on this issue: "It burns me up to be treated like shit by white women who are busy getting their academic recognition, promotions, more money, et cetera, doing 'great' work on the topic of race."

6. Adrienne Rich was also helpful in pointing out this issue to white feminists; as she collected her essays into volumes, she added notes and prefaces at times questioning her former positions and bringing attention to the developing awareness of her own class and racial privilege. See, for example, her 1978 essay "Disloyal to Civilization: Feminism, Racism, Gynephobia," in *On Lies, Secrets, and Silence: Selected Prose 1966–1978* (New York: Norton, 1979), 275–310. *This Bridge Called My Back,* rev. ed. (New York: Kitchen Table: Women of Color Press, 1983), edited by Cherríe Moraga and Gloria Anzaldúa, was another widely influential text.

7. In *Teaching to Transgress,* hooks also admonishes black women: "The presence of racism in feminist settings does not exempt black women or women of color from actively participating in the effort to find ways to communicate, to exchange ideas, to have fierce debate" (110).

8. Cambridge: Harvard University Press, 1992. See also Morrison's influential essay "Unspeakable Things Unspoken" for a brilliant analysis of whiteness in Melville and the American romance. *Michigan Quarterly Review* 28 (winter 1989): 1–34.

9. Gloria Anzaldúa, *Borderlands/La Frontera: The New Mestiza* (San Francisco: Spinsters-Aunt Lute, 1987), 194.

10. Anzaldúa, 202–3.

11. Anzaldúa, 84, 85.

12. I want to acknowledge here that I am in complete agreement with various scholars who have argued against an "additive approach" to "correcting" the canon. In our discussion of texts, gender is a construct that affects not only Emily Dickinson but Ernest Hemingway too; race and culture are issues not only for Leslie Marmon Silko but for Kate Chopin as well. See Gayatri

Spivak's theoretical analysis of the kind of curricular transformations that are necessary, "Scattered Speculations on the Question of Cultural Studies," in *Outside in the Teaching Machine* (New York: Routledge, 1993), 255–84. Peggy Pascoe, "At the Crossroads of Culture," *Women's Review of Books*, February 1990, 22–23, discusses some of the pitfalls and possibilities of the practical effects of integrating "minority" texts into an American history survey course.

13. Mario T. Garcia, "Multiculturalism and American Studies," *Radical History Review* 54 (fall 1992): 50.

14. Elsa Barkley Brown, "African-American Women's Quilting: A Framework for Conceptualizing and Teaching African-American Women's History," *Signs* 14 (summer 1989): 921.

15. Linda Alcoff, "The Problem of Speaking for Others," *Cultural Critique* 20 (winter 1991–92): 9.

16. Alcoff, 17, 20.

17. Alcoff, 22.

18. Alcoff, 23.

19. See *Breaking Bread: Insurgent Black Intellectual Life* (Boston: South End Press, 1991) for her dialogue with West; "A Conversation about Race and Class," in *Conflicts in Feminism,* ed. Marianne Hirsch and Evelyn Fox Keller (New York: Routledge, 1990) for her conversation with Childers; "Building a Teaching Community: A Dialogue," in *Teaching to Transgress* for her exchange with Scapp.

20. Alcoff, 24.

21. Alcoff, 29.

22. Hazel Carby is much less optimistic about the possibility of extending such insights beyond the classroom. In fact, she has argued that "[f]or white suburbia, as well as for white middle-class students in universities, these texts are becoming a way of gaining knowledge of the 'other': a knowledge that appears to satisfy and replace the desire to challenge existing frameworks of segregation"; see her essay "The Multicultural Wars," *Radical History Review* 54 (fall 1992): 17. I cannot share this particular stance, at least not yet, because "multiculturalism" is such a recent phenomenon that I don't think we can evaluate its impact fairly; the current generation of college students who have been influenced by it has not yet come of age in terms of entering into public discourse.

23. My students' identification of pregnancy with heterosexuality is understandable, but of course not necessarily true.

24. Adrienne Rich, "Compulsory Heterosexuality and Lesbian Existence," in *Blood, Bread, and Poetry: Selected Prose 1979–1985* (New York: Norton, 1986), 51–52.

25. Rich's model also allows us to recognize that very effective models of

lesbian and gay scholarship may come from heterosexual scholars. The work of Eve Kosofsky Sedgwick comes most immediately to mind.

26. Chela Sandoval, "U.S. Third World Feminism: The Theory and Method of Oppositional Consciousness in the Postmodern World," *Genders* 10 (spring 1991): 15.

27. Chandra Mohanty, "On Race and Voice: Challenges for Liberal Education in the 1990s," in *Between Borders: Pedagogy and the Politics of Cultural Studies*, ed. Henry A. Giroux and Peter McLaren (New York: Routledge, 1994), 154.

28. I have found Gayatri Spivak's analysis of this issue helpful. Concerning white bourgeois students who feel they lack the authenticity to discuss the Third World, she writes, "you will of course not speak in the same way about the Third World material, but if you make it your task not only to learn what is going on there through language, through specific programmes of study, but also at the same time through a historical critique of your position as the investigating person, then you will see that you have earned the right to criticize, and you [will] be heard. When you take the position of not doing your homework—'I will not criticize because of my accident of birth, the historical accident'—that is a much more pernicious position. In one way you take a risk to criticize, of criticizing something which is other—something which you used to dominate. I say that you have to take a certain risk: to say 'I won't criticize' is salving your conscience, and allowing you not to do any homework"; see "Questions of Multi-culturalism," in *The Post-Colonial Critic: Interviews, Strategies, Dialogues*, ed. Sarah Harasym (New York: Routledge, 1990), 62–63. Spivak focuses on earning the right to criticize in these remarks, but they also may be extended to analyze the difficulty of speaking for and about more generally.

29. Henry A. Giroux, "Living Dangerously: Identity Politics and the New Cultural Racism," in *Between Borders: Pedagogy and the Politics of Cultural Studies*, ed. Giroux and McLaren, 49.

30. Kenneth Mostern, "Decolonization as Learning: Practice and Pedagogy in Frantz Fanon's Revolutionary Narrative," in *Between Borders: Pedagogy and the Politics of Cultural Studies*, ed. Giroux and McLaren, 256.

31. For a flawed but provocative leftist critique of multiculturalism, see Jeff Escoffier, "The Limits of Multiculturalism," *Socialist Review* 21, nos. 3–4 (July–December 1991): 61–73. Cornel West has also criticized unexamined, simplistic calls for multiculturalism in *Beyond Eurocentrism and Multiculturalism* (Monroe, ME: Common Courage Press, 1993).

32. Michele Wallace, "Multiculturalism and Oppositionality," in *Between Borders: Pedagogy and the Politics of Cultural Studies*, ed. Giroux and McLaren, 181–82.

33. Arthur M. Schlesinger, Jr., *The Disuniting of America: Reflections on a Multicultural Society* (New York: Norton, 1992), 15, 18.

34. C. Vann Woodward, "Equal but Separate," *New Republic,* 15–22 July 1991, 43.

35. Joan Scott presents a similar argument in "The Campaign against Political Correctness," *Radical History Review* 54 (fall 1992): 67–68.

36. Scott, 77.

BIBLIOGRAPHY

Alcoff, Linda. "The Problem of Speaking for Others." *Cultural Critique* 20 (winter 1991–92): 5–32.

Anzaldúa, Gloria. *Borderlands/La Frontera: The New Mestiza.* San Francisco: Spinsters-Aunt Lute, 1987.

Brown, Elsa Barkley. "African-American Women's Quilting: A Framework for Conceptualizing and Teaching African-American Women's History." *Signs* 14 (summer 1989): 921–29.

Carby, Hazel. "The Multicultural Wars." *Radical History Review* 54 (fall 1992): 7–18.

Collins, Patricia Hill. *Black Feminist Thought: Knowledge, Consciousness, and the Politics of Empowerment.* New York: Routledge, 1991.

Escoffier, Jeffrey. "The Limits of Multiculturalism." *Socialist Review* 21, nos. 3–4 (July–December 1991): 61–73.

Freire, Paulo. *Pedagogy of the Oppressed.* New York: Continuum, 1989.

Garcia, Mario T. "Multiculturalism and American Studies." *Radical History Review* 54 (fall 1992): 49–56.

Giddings, Paula. *When and Where I Enter: The Impact of Black Women on Race and Sex in America.* New York: Morrow, 1984.

Giroux, Henry A. "Living Dangerously: Identity Politics and the New Cultural Racism." In *Between Borders,* ed. Giroux and McLaren, 29–55.

Giroux, Henry A., and Peter McLaren, eds. *Between Borders: Pedagogy and the Politics of Cultural Studies.* New York: Routledge, 1994.

hooks, bell. *Teaching to Transgress: Education as the Practice of Freedom.* New York: Routledge, 1994.

———. *Yearning: Race, Gender, and Cultural Politics.* Boston: South End Press, 1990.

hooks, bell, and Mary Childers. "A Conversation about Race and Class." In *Conflicts in Feminism,* ed. Marianne Hirsch and Evelyn Fox Keller, 60–81. New York: Routledge, 1990.

hooks, bell, and Cornel West. *Breaking Bread: Insurgent Black Intellectual Life.* Boston: South End Press, 1991.

Hull, Gloria T., Patricia Bell-Scott, and Barbara Smith, eds. *All the Women Are White, All the Blacks Are Men, but Some of Us Are Brave: Black Women's Studies.* Old Westbury, NY: Feminist Press, 1982.

Jones, Jacqueline. *Labor of Love, Labor of Sorrow: Black Women, Work, and the Family from Slavery to the Present.* New York: Basic Books, 1985.

Lorde, Audre. *Sister Outsider.* Trumansburg, NY: Crossing Press, 1984.

Mayberry, Katherine J. "White Feminists Who Study Black Writers." *Chronicle of Higher Education,* 12 October 1994, A48.

Mohanty, Chandra. "On Race and Voice: Challenges for Liberal Education in the 1990s." In *Between Borders,* ed. Giroux and McLaren, 145–66.

Moraga, Cherríe, and Gloria Anzaldúa, eds. *This Bridge Called My Back: Writings by Radical Women of Color.* Rev. ed. New York: Kitchen Table: Women of Color Press, 1983.

Morrison, Toni. *Playing in the Dark: Whiteness and the Literary Imagination.* Cambridge: Harvard University Press, 1992.

———. "Unspeakable Things Unspoken: The African American Presence in American Literature." *Michigan Quarterly Review* 28 (winter 1989): 1–34.

Mostern, Kenneth. "Decolonization as Learning: Practice and Pedagogy in Frantz Fanon's Revolutionary Narrative." In *Between Borders,* ed. Giroux and McLaren, 253–71.

Pascoe, Peggy. "At the Crossroads of Culture." *Women's Review of Books,* February 1990, 22–23.

Rich, Adrienne. "Compulsory Heterosexuality and Lesbian Existence." In *Blood, Bread, and Poetry: Selected Prose 1979–1985,* 23–75. New York: Norton.

———. *On Lies, Secrets, and Silence: Selected Prose 1966–1978.* New York: Norton, 1979.

Sandoval, Chela. "U.S. Third World Feminism: The Theory and Method of Oppositional Consciousness in the Postmodern World." *Genders* 10 (spring 1991): 1–24.

Schlesinger, Arthur M., Jr. *The Disuniting of America: Reflections on a Multicultural Society.* New York: Norton, 1992.

Scott, Joan W. "The Campaign against Political Correctness." *Radical History Review* 54 (fall 1992): 59–79.

Spivak, Gayatri C. *Outside in the Teaching Machine.* New York: Routledge, 1993.

———. "Questions of Multi-culturalism." In *The Post-Colonial Critic: Interviews, Strategies, Dialogues,* ed. Sarah Harasym, 59–66. New York: Routledge, 1990.

Walker, Alice. *In Search of Our Mothers' Gardens: Womanist Prose.* New York: Harcourt Brace Jovanovich, 1983.

Wallace, Michele. "Multiculturalism and Oppositionality." In *Between Borders,* ed. Giroux and McLaren, 180–91.

Walther, Malin LaVon. Letter. *Chronicle of Higher Education,* 26 October 1994, B3.

West, Cornel. *Beyond Eurocentrism and Multiculturalism.* 2 vols. Monroe, ME: Common Courage Press, 1993.

———. *Race Matters.* Boston: Beacon, 1993.

Woodward, C. Vann. "Equal but Separate." Review of *The Disuniting of America,* by Arthur M. Schlesinger, Jr. *New Republic,* 15–22 July 1991, 41–43.

3

Straight Teacher/Queer Classroom: Teaching as an Ally

BARBARA SCOTT WINKLER

In the 1970s and 1980s, many female women's studies teachers assumed that they had more in common than not with the women students who made up the majority in their classrooms. Their assumption was in part a result both of a politics that claimed a universalistic female identity based on the oppression of women and an optimistic confusion between women's standpoint and feminist conclusions. Scholars of feminist pedagogy, grappling with the authority conveyed by their institutional positions, attempted to relocate their leadership on more legitimate, because feminist, grounds. They did this by emphasizing their shared experience of oppression with women students or by establishing their vanguard position as feminist faculty. Caroline Shrewsbury, for example, speaks of feminist leadership as "a special form of empowerment which empowers others."[1]

In contrast, poststructuralist or postmodernist feminist educators of the late 1980s and 1990s are less sanguine about assuming a common identity with their students, or maintaining that radical faculty are automatically at the center of the empowerment process and able to provide students with oppositional or liberatory knowledge they would not otherwise have.

The feminist classroom has therefore emerged in the pedagogical literature as more potentially fragmented, less "safe," and less free of power relations than previously described. The insight that feminist and liberatory education is not "innocent" could lead feminist and other progressive educators to despair. However, our recognition of how education, including "emancipatory" teaching and learning, is enmeshed in power relations need not dishearten us as faculty and students or lead us to abandon our insights into the relationship between knowledge and power. Instead, our classrooms can be places in which we embrace our own and our students' partial knowledge, in which we learn from and struggle to trust one another.

In the spring of 1994, I offered for the first time a special topics course, Sex and Sexuality in American Culture, as part of the women's studies program at West Virginia University.[2] I taught the class again in the spring of 1995 and will be petitioning to make the course a permanent part of the curriculum, both in women's studies and as part of a projected new minor in lesbian, gay, bisexual, and transgender studies. The class helped me find a metaphor and strategy for teaching that does not shy away from the recognition of difference and power in the feminist classroom: "teaching as an ally." As a straight teacher I explored what it meant to teach as an ally in a course that had a strong lesbian, gay, and bisexual (lesbigay) component, both in content and through support by an organized lesbigay student constituency.

While preparing to teach the course for the first time, I found the concepts of coalition and alliance building, taken from feminist political organizing, suggestive guides for dealing with difference. Teaching as an ally became a metaphor for my approach to authority and to the creation of classroom community as a condition for the production of knowledge and transformation of consciousness. Abandoning a priori assumptions of sisterhood and certainties about the teacher as the "origin of what can be known and ... what can be done,"[3] I found myself in the less comfortable but equally committed and enthusiastic stance of teacher as ally.

I am, therefore, proposing the concept of "teaching as an ally" to describe what faculty from dominant groups can do to share power, build trust, and create an atmosphere of mutual respect in which to create knowledge with students from nondominant groups. Groups are not monolithic in their experience of privilege and oppression, and differently oppressed groups can form alliances.[4] However, I will be focusing in this essay on faculty acting as allies to students who, on some dimension, have less privilege and power than the faculty— in society as well as in the academy.

Alliance and coalition emerged as strategies of feminist organizing in response to the recognition that women do not automatically share a common set of experiences and a common agenda based on gender.[5] Feminists of color especially challenged any unified definition of "woman" founded on the construction of white womanhood. They emphasized the ways we experience multiple, intersecting social structures that shape experience and identity. Bonnie Thornton Dill, for example, in an article in *Feminist Studies* published in 1983, argued for "the abandonment of the concept of sisterhood as a global construct based on unexamined assumptions about our similarities." She called instead for a "more pluralistic approach that recognizes and accepts the objective differences between women," and for a politics of "building coalitions around issues of shared interest."[6] Similarly, Bernice Johnson Reagon, in a speech given at the West Coast Women's Music Festival in 1981, argued the necessity of doing the uncomfortable work of coalition, maintaining that our desire to "be only with people who are like [us]" is illusory and dangerous.[7]

Although the concept of teaching as an ally has not been fully developed in the educational literature, other writers on feminist pedagogy have referred to concepts of alliance and coalition building taken from feminist activism. For example, John Schilb, in an article published in an anthology on feminist teaching in 1985, invoked Sara Evans's call for a flexible organizing mentality in doing coalition work as a guide to avoiding rigidity or purity in applying feminist pedagogical principles. Schilb, a man teaching women's studies to an

economically advantaged student population, often felt less distanced
from the women and men students in his introductory courses by his
maleness than by his feminist politics. The concept of flexibility, of
trusting "the complexities of the organizing process itself," helped
him develop a strategy to fit the particulars of his classroom and
school environment.[8]

Mimi Orner also turned to the concept of teacher as ally in an
article published in 1992 on the problematic treatment of student resistance and the difficulties with calls for "student voice" in feminist
and critical pedagogy.[9] Orner, raising questions about the emancipatory role of the teacher, asks, "How do we understand our own embodiment of privilege and oppression, both historical and current?
How do we teach as allies to oppressed groups of which we are not
a part? What does it mean to teach as an ally?"[10]

Elizabeth Ellsworth, in an article that criticizes the foundational
assumptions of critical pedagogy, also discusses coalition and alliance
building in relation to her class on Media and Antiracist Pedagogies.
Ellsworth shifts her attention from the self-understanding and responsibility of the faculty member to the class as a whole. Remarking
on the creation of student-generated affinity groups outside the classroom, she maintains that the class came to see itself as "building a
coalition among the multiple, shifting, intersecting, and sometimes
contradictory groups carrying unequal weights of legitimacy within
the culture and the classroom."[11] (Halfway through the semester, the
students renamed the course "Coalition 607.")

Such a definition of coalitions as constantly responsive and shifting
avoids a simplistic polarization of students and faculty into discrete
groups of "oppressed" and "oppressors." Ellsworth found that assumptions about who would develop alliances were often wrong, because class members shared commitments in nonstereotypical ways.
Ellsworth also described what her new understanding of the classroom gave her as a member of the faculty. She gained a greater appreciation of classroom practices that would avoid premature closure

or fixity of identity (which she calls a kind of "unknowability").[12] Teaching as an ally, therefore, does not mean reducing an individual's life to a single factor or polarizing groups within the classroom into "oppressor" and "oppressed."[13] It does, however, result in a redefinition of authority and an examination of how faculty as well as students embody both privilege and oppression, as Orner suggests.

Writers on feminist organizing describe precisely what coalitions and alliances entail. In their anthology *Bridges of Power: Women's Multicultural Alliances,* Lisa Albrecht and Rose M. Brewer distinguish between coalitions, as temporary commitments, and alliances, which are more long-term political relationships. In coalitions, "groups operate autonomously and are usually not connected to each other," while alliances require a "level of commitment that is longer-standing, deeper, and built upon more trusting political relationships."[14] While some students may have established political connections with one another before taking a course, most will have only a limited relationship to other class members and to the material. Therefore, the concept of "alliance" cannot be transplanted too exactly from organizing to the classroom. However, as a member of the faculty, I found the concept of "ally," which stresses a deeper dedication, instructive and descriptive of my experience.

While we can make commitments to teach as allies in every class, analysis of a course such as the "sexuality class," which emphasizes material on oppressed or marginalized groups and which is taught by a faculty member who is not a member of those groups, can help us focus more directly on what it means to teach as an ally. A description of the creation and teaching of the course Sex and Sexuality in American Culture can therefore, I believe, provide an instructive example of ally teaching.

In January 1993 I received a three-year appointment as the first visiting assistant professor in women's studies at West Virginia University. WVU is the flagship school of the state. Morgantown has a summer population of twenty-six thousand that is almost doubled when students return in the fall. While the campus culture is conservative, there is a small but relatively organized lesbigay community, which includes university and nonuniversity people. A gay bar, an important hangout for students as well as townspeople, is located in the downtown area near the university. A community-based group, "Equal Rights Not Special Rights," successfully fought for an antidiscrimination clause in the employment policy of the city government. Students and staff of the university participated in this effort.

The school has a very progressive antidiscrimination policy that covers sexual orientation as well as race and gender. There is a supportive social justice office, created by the outgoing university president. The Bisexual, Gay and Lesbian Mountaineers (BIGLM), a student group founded in 1987, has a significant presence on campus. Through university-wide activities and programming, including Gay Pride Week, BIGLM raises awaren ss around lesbian, gay, bisexual, and transgender issues. The group played an important role in my hiring and in the creation of the sexuality course.

The WVU Center for Women's Studies has been in existence in one form or another since 1980. Like many women's studies programs, the center originally relied on the founding coordinator (an English department professor) and other departmental faculty for course offerings.[15] Obtaining a full-time women's studies faculty position, even a temporary one, required much organizing by students as well as by center staff and affiliated faculty.

Staffing the introductory course was the primary justification for establishing the position. However, the center was also concerned with internal curricular development. BIGLM was especially interested in ensuring that whoever was hired would offer a course in lesbian and gay studies. I was asked during my hiring interview whether I would be willing to do so both by students and by the social justice officer.[16]

I had just received my doctorate in American studies from the University of Michigan six months before, where new courses in the history of sexuality and culture of gays and lesbians were being offered through the history department and the American culture program. Coursework in this field had not been available to me before I started my dissertation. However, I had read in the area on my own and believed that as a social and cultural historian I could offer a course that focused on the issues and on key theoretical concepts in the history of sexuality in the United States. Equally important, as a feminist and women's studies scholar, I was committed to antiheterosexist teaching and supported a women's studies program making a contribution to the scholarship and curricula in lesbigay studies. These commitments were personal as well as intellectual, and stemmed in part from relationships with lesbian friends and colleagues. As I told the BIGLM representative, the opportunity to teach such a course was therefore very exciting to me.

At the hiring interview I offered to teach lesbigay studies as part of a course on the history of sexuality in the United States that also explored changes in heterosexuality. The course would look at how race and class helped shape those experiences as well. There was no such course on campus, and as a student of American studies with a history background I felt this approach would best tap my skills and knowledge as a scholar, as well as my own subjectivity. This was, therefore, not to be an exclusively lesbigay studies course. However, the extensiveness of lesbigay content as well as questions and themes that would structure the course, such as the emergence of a "homosexual" identity and the creation of a "heterosexual norm," would make it a class substantially informed by scholarship in this area.

After I was hired and before I put together the syllabus, I met with BIGLM. I wanted to hear what their expectations were for such a course. I also invited discussion of the impact that my sexual identity as a straight woman might have on the class, including recognition of the possible limitations this could impose.

I could not meet all the BIGLM students' expectations for the course. For example, I was not an expert on representations of same-sex intimacy in ancient Greece, and I wanted to limit the focus to the United States. Also, while I felt that a statement of my subjective position was a responsible strategy, it did not always produce the effect I intended. Later, one of the older lesbians in the group told me that my declaration had confused her. She wondered if my self-labeling as straight indicated that I would "back off" from committing to exploration of lesbian, gay, and bisexual material. Fortunately, she took the course. She later assured me that she concluded there had been nothing to worry about. If I were to replay the BIGLM meeting, I would make a similar statement, since I believe it challenges notions of objectivity and disinterested authority. However, instead of speaking solely of my identity as a straight woman, I would also refer to my political and intellectual commitments as a feminist and antihomophobic teacher.

Meeting with BIGLM helped me think about who would take the course the first time I offered it. I was told that there was a great deal of "pent-up demand" for the class, and I was aware of the particular constituencies that were most likely to take the class: in particular, lesbian, gay, and bisexual students and feminist-identified straight students. I hoped for a student group that was diverse and gay-positive.

Thirty students enrolled, a large number for a seminar. They included a number of activists in BIGLM and in the lesbigay community at large. Lesbian, gay, and bisexual students who enrolled in this first session may or may not have had acquaintance with scholarship on the history of sexuality, including lesbian, gay, and bisexual studies, but they had considerable life experience in dealing with many of the issues we dealt with in the course. Several were older. Their participation was invaluable in creating a gay-positive classroom community.

When planning the course content, I chose topics designed to engage and inform the lesbian, gay, bisexual, and straight students who wanted to learn more about the history of sexuality in the United States. Lesbigay issues were presented as an integral part of this history.[17] Since the course covered the history of sexuality in the United States from the colonial period to the present, much of the initial material did not directly deal with lesbigay issues, although such topics as cross-gender roles in Native American tribes and Victorian romantic friendships were discussed. Most of the last third of the class did focus more directly on lesbigay concerns, including the emergence of homosexual communities, the political and cultural significance of lesbian and gay bar culture, cross-cultural comparisons and the construction of gayness in communities of color, gay liberation, lesbian feminism, bisexuality, and the moral panic around AIDS. In this section we also dealt with the sexual revolution, abortion and reproductive rights, pornography, and the impact of consumerism on sexuality.

According to evaluations at the end of the course, some straight students overestimated how much time was actually spent on lesbigay material, but most felt that this was a positive experience. As one student wrote, "Bringing homosexual topics into each issue helped me, as a heterosexual, to further understand their world." Another wrote, "I learned so much about a culture I knew almost nothing about—it really opened my eyes."[18]

In this first semester, a significant percentage of the students were lesbian, gay, or bisexual. A student's anonymous survey of class members revealed that half of the students who reported their sexual identity were lesbian or gay male, and half were bisexual or straight. (She divided the class into two categories: lesbian and gay, bisexual and straight.) My own estimate was that 60 percent of the students were lesbian, gay, or bisexual. Out of thirty students, twenty-five were women. The five men were all gay. While BIGLM played an important role in advocating the course, this was not a "BIGLM class." Students who were not part of BIGLM, including those who were lesbian, gay, or bisexual, enrolled, and not all members of the organization took the course. Eight students who had taken my Fall course, Contemporary U.S. Women's Movements, followed up with the sexuality class.

That the course attracted such a significant percentage of lesbian, gay, and bisexual students in the first semester helped make the classroom a gay-positive or "queer" space, as the students described it.[19] Lesbian, gay, and bisexual students often spoke out of their sexual subjectivity, openly identifying themselves. While straight women actively participated in classroom discussion, they sometimes gave the impression of "overhearing" conversations of which they were not the center. Their group presentations (which I will describe below), however, provided them with the means to speak more authoritatively.[20]

When I offered the course again the following spring term, the class makeup was reversed: closer to 40 percent of the eighteen students who enrolled were lesbian, gay, or bisexual, while 60 percent were straight. This affected the dynamics of the class. Heterosexual feminists were more outspoken, focusing on issues of reproductive rights, the sex industry, New Right attempts to regulate sexuality, teen pregnancy, and welfare. Several of the students in the class had direct experience with welfare or knew friends who did. Several straight and bisexual women students also had friends or acquaintances who stripped in local clubs, providing an interesting slant on the sex industry. The more conservative views on these issues of a straight white male student helped spark some of these discussions.

While bisexual, lesbian, and gay students were again active and vocal participants in the class, many fewer chose to self-label, and such identifications seemed not to be as much at the center of the discussion. The absence of role models, such as the older lesbian students who helped shape such discussions the previous year, also contributed.

There were exceptions. Bisexual students were more vocal than before about the ways both straight and gay communities were prejudiced against them or misrepresented them. Heightened bisexual awareness may, in part, have been a result of the impact of a major bisexual speaker, Lani Kaahumanu, who participated in Gay Pride Week that fall.

In the circumstances of the second class, I felt a greater responsibility to bring diverse lesbian, gay, and bisexual voices into discussions through the readings. Our texts, therefore, became an even more central resource.

Course content also helped counter racial bias. In both semesters the class was primarily white. In the first semester the course was offered, it was exclusively so. The second semester, a feminist-friendly black man whose family was Guyanese enrolled. Students of color make up 5 percent of the total WVU student population, and 6 percent of undergraduate students. Three percent both of total students and of undergraduates are African American.[21] There are very few gays of color who are out on campus. I was concerned that the white experience of sexuality not become implicitly hegemonic. Readings on Native American, Mexican, and African American heterosexual experience, and African American, Mexican, and Chicano lesbians and gay men shifted the center to these groups. The perspective of lesbians and gays of color helped make the "naturalness" of Anglo sexual identities problematic.

In the first semester the class met for a three-hour block in the evening. Various class activities helped promote a "lesbigay-friendly" classroom environment. In both the first and second years I emphasized in the first class meeting that a good portion of the course content would be on lesbian, bisexual, and gay issues.[22] Questions raised by such material—for example, social constructionist and essentialist explanations of sexual identity or mechanisms of sexual regulation and marginalization—were then integrated throughout the semester. In the first semester, a lively discussion of the benefits and drawbacks of labeling also took place the first evening, and the class later returned to the topic when we discussed community and identity.[23]

I also asked the students to brainstorm topics for required group projects (or in the second semester, individual paper topics). We filled the board with a variety of possible subject areas, including sex education in the schools, marital rape and the law, femme/butch in the lesbian community, straight and gay experiences of pornography, lesbians and gays in the military, and others. In the first semester the group project "brainstorm" closed the class meeting, producing a high level of collective class energy by tapping student interests and creativity. (Since in the second semester the class met twice a week for shorter time periods, I asked students to bring in topics for a brainstorm during the second meeting.) The brainstorming made it clear that students were expected to be active participants in the class and that this was a course where lesbian, gay, and bisexual themes were welcome—without promoting possibly risky self-disclosure in the first session.

While coalitions and alliances can develop in the classroom, not all students may wish or be ready to make the commitment that is required of faculty who teach as allies. Throughout both semesters, I was acutely aware of my own position as a straight if gay-positive feminist teacher. In class I called attention to my own social privilege in discussing the institutionalization of heterosexuality.[24] I worked to understand life experiences I had not had and encouraged students to become more aware of how their identities are relational, a part of group relations. However, while I hoped students would be open to lives different from their own as they participated in the course, I did not assume that every class member had the desire or ability to make a further commitment to understanding or action.[25] Still, collective in-class and out of class activities can help build knowledge of others, and even commitment and trust.

We made space for announcements of relevant events. This situated the class in larger social struggles and acknowledged students' commitments outside the classroom. In the first year there were announcements of a workshop led by a member of the National Gay and Lesbian Task Force on New Right backlash. There was discussion of the formation of a university-wide Council on Sexual Orientation and evaluation of what effect the university's antidiscrimination clause had on faculty and student attitudes. In the second year, class members discussed attacks by a local politician on BIGLM. A Take Back the Night rally and march, which included protest against hate crimes targeting gays as well as rape and domestic violence, was announced by students who were taking a leadership role in organizing the event.

Group projects in the first semester also contributed to breaking down isolation between class members and helped clarify and bridge differences among students in their identities and their political approach to issues. Students chose topics, usually from the list developed in the brainstorm, and collaboratively researched in-class presentations, after providing me with a group proposal. The students were then required to write individual papers incorporating material from their group presentation. Many straight students demonstrated their desire to act as allies through their choice of project topics or participation in gay-straight project groups. Lesbian, gay, and bisexual students also negotiated their differences and affirmed solidarity through class projects.

One of the more successful presentations, on pornography, was done by a group of students who were mixed both in gender and sexual orientation and who collectively explored how their different subjectivities shaped their responses to the topic. While they engaged in collective activity and discussion—for example, going to a pornographic bookstore together—members of the project group did not feel any need to come to agreement. Their multiple perceptions, sometimes overlapping, sometimes differing, were the center of their class presentation.

Another presentation, on gays in the military, became the basis for a joint evening with BIGLM. Armed forces policy toward gays in the military had become a hot campus topic because of the vocal opposition of ROTC members to any changes. While I and members of BIGLM who were participants in the class arranged the invitation with the BIGLM programming coordinator, we first got the agreement of the class. Since the group of students who presented that evening were the first to share their research project with the class, the evening felt particularly special. In addition to the group presentation, we also showed the film *Comrades in Arms*, a British recreation of the experience of gays and lesbians in the military during World War II.

Group project presentations swallowed up most of class time in the latter portion of the course, making it difficult to explore course material, especially lesbigay material, as thoroughly as I and the class would have liked. I therefore reluctantly abandoned the collaborative projects the second time I taught the course. Instead, to give students the experience of collaborating with other students, I substituted two activities: giving each student a partner who would provide feedback on the drafts of thematic/research papers, and asking students to bring in discussion questions every week. I was dissatisfied with the outcome of the first activity: a few students chose the draft and critique deadline to disappear from the class, and we all agreed that the partnered critiques were not "public" enough discussions of what class members were doing.[26]

The second experiment, however, was extremely successful. On Tuesdays most students consistently brought in questions on our weekly readings, which I typed up on one or two sheets and disseminated for our Thursday sessions. I would group questions to suggest themes. Sometimes I would start us off with a question I particularly wanted to pursue. Still, Thursdays became known as the days students set the agenda for the class.

The questions offered by students deepened our understanding of the issues by providing collective readings of the material. Students felt that the questions democratized the class and built trust among students and between faculty and students. As one student wrote on the year-end evaluation, "I really enjoyed the class discussions on Thursdays. I learned a lot from the other people in the class as well as the material we read!"[27] Another wrote that the student-generated discussion questions "gave us a voice—and also let us see where other people were coming from." This student also maintained that one of the most valuable aspects of the course was "the open environment which nurtured no holds barred discussion."

Successful ally teaching does not preclude conflict in the classroom. Indeed, the articulation of disagreement can mean that a class has become safe *enough* that participants are able to take risks with one another, rather than burying differences in premature agreement or the silence of resistance.[28] In the first semester I was especially heartened when students disagreed with my social constructionist approach to sexual identity, or argued with each other about the best strategies to achieve liberation. Such disagreements emphasized how "knowledge is produced, negotiated and transformed" in the classroom.[29] When students challenged my interpretations or disagreed with other students' political strategies, they demonstrated that pedagogy is interactive and not a matter of knowledge transmitted by the instructor and passively received by individual students unaffected by one another.[30]

Disagreement about the relative value of social construction and essentialism provided an opportunity to encourage students to develop their own interpretations. Some students were especially wary of social constructionist analyses of present-day lesbian and gay identity because such theoretical approaches tended to neglect the relationship between psychology and collective social formation. Others were persuaded by social construction's attempt to historicize sexuality and its emphasis on the mediation of sexual identity by cultural and historical factors.[31] Students who embraced social constructionist theories argued that such approaches freed them from what they perceived as the limitations and denials inherent in all fixed sexual categories, while others were concerned that such explanations were vulnerable to misinterpretation in the current political environment. Like many current gay activists, they preferred a biologically determined "born this way" explanation of sexual identity in the face of right-wing attacks.

To explore student responses to various social constructionist and essentialist explanatory strategies, I asked the students to write about what they liked and disliked and what they found useful in each. This produced a collective text that I reproduced for the students. As a result of this activity, student responses to questions on the final examination about nineteenth-century female romantic friendships and Mexican and Chicano same-sex relations became less polarized. Regardless of their preferred theoretical stance, students did not dismiss any of the models as outside consideration.

My experience of teaching Sex and Sexuality in American Culture has led me to become more aware of multiple leadership in the classroom. Certainly as a faculty member I bring important resources: my training as a historian and a feminist scholar; personal experiences with political activism; and the authority of my position, which gives me greater access to shaping the classroom community than students have. I provided leadership or contributed specific expertise when I engaged the students in historical thinking that challenged received categories. However, students also provided expertise growing out of their experience in organizing around issues that we addressed in the course, their life experience, or their prior knowledge of the scholarship. I agree with educators David Lusted and Patti Lather that pedagogy involves "the transformation of consciousness that takes place in the intersection of three agencies—the teacher, the learner and the knowledge they together produce."[32] I especially strove to create a community of diverse and differing knowers through activities such as the group projects, the evaluation of social construction and essentialism, and the student-generated study questions.

As I have suggested, feminist and other progressive educators have tried to reconceptualize issues of authority and leadership in the classroom. Early feminist educators relied on solidarity between themselves and their often movement-wise students. They expected students to share responsibility for their education. However, as Barbara Hillyer Davis points out, with the successful institutionalization of women's studies, students who were unfamiliar with consciousness-raising or activism in the women's movement became the majority in women's studies classrooms by the 1980s.[33] Many writers on feminist pedagogy responded by de-emphasizing collective responsibility for classroom learning and by paying renewed attention to faculty's caretaking activities.

A redefinition of authority as something to be shared between faculty and students and among students can be seen in the more recent writing by feminist educators. Postmodern feminists such as Ellsworth and Orner deconstruct the role of teacher as "empowerer."[34] Other feminist educators emphasize how students can become "authorities to each other."[35] This renewed emphasis on multiple, diverse, and reciprocal authorities in the classroom has, in part, emerged from recognition of students' individual expertise.[36] But the most significant contributing factor has been the recognition that students, as well as faculty, are members of social groupings with specific (if partial) knowledge. For example, Ellsworth, as a feminist, had developed "sophisticated strategies for interpreting and interrupting sexism" but recognized that her experience of and understanding of racism were constrained by her "white skin and middle class privilege."[37] She contrasted this with the knowledge of her students of color who had life-long experience with racism and had engaged in campus activism and other antiracist struggles.[38]

Teaching as an ally relies on our recognition of partial perspec-

tives—our own and that of our students—and our need to engage
in collaborative efforts to recover and make central the experience of
previously excluded groups in the construction and reconstruction of
knowledge.[39] This isn't always easy. As one feminist teacher, Nancy
Grey Osterud, points out, her white students resisted examining their
own privilege or developing a systematic analysis of racial inequality.
Nevertheless, she wanted to

> create classrooms that prefigure the possibilities of emancipation. That
> means not only sharing authority with students . . . but also . . . critically
> examining . . . and opposing hierarchies of domination and subordina-
> tion based on race, class, and culture.[40]

As members of the faculty, we cannot divest ourselves of our
positions of authority (and responsibility) in our institutions. However, we can acknowledge and use our position and its opportunities
and responsibilities. My own commitment to lesbigay studies grew as
a result of teaching the sexuality course; I was asked to chair the
Education Committee on Research and Curriculum of the president's
Council on Sexual Orientation. Participation in the council, which was
diverse in sexual orientation, gender, and race, gave me both a sense
of community and continued education in institutional strategizing
around lesbigay issues.[41] Both outside and inside the classroom we
can act as allies with our students.

NOTES

1. Caroline M. Shrewsbury, "What Is Feminist Pedagogy?" *Women's Studies Quarterly* (Special Feature: Feminist Pedagogy) 15, nos. 3–4 (fall/winter
1987): 11–12.

2. Special topics courses are not yet permanent offerings in the curriculum
and do not require institutional approval above the program or departmental
level.

3. Elizabeth Ellsworth, "Why Doesn't This Feel Empowering? Working
Through the Repressive Myths of Critical Pedagogy," in *Feminisms and Critical
Pedagogy*, ed. Carmen Luke and Jennifer Gore (New York: Routledge, 1992),
115.

4. On the necessity of oppressed groups with different standpoints forming alliances, see Davida J. Alperin, "Social Diversity and the Necessity of Alliances: A Developing Feminist Perspective," in *Bridges of Power: Women's Multicultural Alliances*, ed. Lisa Albrecht and Rose M. Brewer (Philadelphia: New Society Publishers, 1990), 23–33.

5. See Lisa Albrecht and Rose M. Brewer, "Bridges of Power: Women's Multicultural Alliances for Change," in Albrecht and Brewer, eds., 3. Albrecht and Brewer are citing the work of Bonnie Thornton Dill.

6. Bonnie Thornton Dill, "Race, Class, and Gender: Prospects for an All-Inclusive Sisterhood," *Feminist Studies* 9, no. 1 (spring 1983): 146.

7. Bernice Johnson Reagon, "Coalition Politics: Turning the Century," in *Home Girls: A Black Feminist Anthology*, ed. Barbara Smith (New York: Kitchen Table: Women of Color Press, 1983), 357, 359.

8. John Schilb, "Pedagogy of the Oppressors?" in *Gendered Subjects: The Dynamics of Feminist Teaching*, ed. Margo Culley and Catherine Portuges (Boston: Routledge and Kegan Paul, 1985), 254.

9. Adherents of critical pedagogy see schools as cultural as well as instructional sites, as "arenas of contestation and struggle among differently empowered cultural and economic groups." Through classroom critiques of injustice and oppression, critical pedagogy attempts to contribute to the creation of an "open, self-critical community of inquiring citizens." See Henry Giroux, *Theory and Resistance in Education: A Pedagogy for the Opposition* (South Hadley, MA: Bergin and Garvey, 1983), 74, 190. Poststructuralist feminists like Orner are critical of what they see as insufficient attention to how power relations structure even progressive forums for dialogue.

10. Mimi Orner, "Interrupting Calls for Student Voice in 'Liberatory' Education: A Feminist Poststructuralist Perspective," in Luke and Gore, eds., 75.

11. Ellsworth, 109.

12. Ellsworth, 115.

13. See Margaret Andersen and Patricia Hill Collins, "Shifting the Center and Reconstructing Knowledge," in *Race, Class, and Gender: An Anthology*, ed. Margaret Andersen and Patricia Hill Collins (Belmont, CA: Wadsworth, 1995), 4. Andersen and Collins describe such awareness as "inclusive thinking."

14. Albrecht and Brewer, eds., 3–4. For an additional definition of "alliance," see Gail Pheterson, "Alliances between Women: Overcoming Internalized Oppression and Internalized Domination," in Albrecht and Brewer, eds., 34–48, especially 36.

15. The title "coordinator" was changed to "director" when the center was established as a freestanding unit in 1984. Women's studies has since moved back into the Eberly College of Arts and Sciences.

16. In the academic year 1993–94, the staff adviser for BIGLM and a profes-

sor in the English department brought together a group of faculty, students, and staff to plan a university-wide committee in recognition that greater institutional and faculty support was needed to address the needs of the lesbian, gay, bisexual, and transgender university community. This group, the Council on Sexual Orientation, received the university president's mandate under the guidance of the Office of Social Justice. The Center for Women was also able to hire a second, permanent director, whose appointment is full-time.

17. I believed it was particularly important to problematize heterosexuality by examining the historical and cultural changes in its meaning, expression, and regulation. In this effort, I was guided by our excellent textbook, John D'Emilio and Estelle Freedman, *Intimate Matters: A History of Sexuality in America* (New York: Harper and Row, 1988).

18. See Evaluation Forms—Spring 1994, WMST 191/391/HIST 111, "Sex and Sexuality in American Culture." All evaluations were anonymous.

19. The term "queer" is controversial, and I use it with caution because it can hide differences and tensions among lesbians, gays, bisexuals, and transgender people. Gay, lesbian, and bisexual students called the class in the first semester a "queer classroom," expressing their sense of co-ownership and because it explored political sexual cultures beyond heterosexual domi-nance. For an excellent discussion of the implications of the term "queer," see Lauren Berlant, Michael Warner, et al., "Forum: On the Political Implications of Using the Term 'Queer,' as in 'Queer Politics,' 'Queer Studies,' and 'Queer Pedagogy,' " *Radical Teacher*, issue on lesbian/gay/queer studies, 45 (winter 1994): 52–57.

20. White students experienced a similar initial silence in a course, Women, Race, and Class, taught by Dorothy Haecker and Frances Jones-Sneed at the University of Missouri-Columbia in the mid-1980s. One student, Mary McNamara, maintained that such silence was temporary. When she learned what other women had to deal with *from other students* her reticence dissipated. See Barbara Scott Winkler, *A Comparative History of Four Women's Studies Programs, 1970–1985*, Ph.D. diss., University of Michigan, Ann Arbor, 1992 (Ann Arbor: University Microfilms International, 1992), p. 349, PR 9303838.

21. See *West Virginia University Statistical Profiles, 1992–1993*, 23d ed., table 5, p. 14.

22. In the second year I wanted to include more readings and discussion about transsexuality and transgender. While we did have several articles, the excellent book that I hoped we could order in its less expensive paperback edition before the end of the course became available too late. I intend to

include it next time I teach the course. See Kate Bornstein, *Gender Outlaw: On Men, Women, and the Rest of Us* (New York: Routledge, 1994).

23. Students distinguished between self-identification and labeling by others in the use of terms like "queer," "dyke," and so forth. While some students felt uncomfortable with labels as simplifying their histories and self-understanding, others felt they were useful in creating and identifying community.

24. In the first semester this resulted in a certain amount of good-natured teasing by students who had decided I was just a little bit "bent."

25. I believe that it is important for faculty to keep encouraging involvement and creating support for students with whom we disagree. In all my classes I establish ground rules for mutual respect as the basis for discussion. When sexist, homophobic, racist, or other prejudiced comments are made, I intervene in a way that tries to honor the integrity of each student while helping them step back from their own preconceptions. I ask all of us, including myself, to do this thoughtfully, with compassion, and with humor when appropriate.

26. Interestingly, the critiques had worked well that fall semester in the U.S. Contemporary Women's Movements course. I think the difference may be due to the subject matter.

27. See Evaluation Forms—Spring 1995, WMST 191/391/HIST 111, "Sex and Sexuality in American Culture."

28. While students disagreed with one another and with me, I found that this was usually tempered by good humor and respect. A colleague, Dennis Allen, who had helped found the Council on Sexual Orientation, found this also to be the case in his course Cultural Representations of Sexual Diversity, which he taught for the first time in the fall of 1994.

29. See Jane Kenway and Helen Modra, "Feminist Pedagogy and Emancipatory Possibilities," in Luke and Gore, eds., 143.

30. See Patti Lather, "Post-Critical Pedagogies: A Feminist Reading," in Luke and Gore, eds., 121. On students as academic authorities, see Frances Maher and Mary Kay Thompson Tetreault, *The Feminist Classroom: An Inside Look at How Professors and Students Are Transforming Higher Education for a Diverse Society* (New York: Basic Books, 1994), 130.

31. See Carole Vance, "Social Construction Theory: Problems in the History of Sexuality," in *Homosexuality, Which Homosexuality?* ed. Dennis Altman, Carole Vance, et al. (London: GMP Publishers, 1989), 13, 21.

32. David Lusted, "Why Pedagogy?" *Screen* 27, no. 5 (1986): 3, quoted in Lather, 121.

33. Barbara Hillyer Davis, "Teaching the Feminist Minority," in Culley and Portuges, eds., 245–52.

34. See Ellsworth and Orner, especially 77, 83.
35. See Maher and Tetreault, 130.
36. See Maher and Tetreault, 129, 161–62.
37. Ellsworth, 100.
38. Ellsworth, 99.
39. See Andersen and Collins, 3.
40. Nancy Grey Osterud, quoted in Maher and Tetreault, 160.
41. The Education Committee was successful in obtaining a grant from the WVU Provost's Multicultural Committee to plan a faculty development seminar on the intersection of racial and sexual identities, focusing on lesbigay people of color.

BIBLIOGRAPHY

Albrecht, Lisa, and Rose M. Brewer. "Bridges of Power: Women's Multicultural Alliances for Change." In *Bridges of Power*, ed. Albrecht and Brewer, 2–22.
———. *Bridges of Power: Women's Multicultural Alliances.* Philadelphia: New Society Publishers, 1990.
Alperin, Davida. "Social Diversity and the Necessity of Alliances: A Developing Feminist Perspective." In *Bridges of Power*, ed. Albrecht and Brewer, 23–33.
Andersen, Margaret, and Patricia Hill Collins. "Shifting the Center and Reconstructing Knowledge." In *Race, Class, and Gender: An Anthology*, ed. Margaret Andersen and Patricia Hill Collins, 1–9. Belmont, CA: Wadsworth, 1995.
Berlant, Lauren, Michael Warner, et al. "Forum: On the Political Implications of Using the Term 'Queer,' as in 'Queer Politics,' 'Queer Studies,' and 'Queer Pedagogy.' " *Radical Teacher*, issue on lesbian/gay/queer studies 45 (winter 1994): 52–57.
Bornstein, Kate. *Gender Outlaw: On Men, Women, and the Rest of Us.* New York: Routledge, 1994.
Culley, Margo, and Catherine Portuges, eds. *Gendered Subjects: The Dynamics of Feminist Teaching.* Boston: Routledge and Kegan Paul, 1985.
Davis, Barbara Hillyer. "Teaching the Feminist Minority." In *Gendered Subjects: The Dynamics of Feminist Teaching*, ed. Culley and Portuges, 245–52.
D'Emilio, John, and Estelle Freedman. *Intimate Matters: A History of Sexuality in America.* New York: Harper and Row, 1988.
Dill, Bonnie Thornton. "Race, Class, and Gender: Prospects for an All-Inclusive Sisterhood." *Feminist Studies* 9, no. 1 (spring 1983): 131–50.
Ellsworth, Elizabeth. "Why Doesn't This Feel Empowering? Working

Through the Repressive Myths of Critical Pedagogy." In *Feminisms and Critical Pedagogy*, ed. Luke and Gore, 90–119.

Giroux, Henry. *Theory and Resistance in Education: A Pedagogy for the Opposition.* South Hadley, MA: Bergin and Garvey, 1983.

Kenway, Jane, and Helen Modra. "Feminist Pedagogy and Emancipatory Possibilities." In *Feminisms and Critical Pedagogy*, ed. Luke and Gore, 138–66.

Lather, Patti. "Post-Critical Pedagogies: A Feminist Reading." In *Feminisms and Critical Pedagogy*, ed. Luke and Gore, 120–37.

Luke, Carmen, and Jennifer Gore, eds. *Feminisms and Critical Pedagogy.* New York: Routledge, 1992.

Lusted, David. "Why Pedagogy?" *Screen* 27, no. 5 (1986): 2–14.

Maher, Frances, and Mary Kay Thompson Tetreault. *The Feminist Classroom: An Inside Look at How Professors and Students Are Transforming Higher Education for a Diverse Society.* New York: Basic Books, 1994.

Orner, Mimi. "Interrupting Calls for Student Voice in 'Liberatory' Education: A Feminist Poststructuralist Perspective." In *Feminisms and Critical Pedagogy*, ed. Luke and Gore, 74–89.

Pheterson, Gail. "Alliances between Women: Overcoming Internalized Oppression and Internalized Domination." In *Bridges of Power*, ed. Albrecht and Brewer, 34–48.

Reagon, Bernice Johnson. "Coalition Politics: Turning the Century." In *Home Girls: A Black Feminist Anthology*, ed. Barbara Smith, 356–68. New York: Kitchen Table: Women of Color Press, 1983.

Schilb, John. "Pedagogy of the Oppressors?" In *Gendered Subjects: The Dynamics of Feminist Teaching*, ed. Culley and Portuges, 253–64.

Shrewsbury, Caroline M. "What Is Feminist Pedagogy?" *Women's Studies Quarterly* (Special Feature: Feminist Pedagogy) 15, nos. 3–4 (fall/winter 1987): 6–14.

Vance, Carole. "Social Construction Theory: Problems in the History of Sexuality." In *Homosexuality, Which Homosexuality?* ed. Dennis Altman, Carole Vance et al., 13–34. London: GMP Publishers, 1989.

West Virginia University Statistical Profiles, 1992–1993. 23d ed.

Winkler, Barbara Scott. *A Comparative History of Four Women's Studies Programs, 1970–1985.* Ph.D. diss. Ann Arbor: University Microfilms International, 1992. PR 9303838.

4

The Outsider's Gaze

JANET M. POWERS

As we in women's studies struggle with the Insider/Outsider concept in attempting to teach multicultural literature and theory, we can't help but notice that we are experiencing a pervasive postcolonial crisis of authority, a crisis felt most strongly perhaps by formerly hegemonic Western discourses.[1] Yet the problems we face and the questions they raise are of global significance. We have witnessed in academe such a scramble to recognize and celebrate the other that reactionary attitudes have emerged in resistance. In addition, the Insider/Outsider question has arisen: who in fact should teach multicultural literature and theory? Twenty years ago, I found nothing wrong with my teaching an entire course on African American literature, because there wasn't anyone else on our campus who might do it. Now, however, I wouldn't think of teaching such a course, even if there were no minority faculty available, and I'm astounded by my own arrogance in once thinking that I could. The scenario has changed: now there are well-trained African American faculty who represent their culture as Insiders, and who may resent the idea of an Outsider speaking for them.

Yet I continue to teach courses in the civilization and literature of India, the field for which I was trained, and, perhaps more germane to world feminism, I teach a course entitled Contemporary Women's Writing: Cross-Cultural Perspectives. The latter course includes not only African American writing, but also writing by Native Americans, Hispanics, Asians, and Africans. The women's studies program at my college recognizes the need to teach works and perspectives of women of color from our own culture as well as the postcolonial world; indeed, we have committed ourselves to that goal. Yet in the process of teaching those works, one begins to question the appropriateness of Outsiders speaking on behalf of Insiders. In essence, one is disturbed by some of the same questions James Clifford raises in relation to ethnographic authority: who has the authority to speak for a group's identity or authenticity? What are the essential elements and boundaries of a culture? How do self and other clash and converse in encounters of ethnography, travel, modern interethnic relations? What narratives of development, loss, and innovation can account for the present range of oppositional viewpoints?[2]

The first of these questions is of great relevance to women's studies as an issue of pedagogy: who has the authority to speak for a group's identity or authenticity? To those of us who have undertaken the mission of trying to teach one society to another, the question seems urgent. As Clifford observes, " 'cultural' difference is no longer a stable, exotic otherness; self-other relations are matters of power and rhetoric rather than of essence. A whole structure of expectations about authenticity in culture and in art is thrown in doubt."[3] What gives me, an Outsider, the right to teach a work of African American literature and claim to be teaching its essence? Can I take refuge in the fact that I have read a great deal of African American literature and have gained a sense of African American culture from my forays as an Outsider into the pages of an Insider's novel? Or can I, in the manner of an ethnographer, claim the knowledge of a participant-observer because I have African American friends and am welcome in their homes?

The same questions, applied to my teaching of South Asian culture and literature, seem even more acute. In this area, I can claim the rigors of doctoral work, a dissertation, fieldwork in the Indian subcontinent, numerous South Asian friends, repeated research trips to many parts of India, and knowledge of Indian languages. Indeed, I am more at home with Indians and certain parts of the subcontinent than I am in my own culture. Yet I am surrounded by articulate South Asian scholars who speak with a great deal more authority about their culture than I possibly could, even though they may know only a small corner of it. Worse, as I teach South Asian literature, I sometimes feel myself guilty of trying to interpret attitudes and experiences that are not mine and that perhaps I cannot represent authentically.

Trinh T. Minh-Ha writes of how the dominant culture has moved "from obnoxious exteriority to obtrusive interiority," how our quest for

> the so-called *hidden* values of a person or a culture, has given rise to a form of legitimized (but unacknowledged as such) voyeurism and subtle arrogance—namely, the pretense to see into or *to own* the others' *minds*, whose *knowledge* these others cannot, supposedly, have themselves; and the need to define, hence confine, providing them thereby with a standard of self-evaluation on which they necessarily depend.[4]

These words lead me to raise new questions about what I am trying to do in the classroom, particularly when international students or Asian-American students are part of the dialogue. Does what I say about Indian culture have any validity as interpretation, and if my interpretation varies from that of a South Asian, am I in some way limiting the Insider's sense of self?

Even in the field of women's studies, where there ought naturally to have been a sense of sisterhood and shared purpose, there has been a belated recognition that not all women in our culture share the same experiences and that our agendas and our syllabi need to be more inclusive. Yet as my colleague (also white) and I taught an Introduction to Women's Studies course, and deliberately paired every article about the dominant culture with another that dealt with women of color, our affluent, white students constantly complained in their journals that they could not relate to many of the articles. The whole enterprise took on reality only when we brought into the classroom an African American woman, who talked about growing up black in Gettysburg and being discouraged by her high school guidance counselor from aspiring to college; and a Hispanic woman, who told of challenging her father and paying for her own high school education, in order to transcend the cultural expectations for women in her Mexican community. Clearly, the two white instructors could not speak with the same authority because, even though we might have known about these things, our knowledge was secondhand.

In teaching works by women of color, white women inevitably claim an objective similar to that of ethnographers and filmmakers: "to grasp the native's point of view" and "to realize his/her vision of his/her world." The injunction to do so, as Trinh T. Minh-Ha points out, lies at the center of every polemical discussion on "reality" in its relation to "beauty" and "truth."[5] Yet the question of representing the other has become fraught with issues of rhetoric and power, as postcolonial theory takes the issue to sophisticated levels of interpretation, and political correctness becomes a creed rather than the result of changed perception. Indeed, suggests Minh-Ha, allowing the other "an aura" has become a kind of game, for even when the other is being privileged, she is also reminded of the favor she enjoys in being permitted to speak her mind.[6]

Homi Bhabha, in turn, seeks to shift the conversation "from *identification* of images as positive or negative, to an understanding of the *processes of subjectification* made possible (and plausible) through stereotypical discourse."[7] By focusing on the stereotypes Colonizers have typically used in describing the other, Bhabha recognizes that both "the recognition and disavowal of 'difference' is always disturbed by the question of its re-presentation or construction."[8] His observations raise new questions about the content of my syllabi. What am I teaching when I teach *The Bluest Eye* by Toni Morrison or Bharati Mukherjee's *Wife?* Am I teaching the other as the other perceives herself, or as the other filtered through an Anglo understanding of what the other might be? Do I yield to stereotypes in my attempt to represent the other? How do I explain what I do not fully understand myself, even though I recognize its existence?

Bhabha's understanding of stereotypical discourse is complicated:

> Stereotyping is not the setting up of a false image which becomes the scapegoat of discriminatory practices. It is a much more ambivalent text of projection and introjection, metaphoric and metonymic strategies, displacement, overdetermination, guilt, aggressivity; the masking and splitting of "official" and fantasmatic knowledges to construct the positionalities and oppositionalities of racist discourse.[9]

For Bhabha, stereotypes, and indeed colonial discourse in general, is "a complex articulation of the tropes of fetishism . . . and the forms of narcissistic and aggressive identification available to the Imaginary."[10] He perceives stereotypical racial discourse as a four-term strategy linking the metaphoric (or masking) function of the fetish and the narcissistic object-choice on the one hand and the metonymic figuring of lack with the Imaginary on the other. Here, Bhabha addresses the Colonizer's fascination with the other, his simultaneous need to denigrate and adore that which he perceives as weak and different.

Perhaps most useful in Bhabha's analysis of the stereotype is the recognition that what it dramatizes is *separation*—"*between* races, cultures, histories, *within* histories—a separation between *before* and *after* that repeats obsessively the mythical moment of disjunction."[11] If separation is the essential message of the stereotype, then it must follow that separation is the notion to avoid. Does negating separation mean that I should be focusing on similarities rather than differences? If so, wherein lies the value in exploring the other? What am I asking my students to do when I ask them to stretch their notions of what is possible and what is beautiful? Wherein lies *my* fascination with the other? Is it a concern for the weak, which gives me a notion of power? Is it a delight in the exotic, which makes me something of a voyeur?

Is it a reveling in things imagined, which causes me aggressively to explore the boundaries of what is possible? Or is it the desire for an originality, so lacking in myself, that I must appropriate another's?

Minh-Ha might say that in asking these questions I am opening a space for the other, yet "the space offered is not that of an object brought to visibility, but that of the very invisibility of the invisible within the visible . . . the space of an activity in which everything takes on a collective value in spite of skepticism."[12] I still do not see the Insider except as the other, even though I may attempt to teach her culture. And though I, as the Outsider, am more than happy to accord recognition to and celebrate the Insider, a new set of negativities and positivities emerges in questioning and renaming otherness and unnaming the Colonizer and the other.[13] I am still the Outsider, still looking in, still trying to discern the nature of the other, still gazing at skin, language, habits of conversation, music, ways of relating that are different from my own. Yet, I have taken upon myself the mission of showing what I see to others who are younger, less experienced, more afraid. How can I avoid teaching them to gaze in the same way that I do? If my own fascination with other cultures is suspect, why should I hope that they too will come to identify with the other as I do?

As a way out of this predicament, I would like to propose that we reexamine four modes of authority claimed by ethnographers, with the understanding that what we do in the classroom is, by analogy, similar to what an ethnographer does in representing the other.[14] When we teach literature written by persons from cultures other than our own, we attempt to convey the essence of those cultures based on words and narratives constructed by native speakers. Like ethnographers, we offer our students enhanced access to the worlds of the other. Although any reader might conceivably gain such access via the printed page, a teacher promises additional cultural knowledge, gained either by direct experience or by scholarly work, that will fa-

cilitate the student's access. Presumably, teachers claim as well superior ability to make sense of the words and narratives constructed by
the other. The ethnographer's strategies, therefore, are useful to the
teacher in the dual processes of access and representation.

The first such strategy is that of the participant-observer, already
referred to, and perhaps best known as a technique for anthropological fieldwork. The second, interpretation, consists of the ethnographer's attempt to analyze his data and present it in the realm of public discourse. The third strategy, the dialogical mode of authority,
recognizes the fact that native control over what is observed and
known by the fieldworker can be considerable. Last, the polyphonic
strategy recognizes not only the views of the fieldworker and the
effect of his gaze on the native subject, but also the creative activity
of the reader. Although each has its limitations, these modes of authority offer strategies of representation that may be used in the classroom.

Clifford describes participant observation as "a continuous tacking
between the 'inside' and 'outside' of events: on the one hand grasp-
ing the sense of specific occurrences and gestures empathetically, on
the other stepping back to situate these meanings in wider contexts."[15] Those Euro-Americans who have lived abroad, attended a
Martin Luther King celebration, celebrated a holiday or birthday with
a Hispanic or Native American family, shared a room with someone
of a different race, have experienced, however briefly, the role of participant-observer. "Experiential authority is based on a 'feel' for the
foreign context, a kind of accumulated savvy and a sense of the style
of a people or place. . . . Like 'intuition,' it is something that one does
or does not have, and its invocation often smacks of mystification."
How does one draw on such experiences? An instructor's anecdote,
understood to be and presented as that of the Outsider/Insider, is
often arresting and appreciated, and it serves to make a piece of information memorable. Relevant students' experiences should be elicited to achieve the same effect whenever possible. Students must be

encouraged to recognize and seek participant experiences, even if they do not fully understand their role of observers until later.

Clifford goes on to suggest that one "resist the temptation to translate all meaningful experience into interpretation. If the two are reciprocally related, they are not identical."[16] Indeed, the instructor simply telling of an experience with an acknowledgment that she has not fully understood what happened can be more effective in claiming authority than reams of interpretation aimed at understanding a common, meaningful world. The details of concrete experience suggest a sensitive contact with that world, as well as a rapport with its people. The flaw in the participant-observer mode of authority, however, is that it is, in the end, personal. It is "my experience" that is being related, and for everyone else, it lacks the concrete perception that has inscribed it indelibly in the mind of the participant.

Interpretation as a mode of authority involves looking at a culture as an assemblage of texts to be interpreted by a single thinker. In the classroom, we can often work with texts that have already become autonomous, available to the public domain. The interpretive process is thus separated from the text and from the fictive world generated by the text. Clifford notes that the ethnographer-interpreter may be compared with the literary interpreter, or better yet, "with the traditional critic, who sees the task at hand as locating the unruly meaning of a text in a single coherent intention."[17] I rather like his use of the term *unruly*, for it conveys the notion of information that has a life of its own and that must be approached assertively, perhaps even "tamed," before it is ready for presentation in the classroom. The act of preparing to teach a new text is very much like that: one first reads it, notes the major ideas and themes, savors specific imagery, wrestles with disturbing elements, and attempts to organize them all into some sort of coherent perception that can be passed on to students.

The trick here, I think, is in inviting students to do the same, to deconstruct the text by focusing on disturbing elements, ones that don't fit neatly into conventional explanations or previous ways of seeing. It is sometimes difficult not to tell them, if one has already figured everything out, what they should see and understand. Interpretation is an art that can be taught, but it takes time, and it sometimes goes astray because students have not had the observer-participant experience discussed earlier. Leslie Marmon Silko's *Storyteller*, for example, appears at first to be a randomly gathered mélange of stories, personal recollections, and poems. Yet certain themes must be teased from what is actually an intricate narrative chain, to illuminate Native American attitudes toward gender, sexuality, and cultural confrontation. The vulnerability of interpretation lies, of course, in the way it too is subject to the potentially flawed understanding and expressivity of the interpreter, or, in the case of a class, interpreters. An attempt at interpretation may dissolve into participant-observer anecdotes, or it may emerge with such abstraction as to fail in its intent to illuminate.

Perhaps more desirable is "a process of dialogue where interlocuters actively negotiate a shared vision of reality."[18] If one is lucky, she has multicultural students in the classroom to help show the way. An insensitive professor, however, may overdo the consultative process. Such students need space in which to disagree if they need to. One can also make use of recognized Insider interpretations, which, claiming their own authority, map the way for students and professors alike. Pulling in a significant critical observation at the right moment will often push the interpretive process in a productive direction. Being able to insert a point from a lecture by Gloria Naylor, that "women are circumscribed by words," illuminates our discussion of *Bailey's Cafe*. Finally, at the risk of concentrating the Outsider's gaze into a high-powered laser beam, bringing into the classroom someone the students can interact with, listen to, and ask questions of is inevitably a successful way of at least demonstrating a linkage of authenticity. The fact that the professor knows and is able to produce such informants garners her some authority. However, the recipient of the gaze may well view this opportunity to tell her story as potentially dangerous: "what is given in the context of power relations is likely to be taken back according to where the wind blows."[19]

Perhaps the most workable mode of authority, however, is the polyphonic one, exemplified by Bakhtin's analysis of the "polyphonic novel," which "represents speaking subjects in a field of multiple discourses."[20] As Clifford observes, for Bakhtin the polyphonic novel is "a carnivalesque arena of diversity ... a utopian textual space where discursive complexity, the dialogical interplay of voices, can be accommodated."[21] For the ethnographer, this strategy may amount to a sort of "plural authorship that accords collaborators not merely the status of independent enunciators but that of writers."[22] Indeed, suggests Clifford, the creative activity of a reader, as enunciated by reader-response theory, may also contribute to the coherence of a text. Ultimately, there is always a possible variety of readings beyond the control of any particular authority. Being able to relinquish one's own sense of a work, however, is sometimes difficult, particularly when students insist on simplistic, Disneyesque, or overly specific religious and/or political readings.

Yet this model of the polyphonic novel is perhaps the most desirable mode of authority for the classroom of the nineties, for what Bakhtin values is precisely the resistance of certain novels to totality, their inability to be subsumed under a single coherent critical perception. By acknowledging a variety of voices and possible interpretations, one avoids the possibility of the Outsider's gaze falling painfully and stereotypically on the Insider. Although the possibility of stereotyping cannot be eliminated, particularly with students reading a text in various ways, the instructor as Outsider can always gently question whether a student's reading of the text falls into the realm of stereotype. Accordingly, I have had to defuse observations about Asian reticence in a discussion of *Bone* by Faye Myenne Ng. Such an approach, however, assumes an initial discussion of what is involved in a stereotype, and although Bhabha's discussion is difficult, it is illuminating.

In order to provoke a multivalent reading of a novel, the instructor must not ask the question, "What does this statement mean?" Rather, she must ask a sequence of questions: (1) "What possible meanings could this statement have?" (2) "Are any of these meanings more likely than others?" and finally (3) "Why?" Theory by and about women of color is just as likely to resist simple explanation and to lend itself to polyphonic interpretation, if one asks the right questions of it. Open-ended questions like, "What might have led her to say this?" or "What sort of experiences might lie behind such a statement?" will go a long way toward allowing the texts to speak for themselves in many tongues. Acknowledging the polyphonic voices in the classroom, as well as the text, is of course a key to any successful discussion in a women's studies class. Such an approach makes possible the teaching, by Outsiders, of multicultural literature and theory in a manner acceptable, although perhaps not ideal, for students of varied ethnic backgrounds.

To conclude, I would like to cite three texts, used in teaching an introduction to women's studies course, that elicited something like real understanding from my white, upper-middle-class students, and perhaps even empowered them to work at trading eyes with Insiders. Each addresses the Insider/Outsider predicament and models ways of traversing the slippery terrain of perceived difference. The first, used at the beginning of the course, became a touchstone for everything else that we read all semester: an article by Maria Lugones, entitled "Playfulness, 'World'-Travelling, and Loving Perception" (1990). Two phrases in particular from this article were used by students repeatedly in journals and discussion: *"world"-travelling* and *arrogant perception*. By "world"-travelling, Lugones means that one can "travel" between the worlds that construct us and can inhabit more than one of these "worlds" at the very same time. The shift from being one person to being a different person is what she calls "travel."[23] "Arrogant perception," on the other hand, is an attitude that gets in the way of "world"-travelling, and in particular, inhibits the playfulness involved in it: "the agonistic traveller is a conqueror, an imperialist."[24] Lugones's article spells out very clearly what an Outsider must do to participate in the culture of an Insider. "World"-travelling, or openness to reconstruction (which sometimes means being a fool), cancels the sense of separation that results in stereotyping. It requires a sense of adventure, but—also important—it's fun.

A second article that seems to me quite extraordinary is "The Social Construction of Black Feminist Thought," by Patricia Hill Collins. In this work Collins notes that "values and ideas that Africanist scholars identify as being characteristically African American often bear remarkable resemblance to ideas claimed by feminist scholars as being characteristically female."[25] A generous act of revelation on the part of a woman of color, this essay is an attempt to open to the Outsider the epistemology of the Insider by calling attention to four ways of constructing knowledge (not surprisingly, devalued by academe and the patriarchal culture) that they have in common: (1) living as a black woman requires wisdom and "connected knowing"; and therefore, concrete experience is valued as a criterion of meaning;[26] (2) African American women develop knowledge claims through dialogues with others in a community; the very act of speech involves affirmation of the speaker;[27] (3) the ethic of caring validates the appropriateness of emotions in dialogue for both black women and women in general; "ideas cannot be divorced from the individuals who create and share them";[28] (4) the ethic of personal accountability, in which "all views expressed and actions taken are thought to derive from a central set of core beliefs that cannot be other than personal," is shared by black culture and women in general.[29] By revealing commonalities, Collins invites the Outsider in, bridges the gap between, and suggests that Insiders and Outsiders occupy the same space.

Finally, in "The Master's Tools Will Never Dismantle the Master's House," Audre Lorde challenges women "to reach down into that deep place of knowledge inside herself and touch that terror and loathing of any difference that lives there. See whose face it wears."[30] Insisting that it is not the place of women of color to educate white women as to their existence, differences, and relative roles in joint survival, Lorde suggests that not to study the other is an evasion of responsibility. From these three articles, we must conclude that although difference is perceptible, it is also bridgeable. Lugones and Collins show us ways to tear down the walls between the Outsider and the Insider; Lorde tells us that we must.

Minh-Ha writes of how the dominant culture has moved from caring nothing about the internal lives and emotions of non–Anglo-Saxon peoples to caring about little else. Thus we seem obsessed sometimes by the need to uncover or somehow get at Insiders' sense of self, "supposedly through the definitions they have of themselves."[31] For the Insider, submitting oneself to the Outsider's gaze can be an exhausting prospect, particularly when the Outsider shows so little willingness to engage in the sort of "world"-travel that is constantly required of minorities in Western culture. And it may be that the Outsider can trade eyes with Insiders only in fragmentary moments, unless she dwells for an extended period within the other culture and experiences the distortion of her own gaze. Nevertheless, I am heartened by women of color such as Lugones, Collins, and Lorde, who encourage and exhort the Outsider to stop gazing and start interacting, to stop being self-conscious but not lose her sensitivity, to pay attention to what Insiders are saying about themselves, and above all, to engage in "loving perception."

NOTES

1. James Clifford, *The Predicament of Culture* (Cambridge: Harvard University Press, 1988), 8.

2. Clifford, 8.

3. Clifford, 14.

4. Trinh T. Minh-Ha, *When the Moon Waxes Red: Representation, Gender, and Cultural Politics* (New York: Routledge, 1991), 66.

5. Minh-Ha, 65.

6. Minh-Ha, 186.

7. Homi Bhabha, "The Other Question: Difference, Discrimination and the Discourse of Colonialism," in *Literature, Politics and Theory*, ed. Francis Barker et al. (New York: Methuen, 1986), 149.

8. Bhabha, 169.

9. Bhabha, 169.

10. Bhabha, 164.

11. Bhabha, 170.

12. Minh-Ha, 187–88.

13. Minh-Ha, 187.

14. Clifford, 53.

15. Clifford, 34.

16. Clifford, 35.

17. Clifford, 40.

18. Clifford, 43.

19. Minh-Ha, 186.

20. Clifford, 46.

21. Clifford, 46–47.

22. Clifford, 51.

23. Maria Lugones, "Playfulness, 'World'-Travelling, and Loving Perception," in *Making Face, Making Soul: Haciendo Caras*, ed. G. Anzaldúa (San Francisco: Aunt Lute Foundation Books, 1990), 396.

24. Lugones, 400.

25. Patricia Hill Collins, "The Social Construction of Black Feminist Thought," in *Feminist Frontiers III*, ed. Laurel Richardson and Verta Taylor (New York: McGraw-Hill, 1993).

26. Collins, 22–23.

27. Collins, 24.

28. Collins, 25.

29. Collins, 26.

30. Audre Lorde, "The Master's Tools Will Never Dismantle the Master's House," in *Feminist Frontiers III*, ed. Richardson and Taylor, 11.

31. Minh-Ha, 66.

BIBLIOGRAPHY

Bhabha, Homi. "The Other Question: Difference, Discrimination and the Discourse of Colonialism." In *Literature, Politics and Theory*, ed. Francis Barker et al. New York: Methuen, 1986.

Clifford, James. *The Predicament of Culture*. Cambridge: Harvard University Press, 1988.

Collins, Patricia Hill. "The Social Construction of Black Feminist Thought." In *Feminist Frontiers III*, ed. Laurel Richardson and Verta Taylor. New York: McGraw-Hill, 1993.

Lorde, Audre. "The Master's Tools Will Never Dismantle the Master's House." In *Feminist Frontiers III*, ed. Richardson and Taylor.

Lugones, Maria. "Playfulness, 'World'-Travelling, and Loving Perception." In *Making Face, Making Soul: Haciendo Caras*, ed. G. Anzaldúa. San Francisco: Aunt Lute Foundation Books, 1990.

Minh-Ha, Trinh T. *When the Moon Waxes Red: Representation, Gender, and Cultural Politics*. New York: Routledge, 1991.

Morrison, Toni. *The Bluest Eye*. New York: Washington Square, 1970.

Mukherjee, Bharati. *Wife*. New York: Penguin, 1987.

Naylor, Gloria. *Bailey's Cafe*. New York: Harcourt Brace Jovanovich, 1992.

Ng, Fae Myenne. *Bone*. New York: HarperCollins, 1993.

Silko, Leslie Marmon. *Storyteller*. New York: Little, Brown, 1981.

5

No Middle Ground?
Men Teaching Feminism

J. SCOTT JOHNSON, JENNIFER KELLEN,
GREG SEIBERT, and CELIA
SHAUGHNESSY

"What does it matter who is teaching feminist political theory? What does it matter who is teaching?" This is how we four responded to the question whether one of us (Johnson) should or should not be teaching a course in which the other three were enrolled. But answering a question with a question is not particularly satisfying, nor were we content with the responses we received from our peers. When we presented a talk to faculty on teaching about gender and the relation of gender to the content of a course on the classics of political theory and a course on feminist theory, we were surprised by hostile skepticism from tenured women faculty in three different departments. The discussion quickly polarized. Some senior women faculty who had fought to get gender issues and feminist concerns into the curriculum were not willing to entertain the possibility that a man could teach feminism, because they felt gender was a blinding filter. Apparently the position they were attacking was one that held that anyone could teach feminist theory because gender doesn't matter. There is no middle ground between these positions as they saw them. However, denying men the opportunity to teach feminist theory is a precaution that feminist theory does not need to take. All that is required is a recognition that gender does matter in teaching, and that this acknowledgment should not prevent teaching. In fact, appreciating the role that gender plays can often improve a course regardless of the gender of the professor. This essay reflects our experiences surrounding a course on feminist political theory that was taught by a man.

Government 313: Feminist Political Theory was offered for the first time at Saint John's University and the College of Saint Benedict during the fall semester of 1994. Seventeen students, eleven men and six women, enrolled in the class. We began by comparing Susan Estrich's argument in *Real Rape* to the discussion by Katie Roiphe in *The Morning After*. Following that we surveyed some of the claims made in the history of political thought from Plato, through Rousseau, to Freud. Most of the semester required an investigation of the feminist response and positive critique. We used Rosemarie Tong's introductory textbook and read selections from theorists representing liberal, existential, Marxist, radical, and socialist feminisms. We considered the debate over Adrienne Rich's "Compulsory Heterosexuality and Lesbian Existence" as well as that over Gilligan's theory of *A Different Voice* and an ethic of care. Finally, we considered Naomi Wolf's conception of power feminism and tried to see whether it fit easily into any of our original categories. The course was challenging and the reading load heavy, but most of the students were successfully able to examine critically the ideas presented.

Feminist political theory is often assumed to be more than theory because the point of feminism is to change the world; in other words, feminist theory without action is not really feminist theory. Feminist political theory is a human activity through which women have sought to establish their equality, though different versions of feminist theory have different programs for change. Historically, women also have used feminist theory to argue for greater particularized benefits for themselves as a class or group. Students sometimes have difficulty separating the analytic portions of a theory from its policy recommendations. They often want the right answer and unreflectively accept whatever is placed before them unless they suspect that it has a partisan bias. Of course, feminist theory is unabashedly partisan in favor of the equality of women and men, so many students seem to think of it as propaganda instead of a proper subject for study. On the other hand, some may feel that men cannot present feminist theory sympathetically because they are not supposed to belong to the group that feminist theory is meant to benefit. We argue that both positions are mistaken. Feminist theory simply cannot be dismissed as political indoctrination, but because of the baggage that the recent backlash has attached to the subject, special care must be used in its teaching.

As a group, we believe that a critical approach to feminist political theory allows all students, male and female, to gain a hold on difficult material, assess its strengths and weaknesses, and decide for themselves whether to adopt the perspective advocated by each variety of feminist thought. We maintain that it is not possible to simultaneously and consistently hold and act on all the varieties of feminist political theory, since the debates and differences among feminists are significant and real. We obviously do not believe that men teaching feminist theory are essentially any better than women at maintaining a critical perspective on the subject matter, but we suspect the tension between teaching feminist theory and engaging in political activity, which is inherent in the subject matter itself, explains some of the questioning each of us experienced during the fall of 1994. In what follows we will describe those experiences.

Shaughnessy's Experience

The first person I told that I was taking feminist theory from Scott Johnson immediately had a question: "Is he qualified?" It struck me as odd that this person could not believe that a male could ever be qualified to teach feminist theory. Others asked similar questions, such as, "Why would he want to teach that?" and "What interest does he have in women's issues?" No one had ever questioned the qualifications of any of my other professors. Furthermore, when we gave the talk midsemester, Johnson's senior colleagues dismissed my ability as a student to talk about what I had learned in his class, and they often ignored what he had to say. The room was tense. It looked to me as if it had become a power struggle between two young students as new wave feminists and an older generation of women protecting their authority as longtime feminist scholars. Men were excluded. It seemed that they thought gender was only about women and only women could teach or talk about it.

I, on the other hand, thought it was a great idea that a male was teaching feminist theory, because it could bring a fresh perspective to issues I thought demanded a new look. I was surprised that people assumed that because Johnson was male, he was either unqualified or lacking legitimate interest in the subject matter. I felt that questioning the qualifications of my professor in this class but not in others was injecting partisan concerns into the realm of academics. When we gave the talk, Johnson's senior colleagues even seemed to dismiss my experience as a woman because I was learning about gender and feminism from a man. My friends' responses to the class reflected the polarizing public debate over feminism. Women could love or hate feminism, but not choose the middle ground. Men, on the other hand, were expected to oppose feminism and rarely allowed to be sympathetic or supportive. Treating feminism like any other academic subject—a middle position—was not acceptable. So it seemed the idea of a man being an authority on feminist theory was simply not believable.

From the beginning, I was comfortable in the classroom. For the first time, as a woman, I didn't feel nervous about the possibility (and later the reality) of disagreeing with the feminist mainstream. Johnson did a wonderful thing: he never once laid out what he thought feminist theory was or should be. That was the question that (thank-fully) plagued us through the entire semester. His refusal to define it for us was a key reason the class worked for me. In some ways he was more of a very educated sounding board. I could ask any question or bounce my ideas off him and usually get a ton of questions back. He would never insist that there was a single set way of viewing these ideas. We weren't forced to accept or reject a standard definition of feminism.

As a woman and a student, I found this important. I had always felt uncomfortable being called a feminist because I wasn't really sure that I agreed with all the standard popularized definitions. In this class, I was given the room to find and grow into my own definition of feminism. Johnson would constantly question parts of the definitions that each of us came up with, so that by the end of the semester, I understood and could defend exactly what I believed in.

I felt that Johnson was open to many new ideas and new theories, some of which were highly critical of earlier versions of feminist thought. He gave us a wide variety of readings offering many visions of feminism. This gave us, as a new generation, an opportunity to see that along with the liberal, Marxist, radical, and socialist feminists there were lesbian, minority, and even conservative feminists. To know the history and development of these different strands of theory is of course important and necessary. But we need to know where feminism is today and where it is going in the future.

In my opinion, the historical struggle to form a cohesive women's movement ironically resulted in a loss for individual women of the opportunity to choose their own personal identities. The individual "I" was subsumed in and lost to the ideological "we," defined as all oppressed women. Older versions of feminism obviously can speak for and about all women, but less and less do they speak for and about individual women. They certainly don't speak to me. I think these older versions of feminism have become authoritarian. They seem like a club with particular rules, like those proscribing the enjoyment of sex because women's sexuality has been created by the male patriarchal structure for men's enjoyment, or rules insisting that men cannot be part of the solution because they are the problem. I don't think that that kind of feminism, as it has been popularized and satirized in the media, will work for me or my generation of individual women and men working together for greater equality.

Maybe Johnson presented a more humanistic approach to feminism. By more humanistic, I mean more inclusive and maybe more cooperative. I now believe that feminist theory does not have to divide men and women but can lead to a better search for human equality. I learned that feminism should not make me feel as if I had to choose between men and women. This made me realize that both men and women have to take responsibility and action in order to change thoughts and institutions. I did not have to be a male-basher to be a feminist. Nor did I have to feel left out of the fight for equality just because I did not agree with nor accept all the philosophy or theories that women before me had believed in.

With Johnson's knowledge, guidance, and support, I was able to see the males and females in my class, as well as my professor, as all part of the same struggle to recognize the equality of all human beings. I don't know whether Johnson was more open to this because of his identity. Maybe he was trying to make a genuine effort to reflect on how everyone, including himself, is implicated in the problems, concerns, and triumphs of feminism. This attempt at reflection shows us a human view of equality and feminism. It is what made the class work for me.

Seibert's Experience

Every college student knows how important the choice of professor is to the success of a course. If you find the perfect professor, then even the worst class you can think of can be made worthwhile. However, even the most interesting subject matter can be made deathly dull by the wrong professor.

These thoughts occurred to me as I signed up for a class on feminist theory, a class being taught by, I might add, a man. For some reason it did strike me as odd that a woman was not teaching the course, but I had to take the course anyway so I signed up. Initially, I thought a male professor in this class would have to be either completely effeminate—bordering on gay—or else totally opposed to everything he was teaching. On the other hand, I thought any woman teaching this class could not help but become adamant about one aspect of the movement or another because of her personal experiences. I couldn't see any middle ground between these positions. As I look back, it is clear to me that the gender of the professor affected the view I took of the class.

Feminism has always given me the creeps. In part, this is because I had been confronted with only the most radical, abrasive, and outspoken examples of the feminist movement. These are the ones that make good press and grab the spotlight. None of the history behind feminism is ever presented, and we men are not often allowed to see the real tenets behind the different waves of feminism. It is difficult to discover the entire picture of feminism because of the media's distortions. For men to be sympathetic to feminism, they need to see the origins of the movement and the reasons for its existence.

I will be the first to admit that the fact that Johnson was a male helped me in this class. I knew full well that he was bringing his own prejudices to the classroom and that these prejudices were as much a struggle for him as mine were for me. Because he is a man, I was more open and felt more comfortable asking the questions I thought were important. I did not feel I was being viewed as the enemy. I believed he had probably gone through all the same struggles that I have in trying to figure out who he is in relation to the material he was trying to teach us.

In the past, whenever I tried to discuss with women issues like rape, gender identity, power, and the family unit, they always made me feel as if I had no clue whatsoever about what was happening in their world. I was made to feel as if I were incapable of empathizing with them and their plight. Encounters such as these made me think that I had no way of ever understanding what was happening to them because I was not a woman. Sitting there in class listening to and talking with another man who was obviously well versed in the tenets of feminist theory made me see that I did have the ability to grab hold of the concepts involved. Accusations were not thrown at the class at any point with regard to patriarchal structures or the rape of women. When we examined these topics, we examined hypothetical causes in light of the evidence that was presented by the theorists. Arguments, not accusations, were the central subject of the class. This shifted the focus away from what men had done to women over the years and toward a consideration of the implications of those actions and the question of what we should do now. Thus ideas were always fair game, but the individuals in the class were not.

I found myself becoming a better man for struggling through the course. Johnson knew what he was talking about, and that is what made the class run the way it did. I am glad that he allowed the class to run itself when it would, and could keep it going when the tone of the class required intervention. He had no problem acquainting us with the theoretical frameworks of the wide variety of feminist theories, but at the feeling level he seemed to be learning right along with us. This provided the atmosphere that people need in order to learn. The class became a group endeavor. The process becomes much more effective if the person you are looking up to is trying as hard as you are to really grasp the impact of the issues involved. Johnson let us see what it was like to struggle through the issues. I do not think the gender of my professor hampered the class or in any way diminished the knowledge I gained. If the world wants men to become better men, then more men should teach feminist theory and more men should take classes in it. The information and theories contained in the movement hold the power for both halves of the population to be liberated.

Johnson's Experience

It might help for you to know that I am a political scientist, broadly trained in public policy and political theory at Carleton College, the University of Chicago, and Stanford University. I have worked closely with Susan Moller Okin, Elisabeth Hansot, and Jennifer Ring, as well as other political theorists here and there. I teach political theory and American politics at Saint John's University, an all-male college offering a coeducational curriculum in conjunction with the all-female College of Saint Benedict located a few miles down the road. About a third of my teaching focuses on gender issues: male, female, straight, and gay. I participated in the construction of a new gender studies and women's studies minor and work on a men's development research group. I designed the course taught last semester based on syllabi from Okin and Ring, and I teach it here because no one else in my department has the training and desire to offer the same kind of course, despite the obvious need for one in our department.

Since I am writing this essay with three of my students as an opportunity for each of us to reflect on who we are in relation to the class, I think it helps to have some idea as to who I am, especially as my students were often asked whether I knew anything about the subject or why I had an interest in teaching feminist theory. I have learned a lot about myself by teaching this course and writing this essay. The sections about my coauthors' experiences suggested to me that they learned more from the class than I could possibly have put into it, and surprisingly, each of them seems to have taken a slightly different class.

Of the many things that unnerved me during the semester I taught

Feminist Political Theory, some of the comments written by my coauthors were the most disturbing. When I first began studying feminist
theory, the backlash against the movement had barely moved into
full swing. While it seemed that few men were truly interested in the
material, no one, male or female, appeared really put off by the work.
Everyone in the classes I had taken was there because they wanted
to be. Therefore, when I walked into Feminist Political Theory, I was
somewhat unprepared for a hostile female audience in a class with
almost twice as many men as women enrolled. None of the men were
pro-feminist; at best they were indifferent. Some students had signed
up for the class simply because they needed a political theory class
that semester and had no idea, much less cared, what the topic of the
course would be. Even my coauthors report that they initially came
into the class with their prejudices firm and their critical capacities
somewhat dormant.

I suppose I always had known that by teaching this class I was
going to step on toes and tweak a few noses, so I should not have
been surprised by the reported assaults on the course's legitimacy
based solely, as it seems, on the fact that I am male. Some of the
questioners were students, but others were faculty. Earlier we discussed the polarized reception to a public talk we gave on teaching
gender in a variety of courses. Some of my students have reported
that they were contacted by senior faculty and questioned about the
class content and my approach. When faculty privately question another professor's credibility, that can have a serious effect on a class,
even if those questions never become public. For all these reasons, I
was surprised that the course worked as well as it did. Fortunately,
my department has approved the course as a regular offering for as
long as I would like to teach it.

I teach my upper-division undergraduate courses by using discussion. As one student has already reported, in class I see my role as
being a highly receptive, highly concentrated, highly critical audience

of one who reflects information back to students in order to help them improve their performance. The more I can leave initiative to the students, the better. A teacher must use the energy and experience that the students bring to a class meeting, and the students must be aware of how I see my role as well as theirs.

The philosophy of teaching that I am describing here, the development of the professor into an audience of one, puts an obligation on the student to take responsibility for his or her own learning. A teacher as an audience of one cannot work effectively if the students do not do their work competently. This means that I am often only as good as my students; but it also means that as an attentive audience, I take whatever they bring to the classroom and mold it through careful criticism. I reflect their input, individually and collectively, so they can better see themselves and what they are learning.

When playing the role of an audience of one, I may appear to be doing nothing to the casual outside observer, but by the intensity of my concentration, by the focus of my attention, I will be communicating to the students what they need to know. This self-effacement does not come easily, but I believe it is a necessary characteristic of good teachers. It also hides the amount of preparation that goes into the design of a syllabus, the selection of the readings for each day, the thinking through of the possible as well as the probable course of that day's conversation, and the effort that effective reflection requires to draw out the students' criticisms of the reading.

I developed this approach to teaching from my work in theater. Tyrone Guthrie first argued that a director is primarily an audience of one in the same way that I have suggested a teacher is. Much research on teaching suggests that a student-centered approach helps students go beyond mere knowledge acquisition and begin applying the concepts they have learned. It was only after having settled on this philosophy of teaching that my research on feminist theory uncovered several discussions of feminist pedagogy that recommended a similar approach. These found that while men tended to be granted authority in the classroom automatically, women were often denied it. The authors of these discussions then tried to design a feminist pedagogy that simultaneously made a virtue out of an unfortunate reality.

In my classes, I attempt to shed the authority normally granted to professors so that my students can see me as a learner, much like them, who simply has been studying feminist political theory for a bit longer than they have. I certainly do not want them to confuse my opinions with the right answers to the many questions I ask in my classes. In fact most of my questions have no single right answers even though some have demonstrably wrong ones. It was ironic that an older generation of feminists did not accept my authority to teach feminist political theory even though my philosophy of teaching was based on shedding some of that authority in the classroom. The attack on my authority by others not in the class actually helped break down the barriers between the students and myself as their professor.

This teaching strategy cannot guarantee successful learning any more than its alternatives. By successful learning I mean that the student has critically engaged opposing arguments and found ways to discover or strengthen his or her own position. A failure occurred when a student could never quite see past his or her own prejudices and his or her critical faculties remained in hibernation. Thus a failure doesn't mean the student declined to become a feminist, only that he or she declined to think. A student who still cannot distinguish between MacKinnon and Okin yet believes in everything each says without noticing or questioning their differences is a flop, yet a student who spends an entire semester engaging in the arguments while still rejecting all feminist theory in favor of traditional patriarchal family values can count the course as a successful learning experience if and only if he or she has thought through the reasons for and against patriarchy and can construct a cogent argument for their traditional position. The main goal informing my philosophy of teaching is getting students to think for themselves, which ultimately may allow them to change their beliefs but does not require it.

In reflecting on who I am in relation to my teaching style and the particular subjects I teach, I believe the key factor has been comfort. I am comfortable with who I am and how I go about what I do. I can shed authority in the classroom because the loss of rank does not threaten my sense of who I am, and I think students can read that in my approach to them. This allows my students greater freedom to find themselves in relation to the difficult issues raised in the books and articles assigned and discussed. Shedding authority might be easier for men because they are automatically granted it, but the main point I want to emphasize is that a cooperative style of teaching that empowers students to make their own learning choices and then holds them responsible for those choices is an effective teaching strategy regardless of subject matter or the teacher's gender.

I am not female and cannot actually experience for myself much of what some feminists theorize. But I am also not Plato, nor Hobbes, nor Rousseau, and I cannot directly experience much of what they wrote about either. For me the fact that I am neither female nor Plato has some effect on my teaching, but it does not prevent me from challenging my students to reflect on who they are in relation to the material at hand or who the authors were in relation to what they wrote. Being male does affect how I see the world, but I can recognize that bias and must accept it in order to work through it. Being male gives no extra insight into knowledge. Who I am is simply a precondition, a set of changing filters, through which I experience the world. The identities of readers and writers, teachers and students, are clearly germane to many classroom discussions, but only to the extent that such discussion furthers the consideration of ideas. If the discussion of identity degenerates into ad hominem attacks as a way of avoiding ideas and critical thought, then no one is learning.

Kellen's Experience

When I first signed up for this class I thought that I would be very closely related to the subject matter, simply because of my gender. I expected the course to focus primarily on women's experiences and issues that had been excluded from the political canon (and history in general) and on how this exclusion had affected and, more important, hindered women. I was more or less expecting to hear a one-sided version of the story—the one side of the story that had been lost in history, the one side of the story that had been forced to take a backseat to the male version of the story. I was drawing this conclusion under the assumption that the experiences, issues, and events that had already been published in the political theory canon (and history) were "male."

I also had several questions about what feminism was, or how it could be defined, and what the role of feminist theory has been and could be. Above all, I wanted to know how I, as a woman, fit into all this (feminism, feminist theory, etc.). As the class progressed, I learned that most feminist theorists, especially the political theorists, have written their texts in response to or as rebuttals of the standard, widely accepted canon composed of works by Locke, Hobbes, Plato, and so on, all of whom have excluded women and women's experiences from their texts. One of the chief reasons for feminists' responses is an attempt to redress the imbalance and the imperfect vision of the political theory canon. These attempts at intervention reexamine aspects of human experience that have been ignored because they have been assumed to be just like the male experience. A second reason for the responses is that participation in the canon is in part determined by reflection and redeployment of issues already extant in the canon. Locke responds to Filmer and Hobbes, Wollstonecraft critiques Rousseau and Burke. After participating in the class and learning of the exchange between feminist theorists and traditional theorists, I expanded my view of how the world worked. I had a better sense of the relationship between political theory and my politics.

As the course progressed I realized that both women and men had been falsely represented in the political theory canon, as well as in history. Furthermore, approaching the class as something valuable solely for women, or expecting to learn just about women and to "set the story straight" was extremely shortsighted on my part. I had entered the class under the false assumption that the world as we knew it, or as it had been presented to us in the traditional political theory canon, was a true and accurate representation of what is "male." Eventually I began to understand that not only had women's experiences been left out of things, but so had many men's experiences. Traditional, unreflective conceptions of gender roles had been damaging for both genders—hindering all our experiences. Therefore, to experience the vast spectrum of characteristics that our humanity is composed of, we need to begin to recognize and understand that all of us have been limited by the canonical expectations.

To understand the world, we need to understand both sides of the story, and we need to fuse both fragments together to see the big picture. It is fairly accepted that to argue effectively it is advantageous to know your opponent's argument. I think the same strategy can be applied to understanding "how the world works"—we need to gather all the information and viewpoints and experience that we can from all the fragments that constitute the world, then we need to fuse them together, and hopefully, looking at this big picture, we will gain some insight on how to understand things.

The claim that only women can teach feminist political theory is based on the false assumption that only women can learn, understand, or teach about issues related to women. This is a damaging assumption not only because it limits men, but because it limits women as well. From what I learned in class, and the way I understood it, the women's movement is working toward equality that will allow women (and men) to experience their full humanity. This equality suggests an abolition of essentially gender-specific roles of the kind that divide all activities into women's work and men's work. If only women can teach feminist theory because it is about women, then the standard feminist charge against the mainstream (male) canon suggests that women cannot teach political theory because it is only about men. This is both ironic and sexist. Women are capable of teaching, learning, and understanding subjects that they have been historically excluded from, and so are men. Feminism, as I now understand it, expands how we approach, view, and understand the world.

It is important to view feminist theory in an objective way, although the subject matter is often very conducive to a subjective approach. But I think it is dangerous to approach feminist theory in a narrow and fragmented way. As with any subject, approaching feminist theory in a narrow way limits and excludes valuable information. Studying, learning, or understanding feminist theory in narrow and noninclusive fragments seems to be contrary to what feminist theory is actually trying to do—broaden the information in the old canon, expand our understanding and definition of equality, and expand our understanding of female and male.

This course had a tremendous impact on me. We need to understand men and women in order to understand how the world works. If men are included in the quest to learn from, understand, and teach feminist political theory, we all might better be able to gain new insights from the old canon as well as develop new political theories about how the world works and why. More important, this course helped me understand that feminism was just one version of the human quest for equality for all. I have come to believe that it is impossible to achieve equality in a one-sided manner, or by focusing on only one side. True equality would inevitably affect all people; therefore, it cannot be approached as something one side fights for, or something one side "gives" the other side. It needs to be approached as something that we all work toward together—something that we all need, deserve, and owe to each other, together.

Conclusion: No Middle Ground?

Feminist political theory is an appropriate academic subject for undergraduates to learn and faculty to teach. There is a distinctive core to the subject: it is grounded in the study of the relationship between equality and difference with regard to sex and gender. Part of the rhetoric that was used to justify the inclusion of women's studies as an academic discipline was the claim that all previous work has been the study of men by men. In part this claim was true, but most if not all of that work never considered questions of gender or what being a man really meant. Even today some versions of the new men's studies movement try to borrow the insights of feminist theory and apply them directly to the study of men, thus once again failing to consider critically what differences there might be between men and women. Other versions of men's studies are crude illustrations of the backlash against the gains of feminist political activity, and once again ignore the actual study of men and their differences from women.

Feminist theory focuses on the relationship between gender difference and gender equality. This study can be done by men or women. To prejudge the conclusions of such study based on the gender of the investigator reflects poorly on the holder of that prejudice. This is not to say that all prejudices or assumptions can be ignored. They must be sought out, identified, recognized, and analyzed. What we tried to do in this class was to examine a wide variety of texts and notice how certain assumptions held prior to the research would make the conclusions of the studies congregate within narrow ranges. Radical feminists will find that men as a class dominate women as a class, while liberal feminists will find that changing the rules may allow the supposed domination to lessen over time. In no case did we find that the gender of the writer was the most important assumption needed to get to the conclusion. We found that regardless of gender, those who chose to work in a radical framework would come to radical conclusions, just as if we chose to use liberalism as our frame we would come to conclusions consistent with its predictions.

Teaching feminist political theory unsympathetically or uncritically calls into question political theory—not just feminism—as well as the merits of the professor. We do not expect any theory to be taught as if it were unquestionable, but we also do not expect theories to be taught as if they have no merit. If the course were designed to prevent students from becoming feminists or political theorists, then the course would be a failure. But teaching feminist theory as an academic subject need not create a classroom of feminists. Nor should teaching feminist theory simply be preaching to the choir. Our argument is plainly that a critical approach to thinking about feminist theory leads to a better understanding of its variety and impact and does not depend on the gender of the professor or the student.

The identity of the professor is germane to a conversation about teaching only to the extent that identity affects or biases ideas. Of course identity serves as a filter, but that filter need not remain unexamined. Like all assumptions, identity too should be examined, or it certainly might bias conclusions. But the contrary assumption we faced in this course—that males are essentially unqualified to teach feminist political theory—suffers from a lack of critical examination. In our experience in this course, identity did matter, it was examined, and it helped us all toward a better understanding of the material. We believe that those who challenged the course failed to consider adequately their own assumptions and grounds for their challenge. While we started with the polarized debate whether men can or cannot teach feminist political theory and found little middle ground in this binary opposition, we ended with a different formulation of the issue. By looking at what we feel must have been the reason behind the opposition, we think we have found a solution. This is the obvious compromise: identity is an assumption that should be examined by everyone when teaching or learning feminist theory. The claim that suggests that only male identities be examined seems to us just as untenable as the claim that only women have a gender. Each of us, male and female alike, learned about ourselves as we learned about feminism.

NOTE

The authors gratefully acknowledge the help received from Gail Wise, Jane Opitz, and Katherine Mayberry.

BIBLIOGRAPHY

Cole, Toby, and Helen Krich Chinoy, eds. *Directors on Directing.* Indianapolis: Bobbs-Merrill, 1976.

Culley, Margo, and Catherine Portuges, eds. *Gendered Subjects: The Dynamics of Feminist Teaching.* Boston: Routledge and Kegan Paul, 1985.

Downing, David, ed. *Changing Classroom Practices: Resources for Literary and Cultural Studies.* Urbana: National Council of Teachers of English, 1994.

Estrich, Susan. *Real Rape.* Cambridge: Harvard University Press, 1987.

Gilligan, Carol. *In a Different Voice.* Cambridge: Harvard University Press, 1982.

Keohane, Nannerl, Michelle Rosaldo, and Barbara Gelpi, eds. *Feminist Theory: A Critique of Ideology.* Chicago: University of Chicago Press, 1982.

McKeachie, Wilbert. *Teaching Tips.* 8th ed. Lexington: D. C. Heath, 1986.

Phillips, Anne, ed. *Feminism and Equality.* New York: New York University Press, 1987.

Rich, Adrienne. *Blood, Bread and Poetry.* New York: W. W. Norton, 1986.

Roiphe, Katie. *The Morning After.* Boston: Little, Brown, 1993.

Sunstein, Cass. *Feminism and Political Theory.* Chicago: University of Chicago Press, 1990.

Tong, Rosemarie. *Feminist Thought: A Comprehensive Introduction.* Boulder: Westview Press, 1989.

Wolf, Naomi. *Fire with Fire.* New York: Random House, 1993.

II

The Class Roster

6

The Discipline of History and the Demands of Identity Politics

CHRISTIE FARNHAM

"When Christie Pope [Farnham] entered the room, there was immediate whispering and shock. One question that quickly entered everyone's mind was, How could a white professor teach black students about African-American history?" This quote from the April 1991 newsletter of the Black Cultural Center at Iowa State University posits the problem of identity politics in a nutshell. It raises questions of both authenticity and authority, not out of concern for some philosophical abstraction, but out of the increasing anger and alienation that characterize so many African American youth on today's college campuses. They feel that, historically, the treatment of African Americans has been so cruel and inhuman, so contemptuous and still unrecompensed that any normal black student must, on at least some level, be enraged that a white, whose ancestors came willingly rather than in chains to this country to take advantage of the wealth that slavery created, would have the audacity to lecture African Americans on their history.

Blacks, however, are not the only students who register for my upper-division survey courses in African American history. In fact, they are outnumbered by white students who represent a self-selected group whose interest in the subject grows occasionally out of personal relationships with blacks but more frequently out of an abhorrence of the injustices African Americans have suffered in a society that idealizes freedom and equality. The white students differ from their black peers, however, in their commitment to the notion of a color-blind society.[1] Yet this commitment is occasionally accompanied by an unexamined tendency to judge black experiences by white norms, which accounts for their often silent dissent from the insistence by African American students that black cultural differences be validated.

While whites come to the subject from a different perspective, many accept the same notion of authenticity and authority that animates the quote at the beginning of this essay. Although I have devoted many years to reading and researching in the field of African American history, white students want to hear the views of the black students on the issues raised. This is not simply a matter of being interested in the input of students from the group whose history is under discussion, as important as that is. It is also the belief that, no matter that the interpretations I present are often the results of black scholarship, what African American students have to say is the "real truth" on the subject.

In this regard, white students are no different from white administrators and faculty who often appoint black faculty to positions in the field of black studies on the basis of the color of their skin rather than on the focus of their research. For example, the black male appointed by the dean of the College of Liberal Arts and Sciences to head the African American studies program at my institution last year teaches in the department of chemical engineering.

Permitting pigmentation to impute an aura of authenticity and authority is a type of stereotyping to which social science research on the nature of prejudice over the past thirty years should have sensitized all Americans. Yet even African Americans are capable of stereotyping white faculty. The current climate of intolerant conservatism encourages many of them to assume that no white will see anything positive in Nat Turner and resistance or in Marcus Garvey and cultural nationalism, for example. Nor would they expect to see a significant portion of the syllabus in an African American history course taught by a white instructor begin with a lengthy overview of African history and culture. The assumption is that whites will not teach anything damaging to the reputation of whites, like the rape of black women by white men, and that courses taught by whites will be formulated from a Eurocentric perspective—that is, whites will view the experiences of African Americans only in relation to the history of whites. In other words, critics of white instructors, who often include those with no firsthand knowledge of the courses in question, like other students on campus and members of the larger academic community, stereotype white instructors by assuming that being white is a subject position from which it is almost impossible to present an unbiased account of African American history.

Stereotyping on the basis of color foregrounds the question of pigmentation, which is more complicated than Americans of all races generally realize. In most of the Western Hemisphere there are numerous nomenclatures to designate persons by degree of intermixture, and only full-blooded Africans are referred to as blacks. The exceptions are the United States and Canada, where a "one drop rule" categorized those with any visible black African ancestry as black.[2] The immigration of small numbers of largely male Europeans to Latin America and the Caribbean led to greater miscegenation there than in British North America. As members of an interstitial group, people of mixed ancestry were able to provide those goods and services that were uneconomical for commercial producers (slaves, peasants, and miners) to provide and for which there were too few whites to supply. This provided them with a claim to an intermediate status in society above that occupied by slaves. In contrast, British North America was colonized by entire European families almost from the outset, and they always greatly outnumbered Africans. Since slavery and further exploitation in its aftermath under the auspices of Jim Crow were dependent on the maintenance of racial boundaries, a bipolar racial society acquired the aura of being simply a fact of nature.

Yet most African Americans have some white ancestry (and many some Native American admixture as well). The early colonial inter-mixture before the racial caste system hardened, the vulnerability of African American women to sexual exploitation under slavery and later as well, and a small but significant pattern of voluntary interra-cial relationships, which continued throughout the centuries despite all efforts to eliminate it, contributed to this demographic outcome. The forces of discrimination have been so strong, however, that de-spite some "passing," most African Americans of whatever propor-tion of African, Native American, and European ancestry have identi-fied as blacks, whether by necessity or choice.

Nevertheless, race mixing has not ended. For example, 10 percent of non-Southern black males marrying in 1986 chose white brides.[3] These intermarriages, together with a trend in the United States to-ward widespread racial and ethnic mixing, are creating a movement to challenge commonly accepted categories. The Census Bureau is be-ing urged to add new categories for persons who insist that the old "one drop rule" is inaccurate.[4] Many children who are products of interracial unions now want to acknowledge both sides of their heri-tage. What impact this will have on challenging the concept of iden-tity politics is unclear; however, it does not seem to be undermining various forms of racial fundamentalism based on essentialist beliefs. Although most scholars today argue that race is less a scientific con-cept than a social construct, the public seems to be largely unaware of this argument. In my teaching experience, I have found that black students who have been adopted by white families, or persons of interracial unions who wish to acknowledge a wider allegiance often have been placed under intense pressure by African American stu-dents to maintain racial solidarity. As a consequence, many drop the class or stop coming rather than subject themselves to such intense pressure.

This move to maintain racial solidarity is partially a reaction against the cultural politics of intolerance engendered by the ascendancy of the right, which is also the impetus behind the current trend toward an emphasis on victimization and a rhetoric that demonizes whites. If black students see their opportunities to change society diminishing, they can at least enjoy the moral high ground in the national debate. The ability to maintain a sense of moral superiority as a means of both resistance and empowerment should not be underestimated, for, although it can represent a retreat into the realm of words, not actions, it has the potential to engage students in ways that can lead to positive political involvement.

In this instance, however, an "us against them" mentality confronts white students with a dismissive attitude that denies their sympathies and concerns. To many black students, whites are an undifferentiated category, all equally complicit in the injustices of even the remote past. And the white students accept this complicity even though most of their ancestors arrived in this country *after* the ancestors of most African Americans. Large numbers of my students are descendants of European immigrants who came in the late nineteenth and early twentieth centuries, settling in the prairie and plains states, never having had any connection with slavery. Certainly, an argument can be made that whites today, no matter how recent their arrival, are guilty by virtue of the fact that they benefit from the development of the nation on the backs of slave labor. But if that argument is made, so must analogous ones that implicate the nation as a whole, including African Americans, in the current exploitation of Third World workers and the privileging of Americans in terms of the nation's share of the consumption of the world's resources. Few students notice, for example, that the price of their clothes is considerably less than would otherwise be the case were it not for the fact that they were made by prison (slave) labor in China or child labor in other parts of the world.

Nevertheless, as Malcolm X and immigration scholars have

pointed out, part of the assimilation process for white immigrants was the acceptance of racism. But the white students who enroll in African American history courses, because of self-selection, seldom share the racism of their immigrant forebears or even the racism of some of their parents. This phenomenon of white guilt has always proved frustrating for me. Personally, I find it inconceivable that individuals should be held responsible for what other individuals and entire societies did before they were even born. Even though I am white, I do not feel any responsibility for slavery—I was not there. But if I encounter racism *today* and fail to confront it, then I ought to feel guilty. Or if I live in a society that harbors racism and do nothing to change that society, then I should consider myself culpable. And, of course, the same holds true with regard to other types of injustice, like sexism and anti-Semitism.

Without problematizing pigmentation, then, it is easy to understand the demand for black instructors to teach black history. There is the assumption that they have the necessary authority deriving from the authenticity of their experiences and their morally superior position inherent in their relation to the victims rather than the oppressors. Experience serves another purpose as well. It provides a "comfort zone" in which shared understandings do not even have to be verbalized to be communicated. As a specialist in women's studies as well as black studies, I have experienced the camaraderie and sense of rapport deriving from all-female discussions. The atmosphere is different: the level of emotion is more apparent; the self-disclosure and support more revealing; the identification with the subject matter more intense; the ability to say what you think less subject to censure. The same atmosphere is often found in classes of largely black students taught by African Americans. The students are more expressive; there is less concern for papering over the harsh truths of black experiences in the name of civility; there is a greater sense of solidarity in struggle. In both cases common experiences promote a feeling of common identity. Undoubtedly, the introduction of a male instructor in women's studies classes or a white instructor in black studies courses changes this class chemistry. For some students this may indeed mean that opportunities for leadership and independent thinking are lessened and that learning itself is impaired by the resulting anger and frustration. That is one of the reasons we have black cultural centers and women's centers—they provide safe places to be oneself; yet these largely segregated sites are meant to be only way stations on the path to equality and freedom in the larger society, not final destinations.

Some academicians see these alternative patterns of class interaction as evidence of different learning styles. Whereas I have no doubt that different learning styles exist and that more of one type will be found in some groups than others, largely as a result of socialization and cultural differences rather than essential differences based in gender or race, these cannot be permitted to argue for race- or sex-segregated teaching and instruction in history, or a history pedagogy that emphasizes racial identification over substantive content. Having come of age under segregation, I am convinced that a segregated learning situation, whether it be of the "ins" and the "outs," the whites and the blacks, or the males and the females, in the long term is always an impoverished one, because exclusion leads to misperceptions of the other and the rank ordering of groups in which the dominant social order is maintained.

It is also clear to me that mastering the substance of a subject is the best way to raise self-esteem. Teaching resource centers throughout higher education are presently promoting "active learning," a variation on John Dewey's and subsequent efforts to engage students by avoiding viewing them as passive receptacles of their instructors' wisdom.[5] The profundity of this insight, however, is often lost in the pressure placed on instructors to reject the lecture method in favor of discussions. Whereas the discussion method is an excellent pedagogical tool in many instances—for example, literature and composition classes—it is not always the most useful in large history surveys enrolling one hundred or more students, so I make use of it only in a limited fashion in conjunction with a lecture format.

I agree with Nathan Huggins that "there is an irreducible body of information" that students ought to know in history, simply as a skill.[6] Identifying with the subjects under study and appreciating the social dynamics in which they were enmeshed are necessary, but not sufficient. Therefore, an African American history course cannot compromise content for a journey of self-discovery based on personal experiences. To do so would be to deny one of the primary purposes of education—to acquire the new knowledge a discipline has to offer. Joan Wallach Scott argues that, by forgoing dependence on disciplinary expertise, the instructor has "no protection from the charge that she is 'silencing' the opinions of some of her dissenting students, no way to prove that her criticisms of their work have not denied them freedom of speech."[7] Indeed, my own experience supports the view that, when one is dealing with controversial issues, restricting one's presentation to scholarship on the subject is the safest strategy. Even so, active learning invariably takes place, because the subject matter is relevant to contemporary society and the presentation of competing historical interpretations compels students to choose among them on the basis of the historical data.

Many African American students view black studies courses as "theirs." Thus, they feel that these courses should serve their perceived needs for self-validation, the celebration of black culture, the building of self-esteem, and, in some cases, even a boost in their grade point average. Viewing it as their turf, they not surprisingly object to its apparent appropriation by white students and faculty. Although such attitudes are understandable, and many of these demands have some validity in other contexts, they stand in conflict with the standards of the historical profession. Self-esteem may well result from the study of the African American past, but the discipline of history is not designed to serve this end.

Several points in relation to history as a discipline are important to keep in mind here. First, history is predicated on the notion that the field is not esoteric but can be learned by anyone, just as universities are based on the belief that all knowledge is in some sense universally knowable and therefore can be taught to others. One does not have to be a Nazi or a Jew to understand the Holocaust. To quote Nathan Huggins again, "Black Americans, for instance, who fail to recognize that they are not the same as slaves will never understand slavery. The present provides us with a different perspective as well as a different knowledge of the past."[8] To insist that only blacks can teach or study African American history would also mean, by that logic, that they would be unable to learn about or teach the history of Europeans or Asians. Such positions would lead inevitably to the ghettoization of black studies departments and programs, destroying their intellectual integrity and credibility. Even more damaging, such logic could be used to exclude African Americans from other areas of study, placing them on an inferior academic track.

Second, postmodern analysis has had only a limited impact on the historical profession, which had earlier recognized the impossibility of locating absolute historical truth by means of some type of objective, empirical, method.[9] But, contrary to assertions by the more skeptical postmodernists,[10] one historical interpretation is *not* deemed as good as any other. Because historical facts do have a concrete existence, all interpretations must be measured against them. Slavery *did* occur after all.[11] Nevertheless, contemporary historians recognize that work done in the discipline provides only partial truths and that subject positions must be considered and respected. The bias of earlier historical interpretations is understood to result in part from the dominant subject position of the authors. Yet the potential for self-correction inherent in the historical method by virtue of its requirement that interpretations be systematically assessed against the facts, a requirement enhanced by the current openness of the field to scholars from a multitude of standpoints, largely accounts for the profession being comfortable with the view that past events, if not interpretations, have an existence independent of language and author and can, therefore, form the basis of a realistic understanding of the past.

Finally, the historical profession traditionally has decried presentism in historical writing and deplored a research agenda that seeks a usable past. Today, however, feminist historians, African Americanists, and other scholars actively seek a transformation of American society and hope that their scholarship will provide a spur to achieving social justice. Although presentism still is deplored by most traditional historians, even they would probably agree that each generation asks its own questions of history, questions necessarily arising out of their contemporary social context.

Having said this, however, I must point out that how historians do their work, despite major shifts in focus and types of data assessed, has changed relatively little.[12] Although the ascendance of social history over the political history writing of the past redirects the focus on new historical actors, and the introduction of fresh data, new questions, and "bottom up" perspectives brings major advances to the discipline, the day-to-day approach to the data is still one of collecting and evaluating evidence in a systematic fashion. It is true that to traditional archival textual materials have been added oral histories and examination of cultural artifacts and statistical analyses of all things quantifiable, but whether the historian is emotionally engaged or intellectually detached, the reality remains unaltered: like the sleuth in search of the killer, historians meticulously and systematically analyze the facts they have dug up to see whether they fit the theories they have developed to explain events. And a jury of other historians and scholars uses this same standard to judge the outcome.

The problem for the history instructor is that some of what goes for African American history in today's black communities does not meet these evidentiary standards. Ideas are being fostered in many public school systems in inner cities where African Americans, in an attempt to take control of their children's education, have turned to speakers, popular writers, and scholars trained in other areas to construct their curricula.[13] As a consequence, when these students arrive in upper-division university courses in black history, they charge instructors with giving them inaccurate information. Not surprisingly, given the way history is taught in the nation's public schools as a series of indisputable facts and conclusions, any attempt to offer more than one interpretation for consideration, much less to point out which interpretations have given rise to consensus in the profession and which are still subject to debate, is seen as a rejection of their true history. If the instructor is an African American, such a challenge to their accepted belief system is called a "sellout"; if the instructor is white, this is seen as yet another instance of whites lying to blacks to preserve their own self-interest.

The onus to challenge the false claims of Afrocentrism falls most often on historians, for these claims often remain ignored in other disciplines. In English classes, for example, the focus is on writing, not historical content; and, in any case, the instructor, often a graduate student or newly minted Ph.D. teaching numerous sections of the required first-year composition course, probably does not have the expertise to separate fact from fiction, especially since most Americans have encountered very little African American history in their own secondary and higher education experience.[14] Outside class, many Afrocentric speakers are being brought to campus, but they draw audiences almost exclusively from African American students. Thus, their speeches receive little or no critical commentary, leaving even the more extreme positions unchallenged, which gives them the appearance of credible, scholarly, "cutting edge" research, as far as students are concerned.[15]

Much of what these speakers have to say may best be characterized as myth. Myths are difficult for an instructor to address, especially because all myths are constructed of *both* fact and fiction and therefore require a more sophisticated approach to learning than is generally demanded of students. And resistance is to be expected, because many African American students have something of their self-perception tied up in these myths. This situation undoubtedly will become even more widespread as elementary and secondary teachers adopt materials, like those written by Molefi Asante, with "easy to identify symbols which challenge students to internalize history onto an emotional, personal, level."[16] American history itself has not been without its grand narratives like the triumphalist myth that paints a picture of the nation's past as one of invincible progress. Many historical myths serve the function of legitimating a society's origins, for example. But the purpose of history is to seek the truth about the past, not perpetuate myths. One of my black students insisted that myths should be taught even if they do not conform to the facts, because they build self-esteem; but it is my contention that, while this might be the initial effect, subsequent understanding that this self-esteem was not based on a true reading of the historical record would in the long run undermine self-esteem even more.

Many of the myths that African American students bring to the study of history may be characterized as Afrocentric. Although these ideas have been around for a long time,[17] receiving popular attention in the early seventies, they are now being rediscovered by students on university campuses who are unaware of their earlier exposure. It is this historical amnesia that permits students to see such ideas as "cutting edge."

Afrocentrism refers to an approach to the study of the history and culture of people of African descent that attempts to examine them from their own perspective. In this sense Afrocentric history is the story of blacks as agents, not objects, in society. The focus is not simply on race relations or even black contributions to the dominant culture, because this has the effect of depicting them as appendages of peoples of European descent. Most historians working in the field since the seventies are Afrocentrists in this sense,[18] and I count myself among them. However, some Afrocentrists have taken this position further and developed a paradigm centered on ancient Egypt. A few even tout a rhetoric of anti-Semitism and theories of racial supremacy based on melanin.[19] The recent visibility of these views in the national media has resulted in a shift in popular usage of the term "Afrocentrist" to refer to those who see Egypt as a touchstone for black history, and I so employ the term in the remainder of this essay.

Afrocentrists have two goals: to gain respect for African Americans by providing them with a glorious origin in the remote past to counter long-held racist assertions that Africa, the "Dark Continent," never produced any great civilizations; and to give black studies a distinct subject and methodology in order to provide legitimation as an academic discipline.

The glorious past refers to ancient Egypt, which Afrocentrists argue was the first civilization. They further claim that it was a black African civilization and that therefore much of the knowledge that Europeans credit to the Greeks and Romans should go to Africans, for they took their seminal ideas from the Egyptians. For Afrocentrists, Egypt constitutes a paradigm for understanding cultural achievements analogous to that which classical Greece and Rome constitute for Western European thought and culture, and they demand that even courses in the history of African Americans begin with the study of Egypt. Such a view counters the racist assertion that nothing great ever came out of Africa by turning it on its head, making European civilization derivative of African.

The Afrocentrists not only claim original achievements in the advance of high culture, but also insist on a cultural unity between the early Nile Valley and the rest of black Africa and its diaspora down to the present. Cultural values from the Nile Valley flow primarily from the significance placed on community and cooperation and are discussed in opposition to European civilization, which is seen as a cultural unity emphasizing individualism and aggressiveness.

By setting up such an oppositional paradigm, Afrocentrists believe they offer the key to deliverance. Molefi Asante says that "when a person believes that the society is only to be used, that people are only to be victimized, that neighborhoods are alien, he or she is capable of the worst kinds of actions. Afrocentricity creates a framework for dealing with this type of dislocation."[20] Deliverance, rather than coming through social action, results from a reform of the individual— from "recentering" one's life through a commitment "to internalize an African-centered consciousness in everything we do or think."[21]

This belief in the contemporary efficacy of the Afrocentric perspective in part accounts for the sense of urgency and missionary zeal, especially in view of the problems inner cities face in terms of drugs, drive-by shootings, and the feminization of poverty. An additional motivation is the perceived need to delineate a distinct subject and methodology in order to legitimate the new field of black studies, whose first program was initiated at San Francisco State University only in 1969.[22] Despite the fact that advances in scholarship coming out of a variety of interdisciplinary programs call into question the very concept of disciplines as artificial and unnecessarily fragmenting, Afrocentrists feel that providing the field with a distinctive subject and methodology will legitimate its position in academia. This position is also an effort to increase respect for African Americans, because black studies has been marginalized within the academy as intellectually "soft." Afrocentrists are working to enlarge the field to incorporate the study of all peoples of African descent, whereas most black studies programs currently focus on African Americans, while separate programs, originally begun in the fifties and staffed primarily by whites, focus on Africa. Afrocentrism also provides a theoretical base in terms of a set of key concepts and a paradigm (Egypt and its cultural hegemony). The methodology centers on the notion that "there exist different, culturally-bound ways of knowing the universe."[23] In this case, knowledge is seen to derive from an intertwining of both the material and the spiritual and is thus a rejection of Western empiricism. "In Africology," according to Asante, "language, myth, ancestral memory, dance-music-art, and science provide the *sources* of knowledge, the canon of proof, and the structure of truth."[24]

Black studies, like women's studies, has always had a commitment to the community and to liberation; and some of their proponents have sought to challenge empiricism as objective truth, because it has long been used to maintain the subordinate status of both blacks and women. The oppositional nature of these two movements against deeply embedded forms of social injustice has led to many similar strategies. A case could even be made that the belief of some feminists in an early period of goddess religions leading to the development of nurturant and peaceful societies[25] is analogous to the Afrocentrists' conception of ancient Egypt.

The black studies movement initially began with a demand for black history courses and the hiring of black faculty. Once ensconced in the university, it turned to developing new knowledge and frameworks for understanding African Americans. Presently, departments and programs are interdisciplinary in structure and staff and range in emphasis from Marxism to the black aesthetic. Contrary to the charges of some Afrocentrists that these programs tend to teach about blacks from the white perspective, scholars working in history since the early seventies have transformed the field with their new questions and path-breaking research.[26]

Nevertheless, the Afrocentrists are insistent that theirs is the only perspective for black studies. The National Council of Black Studies is currently attempting to disseminate a curriculum that combines the study of peoples of Africa with the African diaspora based on the Nile Valley paradigm.[27] Darlene Clark Hine objects to the criticism of more traditional black studies scholars by Afrocentrists: "In order that the intellectual domain remain healthy each group of Black Studies scholars must engage in continuous critique, not in a quest for academic dominance."[28]

A critique of Afrocentrism is considered an affront by many African American students. Yet it is my professional obligation to point out problems with their version of the historical record. Ralph Austen, an Africanist at the University of Chicago, writes in reference to Asante and his department at Temple, "I personally find their work parochial, misinformed, and trapped in the discourse of the very racism they claim to repudiate."[29] Many scholars of both races have pointed to problems in the Afrocentric perspective.[30] Egypt was not a black African but a multicultural society; many of the contributions to knowledge claimed to be African were indeed borrowed by the Greeks and Romans, but probably not all of those claimed. But perhaps more important, we should ask what civilization is anyway—only bureaucratized urban societies with monumental architecture? What are the linkages between Egyptian culture and those of West and Central Africa and diasporan cultures many centuries later? Are not Afrocentric assertions based on an essentialist view that culture is in the blood? These and many other questions can be raised to challenge some of the central assumptions of the Afrocentric position. This is not meant to dismiss the claims of those outside the historical profession, for they often bring fresh perspectives that lead to critical advances. The point, however, is the right to challenge their claims.

Although I had taught African American history since 1978 without difficulty, much of it as a faculty member in an Afro-American studies department, the rise of Afrocentrism in the early nineties, together with my move to a new university where my track record was unknown, resulted in serious problems.[31] Some black students began to rudely object to portions of my lecture material. Personally, I like a frank exchange—"telling it like it is," as it was known in the sixties—and I had always encouraged questions and discussion throughout my lectures. But this was different. An in-your-face hostility surfaced that intimidated other students, both white and black. I experimented with teaching techniques from teaching resource centers to improve the learning environment, like an open invitation to students to give five-minute presentations on any subject, to provide those with dissenting views a voice. But this only intensified their hostility. Still searching for ways to enhance the learning environment, I began the course in the fall of 1993 with a discussion of the major schools of interpretation in African American history, of which Afrocentrism is one.

Because African American history is an upper-division course, historiography has always been an important component of the subject. I hoped that, by getting the problem addressed early on in the course, tensions could be eliminated or at least diminished. As an example of anti-Semitism, I referred to the Nation of Islam's *Secret Relationship between Blacks and Jews,* even though I had many members of the Nation of Islam in class. I realized that this might prove to be impolitic, but I had decided that it was necessary to confront the growing acceptance by many blacks in my courses of the idea that Jews dominated the slave trade and slavery.

I was also confronting disruptive student behavior for the first time in my career. A Black Muslim freshman constantly objected to the points I was making. When the student refused to leave class after calling me a liar and then threatened me in front of my departmental chair, he was barred from attending class, pending disciplinary procedures. This incident provoked a sit-in of my class by members of the Black Student Association and the African American members of the university staff, including the head of the office of minority affairs, and took place even though a fearful administration had put the student back in my class over my objections and without requiring him to withdraw his threat against me. The sit-in was legitimated by the administration at a subsequent meeting with Black Student Association leaders, provided that the number of persons sitting in did not go over the limits placed by fire regulations. I continued to teach, even though advised by friends to ask for a leave of absence. The sit-in continued for almost six weeks, despite the fact that in an unrelated incident the disruptive student was jailed for bank theft.

During this period, campus and state newspapers carried numerous stories detrimental to my reputation, often including inaccurate charges made by students who were not even members of the class.

As a consequence, I was largely perceived either as a Eurocentric racist or an insensitive instructor. Because of federal and state regulations limiting what can be said publicly about students, I was initially unable to defend myself. Mass meetings were held on campus in which it was claimed that I must be afraid of African Americans; yet, as far as I could tell, none of the speakers knew with whom I vacation, who are my frequent house guests, with whom I party, or anything about me personally. The B.S.A. even rallied on the steps of the administration building to announce that they would get rid of me "by any means necessary."[32]

The ordeal continued throughout the semester and would have lasted longer had I not been previously scheduled to teach abroad the second semester. Without the support of my colleagues in the history department, the chair of the African American studies program, and family and friends, I could not have survived, especially since I was up for tenure that year. But perseverance eventually paid off. The provost stopped the sit-ins, the faculty governing bodies passed resolutions on my behalf, and most important, I was allowed to complete the teaching of the course. The B.S.A. eventually found four students out of the one hundred in the class to bring charges against me of presenting inaccurate information and being disrespectful of a student's religion. I was subsequently exonerated by the grievance committee that handled the charges.[33]

The potential for conflict remains, however, because of the growing influence of Afrocentric claims emanating from rap music, public school curricula, and books for all ages disseminated through a proliferating market for ethnic goods. This influence, unfortunately, has a much larger impact on students than the current lively debate of these issues among black intellectuals in a variety of periodicals.

This essay is an attempt to demonstrate that not all problems arising out of teaching what you are not—in this case, being a white woman teaching black history—can be reduced to pedagogy or personalities. Certainly, if my classes had been limited to fifteen or twenty students, with primary reliance on the discussion method, I might have been able to defuse the situation. But the decision to limit the number of students who can take the course has to be balanced against the reality that this means many who might benefit will be permanently excluded.

The primary problem, in my opinion, is an unavoidable conflict between the standards of the historical profession and the claims of the Afrocentrists—a conflict that exists independently of the instructor. I am not unmindful of standpoint theory, the "linguistic turn" in history, the contributions of Michel Foucault, and the insights of postmodernism. Yet I am committed to the traditional historical method because, despite its faults, it has demonstrated by its ability for self-correction that it is the best method to date for arriving at historical truth. This is not meant to denigrate the contributions of thinkers outside the discipline. They often provide fresh insights— insights that send historians back to the record to check these claims against their own.

It is unfortunate that many of the current Afrocentric claims are offered in a dogmatic fashion and that the debate, even among the African American intelligentsia, has become so rancorous. But even were that not the case, my problem would remain, because the public (including my students) generally adopts intellectual claims like these without their accompanying qualifications. This process of oversimplification is not new and has long afforded history professors the challenge of confronting naive undergraduates with ideas that undermine their parochial worldviews. But this challenge cannot be avoided, for the mission of the university and the history profession is the search for truth—no matter what the consequences.

NOTES

1. Bob Blauner argues in "Talking Past Each Other; Black and White Languages," *American Prospect,* summer 1992, 55–64, that white students locate

racism in the absence of color blindness, a position that places them in opposition to nationalist views. Most black students today feel that for whites to insist on assimilation of dominant values and styles is itself a form of racism.

2. For an analysis of this phenomenon, see, for example, Carl N. Degler, *Neither Black nor White: Slavery and Race Relations in Brazil and the United States* (New York: Macmillan, 1971).

3. Matthijs Kalmijn, "Trends in Black/White Intermarriage," *Social Forces* 72 (September 1993): 124. I am indebted to David James for this citation.

4. The implications of this trend are discussed in Lawrence Wright, "One Drop of Blood," *New Yorker*, July 25, 1944.

5. One of the publications I have found particularly insightful in this regard is Peter J. Frederick, "The Lively Lecture: Eight Variations," *College Teaching* 34, no. 2 (1986): 43–50. A growing body of literature on improving teaching techniques is being disseminated by teaching resource centers of universities.

6. Nathan Irving Huggins, *Revelations: American History, American Myths*, ed. Brenda Smith Huggins (New York: Oxford University Press, 1995), 173. This essay is reprinted from a lecture delivered at the University of California, Berkeley, September 23, 1987.

7. Joan Wallach Scott, "Academic Freedom as Ethical Practice," *Academe*, July–August 1995, 47.

8. Huggins, *Revelations*, 173.

9. For a discussion of this issue, see Peter Novick, *That Noble Dream: The "Objectivity Question" and the Historical Profession* (New York: Cambridge University Press, 1988).

10. For a discussion of the relationship between history and postmodernism, see Pauline Marie Rosenau, *Post-Modernism and the Social Sciences: Insights, Inroads, and Intrusions* (Princeton: Princeton University Press, 1992), esp. chapter 4.

11. For a critique of postmodernism and the historian's practical approach to the problems it raises, see Joyce Appleby, Lynn Hunt, and Margaret Jacobs, *Telling the Truth about History* (New York: Norton, 1994).

12. There are a few notable exceptions, like Simon Schama, *Dead Certainties: Unwarranted Speculations* (New York: Knopf, 1991), which combines fictionalized accounts with narratives true to the historical record.

13. See, for example, Erich Martel, "Afrocentric Historical Claims: An Examination of the Portland, Oregon, African-American Baseline Essays," *World History Bulletin* 8, no. 2: 13–15, which also includes a short, useful bibliography.

14. I have had firsthand experience advising a composition instructor at Iowa State University and reading some of the essays written for this class.

15. An example of someone whose ideas first appeared in the early seventies who has been rediscovered by African American undergraduates and currently appears on many campuses is Frances Cress Welsing. A psychiatrist, she claims that whiteness is a genetic deficiency; and since "color always annihilates, phenotypically and genetically speaking, the non-color white," and since whites are a minority of the world's population, a fear of extinction motivates behavior known as white supremacy. See *The Cress Theory of Color Confrontation and Racism (White Supremacy)* (Washington, D.C.: C-R Publishers, 1970), 6.

16. Advertisement for "the definitive new teaching system for African-Centered Education," published by Peoples Publishing Group of New Rochelle Park, New Jersey, 1995.

17. Examples of Afrocentric writings that have fostered some of these myths include, for example, John G. Jackson, *Introduction to African Civilizations* (Secaucus, NJ: Citadel Press, 1970); Yosef ben-Jochannan, *African Origins of the Major Western Religions* (New York: Alkebu-Lan Books, 1970); idem, *Black Man of the Nile and His Family* (Baltimore: Black Classics Press, 1978); idem, *Africa: Mother of Western Civilization* (New York: Alkebu-Lan Books, 1971); and Cheikh Anta Diop, *The African Origin of Civilization*, ed. and trans. Mercer Cook (New York: Lawrence Hill, 1956).

18. This is especially apparent in studies on slavery that demonstrate that slaves developed their own culture significantly influenced by African retentions. See, for example, John Blassingame, *The Slave Community: Plantation Life in the Antebellum South* (New York: Oxford University Press, 1972); and Lawrence W. Levine, *Black Culture and Black Consciousness: Afro-American Folk Thought from Slavery to Freedom* (New York: Oxford University Press, 1977).

19. Cheikh Anta Diop is the father of the project to make Africa the basis for the development of European civilization and Egypt the touchstone for the culture of peoples of African descent. See *African Origin*. Molefi Asante, who bases much of his work on Diop, is the architect of *The Afrocentric Idea* (Philadelphia: Temple University Press, 1987). Prominent writers in this camp include Wade Nobles, Maulana Karenga, Robert Staples, John Henrik Clarke, Asa Hilliard, and Ak'im Akbar.

The charge that Jews dominated the slave trade and slavery has forced the American Historical Association in 1995 to take an official stand against such a view. One of the best discussions of the evidence is David Brion Davis, "The Slave Trade and the Jews," *New York Review of Books*, December 22, 1994, 14–16. Davis claims that the "extreme example of anti-Semitic accusations masquerading as a documented history of Jewish involvement in the slave trade and American slavery [is] . . . *The Secret Relationship Between Blacks and*

Jews, Volume One (The Nation of Islam, 1991)" (14n). The Anti-Defamation League of B'nai B'rith periodically publishes research reports documenting statements by the Nation of Islam leader Louis Farrakhan, whose lieutenant, Khalid Muhammad, achieved notoriety for a speech espousing these views at a New Jersey campus. Tony Martin also achieved national notice when he was reprimanded by the president of Wellesley, where he is a faculty member, in the wake of complaints following the publication of his book *The Jewish Onslaught: Despatches from the Wellesley Battlefront* (Dover, MA: Majority Press, 1993). See Welsing *Cress Theory of Color*, for an example of ideas about melanin.

20. Molefi Kete Asante, *Malcolm X as Cultural Hero and Other Essays* (Trenton: Africa World Press, 1993), 124.

21. Ibid., 48.

22. An excellent overview of the intellectual history of the black studies movement is Darlene Clark Hine, "The Black Studies Movement: Afrocentrist-Traditionalist-Feminist Paradigms for the Next Stage," *Black Scholar* 22, no. 3 (summer 1992): 11–18. For an explanation of how the Afrocentric movement wants to transform black studies, see *Afrocentric Scholar: The Journal of the National Council for Black Studies* 2, no. 1 (May 1993): 69.

23. Selase W. Williams, "Black Studies: The Evolution of an Africentric Human Science," *Afrocentric Scholar: The Journal of the National Council for Black Studies* 2, no. 1 (May 1993): 69.

24. Asante, *Malcolm X*, 107.

25. A book review by Carol LeMasters provides a good overview of this movement. See "God the Mother," *Women's Review of Books* 11, no. 6 (March 1994): 7–8.

26. The number of scholars in this regard are too numerous to mention; however, the work of feminists like Deborah Gray White, *Ar'n't I a Woman? Female Slaves in the Plantation South* (New York: W. W. Norton, 1985) provide useful examples of some of the transformations to which I am referring.

27. See *Afrocentric Scholar: The Journal of the National Council for Black Studies* 2, no. 1 (May 1993).

28. Hine, "Black Studies Movement," 17.

29. Ralph A. Austen, quoted in "Academic Correctness and Black Scholarship," *Journal of Blacks in Higher Education* 2 (winter 1993–94): 44.

30. Prominent among those African American scholars who oppose the excesses of Afrocentrism are Henry Louis Gates, Jr., Cornel West, bell hooks, and Clarence Walker.

31. For a description of the controversy over my course, see Christie Farnham Pope, "The Challenges Posed by Radical Afrocentrism," *Chronicle of Higher Education*, March 30, 1993, B1–B3.

32. *Ames Daily Tribune,* November 5, 1993, A3.
33. *Des Moines Register,* December 1, 1993, M1.

BIBLIOGRAPHY

"Academic Correctness and Black Scholarship." *Journal of Blacks in Higher Education* 2 (winter 1993–94): 43–45.
Afrocentric Scholar: The Journal of the National Council for Black Studies 2 (May 1993).
Appleby, Joyce, Lynn Hunt, and Margaret Jacobs. *Telling the Truth about History.* New York: W. W. Norton, 1994.
Asante, Molefi K. *The Afrocentric Idea.* Philadelphia: Temple University Press, 1987.
———. *Malcolm X as Cultural Hero and Other Essays.* Trenton: Africa World Press, 1993.
ben-Jochannan, Yosef. *Africa: Mother of Western Civilization.* New York: Alkebu-Lan Books, 1971.
———. *African Origins of the Major Western Religions.* New York: Alkebu-Lan Books, 1970.
———. *Black Man of the Nile and His Family.* Baltimore: Black Classics Press, 1978.
Blassingame, John. *The Slave Community: Plantation Life in the Antebellum South.* New York: Oxford University Press, 1972.
Blauner, Bob. "Talking Past Each Other: Black and White Languages." *American Prospect,* summer 1992, 55–64.
Davis, David Brion. "The Slave Trade and the Jews." *New York Review of Books,* December 22, 1994, 14–16.
Degler, Carl N. *Neither Black nor White: Slavery and Race Relations in Brazil and the United States.* New York: Macmillan, 1971.
Diop, Cheikh Anta. *The African Origin of Civilization,* ed. and trans. Mercer Cook. New York: Lawrence Hill, 1956.
Frederick, Peter J. "The Lively Lecture: Eight Variations." *College Teaching* 34, no. 2 (1986): 43–50.
Hine, Darlene Clark. "The Black Studies Movement: Afrocentrist-Traditionalist-Feminist Paradigms for the Next Stage." *Black Scholar* 22 (summer 1992): 11–18.
Huggins, Nathan Irving. *Revelations: American History, American Myths,* ed. Brenda Smith Huggins. New York: Oxford University Press, 1995.
Jackson, John G. *Introduction to African Civilizations.* Secaucus, NJ: Citadel Press, 1970.

Kalmijn, Matthijs. "Trends in Black/White Intermarriage." *Social Forces* 72 (September 1993): 119–46.

LeMasters, Carol. "God the Mother." *Women's Review of Books* 11 (March 1994): 7–8.

Levine, Lawrence W. *Black Culture and Black Consciousness: Afro-American Folk Thought from Slavery to Freedom.* New York: Oxford University Press, 1977.

Martel, Erich. "Afrocentric Historical Claims: An Examination of the Portland, Oregon, African-American Baseline Essays. *World History Bulletin* 8, no. 2: 13–15.

Martin, Tony. *The Jewish Onslaught: Despatches from the Wellesley Battlefront.* Dover, MA: Majority Press, 1993.

Novick, Peter. *That Noble Dream: The "Objectivity Question" and the Historical Profession.* New York: Cambridge University Press, 1988.

Pope, Christie Farnham. "The Challenges Posed by Radical Afrocentrism." *Chronicle of Higher Education,* March 30, 1993, B1–B3.

Rosenau, Pauline Marie. *Post-Modernism and the Social Sciences: Insights, Inroads, and Intrusions.* Princeton: Princeton University Press, 1992.

Schama, Simon. *Dead Certainties: Unwarranted Speculations.* New York: Knopf, 1991.

Scott, Joan Wallach. "Academic Freedom as Ethical Practice." *Academe,* July–August 1995, 46–48.

Welsing, Frances Cress. *The Cress Theory of Color Confrontation and Racism (White Supremacy).* Washington, D.C.: C-R Publishers, 1970.

White, Deborah Gray. *Ar'n't I a Woman? Female Slaves in the Plantation South.* New York: W. W. Norton, 1985.

Williams, Selase W. "Black Studies: The Evolution of an Africentric Human Science." *Afrocentric Scholar: The Journal of the National Council for Black Studies* 2 (May 1993): 65–72.

Wright, Lawrence. "One Drop of Blood." *New Yorker,* July 25, 1944.

7

Teaching What I'm Not: An Able-Bodied Woman Teaches Literature by Women with Disabilities

BARBARA DIBERNARD

I had no awareness of disability issues when I saw a sign at a busy intersection of carpeted footpaths at the Michigan Womyn's Music Festival in 1985: "Be aware of slow-moving Amazons." This sign made me look at my surroundings in a different way. When I did, I realized that women with many kinds of disabilities were participating fully in the festival, and that I wasn't used to seeing these women in my daily life. Yet I knew instantly that they were there; it was my awareness that had changed. Since inclusiveness was one of my goals as a feminist teacher, I resolved to seek out literature by women with disabilities and teach it. This was the beginning of a journey that had a profound impact on me and on my teaching.

The first writings by women with disabilities that I read were in *With the Power of Each Breath: A Disabled Women's Anthology*. I knew immediately that I would use this book in my teaching. In the fall semester of 1988 I ordered it for a senior graduate-level course, Twentieth-Century Women Writers. I looked forward to the class, a night class that I knew would have a number of nontraditional students, and was quite pleased with my decision to integrate literature by women with disabilities into the class. However, my complacency was quickly shattered the first night when a woman in a wheelchair wheeled into the room. My first reaction was, "How are we going to talk about disability with *her* here?" I knew then that I had a lot of work to do in coming to terms with my own relationship with and feelings about disability and my identity as an able-bodied person. One of the complications of "teaching what you're not" I had not foreseen is "teaching what you're not in the presence of those who are."

Joni, who had had polio as an infant and had therefore lived virtually her entire life as a person with a disability, helped to educate us all. One evening when students were getting very excited and angry in discussing the way the media portray women as sex objects, Joni stopped us cold. "Who are you talking about when you say 'women'?" she asked. "I have never seen a woman who looks like me used as a sex object to sell a car. In fact, I would like someone to look at me as a sex object sometime." It was one of the most profound moments I have ever experienced in a classroom. In an instant, Joni revealed that our use of the word "women" did not include her, a woman sitting in the room with us at that moment. On a broader scale, her comments showed one of the problems with "identity politics"—we are allowed to "be" only one thing at a time; our identities are reduced to one dimension, and differences are erased or overlooked. Joni was visible as a person with a disability, but not as a woman. The rest of us in the room, all of whom would be seen as "able-bodied" by others, had not taken account of our able-bodied locations. Without a doubt, we saw ourselves at the center, Joni at the margin, ourselves as "women," Joni as "disabled."

Through my teaching of literature by women with disabilities, I have tried to do what Adrienne Rich suggests we must do with other privileged locations such as whiteness: "to experience the meaning of [our able-bodiedness] as a point of location for which [we need] to take responsibility" (219). Although I started out at the first stage of curriculum integration by "adding and stirring" literature by women with disabilities into a course on twentieth-century women writers, reading and teaching the literature have changed my perceptions of myself and the world. I feel my identity now not as a woman who "happens to be" able-bodied, but as a woman whose able-bodiedness is a location for which I need to take responsibility. I need to acknowledge it overtly as the place from which I experience the world and from which I do my work. I hope the same for my students by the end of the semester, although developmentally it's a long journey to make in fifteen weeks if people with disabilities have not even been visible before.

While Joni was a significant resource and teacher for all of us, while she generously and thoughtfully shared her experiences as a person living with a disability, she also made it clear that it was important to her that an able-bodied person had chosen to teach this literature, that I saw it as important to teach "what I was not." It was also the first time in four years at the University of Nebraska, she said, that this aspect of her experience had been included in a class. First, it was affirming and empowering to her; second, it made the lives of women with disabilities visible to the other students; third, it complicated the category of "woman" in a way that made a unitary identity politics of gender impossible.

In order to take account of my own location, it seems necessary to ask some seemingly elementary questions. What does it mean to be "disabled"? What does it mean to be "able-bodied"? What are the implications of these identities in terms of the title of this book, *Teaching What You're Not*? Is there an identity politics in disability studies that enables me to be "not" disabled? Unlike some (but not all) identities, being "disabled" can be changeable for some people. Some people who have been blind recover their sight; some people with disabling diseases and conditions go into remission. Being "able-bodied" is a changeable condition as well. I could become disabled in a moment, through accident or disease. Joseph Shapiro points out that

"Fewer than 15 percent of disabled Americans were born with their disabilities" (7). Does this make my being an able-bodied person at this time (or "temporarily able-bodied"),[1] teaching literature by women with disabilities, different from my being a white person teaching African American literature? After all, a white person cannot become African American. Of course, other identities also seem changeable; for example, many people who have lived for years as heterosexual later come to identify as lesbian or gay. Are there some identities that are immutable, biological, and some that are not? Underlying these questions is a larger question about identity politics. Are there some identities that "count" in identity politics? "Gender, race, and class" is a trilogy we often hear recited in academic work. However, I think we must ask what this trilogy excludes, and we must complicate our notions of identity beyond it.

Is disability an identity that "counts" in identity politics? A wide range of conditions and experiences is covered in the term "disability." The editors of *With the Power of Each Breath* write in their introduction that they began working on the book "with a strong political commitment to produce an anthology representative of all disabled women. We wanted the impossible: that this collection would be *the* definitive statement by and about disabled women. It is not" (11). As "disability" is used in the United States, it includes people with visual and hearing impairments, people who are quadriplegic, people who are paraplegic, people with other kinds of mobility impairments, people with heart conditions, people with multiple sclerosis, people with epilepsy, people with medical complications due to diabetes, and people with mental disabilities, among other things. It's clear that the experience of disability will be very different depending on what kind of disability a person lives with. What we call "disabled" is a multiple, not unitary, set of conditions and experiences. Can it then be an "identity"?

Michelle Fine has pointed out that other factors also influence a person's experience of her or his disability, although most researchers have not acknowledged this in their work:

> To date, almost all research on disabled men and women seems simply to assume the irrelevance of gender, race, ethnicity, sexual orientation, or social class. Having a disability presumably eclipses these dimensions of social experience. Even sensitive students of disability . . . have focused on disability as a unitary concept and have taken it to be not merely the "master" status but apparently the exclusive status for disabled people. Paralleling what Hester Eisenstein (1983) has described as the "false universalism" of feminist writing of the 1970s, the disability rights literature has chosen to stress commonalities among all disabled people rather than differences. (141)

Since the term "person with a disability" falsely universalizes as much as 1970s feminist writing did with "woman," it is important to take account of the degree to which the category is socially constructed and the effect this has on a person's identity. Fine states,

> It is ironic to note that the very category that integrates this text, "disabled girls and women," exists wholly as a social construct. Why should a limb-deficient girl, a teenager with mental retardation, or a blind girl have anything in common with each other or with a woman with breast cancer or another woman who is recovering from a stroke? What they share is similar treatment by a sexist and disability-phobic society. (144)

Another way of talking about the socially constructed nature of "disabled" as an identity is to distinguish between "disability" and "handicap." Debra Connors writes that a classmate of hers made this distinction: "A disability, she explained, is a physical or mental impairment. A handicap is a set of social conditions which impede our independence" (92). Michelle Fine elaborates:

> Likewise in the past twenty years, both the study and the politics of disability have undergone transformation. Activists and scholars have insisted that the *disability* (the biological condition) be conceptually disentangled from the *handicap* (the social ramifications) of the condition. Obstacles to education, community and political participation, in-

dependent living, employment, and personal relationships derived not from the incapacities, for example, of individuals in wheelchairs to walk stairs but in the existence of the stairs themselves. If people with mobility impairments could not enter buildings without ramps or ride inaccessible buses, the fault was in the structures and the transportation system, not in their bodies. If people who wished to work could not because of the medical standards that barred anyone with a history of heart disease, cancer, epilepsy, or obesity or anyone with diabetes or visual or hearing impairments, the problem might be one of arbitrary medical standards, and not of a person's inherent incapacity to perform specific job tasks. If young adults with sensory, motor, or learning disabilities were not attaining a postsecondary education, perhaps the problem lay not in their biology but in the institution's architecture, testing requirements, or admissions standards. (143)

Debra Connors analyzes the social construction of disability in a historical context: "Disability is not a medical problem; nor is able-ism just a set of prejudicial ideas about disabled people. Disability is a social institution which has developed alongside capitalism. Our societal position has been shaped by history and is inextricably woven into the fabric of American culture. There is no reason to assume that medical conditions are disabilities or that they should necessarily be stigmatizing" (93).

People with disabilities report consistently on aspects of a "disabled identity" that are attributed to them by other people. They are considered childlike and often treated like children; they are considered asexual, mentally impaired no matter what their disability, dependent, passive, lazy, and unemployable.

However, it is also true that with the advent of a disability rights movement in the United States, many people feel proud to claim their identity as people with disabilities, acknowledging that both the physical and social elements of disability have shaped their experience and therefore their identities. In the film *Positive Images: Portraits of Women with Disabilities*, one woman states that she is insulted when a person says, "I don't even notice that you are disabled." She says that a close friend would never make that statement, because a friend would know how much her disability is a part of her. Joseph Shapiro begins his book *No Pity* with a similar example:

> Nondisabled Americans do not understand disabled ones.
>
> That was clear at the memorial service for Timothy Cook, when longtime friends got up to pay him heartfelt tribute. "He never seemed disabled to me," said one. "He was the least disabled person I ever met," pronounced another. It was the highest praise these nondisabled friends could think to give a disabled attorney who, at thirty-eight years old, had won landmark disability rights cases, including one to force public transit systems to equip their buses with wheelchair lifts. But more than a few heads in the crowded chapel bowed with an uneasy embarrassment at the supposed compliment. It was as if someone had tried to compliment a black man by saying, "You're the least black person I ever met," as false as telling a Jew, "I never think of you as Jewish," as clumsy as seeking to flatter a woman with, "You don't act like a woman." (3)

Shapiro goes on to explain that while he knows that these speakers felt they were sincerely praising Cook, it is now possible for people with disabilities to have pride in being disabled, or at least seek not to hide it as a shameful thing. "As a result of an ongoing revolution in self-perception, they (often along with their families) no longer see their physical or mental limitations as a source of shame or as something to overcome to inspire others. Today they proclaim that it is okay, even good, to be disabled" (4).

My teaching rests on the assumption that there *is* a self-conscious identity of "a woman with a disability." The literature I teach is not by women who "happen to be" disabled; it is by women who have consciously thought about their identities as having both a physical and a socially constructed component. They are women who, even if they are first-time writers, responded to an external or internal call to write about their experiences as women with disabilities. Such self-identification obviously has a significant political component; it makes a political movement possible. This is an important time for people with disabilities to identify as such because previous liberation movements in the United States have largely excluded them. During the 1992 election, for example, a writer for the *Disability Rag* pointed out, "It's the year of the woman in politics, heralded in the press, on TV, by the pols, the pollsters, and the pundits. It's also been the year of gay and lesbian issues. . . . But neither party has given as much as lip service to disability rights" (1, 4).

As a feminist, I know that all oppressions are linked; they have a similar dynamic, and we cannot erase one without working against them all. I know that a woman with a disability experiences her identity as complex, with gender, race, sexual orientation, class, physical ability, and other aspects all factors in how she experiences the world. I believe that including women with disabilities challenges many of our theories and generalities, making our descriptions of the world richer and more complicated. Sandra Harding's description of feminist standpoint epistemology is helpful here. This epistemology is based on the notion that knowledge is socially situated and that in a stratified society, "empirically more accurate descriptions and theoretically richer explanations" result from using the resources of a lower-status group to view nature and society (119). Harding uses gender, but I believe that disability standpoint epistemology operates the same way. Like gender, the standpoint of disability presents a "less partial and distorted . . . picture of nature and social relations" (121) than a conventional view, because "in systems of domination the vision available to the rulers will be both partial and perverse" (Hartsock, quoted in Harding 120).

But Harding cautions that a standpoint is not the same as a point of view:

> In a socially stratified society the objectivity of the results of research is increased by political activism by and on behalf of oppressed, exploited, and dominated groups. Only through such struggles can we begin to see beneath the appearances created by an unjust social order to the reality of how this social order is in fact constructed and maintained. The need for struggle emphasizes the fact that a feminist [I would substitute "disability"] standpoint is not something that anyone can

have simply by claiming it. It is an achievement. A standpoint differs in this respect from a perspective, which anyone can have simply by "opening one's eyes." (127)

As an able-bodied woman, I see myself as a social and political ally by teaching literature by women with disabilities through the lens of disability standpoint epistemology. I am also an activist on disability issues. I have written letters to the editor about ableist language in newspaper articles; I have protested the lack of an adequate and working elevator in a new arts center, including letters to the editor, to university officials, and to a state senator; I have boycotted and urged others to boycott local theaters that are not accessible. For me, feeling I can use disability standpoint epistemology has been the result of reading, talking with people with disabilities, and attending workshops. I have read everything I have come across by and about women with disabilities, disability theory, and disability politics. I subscribe to and read the *Disability Rag* regularly. Women with disabilities have been generous in talking with me and helping me understand the reality of their lives. Workshops by Connie Panzarino and Mary Frances Platt on ableism as a parallel oppression to other oppressions have also been extremely helpful.

Although disability standpoint epistemology requires that we identify a disability perspective, it does not push toward erasing differences or regarding disability as a unified experience. Following standpoint theory, the more multiple our standpoints, the more complete view of the world we will have. Harding specifically explores race and sexuality in writing about feminist standpoint epistemology, for example. This has implications for teaching. As with any other "group" we "teach," we need to be careful to talk about people's experiences as complex and individual, not "*the* woman's experience," or "*the* disabled experience." I try, through a variety of teaching techniques, to make this part of my classes, but it's difficult, especially when it is most students' first effort to consciously focus on the experience of people who are different from them. We are always balancing disability as a physical and socially constructed identity and human experience as individual.

What has actually gone on in the classroom when this white able-bodied woman has taught literature by women with disabilities? What has happened for the students, and what has happened for me?

A look back at my syllabus shows me that the first time I used *With the Power of Each Breath*, it was one of ten books I asked the students to buy and read. It was the only anthology and the only nonfiction book besides May Sarton's *Journal of a Solitude.* I asked the students to read approximately 90 of the 350 pages, and I surmise from the fact that we spent only one class session on the book that I didn't quite know what to do with it. My discomfort, I believe, stemmed from the fact that the authors were not "professional" writers and their autobiographical stories were not amenable to the usual types of literary criticism. The students were not bothered, however; they found the book very powerful and urged me to use it again.

Through my feminist reading and teaching I have come to see that the standards of "good" literature have often excluded the work of women and other marginalized groups. Reading and teaching Tillie Olsen's *Silences*, Joanna Russ's *How to Suppress Women's Writing*, and Virginia Woolf's *Room of One's Own* in conjunction with Alice Walker's "In Search of Our Mothers' Gardens" have radically broadened my notions of "art" and "literature." In her book *Silences*, Tillie Olsen, incorporating the words and ideas of Virginia Woolf, speaks eloquently of what we need in and from writing:

> Read the compass of women writers in our infinite variety. . . .
> Teach women's lives through the lives of the women who wrote the books, as well as through the books themselves; and through autobiography, biography, journals, letters. Because most literature concerns itself with the lives of the few, know and teach the few books closer to the lives of the many. . . .
> Help create writers, perhaps among yourselves. There is so much unwritten that needs to be written. . . . It does not matter if in its begin-

ning what emerges is not great, or even (as ordinarily defined) "good" writing.

Whether that is literature, or whether that is not literature, I will not presume to say, wrote Virginia Woolf in her preface to *Life As We Have Known It, Memoirs of the Working Women's Guild,* but that it explains much and tells much, that is certain.

The greatness of literature is not only in the great writers, the good writers; it is also in that which explains much and tells much (the soil, too, of great literature). (43–44)

As I enacted Olsen's, Woolf's, and others' ideas about literature and art into my teaching, I became more comfortable teaching literature by women with disabilities and more thoughtful about how and why I'm using this literature in my classes. In the past several years, I have integrated writing by women with disabilities thematically into my courses, and have enlarged my sources beyond *With the Power of Each Breath.* For example, in the same class where I once taught ninety pages of *With the Power* in one isolated class period, I now use a packet that includes writings from *With the Power, With Wings: An Anthology of Literature by and about Women with Disabilities,* and *Voices from the Shadows: Women with Disabilities Speak Out.* I have included readings from these books in the sections of the course dealing with growing up, education, creativity, sexuality and relationships, mothers and children, and women bonding and strength. I have also regularly shown the film *Positive Images: Portraits of Women with Disabilities,* which interviews women with three different disabilities about their childhoods and education, and shows them going shopping, at work, dealing with sexual and other relationships, and generally going on with living their lives. What I'm trying to do in my thematic approach and the groupings of the readings is to keep us from unthinkingly theorizing "woman" as white, middle-class, heterosexual, and able-bodied, to avoid any unitary essential concept of "woman." In other words, it's a pedagogical strategy that complicates identity politics. When we did the section on mothers and children, for example, we read about the experience of a black slave woman (Brent, excerpts from *Incidents in the Life of a Slave Girl*), an impoverished white woman during the Depression (LeSueur, "Annunciation"), a black lesbian (Lorde, "Now That I Am Forever with Child"), a white middle-class woman (Kumin, "Making the Jam without You"), a black woman in the rural South of the United States (Walker, "Everyday Use"), an unmarried Chinese woman whose story is told by her Chinese-American niece (Kingston, "No Name Woman"), a woman with MS who was not physically strong enough to hold her baby and who could not make eye contact with her because of vision loss (LeMaistre), a woman paralyzed from the waist down who had a tubal ligation after three miscarriages (Matthews), and a woman with polio whose daughters were twenty months and three weeks when she became disabled (Matthews). I have also taught Anne Finger's *Past Due: A Story of Disability, Pregnancy and Birth* and invited Finger to speak at our campus, and have taught Connie Panzarino's autobiography *The Me in the Mirror*.

One technique I use sparingly, but at least twice a semester, is a round robin in which every student receives a number and speaks in turn. The main rule is that no one can be interrupted; everyone can have the floor for as long or short a time as she or he wants. I encourage students to take notes when others are speaking on things they want to go back to and discuss in more depth later. I have used this format a number of times when dealing with literature by women with disabilities, for several reasons. It allows us to get a large number of responses out onto the floor; it ensures a range of responses, from very personal and emotional ones to more distanced and literary ones; and it allows students to speak in what they feel is a nonthreatening atmosphere. When I first used this technique, my goal was to get everyone to speak, so that students would realize that each of them had important things to say. It was a student who pointed out to me an additional, powerful effect of the round-robins. She told me that she liked round-robins better than usual class discussions because the person who spoke directly after her would be concentrating on her or his own ideas, not attacking her (which was what she expected, and experienced, unfortunately, in many other class discussions). This was an important insight for me. When I used a round-robin for *The Me in the Mirror* this past semester, students' comments ranged from feeling that Connie was overly demanding of her aides to worries about knowing how to react to people with disabilities to admiring Connie for her courage. I think it's important that students perceive the round-robin as a nonthreatening context in which they can voice things they have previously felt silenced about.

My students also write in their journals before we discuss each reading in class. Often in their journals students will express that this is the first time they have ever read about people with disabilities. Some will write about friends or relatives who have disabilities, including older relatives with whom bringing up the topic is forbidden, or friends their age paralyzed in accidents. Other students write about jobs or internships that involve working with children with disabilities. Many students write about their confusion and fear toward people with disabilities they meet on campus. What are they supposed to do? Should they say hello to a person in a wheelchair, even if they don't know the person? Is looking away from that person a form of prejudice? Should they offer to help open a door, to push someone up a steep ramp, to aid someone stuck in snow? Their questions are real, and most say they haven't had any place to ask them safely. They are often very concerned with the "politically correct" language to use in talking about or to a person with a disability and say that their avoidance of people sometimes has to do with their uncertainty about terminology and their fear of being deemed "politically incorrect." I respond to the questions they've raised in their journals privately, sometimes letting them know about experiences I've had, sometimes referring them to other readings, sometimes quoting people with disabilities who are my friends. In this way, students have another "safe space" in which to voice their concerns and fears.

When these questions come up in class, I usually try to get students to talk with each other about them instead of looking to me for an "answer," although I am ready to share my own ideas and responses. What I want them to realize, both in journal responses and class discussions, is that there are no clear-cut rules. Situations and people differ; what is appropriate for one time and place will not be appropriate for another. I teach "what I'm not" as someone who has educated myself in the area, having done a lot of reading, having talked to people with disabilities, having attended anti-ableism workshops, and having engaged in activism on the issue. I don't have the "answers," but I feel I can help guide students toward a useful discussion.

Another technique I use in class is to ask students to temporarily take on the perspective of someone who is disabled. One exercise that I use regularly with different pieces of literature by women with disabilities is to ask students to imagine themselves as the woman with a disability that we have read about. In a timed anonymous free writing I ask them to describe, in detail, their day up until they came into this classroom. I ask them to be very specific. As a prompt, I ask them to think about how they would wake up, get out of bed, brush their teeth, get dressed, eat breakfast, and so forth. When we are done writing, I ask a student to collect all the writings and then redistribute them, so presumably no one has her or his own. Then I ask volunteers to read their writings aloud, and have several read before opening up a discussion of what it was like to do the exercise and what we learned. Some students seem simply unable to do the exercise; they cannot imagine what it would be like to be paralyzed or blind; they cannot imagine, even after reading the literature, what adaptations they could make to function. Others do extraordinarily well in putting themselves into someone else's experience. Regularly, some students realize that they don't know whether the building we are in has an elevator or where the accessible entrance is; they don't know whether there is public transportation that accommodates wheelchairs; they don't know whether the doors of our classroom are wide enough for a wheelchair. In this exercise, I want them to realize the practical implications of having this disability in our town, attending our university. I want them to realize that a woman who uses a wheelchair might be necessarily more concerned about whether or not she can physically get to a certain class than the fact that some women are often treated as sex objects in advertising. I want for them what I want for myself, to have a more complete view of the world. I believe disability perspectives and disability standpoint epistemology can help.

In other exercises I design for class, I try to help students go beyond their "politically correct" anxieties about which language to use when talking with or about a person with a disability or what to do on meeting a person with a disability on campus. Sometimes, instead of asking them to take on the persona of a woman with a disability, I ask them to take on the persona of an able-bodied person dealing with a person with a disability, a situation closer to most of their own standpoints. In the section on creativity, for example, we read Deborah Kendrick's poem "For Tess Gallagher," in which an aspiring poet wishes to talk with the famous poet after her reading. The narrator hopes to talk to Tess Gallagher "Of line and phrases and meter . . . and laugh like conspirators, over children,/ Pets, and lovers we have known." But the poem ends:

> All we talk about instead
> Is the only
> Other
> Blind person you have known.
> (84)

I have asked the students to do the following assignment in small groups: "You are Tess Gallagher. Write your own version of the evening Deborah Kendrick writes about in her poem 'For Tess Gallagher.' This can be a poem or prose." In response, students have been able to voice the complexities of a "famous" person meeting someone she does not know who admires her, as well as of a sighted person meeting someone who is blind who wants to strike up a conversation. I have found that, in general, small groups work well for these kinds of assignments. Collectively, the students talk out complications within the still practical framework of getting an assignment done, and getting it done on time. It's good practice for community activism, I think.

In another small group exercise I have used with "For Tess Gallagher," I ask students to "Prepare a performance/reading of 'For Tess Gallagher' to present to the rest of the class." Obviously students must work closely with a poem and understand its complexity in order to respond adequately to this assignment. Most do well, and some absolutely astonish me with the creativity and risk taking they demonstrate in the limited amount of time they have to do the work.

In the section on creativity we also read Nancy Mairs's story "Shape," about a woman sculptor who has MS who is shaping a clay head (she has already had to give up working with wood after cutting herself several times). Because her energy is limited, she tells her daughter she can't take her and a friend to the movies that night. Her daughter responds, "No wonder Father left you. . . . Harriet's right— you're nothing but a damned cripple" (96). One or more groups have this assignment: "You are Abby, Pamela's daughter in 'Shape.' Write/ tell your own version of the events your mother tells in 'Shape.' " I should emphasize here that for me such class activities work well in a class in which students know they will be asked to interact with the material in a direct way in class, and in which we have developed some trust and experience in working together and hearing many voices.

My exercises are sometimes more pointedly activist. I have asked students to read a handout on language use called "Unhandicapping Our Language." In one group assignment I tell them, "You are responsible for introducing 'Unhandicapping Our Language' to the office where you work. How will you introduce the handout, what will you do to let people know it's important? What will you do to help people begin to make the language changes it suggests?" Another group has this task: "Based on what we have read and seen so far by women with disabilities, what actions do you recommend that people can take to be allies to these women in eliminating barriers and discrimination?"

I added another dimension to my teaching of literature by women with disabilities in the fall of 1993, when I invited Anne Finger to campus. My sophomore-level women's literature class read her autobiographical book *Past Due* and was required to go to either a reading or a talk on disability that she gave. In their journals on *Past Due*, before they had met Finger, students wrote about a variety of things. One student wrote movingly about her profoundly disabled brother and the toll caring for him takes on her family, especially her mother. Another wrote about her own rheumatoid arthritis, and the uncertainty and scariness of not knowing how it would develop. Another wrote about her aunt who had had polio. Several students noted that they had never read a description of childbirth as graphic as Finger's. Some were uncomfortable with this; others thought about their mothers and the physical pain that their births might have caused them. A couple of students initiated conversations with their mothers about their births. The three mothers in the class wrote about their own childbirth experiences. Many students liked the fact that the book made them think about difficult issues. Specifically, a number of students thought about what they would do if they were pregnant and found out their fetus was likely to be disabled.

On the first day of class discussion, we did a round robin. Students spoke of many of the issues they had written about in their journals, although not some of the most personal. Most people commented in their next journals that they found the round-robin worthwhile and that they had learned a lot from their classmates' responses. The next class period I asked students to write down a passage that moved them emotionally, angered them, or made them think, with a few notes as to why it affected them so. Then I asked them to share this with one other person. After that, I opened up class discussion by asking dyads to share what they had talked about. The discussion again was complex, serious, wide-ranging.

But some interesting and unexpected things happened when the students got to hear Anne Finger. For her evening speech, I had asked Finger to do what I called "Disability 101"—that is, to assume that most of the audience was quite new to disability issues. She did, I thought, an excellent job, using lots of personal examples from her own life and other people's to show the kinds of institutionalized and unquestioned assumptions made about people with disabilities, and the handicaps in the form of barriers that able-bodied people put in their way. I felt that Finger's tone was direct but mild and was effective for getting her points across. I was somewhat startled to hear that several of the students found her tone very negative and were uncomfortable with what they perceived as Finger's anger toward them as able-bodied people. These students felt more negative after hearing her than after reading the book. One example that came up over and over again in their written reports on her talk was her remark that when she uses a wheelchair, many more people open doors for her than when she uses a cane, even if she is balancing a load of books on one arm and leaning on her cane with the other. Some students responded very defensively. They "heard" Finger saying that she was not grateful when people opened doors for her, and they expressed anger at her, saying they "were just trying to help," and "she should appreciate people helping her." They felt she was accusing all able-bodied people of being insensitive.

Another example was Finger's analysis of the Jerry Lewis telethon. She talked about the way the telethon presents people with disabilities as eternal children; even fifty-five-year-old men are "Jerry's kids." She talked about the telethon's "false promise of a cure," implying that it was terrible to be disabled and that only a cure was worth our contributions, not technology to make living with a disability easier.

She talked about the threatening implications of the pitches to send money—"You don't want this to happen to you." She talked about the broader issue of why people with disabilities have to beg on television for donations. But what some students "heard" was that she was being unfair to Jerry Lewis, that after all, he was just "trying to help."

There is a consistent thread here. The students who were most uncomfortable and angry at Finger wanted to remain subjects and central, while Finger and other people with disabilities remained "other" and marginal. They did not want to take responsibility for their able-bodiedness, their privilege; they did not want to see it as the location from which they experience the world. They wanted to be in the position of choosing when to "help" unfortunate disabled others, and to receive gratitude for doing so. Finger had said, "If you are disabled and conscious, you go around in a state of rage." They did not want to hear of her rage. To one of these students, I wrote this journal response:

> maybe you can understand why Finger chose to tell us about some of the negative things about being disabled. Where else are we going to hear them? As she said, when we hear anything, it's usually "The ——— Story," of how someone triumphed over all difficulties, overcame all obstacles. Yet, what about the disabled women who are sexually abused, why is the unemployment rate among disabled people who want to work 66 percent, why did a person assume Finger was looking for the Communications Disorders Clinic when she said she wanted to return a key to the Communications Dept.? She lives with this every day, and I guess I don't mind if she tries to tell me, as an ablebodied person, what it's like.

Still, I don't think that students who had this response are going to come out of my class informed disability activists. They are perhaps conceptually not ready for the kinds of complexities Finger was talking about. They are fearful, I think. They do not want the world as they know it to be challenged or changed. They cannot see privileged locations as locations. They do not see knowledge as socially situated.

I don't think that in a fifteen-week semester I can completely transform these students' view of the world. What I can do is offer some
reading, some experiential exercises in class, some challenging journal
responses, and hope that someday they will have enough other experiences and have lost enough of their fear to look past their own
supposed centralities.

This opens up the larger question in "teaching what I am not"—
am I accomplishing my goals of being an ally of people with disabilities, creating allies in some of my students, and helping give students
a sense of the individuality and complexity of the lives of the women
we read about? I notice as I type this that there is a seeming contradiction between the first two goals and the third. In order to be a political
ally, I must see myself as "able-bodied" and a group of other people
as "disabled"; this kind of identity politics is hard to reconcile with
the aim of seeing the complexity of anyone's individual experience,
where disability will be just one factor among many. This is the
dilemma I have been struggling with through my teaching and
through the course of writing this essay. Like all dilemmas, it is too
neat and false when it implies I must do one or the other. I believe
that at this historical time and place, it is important for me to teach as
if identity politics has a reality and unity I do not believe it has while
actively teaching against it. It's important to me to be part of the
disability rights movement as an ally, as an able-bodied person who
also has many other aspects to her identity. It's also important to me
to teach the complexity, individuality, and social constructedness of
all our identities.

It seems appropriate to end with the words of some of my students.
I ask them to write final journals in which they identify five aspects of
the course that they felt had the most impact on them. Some of them
pick the writings by women with disabilities. In the way they write
about their perceptions and understandings, I worry sometimes that I
may be encouraging stereotypes rather than breaking them down. The

most notable stereotypes are those of the pitiable "cripple" and the "Super-Crip," material for a made-for-TV movie. I also read in their journals, however, a struggle with the complexity of identity and how to deal with "what I am not" that seems to me real, admirable, and a place from which much more can grow. Each of these students has given me permission to use her words in this essay, hoping they will be useful to other students and teachers.

> Connie Panzarino's book *The Me in the Mirror* was also a personal favorite. Issues that face individuals with disabilities have always been an interest of mine. Connie is an inspiring woman who has done so many things for Handicapped rights. I loved reading about her personal struggles and triumphs. (Michelle Karmazin)

> Reading Connie Panzarino's book was an incredible revelation for me. . . . Her story, her life, totally opened my eyes. I began to *see* everyone differently, people with disabilities and people without disabilities. My favorite class period when we were reading this book was the one that you had us write as if we were Connie. We had to write in detail everything we did from the time we woke up to when we went to bed from Connie's perspective. It was definitely an eye-opening experience. It literally *forced* me to think about life and what it would be like in a completely different way. It also made me extremely appreciative and more aware of my own ableness and how quickly it could all be taken away from me. I think that sometimes we look at people with disabilities the same way we do the homeless and serious criminals—if we keep them on the fringes of society they can't touch us, they can't affect us. If we keep a wall between "us" and "them" then what happened to "them" won't happen to "us." (Kim Hansen)

> Reading *The Me in the Mirror* by Connie Panzarino was a definite learning experience for me. I had never before considered many of the struggles that a person with a handicap faces in their life. And, I had never stopped to think of what a day in the life would be like. This book was very eye-opening for me. The book offered a look at the personal and political struggles that Connie faced throughout her life. The experience of reading this book was immeasurable as to the increased awareness I gained. I began to question the construction of handicapped entrances in the backs and sides of buildings. And, some-

times I've looked for entrances and they haven't been there at all. The other day I met this woman named Michelle. It was cold and rainy and I was really happy that she asked for my help on our walk to class. She held my umbrella for us while I pushed. Her destination was Avery and we started talking about the total inconvenience of the entrance being so far out of her way. She also expressed concern about the low bushes that line the entrance. It scares her when she is out at night. I believe that if I had not been exposed to the book and the discussions that accompanied, I may not have felt comfortable talking to Michelle about her disability. (Sunshine Black)

I am so glad that you brought the issue of disabilities into our class. You know, you can learn about types and causes of disabilities, but nothing can educate a person more than to talk to a person with a disability. Connie Panzarino educates her readers in this way. She gives people with disabilities a voice by sharing her experience. I think that for so long non-disabled people tended to think that people with disabilities weren't real people—like they didn't have real emotions, ideas, and thoughts. I am so thankful that this is changing, it is literature like this that can change people's attitudes and lives. (Kelly Schreiner)

[The poet Chrystos] makes us feel like we are all connected and are standing in one huge, earth-sized circle, holding hands and supporting one another. When I read her poem "Ceremony for Completing a Poetry Reading" I can vividly picture thousands of women in the circle, with Chrystos standing among us with a basket of gifts, talking and passing beads and feathers and other things around the circle. . . . A few months ago, Connie Panzarino was not a woman I would have pictured in the circle of women I envision above. All the women would have been standing, able to pass the gifts around just as I would. Most would have been white, heterosexual, American—just like me. Now my circle includes women of different abilities and colors and personalities. This is not to say that I don't have any more to learn or I have completely conquered my prejudices and fears about other people. But the more I read and the more I learn, the bigger and more diverse my circle gets. (Christy Johnson)

NOTE

1. This term "originated among disabled people and has recently been used by some U.S. feminists to refer to people who used to be called 'able-

bodied.' " Cheris Kramarae and Paula Treichler, *A Feminist Dictionary* (Boston: Pandora Press, 1985), 444–45.

BIBLIOGRAPHY

Asch, Adrienne, and Michelle Fine. "Beyond Pedestals: Revisiting the Lives of Women with Disabilities." In *Disruptive Voices: The Possibilities of Feminist Research*, 139–71. Ann Arbor: University of Michigan Press, 1992.
Browne, Susan E., Debra Connors, and Nanci Stern, eds. *With the Power of Each Breath: A Disabled Women's Anthology*. Pittsburgh: Cleis Press, 1985.
Connors, Debra. "Disability, Sexism, and the Social Order." In *With the Power of Each Breath*, ed. Browne et al., 92–107.
"Election 92: The Year of the Gimp . . . Not!" *Disability Rag*, Nov./Dec. 1992, 1, 4.
Finger, Anne. *Past Due: A Story of Disability, Pregnancy and Birth*. Seattle: Seal Press, 1990.
Harding, Sandra. *Whose Science? Whose Knowledge? Thinking from Women's Lives*. Ithaca: Cornell University Press, 1991.
Harrison, Julie, and Marilyn Russo. *Positive Images: Portraits of Women with Disabilities*. 1989. Available from Women Make Movies, New York. Videotape.
Hartsock, Donna. "The Feminist Standpoint: Developing the Ground for a Specifically Feminist Historical Materialism." In *Discovering Reality: Feminist Perspectives on Epistemology, Metaphysics, Methodology, and Philosophy of Science*, ed. Sandra Harding and Merrill Hintikka. Dordrecht: Reidel, 1983.
Kendrick, Deborah. "For Tess Gallagher." In *With Wings*, ed. Saxton and Howe, 84.
LeMaistre, JoAnn. "Parenting." In *With the Power of Each Breath*, ed. Browne et al., 284–91.
Longmore, Paul K., and Dianne B. Piastro. "Unhandicapping Our Language." Los Angeles: Criptography Incorporated, n.d.
Mairs, Nancy. "Shape." In *With Wings*, ed. Saxton and Howe, 94–100.
Matthews, Gwyneth Ferguson. *Voices from the Shadows: Women with Disabilities Speak Out*. Toronto: Women's Educational Press, 1983.
Olsen, Tillie. *Silences*. New York: Delacorte Press/Seymour Lawrence, 1978.
Panzarino, Connie. *The Me in the Mirror*. Seattle: Seal Press, 1994.
Rich, Adrienne. "Notes toward a Politics of Location." In *Blood, Bread, and Poetry: Selected Prose 1979–1985*, 210–31. New York: Norton, 1986.
Russ, Joanna. *How to Suppress Women's Writing*. Austin: University of Texas Press, 1983.

Saxton, Marsha, and Florence Howe, eds. *With Wings: An Anthology of Literature by and about Women with Disabilities*. New York: Feminist Press, 1987.

Shapiro, Joseph P. *No Pity: People with Disabilities Forging a New Civil Rights Movement*. New York: Random House, 1993.

"Temporarily Able-Bodied (TAB)." In *A Feminist Dictionary*, ed. Cheris Kramarae and Paula A. Treichler, 444–45. Boston: Pandora Press, 1985.

Walker, Alice. "In Search of Our Mothers' Gardens." In *In Search of Our Mothers' Gardens: Womanist Prose*, 231–43. New York: Harcourt Brace Jovanovich, 1983.

Woolf, Virginia. *A Room of One's Own*. New York: Harcourt Brace Jovanovich, 1929.

8

Theory, Practice, and the Battered (Woman) Teacher

CELESTE M. CONDIT

Pedagogy—understood as the formal theorization of teaching practices—has become increasingly fashionable of late. This trend was led by the elite private schools, but even the major state-supported research institutions have recently become enamored of the concept of "teaching as scholarship." A wide variety of factors have produced this trend, including intensified competition for student enrollments, pressure from state legislatures, and authentic feminist concerns that we attend to teaching (perceived as a nurturing practice) over research (perceived as a status practice).

Whatever the causes of this trend, one of its characteristic features is the argument that teaching practices need to be brought more into line with "cutting edge" theoretical discourses. The particular theories with which various scholars would have teaching be realigned vary from radical democratic theory to Foucauldian power-knowledge to standpoint theory to "invitational rhetoric." Whatever the theory, however, I believe that using theories as cookie cutters to delineate teaching practices is doomed to failure. Theorizing teaching damages human beings because theorizing, as a reductivist activity, fails to deal with the embodied diversity of both teachers and students and fails to account for the complexity of their interactions. I will advance this argument by describing the assumptions implicit about the teacher's ethos in efforts to theorize teaching, and by describing my own experiences as a woman teacher dealing with male students, experiences that belie these assumptions. I will then offer "critical common sense" as an alternative to organizing our teaching around theory.

Who Is a Teacher?

In any speaking situation (and teaching is invariably a speaking situation), all speakers arrive with and develop what classical rhetoricians called "ethos." One's ethos is one's perceived character or persona.[1] It is who the audience thinks you are. Ethos is derived from social roles, personal appearance, voice quality, management of language, selection of reasons, and a complex amalgam of expectations and behavioral interactions. It strongly influences both the nature of the affective relations between speaker and audience and the persuasiveness of the message that the speaker offers.

Those who wish to impose cutting edge theories on teaching practices generally presume a certain kind of ethos for the teacher. They presume that the teacher is powerful, probably excessively powerful, and that the teacher has high credibility with the students. They worry that the teacher's power and credibility will cow the students and take away the students' ability to find their own identity or develop their own "voice." In this version of the ivory tower, the professor is in control. Even when the professor decides to "share power" and engage in a collaborative model of teaching, it is the professor who makes that decision. Moreover, this teacher is a rational animal. The teacher rationally and thoughtfully matches theory to practice. Even when the professor decides to abdicate authority and engage in dialogue, this is only a strategy. It is still the teacher, in conversation with other theorists, who decides what rationally devised "theory" is to be presented (or embodied) in the classroom.

I do not live in this theoretical university. When teaching undergraduates, I often feel less like a confident, rational professor than a battered woman who cannot escape a bad marriage. For me, undergraduate teaching is not a matter of thoughtful direction of delicate student minds, but more like a desperate attempt to make a relationship work while the other party maneuvers energetically and angrily to shell me. The regnant theories of teaching thus fail me, and call me to search for some alternatives.

To reach for these alternatives requires that I share with you some of my experiences from the classroom. To some extent, these experiences are grounded in gendered experience. To a large extent, however, these gendered experiences raise a more general set of issues about the power of the teacher. Unfortunately, like most members of most oppressed groups, I am not good at drawing the line between those experiences—it is all too easy to see all trauma as gendered. So I will leave it to the men to say which experiences they share. Before I begin, I want to mention that the teaching experiences I describe below will appear very bleak, and that they do not constitute an accurate picture of all of my teaching experience—there are many joyful moments in teaching. However, it is important to attend to the bad side of teaching, and I have had too many of these bad experiences at the University of Georgia, a large Southern "research" university, named by *Money* magazine as one of the "best buys" in the nation.

When I came to teach at Georgia, I came to an entirely new set of experiences of teaching. One of the most shocking elements of that experience was the repeated nonverbal behaviors of male students. Most notably, whenever they wanted me to change their grade or give them an "excused absence," they would put their arms around my shoulders or place their hands on my knee. The first time this happened to me, in the middle of a classroom, with other students milling around, I was so stunned I could not react other than by shrugging and backing away. Later, I was to get angry and tell them not to touch me, for which I was verbally accosted. Later still, I learned to give them a quiet, unthreatening explanation about nonverbal behavior and professional gender norms. But as I watched the world around me, I discovered that this mannerism was a routine way in which white Southern males exhibit their dominance over females. Because it was so routine, there was no way (other than submission) that I could react to this behavior without being labeled a "bitch." In the worst cases, that label is overtly used; a female colleague of mine has even been chased by a male student down the hall yelling at her for assigning him a low grade. I myself have been physically threatened and have had to ask for the protection of campus police.

These are the clearest examples of male control in the classroom to which I can point, but they are not the only type of control that is exercised, and probably not the most important one; gender manifests itself in a variety of ways. On a regular basis, male students challenge not only my arguments, but my right to tell them what to do. It is difficult to describe the nonverbal behaviors by which these challenges are made. It is a glare, a lifted chin, a defiance. Occasionally these gestures break out into verbal form, as with the eighteen-year-old who told me (a middle-aged full professor), "you have to earn my respect." The control is also issued in other ways. Male students talk more, and they make it very difficult for me to address female students and raise issues that I perceive are more salient for female students.

When I walk into the classroom each quarter, I dread the new term, for I know that, each time, I am going to have to go through a battle establishing my authority; and in classrooms with a hundred students, authority is a necessity. This is not the game I came to the role of teacher to play. It is not the role that my feminist theory would have me play. But I have learned that I am forced to play it, or I cannot be a teacher here. I am now fairly good at waging this battle. I do not lose very often anymore, but I am sapped, and I flinch from teaching undergraduates so that I can avoid these battles.

I believe that this "battle of the sexes" that plays itself out in the

South is merely an extreme form of something that goes on in most classrooms in America. To put it bluntly, students are not our pawns. They are not sheep that we decide to teach "actively" or "passively." They are highly motivated, highly skilled, and enormously self-interested people who feel themselves forced to share a classroom with us, often against their desires, and they intend to minimize the pain we cause them, and sometimes to maximize the pain they inflict on us.

The ethos of "student" has probably always contained more resistance to teachers than our formal theorizing has recognized. The records show that students at Georgia were throwing things at professors and spitting in classrooms and skipping classes in the nineteenth century, and of course demonstrations against the authority of the university were common and loud in the sixties even in the South. However, there are a variety of institutional factors that seem to enhance this power in our own era.

The first institutional support for student power is the use and character of teaching evaluations. Let me say first that I believe that students have a right to give anonymous feedback, and, except in exceptional circumstances, I tend to get high teaching evaluations numerically. However, I do this *not* by being a good teacher, but by catering to the prejudices of the students and avoiding irritating their prickly tempers. Nonetheless, I have been attacked in the "open-ended comments" on teaching evaluations, and my younger female peers are even more prone to punishment via this means. Repeatedly, women-oriented content (it needn't be "feminist") garners the ire of male students. They readily report on teaching evaluations that one is "too feminist" or is "biased." This is not in any way an objective evaluation. Even by introducing two or three speeches by women and another two or three speeches by blacks, a female teacher in a speech class can earn this sobriquet on her evaluations. "Too feminist" means simply that one expresses the view that women speakers have had special problems and were historically silenced. It does not mean that one enacts the speaking style or values and arguments of Andrea Dworkin. In other words, for these students, any equality is too much equality.

In my experience, male colleagues do not take this kind of abuse. If they do teach feminist content, they are not suspected of being a "biased special interest" (my geologist husband gleefully calls all dinosaurs "she" in his class, and students never complain about his feminism). If males teach conservative content instead of objective or liberal (as in the "liberal arts") content, this is taken as "natural" or "objective" and so not commented on. But even if men do receive political attacks for their perspectives, note two things. First, the point is the same. *Students are exercising enormous power in controlling what is taught in the classroom.* Second, the uses to which these comments are put by administrators are different. Female teachers have their raises and promotions threatened by these comments. Department heads put these comments into year end evaluations as signs of failures of teaching. (I am reporting actual incidents here, not engaging in general hand wringing.) I do not believe the same happens for men. (This may be hand wringing.)

This problem is even greater for female graduate students. I have now had to counsel a parade of female graduate students who received bad course evaluations. In every case, I have gone to observe their teaching in the classroom, only to find them well organized, well prepared, and giving substantive lectures. In each case, the students saw the women as "biased" and "unfair." I believe they did so primarily because of the women's gender. The graduate supervisor, in one case, commented that *he* never had problems with this. Students never challenged his politics. But of course, he fit the profile of a "professor" and its gender expectations, and he sported relatively conservative politics. Judging from his reactions to my graduate students' comprehensive examination papers, I do not think that he is any less biased in the classroom, but he certainly is perceived as less biased. The minute a woman instructor walks into a Southern classroom in pants and short hair she is branded as outside the bounds of the normal—a liberal, a feminist, or a dyke. There is little she can do to dispute that automatic rejection. Male professors have to work a little harder to earn that kind of rejection.

So what happens to the female graduate students? I counsel them to learn to "perform objectivity" for their students, and to drop all the examples that matter to them and their female students. I teach them to lie low, hide themselves and their interests and politics until they become full professors and can tolerate the salary hits. In other words, the vocal, white, male, upper-middle-class undergraduate students get their way.

The misuse of teaching evaluations is, unfortunately, not the sole factor in this battering of the college teacher. There are higher administrative structures that participate in this game as well. One notes first the reward structure of the university. Our university takes great pride in the fact that it "takes teaching seriously," but this means only that it rewards those teachers who please students. Good teaching, in my view, requires a lot of hard work focused on writing and speaking exchanges that require extensive feedback (i.e., lots of time outside the classroom). This kind of good teaching, however, is in no way recognized by the institution. Moreover, many students resent both the time they have to put into such assignments and the fact that your feedback to them inevitably asks them to improve (and therefore implies that they are not perfect just as they are). Thus the university definition of good teaching as catering to the lowest common denominator among student pleasure represents a double whammy to the would-be good teacher. Your salary is imperiled and no awards are forthcoming if you do not soothe the students, and if you do teach well, this will take time away from your research responsibilities, and you will be further imperiled.

All these problems are further exacerbated by the fact that administrations across the country are pushing for larger and larger classes. The battles of one professor against thirty-five are magnified tenfold when it becomes one professor against the anonymous hundred. Here the culture of student resistance becomes enormously powerful. It makes it impossible to run a democratic classroom or an active one. Students, when told to think and argue, break out into the chaos of a mob, and the instructor is chastised for "losing control of the classroom." The culture of resistance enabled in this environment has taught students to challenge every grade structure and every administrative decision of a professor as "unfair" (where fair is defined as "not to my advantage").

Finally, there are "staff" functions, those efforts to "improve teaching," that also batter the (woman) teacher. When faced with the task of teaching classes exceeding a hundred students I diligently began to attend the "large lecture discussion group" on campus. In only a few sessions I learned my lesson. If one admits, before such a body, that one has any type of difficulty teaching, one is immediately attacked for one's bad teaching. One is "at fault." There are no systemic problems, no basic gender difficulties, no bad students. There are only bad teachers. The purpose of these groups is to share successes, which means that elderly male business professors sit around and tell everyone about their wonderful models and many successes, as they bid against each other for this year's teaching awards.

By now it should be clear that I see the professor who would well and truly teach as being required to respond to a powerful student culture, and I see a variety of university structures complicit in enhancing student power over teachers. I see female instructors as particularly vulnerable to this power, but I recognize that the same forces are at work against male instructors (they simply have a few more tools to deal with the problems). To some extent, we are all Doonesbury's Professor Deadmon.

Who Is a Student?

This brings us to the issue of the relationship of our theories to our students as audience. As I have suggested, it appears to me that most of the theories we bring to bear in critical pedagogy presume a need to empower students and affirm their identity. I hope I have suggested that this is not uniformly true. The lesson, however, is not to develop a new theory that describes students as powerful manipulators, for not all students are like that either. I believe, therefore, that instead of generating uniform theories, pedagogy needs to investigate the particularities of the audiences we face. This is in part because our own ethos is dependent on student expectations, but it is also because what it means to teach a person and what one ought to teach that person depend on who they are. Let us consider then, our students as audiences, and their goals.

In the first place, the goals of our students can be compared to our own only on a case-by-case basis (although across time, patterns may appear among groups). The goals of students in private universities are far more likely to be consonant with those of their professors than are those in large public institutions. Further, those of you fortunate enough to teach in institutions with diverse student bodies will find a different set of mismatches between your own values and those of the students than I face with my upper-middle-class and upper-class white male UGA students. But each of us must start our exploration of power and teaching with our own case.

My students—the majority of them, or at least the speaking majority—want the best grade at the lowest cost. Period. In contrast, my goals require much work from them. I am happy to give good grades, but I can get good work from most students only if I tie good grades to that work. I make that link between work and grades because, as a teacher of rhetoric and communication, I have three values that I want my students to adopt: (1) I want them to be better citizens, lovers, colleagues, parents, and neighbors; (2) I want them to become more reflective, slower to judge, and more expansive in the things they come to include in their considerations for judgment; and finally, (3) I hope that I can help them to articulate their reflective selves with eloquence and sensitivity to those with whom they speak.

In contrast to these values, consider a few statements from student assignments I have received recently. I list after these student statements my honest reactions, things I think are the "truth," though I don't usually feel free to express these as responses to the students.

> More and more politicians are fighting for more lenient sanctions for people that break the law. I think that we should go back to the old philosophy of "an eye for an eye; a tooth for a tooth." Do you think that petty shoplifters would not think twice about stealing that aspirin if they knew that they could lose a finger for it?
>
> *(To which I feel compelled to ask, what politicians have fought for more lenient sanctions? And yes, the evidence suggests that severity of penalty is weakly connected to gravity of the crime, but it is more directly connected to the odds of detection, and would you truly value an aspirin over the body of a human being?)*

> Daily we deal with the problem of prisons overflowing. This is absurd. We could eliminate this problem easily. If a citizen is found guilty of murder, that citizen should be executed without question of delay.
>
> *(To which I must say that the number of murderers would hardly make a dent in the prison population; what kind of emotion enables this irrational argument?)*

> Children should study the Bible in school and learn and gain wisdom. You may not agree, but everyone is entitled to their own opinion. But it is only through God's command that a good society will be achieved on earth.
>
> *(To which I must say, how can you manage authoritarian relativism?)*

> I get sick and tired of old grey heads slowing me down on the highway. These old people should be taken off the roads so the rest of us can get on with our business. A two thousand dollar a year driver fee would help solve this problem.

And, just for fun:

> We should shun people like John Lenin who founded communism. . . .
> If we eliminate our corrupt Congress we could still avoid a dictatorship because the President would be elected.

These examples should make it clear that as a teacher in this setting, I am teaching *who* I am not. These students are not at all like me.

Moreover, in any class where you are grading writing and speaking assignments, teaching who you are not is the same thing as teaching *what* you are not. There is no simple separation between ethos and content. If one is to teach a student to be a better writer or speaker, this entails improving the quality of their reasoning, the quality of their evidence, the decency of their emotions, as well as their ability to use commas and vocal pauses. At least if one follows the classical criteria for rhetoric and composition, criteria that extend back to Aristotle, a teacher is enjoined to improve the ethos (character), pathos (emotions), and logos (logic) exhibited in a student's speaking (and writing).[2]

There is, however, a terrible cost to this set of practices, and that cost increases with every increment of difference between the teacher and the student. Students do not want to be told that they are ill-informed, narrow-minded, incapable of consistent thought, selfish, and cruel. They do not want to be compared (even in the most cloaked fashion) to mewling infants who care only for their own warm bottle, and look not beyond the next feeding. They most certainly do not want to be given that as a reason for why they are not going to get an A for the speech they wrote at 2 a.m. last night. Given that many students are relatively empowered to fight back in many institutions, I conclude that professors who feel powerful are powerful only because their goals and views are consonant with their students' and institutions'. The rest of us face a very different set of circumstances, and theories of teaching that do not recognize the different personae who make up teaching and learning situations are of little use to us.

Theories of Teaching

Although I have used personal examples to suggest that the variability of the ethos of students and teachers makes the application of theories to teaching practice treacherous, I would like to deepen that claim by illustrating these pitfalls with regard to three contemporary theories that are being suggested for pedagogy. The first two of these theories are "hot" among progressives in my field and have some interdisciplinary purchase. The third is viewed as "outdated" and "conservative," but, ironically, may be of more use to the battered woman professor.

One of the most important theorists in the humanities across the past two decades has been Michel Foucault. Foucault offers a theory about the relationship between power and knowledge that would seem to be highly salient to pedagogical reflections. Unfortunately, the experiences I have described from teaching seem to discredit Foucault's claims on every count. Foucault's image of the panopticon or the disciplined subordinate does not seem to match my classroom and my students.[3] It is true that students are watched, but they watch back closely, and with power. Students know that power and knowledge are linked, and they are guarding their own systems of power/knowledge closely. There is no single episteme here, but a struggle among many views. Perhaps the students hold hegemony, or perhaps the administrators and students hold hegemony in coalition. But in either case, I find it difficult to claim that it is "knowing" in any meaningful sense that has the upper hand here. Knowledge is weak; self-interest is strong. Emotion, not knowledge, guards the gates of self-interest.

An alternative progressive theory may therefore seem more appropriate. One of the most active areas of research in cultural studies and communication studies in the past decade has been the theory of the "active audience." This theory holds that audiences for mass media are not passive receptors of the dominant ideology contained in most media products.[4] Instead, they are active decoders who use media for their own pleasures and their own political interests. At first blush, this theory would seem enormously consonant with the experiences I have described from my classroom teaching. It would certainly seem to offer a better explanation than the notion of "discipline and punish." There are, however, several incompatibilities here as well. When applying the recent findings of audience research to the classroom, we come to notice that audiences are indeed active. But unlike mass media audiences, who can only be playful and polysemous as decoders, students are actively working in their own self-interest, and effectively targeting their interests against professors. Audience studies also presume that the encoder is producing a message consonant with the dominant ideology and that the decoder has interests that are not consonant with the dominant ideology, but in this case, that is not true.

In part, the theory of the active audience does not work well for pedagogy because students are not simply audiences. They have routes through which to speak, and they use them. These routes include not only the space of the classroom and the office, but also the teaching evaluation and the prerogative to "vote with your enrollment," which is a serious factor in contemporary universities. The multiplicitous character of the role of the "student" thus again makes a single theory inadequate to capture the practice.

Two dominant progressive theories, quite opposite to each other, both fail to capture crucial features of my classroom. So what alternatives are there? What theory is most evident in my classroom, the classroom of a political progressive who thinks a lot about teaching? Shockingly perhaps, one of the strongest components of my classroom is the old-fashioned, outdated Enlightenment theory of "information processing." Enlightenment ideals hold that teaching is mostly a matter of passing information to students and, where necessary, helping them learn the techniques of manipulating that information through demonstrations that they can imitate. This, of course, is not consonant with theories of rhetoric (which is my home discipline) or with progressive thought. So why is it this theory that best describes much (but by no means all) of my teaching?

The answer is that my teaching practices are not dictated by my theories, but by the specific constraints I face. Some of these are institutional (and the institution operates on an information processing theory). Some of these constraints are personal to the students I teach (and they may operate on information processing models). However, the use of these theories is also my self-defensive choice. The information processing model casts me as the "expert" with knowledge the students do not have. It thereby gives me power to levy against the students with their power as consumers. The response to this choice by most progressives (most of whom style themselves as "radicals") today is that we must eliminate these old theories and replace them with new ones. But given the circumstances of each of us as teachers, that is a self-destructive act of a proportion beyond my tolerance. One cannot walk into a classroom that is structured against progressive teaching and simply enact a progressive world. Theory does not override material constraints that easily. In addition, however, theory itself is deficient for practice.

I leave open the possibility that somehow we can reconstruct universities so that they are friendly to progressive teaching. I wish, however, to suggest that the theories we are promulgating for progressive teaching are themselves insufficient. Theory, by its nature, presumes uniformity among the component elements whose relationship it describes. It presumes that each teacher is a unit, of a type, not a "who" with a distinctive (if complex and changing) identity. It assumes that students are interchangeable with each other. It presumes, therefore, that there is a single set of relationships possible and desirable among those units. My experiences belie those assumptions, and I suspect that yours do too.

My conclusion is that trying to fit our teaching practices within a theory is an inappropriate activity that is destructive to the diversity of our lives. This does not mean that theory cannot be useful to teaching. I derive, for example, a great deal of utility from Gramsci's concepts of "war of position" and "war of maneuver" when teaching recalcitrant students.[5] But such pragmatic borrowing, and cutting and pasting, is a different activity from trying to make one's teaching conform to a singular theory. It may be useful, therefore, to have a name for this kind of activity—an activity that would serve the interests of a progressive politics, and the interests of teachers facing varied students and the varied teaching tasks that go with the inevitable mismatch between student and teacher that is inherent to the assumption that teachers have something new for students to learn. I offer the label "critical common sense" to serve that purpose.

Critical Common Sense

The notion of common sense has been almost completely discredited by progressive academics in the past two decades. "Common sense" is a term that has been appropriated most often by conservatives, and much of what passes in common parlance for common sense fails all the tests for radicalness. In fact, it is almost by definition that to be "radical" is to be against whatever is common. (Besides, one guesses that even progressive academics are terrified of the possibility that there is something worth knowing that one does not have to go to college to learn!) If one is not a radical, but merely a progressive, however, this attack on common sense may be seen as overstated. There is a perfectly appropriate meaning of common sense that describes it simply as that which one learns from life experiences. Moreover, common sense is only that which is "common" to a particular community, and that community may be progressive, conservative, or even radical. (There is indeed a set of "common sense" among radicals.) Common sense is not, therefore, inherently conservative. In order to specify, however, that this common sense is a reflective one, one that takes into account not only the lessons of daily experience, but also reflection on how those experiences fit into larger social structures, one can refer to "critical common sense."

Such critical common sense about teaching is garnered by experience in the classroom, discussions with other teachers, feedback from students and administrators, and reflection on teaching in comparison to available theories of communication and social structure. It is different from theory in three major respects. Where theory prescribes a rational, coherent plan from which all of one's teaching choices flow, critical common sense is a pastiche of what works and achieves one's goals in particular contexts. Critical common sense may derive from theoretical structures that are logically inconsistent with one another, but because practice does not require logical consistency, the pastiche works. Second, where theory prescribes a uniformity and consistency to one's teaching across time and situation and with different audiences, critical common sense prescribes that one adapt to the changing circumstances one faces. Thus, when in a large lecture section, one will use different theories than when in a small seminar. Finally, where theory prescribes the same actions for all teachers, critical common sense requires active thought and a personal collage of components. This reference to the personal does not require an essentialist theory of identity. It is compatible with recent insights that suggest that we are not at all rational, homogeneous products of our own free will, but rather products of social codes and social forces. However, critical common sense does require that we believe that there are differences between teachers, and that these differences extend to the level of individuation. That is, although we are each a product of social forces that are shared with many other persons like us, we also each represent a distinctive intersection of multiple social forces that is uniquely embodied in our self, and that this gives rise to creativity and agency.

I am always challenged, when I ask people to step out of rigid theories and to attend to experience, by the claim that "one always operates from an implicit theory." And I used to say "yes, but one needn't always be *merely* articulating that theory." But it is time to make an even firmer rejection of that cliché. Sometimes (and probably most times) one does not operate from an implicit theory. Often one struggles in a situation, using all the theories one has at hand, to patch together survival and defense in a way that no rigorous theorist would find satisfactory. Coherent, internally consistent, well-organized theory is an artifact of academics. It is not descriptive of how people approach living.[6]

Progressive politics have become so tightly linked to theory by some that this proposal of critical common sense will seem to fail to be sufficiently radical. It is difficult to argue that a pastiche will be "pure" enough and "hard hitting" enough to count as radical, given that radical politics seem to be defined by the development of increasingly more thorough-going, totalizing, or absolutist uses of a singular principle. Given the pragmatic failure of radical politics in the United States at the current moment, however, I am not too troubled by the assertion that what I propose is not radical enough in the conventional sense. Discursive purity and progressive social change do not seem innately tied to one another. In practice, theoretically "conservative" pedagogical practices can serve progressive ends, and that is well enough. For example, I am able to turn the classic "information processing" modes of communication to progressive ends. Where my white male elite students resist learning "person-centered" communication practices when presented to them on grounds of diversity or love and care, they accept them when I tell them that these practices are correlated with higher income.[7] If they begin to engage in person-centered communication practices, I believe that they will become better friends, lovers, and colleagues, and the fact that the original motive I used to get their attention was "impure" does not trouble me overmuch.

What kinds of things make up a critical common sense of teaching, then? That can hardly be specified in a single essay. It is a practice we need to share between graduate students and faculty, and in many essays, because the tools are so varied and context-dependent.[8] Some of the prescriptions I would offer in this limited manner, however, would look like this: (1) strengthen the teaching culture of progressive professors; (2) in any classroom do as much as you can (take as many hits as you can, but no more); (3) resist large classes (because they enable recalcitrant students to gang up on you); and (4) special tactics for rednecks: don't lose your cool, out-bully them (quietly), don't try to enact democracy for them, and don't use subtle strategies like contrast or self-deprecation.

To further the project of sharing our critical common sense about teaching, we should encourage venues where situated explanations of our teaching strategies can be presented and varied experiences with those strategies and contexts shared. This might take the form of a story told about a specific teaching episode, the strategies employed in that episode, the consequences of the interaction, and then discussion by those with related experiences for comparison and contrast. Outside the faculty lounge there is no space for such discussions today, and most of us spend very little time in the faculty lounge. Most of us would, indeed, profit from more time spent on rigorous reflection and sharing about teaching, and to that extent the increasing fashionableness of pedagogy is a good thing, but good teaching is not a science that can be reduced to a rigorous and regularized set of prescriptions. The "who" of teaching and learning cannot be reduced to the "what" of science (even science described as progressive theory). Instead of theorizing teaching, we need to talk together to build some critical common sense.

NOTES

1. For a more thorough, albeit regrettably metaphysical, account of ethos and character, see Eugene Garver, *Aristotle's Rhetoric: An Art of Character* (Chicago: University of Chicago Press, 1994).

2. Aristotle, *On Rhetoric: A Theory of Civic Discourse*, trans. with introduction, notes, and appendixes by George A. Kennedy (New York: Oxford University Press, 1991).

3. Foucault borrows the image of the panopticon from Bentham and puts it to his own uses. The Foucaultian corpus is large, but for a relatively clear summary of his ideas on the relationship of power and knowledge, see *Power/Knowledge* (New York: Pantheon, 1980). See also *Discipline and Punish*, trans. A. Sheridan (New York: Pantheon, 1977).

4. Two germinal works from, respectively, the United States and the

United Kingdom are Janice Radway, *Reading the Romance: Women, Patriarchy, and Popular Literature* (Chapel Hill: University of North Carolina Press, 1984); and Don Morley, *The "Nationwide" Audience: Structure and Decoding* (London: British Film Institute, 1980).

5. Antonio Gramsci, *Selections from the Prison Notebooks*, trans. and ed. Q. Hoare and G. N. Smith (New York: International Publishers, 1981–87). My idiosyncratic appropriation of Gramsci is elaborated in "Hegemony in a Mass-Mediated Society: Concordance about Reproductive Technologies," *Critical Studies in Mass Communication* 11 (September 1994): 205–30.

6. The fact that ordinary people, as opposed to political and intellectual elites, are not ideologically consistent is usually interpreted as a vice of the people, rather than as a sign of their good skills at juggling multiple values, interests, and concerns. See M. Kent Jennings, "Ideological Thinking among Mass Publics and Political Elites," *Public Opinion Quarterly* 56 (1992): 419–41.

7. Person-centered communication practices encourage communicators to attend to the needs and concerns of those with whom they dialogue, rather than simply giving free reign to their own emotional state. I recognize that several political critiques are available of this approach, but when applied to male students, the training practice is generally progressive.

8. It is also important to avoid framing suggestions for teaching in a manner that appears to "blame the victim." Repeatedly, when I describe the negative conditions I face, would-be helpful individuals immediately offer strategies for dealing with the problems. This tends to imply that one is a bad teacher, rather than that the situation in which one finds oneself as a teacher is problematic. When someone is having a difficult time teaching, you need to affirm first that the situation is unfair and unpleasant, and then say, okay, now that we know that this is a bad situation, how do we make the best of it?

BIBLIOGRAPHY

Aristotle, *On Rhetoric: A Theory of Civic Discourse*, trans. with introduction, notes, and appendixes by George A. Kennedy. New York: Oxford University Press, 1991.

Condit, Celeste M. "Hegemony in a Mass-Mediated Society: Concordance about Reproductive Technologies." *Critical Studies in Mass Communication* 11 (September 1994): 205–30.

Foucault, Michel. *Discipline and Punish*, trans. A. Sheridan. New York: Pantheon, 1977.

———. *Power/Knowledge* . New York: Pantheon, 1980.

Garver, Eugene. *Aristotle's Rhetoric: An Art of Character*. Chicago: University of Chicago Press, 1994.

Gramsci, Antonio. *Selections from the Prison Notebooks*, trans. and ed. Q. Hoare and G. N. Smith. New York: International Publishers, 1981–87.

Jennings, M. Kent. "Ideological Thinking among Mass Publics and Political Elites." *Public Opinion Quarterly* 56 (1992): 419–41.

Morley, Don. *The "Nationwide" Audience: Structure and Decoding.* London: British Film Institute, 1980.

Radway, Janice. *Reading the Romance: Women, Patriarchy, and Popular Literature.* Chapel Hill: University of North Carolina Press, 1984.

III

Professorial Identities

9

Teaching What the Truth Compels You to Teach: A Historian's View

JACQUELINE JONES

A few years ago I delivered a lecture on Toni Morrison's novel *Beloved* to an audience of college students in New York City. After the talk, two undergraduates approached me and initiated a conversation. They had recently read my book on the history of black working women, *Labor of Love, Labor of Sorrow,* and, they confessed, they were surprised to see that I was white. They had assumed I was an African American, but instead... The young women were too polite to say so, but I realized they had hoped to meet a tall, proud sister rather than a short white girl. One of the students asked how I came to write the book, and so I launched into an autobiographical tale that began with my childhood in a racially segregated small town in Delaware, and continued through my college years as a tutor of inner-city children. I was wending my rhetorical way up to my experiences at Wellesley College, where my mostly upper-middle-class students lacked any understanding of African American history, when I noticed that my listeners were becoming increasingly impatient with my little walk down memory lane. Exasperated, one of them interrupted, "May I ask you a personal question?" I nodded, and she asked, *"Are you married to a black man?"* In response, I could only smile and shrug and say no, and the conversation ended on a rather unsatisfying note for all three of us. The students had been looking

for some personal—even intimate—connection between me and the
story I told in the book, and when they could not find it, they felt
disappointed.

My reaction to this encounter was mixed. On the one hand, as a
graduate student (at the University of Wisconsin, in Madison in the
early 1970s) I had come to believe that "all history is autobiographical." My friends and I were studying history because we had a compelling interest in American society, and we sought insight through
the lens of our own families and communities—hence the self-pro-
claimed "swamp Yankee" from a New England working-class family
writing a history of an early-twentieth-century strike among textile
workers; the granddaughter of Irish immigrants researching the
structure of nineteenth-century Irish immigrant families; the native
Californian exploring the history of agricultural migrant labor in that
state. Within this small circle of graduate students I fit right in; the
subject of my dissertation, the Northern teachers who went south
after the Civil War to teach the freedpeople of Georgia, evoked my
early elementary school years in a Jim Crow school system. By the
time I wrote *Labor of Love* I had a daughter (Sarah, born in 1981; Anna
would come along in 1985), and (I told myself) perhaps motherhood
was the "intimate connection" between the book I wrote and the person I was. In a sense, then, my student-questioners were on the right
track, though I never got far enough in the (admittedly long-winded)
story I was telling them to make that point.

On the other hand, I must confess that I was a bit irritated by the
two students' queries about my decision to write a book about black
working women. After all, I wondered, how many historians are routinely called to account for the subjects they choose to explore? After
a lecture on nineteenth-century financial institutions, is my econome-
trician colleague asked, *"Are you married to a banker?"* Does my colleague in seventeenth-century Puritan studies face routine challenges,
"Is your father a preacher?" Too, I asked myself why I had never heard
of instances where any number of white male scholars of black his-

tory were questioned about the "personal" reasons behind the topics they chose to study—slavery, free blacks in the antebellum period, the freedpeople during Reconstruction, for example. Finally, I suspected that the "motherhood connection" between my subjects and me amounted to a desperate attempt on my part to rationalize, or justify, my topic. In fact, I realized that I began my research on *Labor of Love* in the late 1970s, before I even contemplated having children, and that the real motivation behind it was my desire for something on the topic to assign to my Wellesley students. More significantly, I had an intrinsic interest in the history of black working women and their families, and I realized that very little had been written on these topics. What more did I need to launch a major research project?

To understand why I have chosen to write about certain topics over the last twenty years, one would need to consider the sequence of my four major research projects. In the process of writing my dissertation on the Northern teachers of the Georgia freedpeople from 1865 to 1873, I realized that I would have to learn much more than I already did about the history of African American life and culture. That interest led me directly to *Labor of Love, Labor of Sorrow*. While researching the history of Southern sharecroppers for that book, I was struck by the similarities in the material condition of the black and white families that lived under that system, and I was struck by the efforts of those families to seek out work and better wage and educational opportunities, within a highly circumscribed plantation economy. Those concerns resulted in a study of black and white poverty after the Civil War, *The Dispossessed* (1992). At that point I became intrigued with the highly contingent dynamics of the structure of the American labor force—how certain groups of people came to embrace, or be assigned, certain kinds of jobs throughout history. I am currently at work on a history of the social organization of labor, and especially the ways that the job histories of white women and children have at times converged with, or diverged from, the histories of African American men, women, and children. Over the generations, within a variety of regional economies, black people and white women and children (not to mention a whole host of other groups identified by their marital status, age, and religion, among other personal characteristics) have predominated in certain kinds of jobs, waged and nonwaged, as a result of not only racial and gender ideologies (which have shifted over time in any case), but also military considerations and the availability of large numbers of (certain kinds of) laborers in a particular time and place. Shut out of the paid labor force for whatever reason, or limited to ill-paid seasonal or casual labor, blacks and poor white female household heads have been stigmatized as lazy and lacking in ambition. Indeed, white elites (men and women) have tended to conflate criminality and poverty; hence the currently fashionable view that holds poor women of both races responsible for all the ills that afflict American society today. For example, Richard Herrnstein and Charles Murray, authors of *The Bell Curve,* argue that poor women are the agents of dysgenesis, the process by which "dumb" women reproduce (what the authors might call) the Cognitive Mudsill, children who will supposedly inevitably grow up to be violent and irresponsible members of society.

Labor of Love, Labor of Sorrow, then, represents one stage in the evolution of my professional interests. It should go without saying that none of my books represents some distilled essence of "who I am"; rather, each book is a "text" of my interests at a particular time in my career.

More to the point perhaps is my lack of comprehension about what it means to study or teach "what you are" or "what you are not." Obviously, all of us are composed of multiple, overlapping spheres of identity. Would those who insist that I teach only "what I am" find it acceptable for me to teach white women's history, but not black women's history? Or the history of all middle-class women (black and white) but not the history of poor women? Or the history of women in small towns but not those in big cities or rural areas? Or perhaps I should confine myself to the history of white women academics, preferably those who have married and have had children? Obviously, the whole notion of matching any single personal demographic characteristic to one's teaching and scholarship is absurd on the face of it. This is not to deny the value of collaborative scholarship or the importance of intellectual exchange among people from different backgrounds (at conferences or within the pages of journals); the study of history (or any field, for that matter) thrives on debate, give and take, and the more people involved the better. But it would be difficult to sustain the argument that one particular kind of person will inevitably possess insights into the past based on his or her background or life experiences. The study of history depends on people's research and analytical skills, and the passion they bring to their work, not their psychic powers.

Historical scholarship is a highly politicized enterprise today, and that that politicization is manifested in a variety of ways, in and outside the classroom, within the publishing business, and within the profession itself. Yet I stand by one fundamental principle: scholars must remain free to write about and teach any subject they wish. Debate should focus not on what a person has chosen to research, but rather on how well he or she has done it. Whenever anyone expresses doubts about my work as a white woman writing African American history, I reply (if given the opportunity), "Let's begin the discussion with my footnotes, and go on from there." The vitality of historical—and indeed, all scholarly—inquiry depends on a generosity of intellectual spirit, an openness to the exploration of any number of issues in any number of ways. The field of history is enriched, and enriches life outside the academic community, only to the extent that scholars are free to pursue the study of the past in all its dazzling complexity.

Far too timid about any criticism they might face for writing on topics related to the history of race or ethnicity, some younger white scholars have decided to focus on whites exclusively, on the theory that, for example, African American history is best left to blacks,

Asian-American history to persons of Asian descent, and so forth. Implicit in this attitude is the narrow-minded and misguided conviction that minority historians should study one thing, and one thing only—the history of their own ethnic or racial (or gender) groups. This view is objectionable both on practical grounds and on principle. In practical terms we might note that the number of black men and women going to graduate school in history today is very low, for a variety of reasons—the sagging academic job market; the need for many college graduates (from all backgrounds) to find a job and begin paying off their student loans as soon as they receive their diplomas; the lack of encouragement gifted students of color receive throughout their educational careers, encouragement that is necessary to get anyone into graduate school and keep her or him there.

A larger issue of principle is at stake here—the potential fragmentation of scholarship altogether. Some American historians are preoccupied with sorting out a wide range of personal demographic characteristics—gender, race, ethnicity, regional identification, and class—and parceling out topics to scholars accordingly. Thus we hear serious discussions about whether or not men should write women's history, whether non-Southerners can actually understand "the Southern way of life," and so on and on. Obviously, if we wait for descendants of English indentured servants to step forward and write the history of that group, or if we reserve the study of Florida phosphate miners to people of their own kind, we will be out of luck. In fact, the view that the histories of certain groups of people must be written only by members of their own group shows a veiled contempt for those groups; the idea would seem to be that if no representative scholar steps forward to write that history, who cares? Better we learn nothing about that group than learn it from the "wrong" person. I believe that the bottom line is that no particular piece of the past should be ceded to a particular group; why should our willingness to explore every avenue of history be limited by the economics of the job market and the demographics of the profession?

Over the past few years, the field of American history has been enlivened by attention to groups that received short shrift—if any attention at all—from traditional scholars who focused their sights on "great men" and the wars they waged and the politics they practiced. History was narrowly defined precisely because one group of people—white men of property and privilege—was writing about people in the past much like themselves—white men of property and privilege in the past. While one might argue that the elite should write about the elite—that these men "understand" the culture and values of their forebears, it is clear that as a consequence many generations of American students gained only the most shallow view of the past.

A scholar's choice of topics for research has a clear connection to what he or she teaches in the classroom. To the extent that our departments are inclined to indulge us, we teach about the things that intrigue and inspire us; it is up to us somehow to communicate the love of history to our students, and the best way to do that is to present the most inclusive and expansive view of our subjects. Consider how silly it would be for me, or any other white person, to announce to my classes at the beginning of the semester that I feel uncomfortable talking about black history, because I am not black myself, and so if my students who are interested in the history of the family or labor history want to learn about black families and workers, they should take a course offered through the African and Afro-American studies department—if one is offered that year, or if not, too bad. Stated another way, I would be offended to know that my male colleagues down the hall teaching American survey courses were taking care to omit any mention of the vast scholarship in the field of women's history because they were men and felt it inappropriate for them to do so. Clearly, such a parochial approach would set us back several decades to the time when women, black people, and workers of all kinds were omitted from standard history courses and textbooks.

My course syllabi include a wide range of voices from the American past, and it is ludicrous that I should apologize for it, just because I grew up in a white middle-class family in the mid-Atlantic region (how "white bread" can you get!). In my survey of American women's history, I have assigned a number of Federal Writers Project slave narratives, as well as Maya Angelou's *I Know Why the Caged Bird Sings* and Anne Moody's *Coming of Age in Mississippi.* For a course on Southern women's history I have used Harriet Jacob's *Incidents in the Life of a Slave Girl,* Mamie Garvin Fields with Karen Fields's *Lemon Swamp and Other Places,* and Alice Walker's novel *The Color Purple.* I have taught a survey of American history with a special focus on autobiography, and included Booker T. Washington's *Up from Slavery* and Frederick Douglass's autobiography. The reading list for my modern social history course includes Du Bois's *Souls of Black Folk,* in addition to Federal Writers Project interviews with a variety of black workers, from Pullman porters to Southern midwives, and a collection of interviews of automobile assembly line workers (including black and white men and women) from the 1970s and 1980s.

At this point I should mention the obvious: as a historian, I do not hesitate to teach novels and autobiographies written by African Americans (or by Native Americans or Asian-Americans or Italian-Americans, for that matter). My students must learn to read these works the way they would any other historical texts—there is nothing particularly mystical about the stories these writers tell, or the way they tell them; how irresponsible it would be to suggest that appreciation for these works depends exclusively on one's chromosomes, phenotype, or family rituals practiced back home.

Over the past twenty years or so, I have taught hundreds of students at Wellesley, Brown, and Brandeis, and I know for a fact that a good many of them (Native American, Asian, black, and white men and women, undergraduates and graduate students, from a variety of backgrounds) have gained a deeper appreciation for the study of

American history as a result of reading these works. I cannot conceive of constructing a syllabus around the notion that I must teach only "what I am"—whatever that is: mother, white person, resident of New England, academic? Similarly, the suggestion that I should refrain from teaching what I am not—whatever that is: sharecropper, coal miner, working-class, black?—insults the intelligence of my students, and indeed, the ideals of learning and scholarship altogether. After all, the goal of higher education is (or should be) to introduce students to worlds outside their own, to engage them with complex questions about the human condition, and to encourage them to study the work of serious thinkers.

I reject the whole notion of an "authentic voice" and its corollary—that only persons with certain demographic characteristics may unlock the secrets of that voice. The autobiographies, oral interviews, and firsthand accounts listed above are not "pure" in the sense of being raw or unmediated accounts. For instance, the Federal Writers Project slave narratives were transcribed by interviewers who varied in their views of their subjects. It is important for students to understand the social context in which those interviews were conducted—the Depression-era South, when Jim Crow patterns of racial etiquette pertained—and the point of view of the interviewers themselves. This particular kind of historical source offers a good lesson in the pros and cons of oral histories and interviews.

In a similar vein, Booker T. Washington wrote his autobiography with prospective benefactors and other white patrons in mind. We need to consider his "secret" life as a sponsor of test cases challenging Jim Crow segregation in order to begin to understand *Up from Slavery*; the book itself of course hardly tells us the whole story of his life. To cite another example: perceptive students of any class or color can surely recognize the dramatic forms utilized by Angelou—her selective choice of childhood memories; her license in reconstructing dialogue from many years ago; the series of vignette in which she, or members of her family or community, encounter specific incidents of racism and then, just as surely, seek to regroup and triumph over mean-spiritedness in its various guises. Every text must be read critically; any good teacher can help a student understand how to do that, and any good student can learn how.

My own experiences have taught me that, if the notion of an "authentic voice" is less than helpful in understanding primary texts, it is downright dangerous as an approach to secondary works like historical monographs. Over the last few years I have accumulated a number of anecdotes—some funny, and some not so funny—about people who believed they were reading the "authentic voice" of an African American woman in *Labor of Love, Labor of Sorrow*. There was the African American graduate student who prefaced her comments about my book in her women's history seminar with the observation that it was a relief to move beyond the history written by white women and finally grapple with the more sensitive work of a black woman historian. There was the debate about my race in an undergraduate class, where one student assured her classmates that I was indeed black (despite the suggestion to the contrary offered by my photo on the book jacket); it was just that I was "very light skinned." Or the time I was asked by a magazine book editor to review a new biography of Martin Luther King, Jr. (I had recently reviewed a book by Angela Davis for the same magazine). In the course of the conversation the subject of my race came up, and when I mentioned that I was white the editor responded in dismay, "But I was *assured* you were black," and then promptly retracted the invitation (she felt bad, though, and gave me a book on the history of housework to review instead). I have waited at airports for long periods of time because the person sent to fetch me was looking for a black woman to get off the plane; I have arrived at speaking engagements only to have my hosts profess their disappointment with my appearance, because they had intended that I should serve as a "role model" for their black students. Together, these stories add up to a cautionary tale—the hazards of extrapolating much at all about a person on the basis of the kind of history he or she writes.

A variation on this theme is the criticism my work has received because I am white. I have had my share of uncomfortable encounters at scholarly conferences when I was urged to sit down and refrain from speaking because my presence on a panel devoted to black women's history simply replicated historic patterns of class and racial oppression. (I know for a fact that witnessing one or more of these encounters has been enough to dissuade certain younger white women and men scholars from ever focusing on the history of black women in their own work.) One reviewer of *The Dispossessed* charged that, first, I was guilty of "sentimental racism" because I had an unrealistic and condescending view toward black family life, and second, that I should examine the cultural degradation of my own middle-class white existence before deigning to make any hypocritical comments, scholarly or otherwise, about any aspect of African American life or culture. These public and personal criticisms are of course hurtful, but I would not want to spend much time whining about them. Most scholars who have ever written a book or article or delivered a paper at a conference have endured strongly felt criticism of some type, and indeed, contempt and ridicule are tried and true means of intellectual discourse in a whole host of settings. It's hard to be on the receiving end of such invective, but it is certainly not limited to historians, or to white girls who write about black history. And ironically, personal attacks are easier to deal with than attacks that focus on aspects of my work over which I have some control; in the end (I have to remind myself), I would rather be denounced for the color of my skin than for the weakness of my argument. In the next book I can work on sharpening my argument, but there is not much I can do about my whiteness.

While teaching a new course at Brandeis University in the fall of 1994, I was reminded that my high-minded ideals about the nobility of the scholarly enterprise will continue to collide with some of my students' expectations—personal, political, and otherwise; but as far as I could tell, my race was not a major factor in this particular setting. The course was part of a new "University Seminar" (Usem) program offered at Brandeis; its aim was to group all first-year students in seminars, introduce them to the critical analysis of texts, and help them improve their writing skills.

In preparing the catalogue copy (this was the first time the course was offered), I made the mistake of giving the course a broad, and probably misleading, title: History of American Race Relations. The short course description sent to all incoming students noted that the main theme of the course was the history of blacks and whites in the workforce, from colonial times to the present; but it was not until students arrived in class on the first day and saw the syllabus that they had an idea of what we would be doing:

> This course focuses on the relations between black and white workers, from the country's earliest colonial settlements through the late twentieth century. We shall pay particular attention to place (regional variations in patterns of work and family), change over time (the development of the economy from rural to agricultural to urban and industrial), and varieties of work culture (the ways in which workers resist the demands imposed upon them, and the ways in which they create communities among themselves). Several questions inform our study: What are the shifting meanings of "race" throughout American history? How do the factors of class and gender affect patterns of "race relations" over time? What is the impact of larger economic transformations on the relations among various groups of men and women workers? And how do workers who live in racially segregated communities perceive each other within a racially integrated workplace?

By the time my Usem students saw this fuller description of the course, the damage had been done. Most had expected to spend the semester talking about Rodney King and O. J. Simpson (with the history of the Los Angeles Police Department providing the "context," I suppose). They were in for a rude shock. Over the next few weeks I found that at least some of the students resisted examining their own ideas about race, and some were (in all probability) wondering how they had gotten themselves into such a course. It did not take long for them to realize that their own histories as family and community members, as high school students, and as enthusiastic consumers of late-twentieth-century youth culture were not necessarily going to provide them with any direct connection to the past.

In the course, we examined a variety of full-length texts, as well as a hundred-page packet of short primary documents that I had collected as part of my research over the last few years. These documents included court cases from the seventeenth century Chesapeake; excerpts from the laws of Virginia 1661–62 and 1691; a list of tithables in Northampton County, Virginia, 1666; an early-eighteenth-century New York indentured servant's contract; Samuel Sewall's antislavery and antiblack tract "The Selling of Joseph" (1700); notices for fugitive slaves, servants, and white wives published in New Jersey papers in the eighteenth century; a Virginia planter's misgivings about slavery (1736); slaves' petitions for their freedom during the Revolutionary era; the Ohio black codes of 1804; James Henry Hammond's defense of slavery (1845); newspaper articles written by Frederick Law Olmsted, based on his travels in the South in the 1850s; documents related to the deployment of black and white labor during the Civil War, the violence inflicted on blacks by white workers in Northern cities around the time of the war, the struggles of freedpeople to own their own land and control their own families in the Reconstruction South, the history of trade unionism in the late nineteenth century, and federal policies related to black labor during the two world wars.

I could be wrong, but in terms of shaping the classroom learning that semester, the demographic makeup of the classroom was secondary compared to other factors. Among the eighteen students, half were women, three were African American, and most were probably middle-class or upper-middle-class. The students gave no indication that they considered my race significant one way or the other; they saw me first and foremost as a professor—one of the very first they had encountered in college—and I think they were simultaneously open to my teaching style and wary of the demands I placed on them.

As for the students themselves, I cannot categorize them by race or gender on the basis of how often they talked in class, what insights they brought to bear on the material, or how well they wrote their papers. In other words, no particular *kind* of student was either adept or handicapped at reflecting on the historical significance of the readings. Most had only a tenuous grasp on the chronology of American history, and when it came to examining documents from the seventeenth century, they all started at about the same point in terms of their prior knowledge of the period. They were, essentially, still high school students, and I intended that their first college-level history course should introduce them to a wide range of methodological and historiographical issues. We talked about the problems of using legal statutes, court cases, personal reminiscences, social workers' reports, and newspaper editorials as historical evidence. We used one account written by Olmsted as an exercise in inference; from his description of slaves and poor whites, we speculated about his views on slavery and on poor people of both races. We drew connections among workplaces in antebellum Baltimore, Boston, and Cincinnati, based on the sometimes violent confrontations between black and white workers at certain worksites, in certain jobs, in those cities.

I was intrigued that, toward the end of the semester, almost all the students listed *Maggie's American Dream* (the autobiography of Maggie Comer, edited by her son James P. Comer) as their favorite book for the semester. I think most college students, and first-years in particular, are pretty egocentric, and so for understandable reasons my students found particularly appealing this story of a young woman determined to get a good education and see her children succeed in life. Too, Maggie Comer seemed to live in a world that was not so distant in either time or sensibility from their own twentieth-century urban, industrial society. On the other hand, at times they seemed unable to make the leap of imagination that a study of (for example) the seventeenth-century Southern colonies called for. If an when I offer the course again, I will consider using autobiographies exclusively; most students seem most easily and effectively drawn into the study of history through stories about specific people.

Throughout the semester we considered a wide variety of workplaces, the tobacco fields of seventeenth-century Maryland, the docks and taverns of the early-eighteenth-century seaport city, artisans' shops during the Revolutionary era, antebellum Piedmont cotton fields, Civil War army camps, postbellum plantations of tenant farmers and sharecroppers, steel mills, the parlors and kitchens of middle-class white women, World War II defense industries, and finally, high-tech and corporate offices. We tried to keep in mind a truly bewildering number of factors as we examined each workplace—the ethnic, gender, and racial composition of the workers; the political economy that shaped their work choices (or lack thereof); the physical and emotional demands of the job; and the conditions that shaped their everyday experiences. We talked about the historical processes by which certain groups of workers come to think of themselves as part of a community, variously defined, and about the many forces that have divided American workers over the years. At the midpoint of the semester I asked the class to review what we had learned thus far and was rewarded when one student suggested, "Sometimes race matters—and sometimes it doesn't." This observation was, of course, one of the major themes of the course. I allowed myself some tentative feelings of satisfaction.

The course ended on an ambiguous note. Moving into the more recent period and reading Cornel West's *Race Matters,* the students finally felt free of the historical straitjacket I had imposed on them all semester, and began to talk about racial issues as revealed in contemporary popular culture, the news media, their neighborhoods at home, their circle of high school friends. But these discussions seemed curiously circumscribed and muted, considering the fact that

I thought they would amount to the culmination—or rather, refutation—of a semester-long attempt to censor "easy talk" in favor of close textual analysis. The hard fact of the matter was that glib generalizations did not come so easily anymore. A description of white boys emulating the black "hip hop" style at one student's high school brought the inevitable questions—where is the high school located, and what is the class makeup of the student body? It mattered whether the school was in Manhattan, or Cambridge, or Atlanta— some of the places represented by the students in the class. Stories of family-based prejudices had to be placed in the context of a particular place, ethnic or racial group, and the ages and occupations of its members. Other questions included, What is the significance of skin color today, and doesn't it matter which particular shade you are referring to, and in what setting? And on an on. We had run out of steam; there were so many factors to consider about any one situation.

Still, in broad outlines we could draw some conclusions about changes in the meaning of race and in the nature of biracial workplaces through the centuries. We began the course by examining a 1658 Maryland tobacco plantation worked by white male and female English indentured servants, male African and Native American slaves, and the white landowner and his wife and children. Most laborers during this period were bound (in this case, only the landowner himself was "independent," or "free" in any meaningful sense of the word), and teenaged white servants and black and Indian workers of all kinds were often lumped indiscriminately into a category of rowdy, promiscuous, profane, intractable workers. The contrast between that work setting and the white-collar office place of postindustrial America was striking, to say the least, though if we consider gender, class, and racial configurations in both time periods we might detect some threads of continuity linking the Maryland of 1658 to the America of 1996.

Obviously, I faced a number of pedagogical challenges in teaching this course, but my inadequacy as a white person teaching African

American history was not high on my list. I had to figure out the most effective ways to teach first-year students how to read historical texts, analyze their significance, and see the connections among them; and how to write a well-organized paper and document it appropriately. I had to encourage shy students to overcome their reluctance and speak out in class. Obviously high school preparation affected individuals' literary, analytical, and verbal skills, but a whole host of other factors influenced their engagement with the material. I was paired with thirteen of the students in this class as their faculty first-year adviser, so I made a special effort to get to know everyone outside class; as a result I came to understand better some of the developmental problems first-year students must deal with. One student was homesick; he missed his high school friends. Another student decided very early on that she wanted to try to transfer to the West Coast; her parents were separated, and her mother lived nearby, but she wanted to live near her father. A couple of soon-to-be math and science majors were not happy about taking history seriously; they saw my course as the least of twenty-two other evils they had been forced to choose among. One student spent at least part of the semester comparing me to her beloved high school social studies teacher, and found me lacking. When I think of all the problems my students faced that semester — getting adjusted to a new place to live and to new friends, to a new set of academic demands and a whole new weekly work rhythm — my race quickly receded in significance as an issue of major concern in the classroom.

Offering a variation on my student's succinct observation, I would venture to suggest that in the historical profession today, sometimes race should matter, and sometimes it should not. As historians, we have come to believe that a full and honest rendering of the past necessarily mandates attention to groups long believed unworthy of scholarly study; and we have discovered that throughout American history, whether we are exploring the ratification of the Constitution or the Cult of True Womanhood, the history of the trades union movement or the development of American foreign policy, certain notions about "race" have mattered, and have mattered a great deal. At the same time, when we debate, teach, and otherwise draw on current historical scholarship, the race of a particular scholar should matter much less than the shape of his or her argument, the content of his or her footnotes. In the classroom and at scholarly conferences, in department meetings and the pages of scholarly journals, the advancement of history relies on a diversity of viewpoints. As a means of furthering scholarly inquiry within the historical profession, self-censorship has little to recommend it; and in fact, assigning certain kinds of people to certain historical topics, while ostracizing those who stray from these narrow-minded guidelines, poses a distinct danger to our continually evolving understanding of groups and issues that have received far too little attention from scholars in previous generations.

Over the past few years we have made great progress in opening up the study of history—in breaking down artificial boundaries between men's and women's history, between social and political history, between economic and labor history (for example). The last thing we need to do now is to slip back into a Balkanized view of the world, a view based on dualities between black and white, rich and poor, male and female. Should we as scholars retreat defensively into our respective "camps," or subfields, the whole study of history will be diminished, and accordingly rendered suspect as a scholarly enterprise.

10

Pro/(Con)fessing Otherness: Trans(cending)national Identities in the English Classroom

LAVINA DHINGRA SHANKAR

The starting-point of critical elaboration is the consciousness of what one really is, and is "knowing thyself" as a product of the historical process to date which has deposited in you an infinity of traces, without leaving an inventory.
— Antonio Gramsci, *Selections from the Prison Notebooks*

The foreigner is within me, hence we are all foreigners.
— Julia Kristeva, *Strangers to Ourselves*

Race consciousness is a deadly explosive on the tongues of men. — Zora Neale Hurston, *Dust Tracks on a Road*

Professing "otherness" can, in contemporary literary criticism, privilege critics, allowing them privilege even while decrying it;[1] this is clearly manifest in the case of the multicultural "holy trinity," who have in the last decade been canonized and institutionalized—Edward Said, Henry Louis Gates, Jr., and Gayatri Chakravorty Spivak.[2] Yet the "outsider" who "teaches what she is not" can have a problematic relationship to power and authority, especially in the undergraduate English classroom.

Before discussing the complexities surrounding my own "crossdressing" as a "nonnative" English speaker teaching a language and literature that are not her "own," in what is not Herland, I will briefly analyze *In Other Worlds,* by Gayatri Chakravorty Spivak, a simultaneously mainstreamed and yet marginalized "Third World" intellectual "teaching what she is (not)" in the "First World."[3]

The following discussion of Spivak's identity dilemma functions as an example to highlight just how complex and problematic the issue of identity and identity politics is in the contemporary American academy. My intention is not so much to critique Spivak's "identity politics" per se, but to explicate the convoluted nature of personal and scholarly identity, as well as to warn against the oversimplification that occurs in much multicultural rhetoric of "us" versus "them."

In the context of postcolonial and transnational identities and transcultural educational systems, the boundaries between self and other, East and West, Western and non-Western, First and Third World are fuzzy right from the start. Acclaimed as a "Third World feminist" in the West, Spivak represents "deconstruction American style" for her colleagues in the East.[4] The Bengali Gayatri *Chakravorty* vehemently attacks "majority" "Western" feminists' appropriative gestures to establish a "hegemonic, 'global' theory of feminism" under the guise of "international feminism."[5] And yet, despite Gayatri *Chakravorty's* emphasis on her own "otherness" (read uniqueness) as a non-Western scholar, she herself *is* a "Western" feminist.[6] Hence, the American Gayatri *Spivak* employs the personal pronoun "we" to distance herself from the "rest of the world's women."[7] Gayatri *Spivak's* use of "we" (which Jane Tompkins criticizes Foucault for using in order to become "chummy" with the reader) claims common experiences and thought with her "white" academic readers in the "First World."[8]

Who are the "we" that Gayatri Chakravorty Spivak refers to in her critiques of the "Western" academy's cultural politics? Even after being a member of the American academy for more than half her life, Gayatri *Chakravorty* feels like an "outsider."[9] Nevertheless, because of her "Western" intellectual training, she repeatedly finds herself allied with American academics.[10] Not surprisingly, Gayatri *Spivak* takes over and begins talking in the same breath about Freud, Marx, Nietzsche, and Derrida. The postcolonial subject's confusion of East-West identities began even before she physically entered the West—via her colonial British education. Or, as Derrida himself says in another context, "the outside is the inside."[11]

The postcolonial feminist is indeed caught between her roles in two different and yet similar worlds.[12] As she herself acknowledges, the Eastern-born, Western-educated teacher is "not in a position of choice in this [identity] dilemma."[13] Gayatri Chakravorty Spivak's deconstructive perspective makes her realize the limitations of implementing her brand of "Third World" feminism in the "First World" classroom. She admits,

> I think less easily of "changing the world" than in the past. I teach a small number of the holders of the can(n)on, male or female, feminist or masculinist, how to read their own texts, as best I can.[14]

Whose texts are these, anyway?[15] And who are "they" who have to be taught "their own texts"? Needless to say, in the newly emerging multiethnic, multiracial classrooms, there is no fixed, homogeneous entity, no monolithic "they" who can unproblematically be taught their own texts.

What does it *mean* for a "colored," foreign female, triply an "outsider"—"Woman, Native, Other" in the words of the cultural anthropologist Trinh T. Minh-ha—to assume the position of power and authority in a "First World" English classroom and to echo her (colonial) "master's" voice?[16] The token "minority" faculty member (or student) in a nearly all-"white" English department is often expected to bear the burden of representing *all* minorities, *all* colored peoples, and *all* Third World and postcolonial perspectives. Yet the very *différence* in the teacher's cultural, racial, and gender perspectives can become problematic, especially when the teacher discusses issues about "race."[17]

Discussions focused on cultural diversity, racism, multiculturalism, and global awareness evoke a certain resistance even when a "white" teacher informs "white" upper-level undergraduate and/or graduate students, say, about slavery while teaching Toni Morrison's *Beloved*, or about the Chinese Exclusion Acts while discussing Maxine Hong Kingston's *Woman Warrior* or *China Men*, or about Native American genocide and the Trail of Tears when introducing Louise Erdrich's *Love Medicine*—works that have almost been canonized by many white feminists.[18] But the power dynamics may seem even more threatening to some eighteen-year-olds when the only colored person in the classroom also assumes the position of authority and informs them of the uglier parts of their cultural history, which they would rather not own (up to). In my experience, often the "white" (especially male) students either feel guilty and become silenced, or become defensive and/or (mildly) aggressive when the discussion centers around slavery or colonization.

In another scenario, if students assume that the ("minority") teacher "teaches what she is," the classroom can become a potential site for reverse discrimination. The token "nonwhite" students may feel newly empowered on seeing that the reins of authority reside in a "colored" person and may look to the teacher for validation of their own views; they may even take an aggressive stance toward the "dominant" majority and express their deeply entrenched anger to-ward all "white" peoples.[19] In yet another scenario, "colored" students who, either because of economic or other privileges, have not experi-enced (or at least not perceived) discrimination, may be disbelieving of what they assume to be the teacher's "politically correct" focus on "race"; or there may be yet another "minority" individual or group who, in trying hard to assimilate, may get angered at being segregated from their peers by the teacher's discussions regarding "race." In all the above situations, the teacher—who by virtue of her "color" is assumed to be "teaching what she is"—faces both political and moral dilemmas about which student community to identify with.

That is where my question "who are 'we'?" with reference to

Spivak's identity politics becomes relevant. Should "minority" teachers align themselves with "majority" students and claim how "we"
are to blame for "our" narrow-minded ethnocentrism and "our" tendency for, in Richard Slotkin's words, "regeneration through violence"?[20] Or in forging communities with "majority" students, do
teachers then participate in internalized racism and send them a message of voluntary self-erasure? By negating their own racial identity,
do teachers also delimit "majority" students' acceptance of cultural
and racial differences? And what about the professor's responsibility
to the marginalized nonwhite student(s) who grew up battling the
racism that the foreign-born scholar discusses in mostly pedagogical
terms?

Or, on the other hand, should teachers emphasize their own "minority" position (and perhaps simultaneously accept a certain disem-
powerment vis-à-vis the "majority"), and claim angrily how "we" the
colored, the foreigners, the immigrants, the Easterners, the colonized
(especially female) subjects, the Third World citizens, the "subalterns,"
in Spivak's term, have been victimized and silenced by "you," the
"dominant" "majority"?[21] At the present historical moment, such a
stance might succeed in the upper-level college or graduate seminar,
when the student is the "other," or when a minority faculty member
teaches a course that explicitly professes "multicultural" and "multiracial" perspectives—for example, courses in ethnic American literature, minority literature, black literature, world civilizations/litera-
ture, Third World literature, non-Western perspectives, and so on. But
the "minority" teacher who pits himself or herself in survey courses
against eighteen- or nineteen-year-olds who have not yet crossed the
border into academia's self-conscious, ideological embrace of cultural
and racial diversity might invite their defensive rejection of her or his
viewpoints as well as her or his alien, and hence alienating, "self."[22]

The issue of "teaching what you're not" becomes more complicated
when "white" students (including those who were considered "ethnic" not so long ago, such as Jews, Irish, and Italians) perceive them-

selves as a homogeneous community rooted in "Western culture,"
as opposed to "them," all those "other," "non-Western," "minority"
cultures whose literatures they may view as being thrust on them.

I am thinking of my experience while teaching Paule Marshall's
Brown Girl, Brownstones in an introductory literature seminar.[23] Many
of the students (both male and female) identified or at least empa-
thized with the teenage female protagonist Selina's love-hate relationship with her mother, her search for an adult identity discrete from
her parents, her sexual awakening, her realization of her gendered
identity, her confusions about entering college and making career
choices, her family's pursuit of the American dream, and so on. But
some others consciously resisted relating to the novel, immediately
distancing it as completely alien to their own experiences. When asked
why, a "Swedish-American" male student responded candidly, "I'm
not black, so I can't understand Selina's struggle against racism; I'm
not (and neither are my parents) immigrants, so I don't identify with
the immigrant identity-conflict, or with Selina's mother's obsession
with the American Dream; my family is financially secure, so I don't
know how poverty affects family relations; I'm not a woman, so I
don't have to worry about looking boyish or not menstruating before
my peers."

On a simple level, this student's remark can be interpreted as yet
another protest against the reformation of the canon, but to me it
resonated differently. In one sentence, this student had raised some
important questions about the cultural politics of knowledge, identity,
and identification. Although I cannot honestly say that he was *blaming*
me for choosing a text that he, as the proverbial heterosexual, upper-
class WASP male didn't find worth reading, it certainly made me
question my own motivations for teaching this novel. What was implicit in this (I think, nonconfrontational) well-reasoned argument was
that I was a woman; (he assumed) I was an immigrant; I was "colored"; as a member of a postcolonial nation, I knew of a different
history of Barbados than the spring break haven for American college

students; having grown up in a poor Third World nation, I had witnessed poverty (if not experienced it) and, hence, understood it. In sum, as a complete "other" I had an/other agenda that the novel satisfied and that this student had no use for; my choice of what I taught was based on who I was, not on who the students were.

Was it possible for me to teach this novel without sentimentalizing the images of self/other that I consciously or unconsciously saw in a black woman's text? Or to look at the situation from another perspective, is it possible that even though I wasn't sentimentalizing any more than a "white" feminist might, I was being stereotyped as the "alien" with different experiences, different emotional needs in my appreciation of literature, and, hence, completely different (if not irrelevant) ways of seeing?

The identity dilemma (and that of "teaching what I am") becomes even more complicated when my own educational history is revealed. I grew up on a stronger diet of canonical, white, male, British literature than my American students will ever encounter. And I was introduced to so-called ethnic literatures and minority issues only through the eyes of "white" American feminist teachers. So even though my student may have thought it was my "non-Western" background that made me teach texts by and about "oppressed" "minorities" and "colored" women (and, on a subconscious level, perhaps it was so), it was primarily the legacy of my American "multicultural" education.[24] My concerns (in teaching) were not those of a scholar in the Third World, but of a Third World scholar *in the First World.* Ironically enough, I had internalized the rhetoric of "multiculturalism" and assumed that since I was a "minority" I must, therefore, teach primarily (if not *only*) about others like myself.

But then, as Derrida, Foucault, Althusser, and Lacan, among others, have taught us to question, what is one's "self" anyway?[25] If Harold Bloom's dictum "You are or become what you read"[26] has any validity, and if culture is transmitted by education and not by racial heritage, then isn't the postcolonial feminist teacher also a product of

"Western" civilization, just like her "Euramerican" students? While growing up in post–British independence India, I encountered Charlotte Brontë and E. M. Forster in eighth-grade English class, Jane Austen in the seventh grade, abridged versions of Dickens's *David Copperfield, Oliver Twist,* Hardy's *Mayor of Casterbridge* and *Tess of the D'Urbervilles* in the fifth and sixth grades; numerous Shakespearean plays, *Macbeth, As You Like It, The Merchant of Venice, Hamlet, A Midsummer Night's Dream*—which were read, enacted, memorized, and "possessed" in original Elizabethan verse—between the sixth and the tenth grades; Charles Lamb's prose version of the tales of Shakespeare as early as the third grade, and so on. I don't buy the argument that this education was possible only because it was imposed by another culture, that it was a form of "cultural imperialism" and "colonizing the mind," because concurrently I also learned the literatures of two native Indian languages—Hindi and Bengali—and before I entered college, I had already taken on five languages (and their accompanying cultures), only two of which were European.[27]

In his groundbreaking text *Black Skin, White Masks* (1952), the French Antillean psychiatrist Frantz Fanon asserts that "to speak a language is to take on a world, a culture." Fanon critiques the pernicious effects of "honorary citizenship" that the acquisition of the colonizing "other's" language allows.[28] However, I would like to subvert Fanon's idea by suggesting that acquiring other languages need not necessitate erasing one's "own." At one level, any language acquisition is a form of cultural imperialism; but it also simultaneously facilitates the expansion of one's intellectual and cultural horizons. Multilingualism is not an impossible feat.

To return to the issue of my ability to teach a language and literature that are not a/part of myself, but that of the colonizing "other": My sense of "self" for the first twenty years of my life was a sense of being not an "oppressed minority" but rather a member of the "privileged minority," in a country where it is the majority that is oppressed. However, in imbibing (or unconsciously catering to) the ideological positions of my professors in America (both "white" and "colored," "majority" and "minority," "native" and "foreign," "ex-colonizers" and "ex-colonized") who tried to "decolonize my mind"[29] and deliver me from my British colonial education, my "self" had been (re)defined by another "alien" educational system—this time, American "multiculturalism." I realized then that I had begun teaching "minority" literatures not because I saw them as a reflection of my own views, experiences, or philosophies, but because my so-called liberatory educational training had (successfully) convinced me that I *should* teach only "what I was" assumed to be—that is, teach works representing the racially and socioeconomically "oppressed."[30]

This assumption was, of course, internalized by me; it was intensified by the fact that the few "colored" teachers or scholars that I have encountered, or whose work I have read, do not "teach what they are not," that is, canonical "white" literature. It is difficult for me to decide whether most "subalterns" speak only of their own (or other minorities') experiences because they do not possess the *knowledge* to speak about the "majority," or because they are not granted the *authority* to "teach what they are not." Of course, from an administrative perspective, it is, perhaps, cost-effective for departments to fulfill both their goals of canon expansion and affirmative action by having a "person of color" teach literature written by and about other "colored" folk.

The dilemma of (not) "teaching what you are not" is even more perplexing since, ironically, I often have ideological, political, and even cultural differences with the students I am expected to identify with merely on the basis of their status as racial minorities. For example, as an international scholar who has voluntarily chosen (and who considers it a privilege) to participate in the American higher education system, I cannot identify with African American students whose definition of "race" is embedded in a history of slave ancestors and who feel intensely embittered and angry against the "dominant" "white" culture; similarly, I feel alienated from Asian American females whose immigrant parents have given them such a strong diet of their native culture and traditions that their gender role definitions and religious and moral values, despite their having grown up in the United States, seem closer to my grandmother's than to my own.[31] And if, when I teach Asian-American literature, students assume that "I am what I teach" and expect me to ratify their stereotype that all Asian women are docile, or that all have arranged marriages and bound feet, or that (in order to assert my ethnic identity) I should dress exotically, I refuse to oblige. Besides, at different moments I often find it easier to identify both with fictional protagonists and with students who are completely different from me on one or more categories—of class, gender, race, sexuality, religion, nationality, citizenship, and so on—but with whom I can easily "connect" intellectually and/or emotionally.

The fallacies in the assumption that we cannot teach "what we are not" are too many to enumerate. If the idea is carried to its logical conclusion, it would imply that only men can teach men's texts, only women must teach women's texts, only the British can teach British literature, and so on. The entire question of identity as based on categories such as "race" and "culture" is tenuous. It would even imply that we are not able to teach texts written in a different historical period; for instance, surely, a Norwegian-American or Irish-American male professor in the late twentieth century is not part of fifth-century B.C. Greek culture, or of Renaissance Italy. How could he then teach about the same?[32] A Jewish-American woman is *not* a male poet living in nineteenth-century England. How can she then "teach what she is not"—works by Wordsworth, or Shelley, or Browning? Similarly, a working-class African American female professor's identity and experiences have little in common (except her skin color) with those of an upper-class male Nigerian novelist (or with his fictional protagonists); and a lesbian teacher is very different from the heterosexual authors whose works she may wish to teach. Does it follow from this line of thinking that they cannot, therefore, "teach what they are not"?

If we must only "teach what we are," then we would surely be admitting that the human imagination and ability for gaining knowledge are circumscribed—not to mention completely self-absorbed—from birth until death; that we are incapable of learning from, sympathizing or empathizing with, or understanding any human being who is not identical to ourselves; that we can know only what we have experienced.[33] While teachers surely face an immense challenge and must undertake a huge responsibility in representing the "other" in literature, avoiding that challenge seems to me to go against the grain of the intellectual process itself.

So the question I posed at the beginning of this essay with respect to Gayatri Chakravorty Spivak's identity politics, "Who are we?" has no simple answer; neither does the question about whether we can/ should "teach what 'we' are not." Nevertheless, they have helped me raise larger theoretical questions, with which I will conclude: How can we learn to construct multiethnic communities that comprise neither the colonizers nor the colonized? Is *belonging* to a world (or owning a fixed identity) ever anything more than a fiction strategically employed to disempower or appropriate a critical discourse? How can a privileged "Third World" citizen teach texts about the "oppressed" in the "First World" without sentimentalizing the self/other? Should "non-Western" scholars feel obliged to change the canon and teach "minority" literatures, or can they also teach the "Western" authors that their "majority" students identify with (and with which, ironically, perhaps they may too)? Or, vice versa, must postcolonial "subjects" relinquish teaching canonical authors and be confined to "minority" texts to prove that the process of "decolonizing [their] mind" is complete? What if the "colored" female foreigner is more interested in teaching about gender and class issues in, say, "mainstream" Romantic and Victorian British literature, while academic cultural politics dictate that, as a "minority," she must "teach only what she *is*," that is, teach about "race" in multicultural and multiracial texts?

What about a teacher like myself who is neither British nor American but who has—thanks to her postcolonial education—been immersed in and has, perhaps, even internalized the once "imposed" culture's literature; whose knowledge about "Western" literature and history is more ingrained, sometimes deeper than that of her "Western" colleagues; who may have, since early childhood, identified with the female heroes in British Victorian fiction or with male Romantic poets, whose works sustained her, even helped formulate her sense of "self," perhaps, a decade before her American peers even heard of an Austen, a Brontë, a Wordsworth, a Maugham, or a Shakespeare?[34] And what if she doesn't equate the "decolonizing [of] the mind" with a rejection of "Western culture," or with "going native"?[35] What if she chooses to stake a claim to both "knowing" and "owning" Hardy, Dickens, and Eliot? What if she vindicates her rights to her British intellectual "heritage," so to speak, in addition to her Bengali, or Italian, or Russian, or Urdu, or Finnish, or African, or Chinese, or Chippewa, or Malaysian, or French, or Hindi, or Greek, or American ancestry? What if she believes that knowledge and imagination need not be restricted by one's biological identity; that the brain and the blood of all humans is of the same color?

Unfortunately, the process of being "manufactured" into a race/postcolonial critic (which the identity politics of "teaching only what you *are*" demand) makes the "other" prey to the "majority's" definition of her or his critical sensibilities. The rules of survival in the job market revive racial ghettoization by confining all "others" to the ostensibly multicultural, "colored" corridors of the academy, and result in a *re*colonization of the postcolonial subject(ed) "self." Simultaneously, it makes the "outsiders" exploiters of their own "otherness" (and thus, as Spivak says, "pluralist aesthetes,"[36] consumers of their native culture) for the sake of career advancement in the capitalist academic job market "jungle," where they must "sell" their "selves" yet again as "orientalized"[37] objects for scrutiny under Western eyes.

My personal stake in "self-fashioning"[38] a critical identity by negotiating between East and West increases as I realize my simultaneously privileged and disempowered position as a token "(multi)cultural" teacher compelled to look toward the "East" to establish her professional identity in the "West."

NOTES

Brief sections of this essay were presented at the following conferences: CCCC 1992, MELUS 1995, and M/MLA 1995. I wish to thank Beverly Lyon Clark, Lee Edelman, Sheila Emerson, Rajiv Shankar, and Ruth Spack for their direct or indirect encouragement and support of this project at its various stages.

1. The title of this essay was influenced by the title of Gerald Graff's famous history of literary studies, *Professing Literature: An Institutional History* (Chicago: University of Chicago Press, 1987).

2. One has only to follow the trajectory of these "minority" critics' careers—Gates skipped from Duke to Harvard, Spivak from the University of Pittsburgh to Columbia—to note how the marginalized has been institutionalized.

3. Gayatri Chakravorty Spivak, *In Other Worlds: Essays in Cultural Politics* (New York: Routledge, 1988). Diana Fuss denounces the practices that the term "identity politics" has come to represent. In using this term to refer to Spivak's identity dilemma (as well as strategy), I do not follow Fuss's narrow and extremely critical usage, which seems to imply that identity politics are always merely a *performance* of oppression. See Diana Fuss, *Essentially Speaking: Feminism, Nature and Difference* (New York: Routledge, 1989), 97–112.

4. Gayatri Chakravorty Spivak, "Reading the World: Literary Studies in the Eighties," in *In Other Worlds*, 95–102: 100.

5. Gayatri Chakravorty Spivak, "Feminism and Critical Theory," in *In Other Worlds*, 77–92: 84.

6. Her decision to begin her first book, *In Other Worlds*, with the not-so-other worlds of Dante, Yeats, Coleridge, Wordsworth, and Woolf indicates Spivak's intention to establish herself on firm "Western" academic ground before losing her readership by journeying à la Forster or Conrad into exotic "temples, mosques, caves" or into the "heart of darkness" in the Indian short

stories that follow. Before espousing the cause of Third World feminism, she perhaps wishes acceptance first as a worthy, even "mainstream," literary critic.

7. In the foreword to her translation of the Bengali short story "Draupadi," Gayatri Spivak addresses her Western feminist sisters,

> Correspondingly, *we* grieve for *our* Third-World sisters; *we* grieve and rejoice that *they* must lose *themselves* and become as much like *us* as possible in order to be "free"; *we* congratulate *ourselves* on *our* specialist's knowledge of *them*. (179, emphasis added)

"Translator's Foreword, *Draupadi*," in *In Other Worlds*, 179–96.

8. Jane Tompkins criticizes Michel Foucault for beginning his *History of Sexuality* with the section on "We 'other Victorians' "; by using the first person plural, the male author is being "Presumptuous because it presumes that we [the readers] are really like him [the author]" and it makes the reader "want to cooperate, to be included in the circle the author is drawing so cosily around 'us.' It is chummy this 'we.' " Jane Tompkins, "Me and My Shadow," in *Gender and Theory: Dialogues on Feminist Criticism*, ed. Linda Kauffman (New York: Basil Blackwell, 1989), 121–39: 132.

9. Spivak, "Reading the World," 102.

10. The non-Western feminist criticizes the sexism of her "Eastern" male colleagues in the Indian Subaltern Studies Group: "Male subaltern and historian are here united in the common assumption that the procreative sex is a species apart, scarcely if at all to be considered a part of civil society." Gayatri Chakravorty Spivak, "Subaltern Studies: Deconstructing Historiography," in *In Other Worlds*, 197–221: 217.

11. Jacques Derrida, *Of Grammatology* (Baltimore: Johns Hopkins University Press, 1976), 44.

12. A remark made by Edward Said is, perhaps, applicable to Spivak's work too:

> The sense of being between cultures has been very, very strong for me. I would say that's the single strongest strand running through my life: the fact that I'm always in and out of things, and never really *of* anything for very long.

Edward Said, Interview with Imre Saluzinsky, in *Criticism in Society*, ed. Imre Saluzinsky (New York: Methuen, 1987), 123–48: 123.

13. Gayatri Chakravorty Spivak, "French Feminism in an International Frame," in *In Other Worlds*, 134–53: 135.

14. Spivak, "Feminism and Critical Theory," 92.

15. The canon revision debate is too lengthy to reproduce here. For the

various conflicting positions, see especially Paul Lauter, *Canons and Contexts* (New York: Oxford University Press, 1991); Paul Berman, ed., *Debating P.C.: The Controversy over Political Correctness on College Campuses* (New York: Dell, 1992); Henry Louis Gates, Jr., *Loose Canons: Notes on the Culture Wars* (New York: Oxford University Press, 1992); Dinesh D'Souza, *Illiberal Education: The Politics of Race and Sex on Campus* (New York: Free Press, 1991); E. D. Hirsch, Jr., *Cultural Literacy: What Every American Needs to Know* (Boston: Houghton Mifflin, 1987); Allan Bloom, *The Closing of the American Mind* (New York: Simon and Schuster, 1987).

16. Trinh T. Minh-ha, *Woman, Native, Other: Writing, Postcoloniality and Feminism* (Bloomington: Indiana University Press, 1989).

17. For a discussion of the "origins" of the concept of "race," see Henry Louis Gates, Jr., "Writing 'Race' and the Difference It Makes," in *Figures in Black: Words, Signs and the Racial Self* (Oxford: Oxford University Press, 1987), 4–5:

> Race, as a meaningful criterion within the biological sciences, has long been recognized to be a fiction. . . . Race has become a trope of ultimate, irreducible difference between cultures, linguistic groups, or adherents of specific belief systems which—more often than not—also have fundamentally opposed economic interests. Race is the ultimate trope of difference because it is so very arbitrary in its application.

For a discussion of the debate about "race" among African American scholars, see Diana Fuss, "'Race' under Erasure? Poststructuralist Afro-American Literary Theory," in *Essentially Speaking*, 73–96.

18. See Lauter, *Canons*, for a discussion of the impact of feminist teachers on the American literary canon.

19. I agree with Diana Fuss about the "unwelcome effects of essentialism in the classroom, and with the pedagogy and politics of 'essentially speaking'" (115). However, I am rather wary of Fuss's oversimplification of the issue of identities in the classroom: "in the classroom identities are *nothing* if not commodities" (115, emphasis added). Fuss forgets to mention that the ability to *choose* these commodified identities is itself a sign of privilege; some are born with identities, others have identities thrust on them. Further, Fuss attacks *all* marginalized students who, newly empowered, attempt to dominate and silence the "insiders" without commenting on the teacher's authority as one who negotiates between different groups of "majority" and "minority" students.

20. See Richard Slotkin, *Regeneration through Violence* (Middletown, CT: Wesleyan University Press, 1973).

21. The term "subaltern" has been popularized by Spivak's renowned

essay "Can the Subaltern Speak?" in *Marxism and the Interpretation of Culture,* ed. Cary Nelson and Lawrence Grossberg (Urbana: University of Illinois Press, 1986), 271–313. Its use in Antonio Gramsci's *Prison Notebooks* (written between 1929 and 1935) seems to be elided in contemporary critical discourse. In Gramsci's work, the term *"classi subalterne"* refers to the "subordinate" classes, and is used interchangeably with *"classi subordinate"* or *"classi strumentali."* See editors' footnote to Gramsci, "On Education," in *Selections from Prison Notebooks,* trans. Q. Hoare and G. N. Smith (London: Lawrence and Wishart, 1971), 26.

22. The issue of whether students need to "love" or at least "like" their teachers in order to accept their authority and learn from them is a contentious one, especially among proponents of feminist pedagogy. For discussions on this issue, see *Gendered Subjects: The Dynamics of Feminist Teaching,* ed. Margo Culley and Catherine Portuges (London: Routledge and Kegan Paul, 1985). Constance Penley reminds us of Lacan's insistence on the correlation between knowledge and love: "Transference *is* love ... I insist: it is love directed toward, addressed to, knowledge" (*Scilicet V,* 16, quoted in Penley 132, all emphases from source). Penley further builds on Lacan's viewpoint and explains that "Teaching proceeds by way of seduction; the student wants to learn because he or she loves the teacher insofar as he or she presumes that the teacher *knows.* . . . the teacher in order to be effective, to be a teacher at all, must fully assume the mantle of the subject supposed to know." Constance Penley, "Teaching in Your Sleep: Feminism and Psychoanalysis," in *Theory in the Classroom,* ed. Cary Nelson (Urbana: University of Illinois Press, 1986), 132.

23. Paule Marshall, *Brown Girl, Brownstones* (1959; reprint, New York: Feminist Press, 1981).

24. My introduction to American literature has been through seminars such as American Realism, including texts by minority authors like Sui Sin Far, Maria Christina Mena, Frances Harper, and so on, or a course on Twentieth-Century American Women Writers, including one text each by Leslie Marmon Silko, Louise Erdrich, Toni Morrison, Paule Marshall, Nella Larsen, Maxine Hong Kingston, Hisaye Yamamoto, Janice Mirikitani, Willa Cather, Edith Wharton, and Zitkala Sa, and anthologies of poetry by Native American and Latina writers.

25. That the concepts of a determinate self and of individual subjectivity have been questioned by poststructuralist theory needs no further elaboration.

26. Harold Bloom, *Kabbalah and Criticism,* 96, quoted in Annette Kolodny, "A Map for Rereading; or, Gender and the Interpretation of Literary Texts," in *The Mother Tongue: Essays in Feminist Psychoanalytic Interpretation,* ed. Shirley Garner, Clare Kahane, and Madelon Sprengnether (Ithaca: Cornell University Press, 1985), 258.

27. Cf. Louis Althusser, "Ideology and Ideological State Apparatuses (Notes towards an Investigation)," in *Lenin and Philosophy and Other Essays,* trans. Ben Brewster (New York: Monthly Review Press, 1971); and Michel Foucault, "Docile Bodies" and "The Means of Correct Training," in *Discipline and Punish: The Birth of the Prison,* trans. Alan Sheridan (New York: Pantheon, 1977), 135–94. According to Althusser, formal education is merely a vehicle for reproducing the dominant ideology; for Foucault, the process of discipline and punishment that is necessary for such cultural reproduction begins at school in early childhood. While I accept that there is some validity in these arguments, I think they deny the potential for educated subjects' individual agency once they have learned to think critically.

28. Frantz Fanon, *Black Skin, White Masks,* trans. Charles Markmann (New York: Grove Press, 1967), 38.

29. I borrow this phrase from African postcolonial writer N'gugi wa Thiong'o, *Decolonising the Mind* (London: James Curry, 1986). The author is renowned for his decision to relinquish writing in English and to return to the native languages of precolonization.

30. I discuss the dangerous conflation between "oppression" and "multiculturalism" in contemporary literary discourse in "Historicizing Literacies: (Ir)Responsibilities of Multicultural Representations," in *Multiculturalism and Representations* (Hawaii: University of Hawaii Press, forthcoming). In the development of my thinking about the complex implications of the conflation between multiculturalism and oppression, I have been indirectly influenced by the Brazilian educator Paulo Freire, *Pedagogy of the Oppressed* (New York: Herder and Herder, 1971).

31. Here I do not intend to make a simplistic generalization representing the "native" as "traditional" (misread as backward) and the "Western/foreign" as "modern" (misread as progressive); rather, I would like to suggest the complexities of cultural identity formation.

32. I am indebted to Rajiv Shankar for raising this point and contributing to the following discussion.

33. I believe that knowledge or understanding is not based only on identity. Here I am in agreement with Edward Said:

If one believes with Gramsci that an intellectual vocation is socially possible as well as desirable, then it is an inadmissible contradiction at the same time to build analyses of historical experience around exclusions, exclusions that stipulate, for instance, that only women can understand feminine experience, that only Jews can understand Jewish suffering, only formerly colonial subjects can understand colonial experience.

Edward Said, *Culture and Imperialism* (New York: Knopf, 1993), 31. A similar idea is echoed by Spivak in a much cited section from her essay "A Literary Representation of the Subaltern: A Woman's Text from the Third World," in *In Other Worlds*, 254:

> The position that only the subaltern can know the subaltern, only women can know women and so on, cannot be held as a theoretical presupposition either, for it predicates the possibility of knowledge on identity.

34. Most American students don't encounter many of these authors until college and usually, only if they become English majors—and this is true even for the "good old days" before the so-called capitulation of the "Western canon" to "multiculturalism." In his essay "The Value of the Canon" (1991), in *Debating P.C.*, ed. Berman, 153–71, Irving Howe nostalgically laments that "Several decades ago, when I began teaching, it could be assumed that entering freshmen had read in high school at least one play by Shakespeare and one novel by Dickens. . . . These days, with the disintegration of the high schools, such an assumption can seldom be made" (162). Compare this with my (what seems lifelong) training in British literature.

35. I realize that these opportunities were available to me because of economic privilege; the impact of colonial education would be quite different on others who did not have the same access to the "West."

36. Spivak, "Translator's Foreword," 179.

37. Cf. Edward Said, *Orientalism* (New York: Pantheon, 1978).

38. I borrow this term from Stephen Greenblatt, *Renaissance Self-Fashioning: From More to Shakespeare* (Chicago: University of Chicago Press, 1980).

BIBLIOGRAPHY

Althusser, Louis. "Ideology and Ideological State Apparatuses (Notes towards an Investigation)." In *Lenin and Philosophy and Other Essays*, trans. Ben Brewster. New York: Monthly Review Press, 1971.

Berman, Paul, ed. *Debating P.C.: The Controversy over Political Correctness on College Campuses*. New York: Dell, 1992.

Bloom, Allan. *The Closing of the American Mind*. New York: Simon and Schuster, 1987.

Culley, Margo, and Catherine Portuges, eds. *Gendered Subjects: The Dynamics of Feminist Teaching*. London: Routledge and Kegan Paul, 1985.

Derrida, Jacques. *Of Grammatology*, trans. Gayatri C. Spivak. Baltimore: Johns Hopkins University Press, 1976.

D'Souza, Dinesh. *Illiberal Education: The Politics of Race and Sex on Campus.* New York: Free Press, 1991.

Fanon, Frantz. *Black Skin, White Masks,* trans. Charles Lam Markmann. New York: Grove Press, 1967.

Foucault, Michel. *Discipline and Punish: The Birth of the Prison,* trans. Alan Sheridan. New York: Pantheon, 1977.

Freire, Paulo. *Pedagogy of the Oppressed.* New York: Herder and Herder, 1971.

Fuss, Diana. *Essentially Speaking: Feminism, Nature and Difference.* New York: Routledge, 1989.

Garner, Shirley, Clare Kahane, and Madelon Sprengnether, eds. *The Mother Tongue: Essays in Feminist Psychoanalytic Interpretation.* Ithaca: Cornell University Press, 1985.

Gates, Henry Louis, Jr. *Loose Canons: Notes on the Culture Wars.* New York: Oxford University Press, 1992.

———. "Writing 'Race' and the Difference It Makes." Introduction to *Figures in Black: Words, Signs, and the Racial Self.* Oxford: Oxford University Press, 1987.

Graff, Gerald. *Professing Literature: An Institutional History.* Chicago: University of Chicago Press, 1987.

Gramsci, Antonio. *Selections from the Prison Notebooks,* trans. Q. Hoare and G. N. Smith. London: Lawrence and Wishart, 1971.

Greenblatt, Stephen J. *Renaissance Self-Fashioning: From More to Shakespeare.* Chicago: University of Chicago Press, 1980.

Hirsch, E. D., Jr. *Cultural Literacy: What Every American Needs to Know.* Boston: Houghton Mifflin, 1987.

Howe, Irving. "The Value of the Canon." In *Debating P.C.,* ed. Berman, 153–71.

Hurston, Zora Neale. *Dust Tracks on a Road: An Autobiography.* 2nd ed. Urbana: Illinois University Press, 1984.

Kolodny, Annette. "A Map for Rereading; or, Gender and the Interpretation of Literary Texts." In *The Mother Tongue,* ed. Garner et al.

Kristeva, Julia. *Strangers to Ourselves,* trans. Leon S. Roudiez. New York: Columbia University Press, 1991.

Lauter, Paul. *Canons and Contexts.* New York: Oxford University Press, 1991.

Marshall, Paule. *Brown Girl, Brownstones.* New York: Feminist Press, 1981.

Minh-ha, Trinh T. *Woman, Native, Other: Writing Postcoloniality and Feminism.* Bloomington: Indiana University Press, 1989.

Nelson, Cary, ed. *Theory in the Classroom.* Urbana: University of Illinois Press, 1986.

Nelson, Cary, and Lawrence Grossberg, eds. *Marxism and the Interpretation of Culture.* Urbana: University of Illinois Press, 1986.

Ngugi wa Thiong'o. *Decolonising the Mind: The Politics of Language in African Literature*. London: James Curry, 1986.

Penley, Constance. "Teaching in Your Sleep: Feminism and Psychoanalysis." In *Theory in the Classroom*, ed. Nelson, 129–48.

Said, Edward W. *Culture and Imperialism*. New York: Knopf, 1993.

———. Interview with Imre Saluzinsky. In Saluzinsky, *Criticism in Society*, 123–48.

———. *Orientalism*. New York: Pantheon, 1978.

Saluzinsky, Imre. *Criticism in Society*. New York: Methuen, 1987.

Shankar, Lavina Dhingra. "Historicizing Literacies: (Ir)Responsibilities of Multicultural Representations." In *Multiculturalism and Representations*. Hawaii: University of Hawaii Press, forthcoming.

Slotkin, Richard. *Regeneration through Violence: The Mythology of the American Frontier, 1600–1860*. Middletown, CT: Wesleyan University Press, 1973.

Spivak, Gayatri Chakravorty. "Can the Subaltern Speak?" In *Marxism and the Interpretation of Culture*, ed. Nelson and Grossberg, 271–313.

———. "'Draupadi' by Mahasweta Devi." In *In Other Worlds: Essays in Cultural Politics*, 179–96. New York: Routledge, 1988.

———. "Feminism and Critical Theory." In *In Other Worlds*, 77–92.

———. "French Feminism in an International Frame." In *In Other Worlds*, 134–53.

———. "A Literary Representation of the Subaltern: A Woman's Text from the Third World." In *In Other Worlds*, 241–68.

———. "Reading the World: Literary Studies in the Eighties." In *In Other Worlds*, 95–102.

———. "Subaltern Studies: Deconstructing Historiography." In *In Other Worlds*, 197–221.

Tompkins, Jane. "Me and My Shadow." In *Gender and Theory: Dialogues on Feminist Criticism*, ed. Linda Kauffman, 121–39. New York: Basil Blackwell, 1989.

11

Caliban in the Classroom

INDIRA KARAMCHETI

Now don't get me wrong: I've got nothing against Caliban—at least not more than most people. And I've got absolutely nothing against classrooms—again, not more than most people. But I'm not crazy about the combination of Caliban *and* the classroom, especially when I'm cast in the role of Caliban. I sometimes think that a lot of us academics who are blessed with the "surplus visibility"[1] of race or ethnicity are cast as Calibans in the classroom, lurching between student and blackboard. It seems that our hour has come round at last, that we, who may have been excluded in the past, are at last to take our rightful place in the halls of academe. But under what guise do we make our appearance there, and what is our presence taken to mean? I wonder whether we are here, not in the role of Prospero in charge of the books of magic, but still as Calibans, rough beasts slouching (maybe even shuffling) along in the ivied Bethlehems of higher education.

We are sometimes seen, it seems to me, as traveling icons of culture, both traditional (as long as we're over there) and nontraditional (when we're right here), unbearably ancient in our folk wisdom and childlike in our infantile need for the sophistication of the West. We are flesh and blood information retrieval systems, native informants who demonstrate and act out difference, often with an imperfectly concealed political agenda. We are the local and the regional opposed to the universality of the West, nature to its culture, instinct to its intellect, body to its brain. We are, in fact, encased in the personal and visible facts of our visible selves, walking exemplars of ethnicity and race.

What we are not, however, is objective, impartial purveyors of truth, teachers of fact and method. We always teach, at some level, the personal but usually unspoken story of ourselves in the world. We teach with ourselves as our own most effective visual aids. The contemporary practice of choosing to insert personal, biographical details about the author into critical or theoretical articles deliberately sets out to situate and historicize authority, maybe even reveal the illusory nature of impartiality, objectivity, and authority itself. But the minority teacher does not necessarily have the choice of deliberately engaging the machinery of the personal in order to question authority. Authority has already been problematized by the fact of visible difference. The manifest personal antedates the decision to engage in the politics of the personal. Indeed, the minority teacher is already known, *in personal terms:* ethnicity, race, is, among other things, an already familiar genre of personality. It is a familiar if not always understood category of both analysis and interpretation.

The more elusive issue for the minority teacher is the establishment of authority, of objectivity, of impartiality—that is, of those attributes traditionally associated with the performance of teaching. What I hope to examine in this essay is that problem of the personal as it establishes or works against authority in the classroom for the teacher marked by race or ethnicity. What is the nature of authority in this particular case? What are its sources and limits? In what ways is it dependent on the personal? Can the genre of race be used to create a more supple form of authority in the classroom, perhaps by foregrounding ignorance, active or inactive, or perhaps through the strategies of performance?

The entanglement of the personal—the facts of race and ethnicity—with the professional—a teacher's authority to speak with credibility, and thereby to educate, to lead out—came home to me when I first began teaching, as a teaching assistant, at the start of my graduate school days. I taught freshman composition in the English department at the University of California, Santa Barbara, a predominantly white, upper-middle-class campus in southern California. I realized pretty quickly that my person in the classroom was a bit of a shocker for some students. On the first day of classes, I would deliberately wait until a few minutes into the class period to allow people time to locate a new classroom in a new school, then make my entrance, walk to the table at front and center of the room, and put down my books. It was interesting to have students approach me, and, speaking very loudly and slowly, inform me that that place was meant for the teacher. Correspondingly, during the next several days, a few students—not necessarily the same ones—would come up after class to remark on my amazingly good grasp of the language.

Most students were neither so officious nor so ingenuous. But events of this nature occurred sufficiently often to convince me, first, that I was probably sitting in the wrong place, and second, that it was admirable of me to speak English well, or, possibly, at all. By the time I was ready to leave UCSB, I was curious enough about this matter of race, authority, and the classroom to offer one class the choice of writing about prior experiences with minority teachers as one of several essay topics. And I was intrigued enough by what some students wrote that I saved several of these essays. (I don't mean to imply that this material is in any way a scientific study, an objective, impartial, or even authoritative investigation. It's just personal.) These students of course saw that one of the issues hidden in the essay topic was the question of prejudice. And, of course, that they chose to write on this topic for a teacher they perceived as a minority person influenced what they wrote. Given this context, it's revealing to look at what incidents they chose to narrate, and what rhetorical strategies they employed.

Almost all the essays began with the claim that the author personally had no prejudice; these students claimed to judge whether a teacher was good or not on purely "objective" grounds. One student wrote,

> It was all perfectly normal. I walked into my third period class on the first day of school when I was in seventh grade, and I found, sitting behind the desk, a large black man in his mid forties. "So he's my new math teacher, eh?" I thought as I found my seat. "I wonder if he's a good teacher." It did not even occur to me that he would not be as good a teacher as a white man or woman.

Several thereupon proceeded to comment on how irritating they found it when the ethnic instructor had such a strong accent that they had difficulty understanding. I don't want to take up this particular debate here; rather, I would like to point out the slippage between the references to foreign speakers of English in an essay on racial and ethnic minorities, especially following hard on protestations of lack of prejudice against black and Hispanic teachers.

Some chose thereafter to comment on me, despite the assignment that they discuss minority teachers they had had prior to the current class:

> My first reaction upon you walking into class was, "How can that little lady expect to teach a college course?" When you came in and gave a hearty "Hi" and began talking, my fears were dissolved.

Another student wrote about an African American woman teacher he very much disliked—okay, hated:

> Although my hatred was composed of various elements (injustice, rebellion, frustration, anger, etc.), Mrs. [X]'s ethnicity definitely served to strengthen and perpetuate my abhorrence. Because her racial heritage had an ancient legacy of ethnic slurs and stereotypes, I was supplied with a plethora of powerful, seemingly empirical justifications. In effect, Mrs. [X]'s physical and emblematic ethnicity further reinforced and rationalized my negative perception of her.

Immediately thereafter, the same student chose to describe me to me in these terms:

My only other nonCaucasian teacher is my current English teacher. My first impression upon viewing her Indian ethnicity was a mixture of surprise and skepticism. I was surprised by the novelty of an Indian woman teaching English and was simultaneously skeptical of her proficiency. Despite my initially disdainful response, I was very pleasantly surprised by her competence. Her spoken English was flawless, eloquent, clear, forceful, and concise. I perceived her manner as authoritative but not domineering, poised without arrogance, lighthearted yet not giddy, and open-minded but not indecisive [a description that makes me feel like a decent, moderately priced Bordeaux: "Assertive, yet modest"]. Her literary discussions displayed an "impressive" range and depth of knowledge, commanded by a "very sharp" intellect.

The swollen ego engendered by this flattery, however, was quickly punctured by the next paragraph:

Clearly, in this instance the professor's ethnicity affected my perceptions in a positive manner. Because of racial typecasting and her professional uniqueness [which, of course, is no longer as true now as it was in 1987], I had unusually low expectations. Consequently, the more she established her competency and her affability, my esteem increased geometrically. The ability to speak correctly and articulately or to skillfully direct a literary discussion shouldn't be foreign to any English teacher, but because of my assumption of an ethnic handicap I was overly impressed by her abilities. When she exceeded my ethnic expectations, I then perceived her qualities more favorably than I would have for a Caucasian teacher.

The last of the student essays with which I'll burden you reaches some interesting conclusions that I've increasingly come to agree with. This student makes the point that the competence of minority teachers is directly related to the correlation between their race or ethnicity and the subject they teach: an African American woman who taught physical education ("Not only was this teacher good, but she was doing something we all knew she could do. Are black people not suppose [*sic*] to be more athletic than white?"); a "Mexican" teacher who taught Spanish III ("He, like my PE teacher was doing something that all of us, as students, knew he was capable of, teaching his language"). On the other hand, an African American man who taught biology is judged in retrospect as not competent on the grounds of disorganization and inconsistency. At the time, however, this student writes,

> We let ourselves accept this teacher as "good" even though he really was not. This is very unusual when I think of how we reacted when we had a "not so good" white teacher. This teacher would be criticized without mercy because, in my opinion, we expected more out of him. My Biology teacher was black and because of the stereotype of black people being dumb we just accepted his faults blindly.

The excerpts from these student essays obviously prove nothing. But for me, they are suggestive, if nothing more, in connecting the issues of race—as a category of the personal—and the taking or granting of pedagogical authority. While race or ethnicity alone may undermine classrcom authority, it doesn't end here. The more complex issue is contained in the last essay from which I quoted: the matching of race with subject, the disciplining and containing of ethnicity into its proper and personal field.

Admittedly, these excerpts were drawn from essays written some years ago, in a large state university, where I, like all the other freshman composition instructors, was identified in the schedule of classes in advance only as "staff," so that my appearance in the classroom affronted certain expectations. I now teach in quite a different setting, a small, liberal arts college in New England with a long history of socially progressive thought and ideals. I no longer teach freshman composition, nor do I teach pseudonymously as "staff." Instead, I teach postcolonial literature, which I refer to in more perverse moods as P.C. Lit. Because my university is so small, and because my subject and I exhibit a phenomenological fit, I do not experience the same kinds of issues with authority.

That does not mean, of course, that authority has ceased to be problematic. I have increasingly come to see that my authority, and that of other teachers who work within the differences of race or ethnicity, is granted within the confines of certain more or less clearly defined boundaries. And the boundaries, though flexible, are drawn within the shadow lines of authenticity, the authentic and perceivable racial/ethnic self. "Authenticity," as the ground of authority, creates at least two different genres of personality, two already available dramatic roles and dramatic narratives the ethnic teacher can perform. One role is that of Shakespeare's Caliban (in *The Tempest*) as a kind of native informant, lurching about the island and showing Prospero its sweet and secret places, serving to provide data with which Prospero can then rule. Caliban's claim to authority is based on natural claims— descent by blood from Sycorax. He does not have access to Prospero's source of power, his books.

As a postcolonial person teaching postcolonial literature, my authority, too, is somewhat dependent on my bloodlines, my physical and visible affinity with my subject matter. My authority is somewhat dependent on my status as native informant, providing others with data that can then be theorized, so that I serve as the representative figure for my entire field of study. Since that field covers 85 percent of the world's landmass, this sometimes seems a largish burden. In any case, it's a representational responsibility that's difficult to fulfill. Genetic authenticity is ultimately always on a sliding scale of greater and lesser degrees of raciality: a slippery scale of "more colored than thou." The hierarchies of races and ethnicities in the United States cannot support the construction of genetic authority for very long. The role of native informant is also ultimately thankless to fulfill. In my discipline, real power and authority lie, not in the role of native informant, not with Caliban, but in theory, with Prospero.

At my current university, there is another narrative that has a prepared role for the racialized body: the narrative of resistance. Resistance, as a methodology for the examination of literatures produced by "others," has the real and valuable function of focusing attention on what has been done by those others who have been disenfranchised or exploited by colonialism, institutional prejudice, and so on. Placing "others" center stage has salutary political and disciplinary

effects in the study of literature. But the hunt for resistance on the part
of the subaltern figure can, and in some ways has already, become a
formulaic approach that provides too easy, too gratifying solutions to
long-enduring social, historical, political, and economic inequities that
show little signs of suddenly becoming "okay." According to the
narrative, however, resistance is discovered everywhere, in every margin and periphery. Show me an other, a subaltern, a marginalized
figure; I'll show you resistance. Resistance is so prevalent that it makes
one wonder that anyone has ever been oppressed anywhere, at any
time.

The narrative of resistance has a ready-made role for Caliban: the
authentic, organic intellectual—read revolutionary—seeking to over-
throw Prospero's rule, the postcolonial, the guerrilla fighter waging
battle in the belly of the beast, the revolutionary in the arms of
academe. The politicization of the role is clear, and brings Caliban
closer, if not close enough, to the sources of power, Prospero's books.
But Caliban's resistance is no real threat because he is not allowed
access to those sources of power. Similarly, the postcolonial playing
the role of the academic revolutionary is safely contained by that
recognizable role of resistance rather than made threatening by it. Far
from granting access to the centers of power, where substantive
changes could be made to the university, the role of the revolutionary
can instead serve the purposes of power by seeming to answer oppression with an easily recognized resistance, and, moreover, one provided by the institution itself. The revolutionary can in fact become
the university's very best alibi, while demonstrating that institution's
good intentions and virtue. To take the presence of the racialized
other on university campuses for a sign of substantive change within
society as a whole can create an overly simplistic narrative: a reassur-
ing psychobabble that, while things may be bad all over outside,
inside the world of academia, at least, "I'm okay, you're okay." In the
end, to accept the narrative of resistance at face value is to confuse the
real and important—and political—work that is the proper work of

academia with a misdirected call to popular, "grassroots" action to replace it. The unspoken subtext here is certainly an anti-intellectualism, more certainly a distrust of the native or subaltern intellectual; most certainly a sense that the "authentic" postcolonial is the grassroots peasant, living oppression, not the indigenous or metropolitan intellectual, theorizing postcoloniality. Caliban's authenticity is balanced by another, more culture-based (by which I mean practice-based) notion of authenticity: the figure of hybridity, of authenticity established not in reference to purity of traditions, culture, and race, but on notions of impurity and contamination. Shakespeare's *Tempest* does not offer a figure to encompass this identity, but Aime Cesaire's work *A Tempest*, his revisioning of Shakespeare's play from the viewpoint of the colonized, does. Cesaire's Ariel is not Shakespeare's figure of radical difference, a figure who finally succeeds in escaping the power struggle between Caliban and Prospero. Cesaire's Ariel is a mulatto, the house slave against Caliban's field slave, the native intellectual, having an identity crisis, as Cesaire's Prospero derisively gibes, deeply implicated in the very structures that enslave him, seeking to mediate and achieve synthesis between exploiter and exploited. Within the classroom, this Ariel role becomes that of the mediating figure of the indigenous elite. The Western-trained postcolonial academic, because of his or her cultural familiarity with and ease in the West combined with manifest racial or ethnic difference, is often perceived as the ideal bridge between Western academia and non-Western subject matter. The rewards can be great. At its furthest extreme—think of postcolonial academic superstars—Ariel's flightiness is transformed into transcontinental flight: the hybrid cosmopolite, jetsetting everywhere, at home everywhere, belonging nowhere, alighting in the classroom momentarily to magic up a literary repast, perhaps to lead the class on a whirlwind literary tour of the global, yes, postmodern, literary bazaar.

The last of the potential roles lying in wait for the minority teacher in the classroom is, of course, Prospero himself. The minority teacher can cast himself or herself as the traditional authoritarian personality, the hard-driving, brilliant, no-nonsense professional for whom the personal has nothing to do with anything. This role plays visual and epistemological games, and ultimately, it, too, establishes its own authority in reference to a standard of authenticity. Denying the visual evidence of race or ethnicity, this role insists on the authenticity of guild membership—card-carrying status in the union of academic professionals, usually demonstrated, at least in humanistic fields at the current time, by the use of complex poststructuralist concepts, language, and theory to analyze postcolonial, minority subjects. Caliban can speak with the master's voice, perhaps even be transformed into Prospero.

This cataloguing of some of the various roles available to the minority teacher is of course both schematic and oversimplified. One major missing subject is that part of the personal that cannot be made shapely or safe for pedagogical purposes. Caliban says that Prospero has taught him to speak and his profit on't is that he has learned how to curse. I'm not suggesting that minority teachers need to have their mouths washed out with soap. I am suggesting, however, that marginality, precisely because it is not an inborn, natural category but something learned, teaches its own discourse, its own curses.[2] Built into difference is real resistance to authority, to Prospero's voice. Minority discourse is characterized more by subversion, interrogation, critique than by construction. We are all gadflies to some extent; the best of us carry lethal infection. But teaching, at least traditional ideas of the role of the teacher in the literary studies classroom, insists that criticism be constructive, that analysis lead to the new, improved model. I suggest that minority discourse does not necessarily lead to the construction of a newer model. Yet the pressure to do so is exerted in the classroom by students, and certainly within the world of scholarship by peers and tenure reviewers. The pressure to provide intellectual guides, schema, methods of analysis that will lead to more and more accurate interpretations has already produced analytical blueprints such as blues ideology, signifyin', or the idea of resistance.[3]

The harder issue for me is the problem of anger, the issue of rage named in the idea of cursing. Anger, it seems to me, is antithetical to the dialogue of teaching; yet anger is a real and present fact of the personal. And if minority teachers can be figured as Calibans, Ariels, impersonators of Prospero, at what level does anger move against the children of Prospero and his heirs? This leads me to the last of the points I'd like to make. In fact, as should be no surprise, the personal, while it seems to be the ground on which the minority teacher constructs his or her myths of authority, is not the commodity in which one trades. Rather, the personal remains a matter, if not for repression, much in need of shaping according to some genre or other. One does not present the personal, one represents it. For the minority teacher especially, I think, who has historically been allowed into academia in the guise of the native informant, the use of the personal poses problems. To refuse to engage the personal—to silence it—is one way of resisting the commodification of the multicultural body.

However, the personal in this country is irrepressible; it cannot be silenced. It is inevitably part of the equipment with which one teaches, willingly or not. Perhaps the best way to use that equipment is to be aware of the preexisting roles for ethnicity, and then to playfully, inventively, eclectically subvert them. An authority derived from the ground of authenticity is ultimately self-defeating, but a self-aware, deliberate performance of race or ethnicity can provide a more powerful, more challenging authority. By "performance of race," I mean that students should be encouraged to perceive how much "race" is made by social expectations and constructions, rather than having those expectations fulfilled. It can mean a deliberate evocation of cultural stereotypes about race or ethnicity, in order to puncture them, joke about them, insist on them. Performance of race means to make race visible, and thereby to undermine its authority in the classroom; simultaneously to question its meaningfulness and to insist on its importance in shaping our understanding of the world. This kind of performance is really guerrilla theater, which keeps the audience off balance, and makes them learn by shaking up their assumptions about the nature of the world. If we minority teachers are sometimes cast as Calibans, we also know our hour has yet to come round. If we are not yet slouching toward Bethlehem, yet we may shuffle off to Buffalo, in a neo-blackface minstrel show.

Performance and guerrilla theater are both strategies, and they are, I think, symptomatic. They are strategies for seizing control of the machinery of representation. They are also symptoms of powerlessness—as well as symptoms of the limited kinds of power the minority teacher does have. The demand for the personal is made on the minority teacher in many ways: from the personal levels of teaching, to teaching strategies, to subject matter. The personal is present as the ground for pedagogical authority, and certainly in the power dynamics as well as the erotics of the classroom.

Most important of all, the demand for the personal moves the marketplace into the classroom. The personal is something we produce as part of the package we sell. Academia is neither Bethlehem nor Jerusalem, neither the birthplace of the new Golden Age nor the heavenly city, although part of its mythology is the legend of past virtue that has been lost and the utopia that is to come. But it is useful to remind ourselves that it is also an industry. If academia is neither heaven nor hell, it is preeminently the place where we academics make our living by selling our services, our knowledge, and our symbolic presence. For the minority academic, all three are shaped by the personal, private and public, performed and lived.

NOTES

This essay was originally written for a conference titled "Pedagogy: The Question of the Personal," held at the Center for Twentieth Century Studies at the University of Wisconsin, Milwaukee, April 15–17, 1993. It is being published by Indiana University Press in a forthcoming anthology titled *Pedagogy: The Question of Impersonation* in the center's series Theories of Contemporary Culture.

1. Daphne Patai, "Minority Status and the Stigma of 'Surplus Visibility,' " *Chronicle of Higher Education*, October 30, 1991, A52.

2. See, for instance, the suggestion that one is not born minor but becomes minor, in Abdul R. JanMohamed and David Lloyd, "Introduction: Toward a Theory of Minority Discourse: What Is to Be Done?" in *The Nature and Context of Minority Discourse*, ed. Abdul R. JanMohamed and David Lloyd (New York: Oxford University Press, 1990), 9. Similarly, Rey Chow persuasively demonstrates that one "is not simply ethnic, but *ethnicized.*" *Woman and Chinese Modernity* (Minneapolis: University of Minnesota Press, 1991), 25.

3. See the following, all persuasive and powerful arguments: Houston Baker, Jr., *Blues Ideology and Theories of the Vernacular* (Chicago: University of Chicago Press, 1984); Henry Louis Gates, Jr., *The Signifying Monkey* (New York: Oxford University Press, 1988); and Barbara Harlow, *Resistance Literature* (New York: Methuen, 1987).

12

A Paradox of Silence: Reflections of a Man Who Teaches Women's Studies

CRAIG W. HELLER

People often ask about my students' reactions to me, both as a teacher and as a feminist. I have discovered that this is usually a polite, if thinly veiled, way to ask me the question that is really on their minds, which is, "What the hell are you, a white, middle-class, straight male, doing teaching Introduction to Women's Studies?" The conversation usually goes off in various directions regarding feminism or pedagogy or the politics of exclusion. In truth, the classes I have taught, regardless of how they were listed in the catalog, have always centered around issues central to feminism, and my teaching style, were you to observe me, is feminist pedagogy at its most stereotypic. It was not, however, until I had my first opportunity to teach Introduction to Women's Studies (while completing my dissertation on feminist pedagogy) that I began to examine my own pedagogy in light of my sex.

Research on feminist pedagogy usually sees gender as a unit of analysis both for students and for the construction of knowledge, but rarely has the gender of the instructor been addressed as an issue. Typically, the literature either assumes that feminist teachers are women (which, although smacking of essentialism, makes for a moot point) or, worse, supposes that feminist teachers, whether female or male, need only follow certain pedagogical principles in order to fit the label. One of the purposes of this essay is to point out that the gender of the instructor *is* an important element of one's feminist pedagogy and that "one size does not fit all." In other words, a feminist teacher who is a man and a feminist teacher who is a woman face different issues, and both need to understand the different roles and expectations they fill, both willingly and unwillingly, for their students.

I explore three matters in this essay: first, how my subject positions[1] of "male" and "teacher" have been previously constructed by students long before they enter the college classroom; second, the role of silence in a women's studies classroom when that silence originates from a male teacher; and third, the inherent paradox in a man teaching women's studies—a situation where I use the power afforded me by my white male status to encourage students to challenge traditional patriarchal assumptions and expectations. This strategy, in itself, is merely subversive, but given that my venue is a women's studies classroom and that I am a teacher in a women's studies program, utilizing this strategy evokes a troubling question: How contradictory is it that I may be convincing students of the viability of a feminist message by, at least in some part, fulfilling the patriarchal expectations that many students have of male teachers?

Gender plays a role in all our daily interactions; this is a basic tenet of feminism. Our society's assumptions about gender carry over into the classroom in student/teacher relationships as much as in any other interaction. By the time they reach college, students have had at least twelve years of indoctrination and "practice" at catering differently to male and female authority figures. Research has shown us that students have different expectations for male teachers, believing them to be more competent, more experienced, and "tougher" than female teachers.[2] A recent study found that students see young women teachers as less capable than young men teachers, but that older women are believed to be the best teachers even though they are seen to be on a par with older men teachers as far as the depth of their knowledge is concerned.[3]

Regardless of their gender-dependent perceptions, students are highly experienced at ceding authority to teachers while they themselves adopt a passive stance. In this relationship, students passively consume facts provided by a recognized authority figure, assuming that the information is "truth." This typically results in the type of "banking education" that Paulo Freire has long criticized.[4] Freire describes this situation, which is the norm in Western schooling, as teachers making deposits of facts in students who act as little more than bank accounts for the storing of information rather than the analysis or critique of information. By the time most young men and women reach college age, they subconsciously expect little change in these long-established patterns. A women's studies class is often their first exposure to the idea of and means for challenging these patterns.

Susan Heald has argued that we all hold "a taken-for-granted set of assumptions about the identity of individuals in various categories," which are rigidly defined by the dominant discourses of our society.[5] These categories, or "subject positions," include everything from piano player to lesbian, woman to doctor, teacher to student. Heald cites her own example of having her teenage sense of identity defined and limited through others' expectations of the subject positions of "pianist" and "talented" that were applied to her. We also hold similar assumptions about ourselves, contributing to the creation of a sense of subjectivity, as we occupy various categories. This creation of dominant identities or "subjects" contributes to the stereotypes that reinforce the systems perpetuating sexism, racism, and other social ills. Just as it was long held that Africans were not intelligent enough to care for themselves and thus "needed" the institution of slavery to protect them, there are many beliefs and definitions, based on similar, if less overtly reprehensible, interpretations of subjectivity that bind our own sense of identity as teachers.

Heald goes on to argue, and I would agree, that a part of feminist pedagogy should be to question these established assumptions so that we can upset some of these long-held perceptions about teachers' as well as students' roles.

> Teachers and students are "gendered" subjects, as they are "raced" and "classed" and identified according to sexual orientation, age, and physical ability. In addition, we/they are also what I call *educational* subjects: We have claimed an identity within the range of those laid out by educational institutions. We need to keep trying to uncover just how it is that our subjectivities are formed within these institutions. . . . Feminist pedagogy needs to be grounded in the understanding that education is an apparatus of social regulation and as such participates in the formation of the dominant subject positions of "teacher" and "student."[6]

What are the beliefs, assumptions, and definitions students hold about the identity of the subject position "male teacher"? How do they limit, or perhaps, as John Schilb has suggested, enhance, my ability to teach in women's studies?[7]

For both students and professors, these beliefs, assumptions, and definitions center around the use of power. All students have been taught in the classroom that the teacher holds power and they do not. We are all taught by our society and our culture that men hold power, and women, with few exceptions, do not.

Power and authority have always been recognized as problematic components of feminist pedagogy. The stereotypical image of the feminist teacher as "female nurturer" rather than "male disciplinarian" is all well and good, but we cannot dismiss, as bell hooks points out, that teachers have power over students, and as long as we evaluate students' performance we cannot pretend to give up all our authority as teachers.[8] Some, such as hooks, Nancy Buffington,[9] or Magda Gere Lewis, suggest that this power can be used to good advantage. Lewis asserts that

> the use of institutional power, I believe, should not always be viewed as counterproductive to our politics. Feminism is a politics that is both

historical and contingent on existing social relations. I [have] no problem justifying the use of my institutional power to create the possibility
for privilege to face itself and own its violation publicly. Using power
to subjugate is quite different from using power to liberate.[10]

While I agree that a teacher cannot and should not abrogate all
power and authority in the classroom, I question the use of power as
a pedagogical tool for myself or for any male feminist teacher. Under
certain circumstances, it can be useful and beneficial for a female
teacher to use those strategies that have typically been the reserve of
male authority figures, especially if their use can challenge oppressive
stereotypes. But as a white male teacher, I obviously have no need
to appropriate "the master's tools" of authoritative power. It is my
responsibility as a feminist teacher to promote a discursive space that
not only promotes new interpretations of women's subject positions
but also allows students to challenge the dominant images of men and
men who are teachers.

My students expect me, as a male teacher, to overtly control the
discourse and the classroom environment. To them, a teacher is a
source of information and an "attitude cop," with the grade book
as the nightstick. While being a source of information is a primary
responsibility of any teacher, it should be tempered with an understanding of how students see this second role, especially if one is
committed to a feminist pedagogy.

The students in my Introduction to Women's Studies classes (I have
taught this class seven times now) work in small groups of five or six
for most of the class periods during the semester. The groups have
directed activities, such as role plays and small group projects as well
as broadly outlined discussion agendas to work from, and the students are responsible for maintaining a fruitful discussion within their
own group. I rarely intervene. Within a very few weeks, the students,
partly as a reflection of the subject matter of the course and partly as
an aspect of human nature, form a sense of community with their
group members and, by extension, with the class as a whole. To a

large extent, this sense of community replaces any need on my part to exercise control overtly.

By remaining largely silent, I abrogate my traditional subject position as authority figure, and the students, by virtue of the communities they form within the classroom, have no need of one. When they see that I, the traditional teacher/power figure, am willing not to exercise my privilege to control their discourse, their thinking, *or their learning,* then they are free to learn from the materials, from each other, and from me in whatever way each of them can best profit from. The students, because they feel an obligation and responsibility to their classroom community and to themselves, make the investments of thought, time, and effort that are necessary for a successful learning experience.

I am very active in creating a relationship with my students characterized by a horizontal rather than vertical power dynamic. I expect my students to use my first name and I rarely answer questions directly as if I held secrets for others to discover. I often leave the classroom (after establishing some guidelines) to allow them autonomy in their learning, and I practice a variety of other behaviors designed to shift the focus from me at the center to the academic information and their analysis of it.

After several weeks of a semester, the majority of my students do exhibit a good deal of autonomy and community in the classroom. It takes only two to three weeks for them to stop looking to me for reassurance or reward and to begin relying on themselves and their classmates for interaction. This is not to say that I sit among my students observing a raging chaos. I do have to set boundaries, establish a classroom environment, assign grades, and act as a knowledgeable resource. But by redefining my subject positions, I can do all these things *with* my students, not *for* them.

Regardless of how well or much I "redefine" myself in the classroom, I still, in large part, represent the "norm," and students have been taught that when the "norm" speaks, they should sit up and take

note. Even after weeks of nearly silent participation, I need only raise
my voice or adopt a stern demeanor and my little communities of
learners start to wither, their budding sense of empowerment seeming
to collapse on itself. Clearly, in one fifteen-week semester, I cannot
completely overcome my subject position. Even by the end of the
semester, the majority rarely challenge me directly or export their
autonomous behavior to other classes. The few instances in which this
has occurred I count among my greatest successes.

It has been my perception that students question but do not challenge my unique (in their experience) subject position of male wom-
en's studies teacher; they want to know why, as a man, I am interested
in feminism and women's studies, but they have never challenged
that interest or my professional expertise. My women colleagues, on
the other hand, who teach similar courses in the women's studies
department, do not, in general, go unchallenged by many of their
students, at least the male ones. Their pedagogies tend more toward
the overt use of authority in the classroom, which I agree can be an
important strategy for women. In the same way that students need to
learn that I can be silent, they need to learn that women can represent
authority. But regardless of pedagogical style, these colleagues, particularly the younger ones, regularly experience resistance, not necessarily to the material, but to their sex and their role as teacher.

This is the source of what I see as a paradox. If students are not
questioning my positions and are responding to me primarily as a
man/teacher (rather than a man/feminist or any other subject position), what then are the consequences for my pedagogy? Obviously, I
am in a somewhat unique position. Should I use my patriarchal subject position to further my feminist agenda? If I continue to work
toward less authority-based relationships with my students, will I
reach a point where they stop taking me seriously? This, I feel, is the
major issue facing men in women's studies. On the one hand, we
represent excellent role models for students as men who respect and
support feminist agendas, but, on the other, we represent the patriar-

chy and everything our students expect of it. Where is the balance between male silence and male authority?

Maintaining this balance is a key responsibility of a male women's studies teacher. I wonder, even when I remain verbally silent, what other messages I am sending with my body language, my mannerisms, my very presence—messages that my students are long practiced at recognizing and responding to. As Kampf and Ohmann point out, a man teaching in women's studies "will have to be sensitive about dominating class. He will have to be open to criticism. . . . He'll have to learn when to be quiet and when to disappear. These are all lessons worth learning."[11]

Do I succeed if one of my students comes to believe that patriarchy must be challenged because I say it should? Obviously not. Do I succeed if I make myself so innocuous in the classroom that my students have no respect for me at all? Again, obviously not. I can maintain a balance between these extremes only by subverting my position as male authority figure through the use of feminist pedagogy while asserting my position as teacher, again using feminist pedagogical strategies. I cannot (and should not) shed the evaluative and mentoring authority granted me by my role as a teacher. However, by deflecting the flow of power in the classroom away from me and back to my students so that it flows among all of us in a more or less egalitarian manner, I am able to present myself as a teacher who respects my students' abilities, knowledge, and experiences as well as their lack thereof. This more horizontal power dynamic supports the creation of a community of learners in the classroom who view me as a more knowledgeable member who can be looked to for guidance and leadership rather than as the authority figure from whom the setting and interpretation of rules are expected.

To create such a community, a teacher needs to understand that students are active agents in their own learning processes and to promote an environment that supports this perception among all members. This requires that the teacher agree not to exercise all of

her/his power and to allow the students to explore and experiment
with their own senses of identity—their own subject positions. There
will always be a certain degree of indoctrination that occurs in a
classroom, especially a women's studies classroom, but if we allow
students to contribute to the process, then we can involve them in
their own learning.

NOTES

1. Susan Heald, "Pianos to Pedagogy: Pursuing the Educational Subject,"
in *Unsettling Relations: The University as a Site of Feminist Struggles*, ed. H.
Bannerji et al. (Boston: South End Press, 1991), 129–49.

2. B. L. Goebel and V. M. Cashen, "Age, Sex, and Attractiveness as Factors
in Student Ratings of Teachers: A Developmental Study," *Journal of Educational
Psychology* 71 (1979): 646–53.

3. K. J. Martin and L. R. Smith, "Effect of Teacher Age and Gender on
Student Perceptions," ERIC Document 347162.

4. Paulo Freire, *Pedagogy of the Oppressed* (New York: Knopf, 1970).

5. Heald, 134–35.

6. Heald, 147.

7. John Schilb, "Men's Studies and Women's Studies," *Change*, April 1982,
38–41.

8. bell hooks, *Talking Back: Thinking Feminist, Thinking Black* (Boston: South
End Press, 1989).

9. Nancy Buffington, "When Teachers Aren't Nice: bell hooks and Feminist Pedagogy" (paper presented at the annual meeting of the Conference
on College Composition and Communication, San Diego, March 31–April 3,
1993).

10. Magda Gere Lewis, *Without a Word: Teaching beyond Women's Silence*
(New York: Routledge, 1993).

11. Louis Kampf and Dick Ohmann, "Men in Women's Studies," in *Against
the Tide: Pro-Feminist Men in the United States, 1776–1990*, ed. M. Kimmler and
T. Mosmiller (Boston: Beacon Press, 1992), 389–93.

BIBLIOGRAPHY

Buffington, Nancy. "When Teachers Aren't Nice: bell hooks and Feminist
    Pedagogy." Paper presented at the annual meeting of the Conference on

College Composition and Communication, San Diego, March 31–April 3, 1993.

Freire, Paulo. *Pedagogy of the Oppressed.* New York: Knopf, 1970.

Goebel, B. L., and V. M. Cashen. "Age, Sex, and Attractiveness as Factors in Student Ratings of Teachers: A Developmental Study." *Journal of Educational Psychology* 71 (1979): 646–53.

Gore, Jennifer. *The Struggle for Pedagogies: Critical and Feminist Discourses as Regimes of Truth.* New York: Routledge, 1994.

Heald, Susan. "Pianos to Pedagogy: Pursuing the Educational Subject." In *Unsettling Relations: The University as a Site of Feminist Struggles,* ed. H. Bannerji et al., 129–49. Boston: South End Press, 1991.

hooks, bell. *Talking Back: Thinking Feminist, Thinking Black.* Boston: South End Press, 1989.

Kampf, Louis, and Dick Ohmann. "Men in Women's Studies." In *Against the Tide: Pro-Feminist Men in the United States, 1776–1990,* ed. M. Kimmler and T. Mosmiller, 389–93. Boston: Beacon Press, 1992.

Lewis, Magda Gere. *Without a Word: Teaching beyond Women's Silence.* New York: Routledge, 1993.

Martin, K. J., and L. R. Smith. "Effect of Teacher Age and Gender on Student Perceptions." ERIC Document 347162. 1990.

Schilb, John. "Men's Studies and Women's Studies." *Change,* April 1982, 38–41.

———. "Pedagogy of the Oppressors?" In *Gendered Subjects: The Dynamics of Feminist Teaching,* ed. M. Culley and C. Portuges, 253–64. Boston: Routledge and Kegan Paul, 1985.

IV

The Texts and Contexts of Teaching What You're Not

13

Teaching in the Multiracial Classroom: Reconsidering "Benito Cereno"

ROBERT S. LEVINE

Available in all the major anthologies of American literature, Melville's novella "Benito Cereno" (1855) has emerged as one of the most widely read and taught of his works. In large part, the relatively recent popularity of the text has to do with the fact that critics have come to recognize, over the past thirty years or so, that the novella powerfully and problematically addresses the politics of slavery and race in antebellum America; arguably, it is *the* pre–Civil War antislavery masterpiece. What I want to do here is discuss some of the problems I have encountered in teaching the novella, and to use this discussion as a way of addressing the debate on multiculturalism and the politics of identity. It needs to be emphasized that virtually every attack on multiculturalism, or on teachers who supposedly teach "political correctness," works with synchronic models. These polemicists have little to say about how the vast majority of college professors have wrestled, and will continue to wrestle, with pedagogical issues over time. Thus Dinesh D'Souza, the best-known of these polemicists, in his chapter "Teaching Race and Gender" in *Illiberal Education*, simply calls attention, through the use of anecdotal examples, to what seem to be particularly egregious instances of misguided teaching by a group of unreflective, unselfconscious professors. (An emphasis on the synchronic is evident as well in attacks on multiculturalism in

Paul Berman's *Debating P.C.*, Roger Kimball's *Tenured Radicals*, and Richard Bernstein's *Dictatorship of Virtue*.) All D'Souza's anecdotes (many of which are lifted from the *Wall Street Journal*) are drawn from a very short period of time, and all present a cartoonish picture of "representative" professors who, presumably for the rest of their careers, have locked themselves into a militant 1960s radical authoritarianism, a new form of McCarthyism from the Left.[1]

In this essay I want to complicate such a perspective through a diachronic account of one professor's teaching practices, focusing on my shifting responses to teaching (and reading) "Benito Cereno" over a nearly twenty-year period. By locating my discussion of multiculturalism in the specific context of my attempts to make sense of and teach Melville's novella, I hope to provide a more concrete account of the implications of the curricular, pedagogical, and demographic changes that the academy has witnessed over the past two decades. The sorts of classroom negotiations I will be describing, though based on my personal struggles with a recalcitrant text (and students), are, I believe, much more truly representative of how the vast majority of the professoriate operates from day to day, from year to year, than the crowd-pleasing tales dished up by the monoculturalist polemicists.

Not all that long ago, a mad, word-drunken reading and rereading of Melville's *Moby-Dick* propelled me to apply to graduate school with the hope of teaching Melville's masterpiece to similarly intoxicated souls. But the Melville text that came to obsess and haunt me— as a graduate student, critic, and teacher—was the more spartan and austere "Benito Cereno." Looking back now on this change in energies and sympathies, I can understand how, as an undergraduate, Melville's novella of a slave revolt had had no great impact on my literary (or political) consciousness. I had read the novella only once, as a brief and exotic excursion away from the more spectacular novels of Stendhal, Dickens, Tolstoy, and others, in an honors seminar called

Colloquium on the History, Language, Literature and Philosophy of the Nineteenth and Twentieth Centuries, taught by two of Columbia University's very best literature professors to a group of twelve students who knew, with that special self-regard of the "honors" undergraduate, that we were among Columbia's best and brightest. As I recall the thirty-and-some-odd-minute segment of the class devoted to "Benito Cereno," before we turned to the weightier matters of Conrad's *Lord Jim,* slavery was barely mentioned during the discussion— a discussion that was, as always, boisterously propelled by an unrestrained imbibing of hearty burgundy. Instead, we all agreed—we happy white males who, about ten minutes into our evening seminar, would pass through the gates of what Melville in 1855 called "the paradise of bachelors"—that in "Benito Cereno," Melville, metaphysical as ever, was using black and white symbolism to confront the reader with a universal truth: the reality of evil in the world. Certain of our interpretation, as we were certain of all our interpretations that year, we moved on to address Conrad's universal/metaphysical vision. The year was 1973, more than thirty years after F. O. Matthiessen had offered a similarly allegorical interpretation of "Benito Cereno" and about ten years after serious revisionist work on the novella had begun.[2]

It wasn't until graduate school that I began my own revisionary reconsideration of the novella, and I connect that reconsideration to a very central discovery that I made during my graduate years (a discovery lots of graduate students raised on the New Criticism and various other formalisms were making at that time): the historicity of literary texts. Soon after my late 1970s "fall" into history came my early 1980s discovery of the historicity—or the cultural embeddedness—of the teaching of literature. That discovery, or second fall, generated a series of reconsiderations of "Benito Cereno" as a classroom text—reconsiderations that continue to make teaching "Benito Cereno" one of the most difficult, but in many ways one of the most satisfying, things I do as a professor of American literature.

Like many critics of "Benito Cereno," I read Melville's novella as an antislavery narrative that, by presenting us with the limited perceptions of a sea captain in the midst of a slave revolt, attempts to implicate its readers in the racist worldview of Delano only to expose the mendacity, immorality, and dangers of that worldview. And I'd go one step further to suggest that the novella, through its implicating narrative strategies, possesses transhistorical power as a work of cultural criticism in the way it challenges us to consider our own implication in dominant modes of cultural power.[3] The text's ability to implicate readers in Delano's blindness and thus to remind us of our own analogous forms of complicitous blindness is what I try to get across in the classroom (in addition to the novella's more explicit antiracist and antislavery themes).

But in light of recent debates on multiculturalism and the politics of identity, we might ask, "Who is us?" Does such a unified body of readers exist? Aren't there risks in this sort of consensual interpretation, particularly when applied to a novella that seems to expose Delano's "consensus" reading of the rebellious slaves as a form of cultural blindness? As I've found myself teaching the novella to an increasingly diverse student population, these large questions have necessarily complicated my teaching, and understanding, of Melville's text.

When I first taught the novella at Stanford University, however, not many "problems" arose with my particular reading of "Benito Cereno," at least none that I could see. My students, for the most part economically well off, and all white, were initially fooled by the text (most were unaware that Delano was in the midst of a slave revolt), were then surprised by the revelation of the plot, and then were "educated" by the ironies newly detected in their rereading of the novella. Good students that they were, they readily accepted their instructor's transhistorical reading of the novella, which, in the late 1970s, made the very Palo Alto point that just as Delano was blind to slavery's evil and the blacks' humanity, so these elite white liberals (and students at Stanford were mostly liberal in those days) were blind to the ways their happy idyll at Stanford depended on the existence of the black ghetto in East Palo Alto, conveniently out of sight and mind on the other side of Route 101. It was just the sort of feel-good consciousness-raising about inequality that we all needed before our late afternoon swim or tennis game.

Things became less easy at the University of Maryland. For one, there were now African American students in my classroom; for another, many of my students, particularly the white students, were more ignorant of the history of slavery than my Stanford students; and for another yet, some of my students, white and black, were working-class people who worked twenty to thirty hours a week while taking a full load of courses. What this meant in practical terms was the following: First, given that African American readers had entered into the equation, there was a greater variety of response in the first-time readings of "Benito Cereno" (blacks more than whites were able to detect the slaves' conspiracy early on). Second, given that many of the white students were less subtle readers than my Stanford students, they showed a greater willingness to accept Delano's (and the narrator's) racist views, and thus I faced greater difficulties in convincing students of Melville's ironic, educative, and implicating purposes. Third, because some of the students, black and white, could legitimately claim to be at the lower end of the socioeconomic spectrum, I was perhaps irresponsibly self-righteous in trying to teach these students about their implication in the dominant power structure. Let me now be more specific about these various problems, conflating five years of problems into a paragraph—one that will suggest greater disarray than there actually was (I think)—before I describe my efforts to address these problems.

Generally, I like to teach the novella over two classes, cutting off the reading and discussion just before that point in the novella when Babo and his fellow Africans are explicitly revealed as rebels and conspirators. In this way I can foreground interpretive issues: What

is going on aboard the *San Dominick?* To what extent should we trust
Delano's perceptions of the blacks and Spanish? What are we to make
of the narrator? Because we've not yet read to the point of revelation,
nothing can really be said about the novella with any certainty. And
so most students will confess to being relatively confused about who
is in power, or about what's going on, say, with Atufal's ritual refusal
of apology, or, most crucially, about the role of the narrator in the
novella—an especially pivotal problem in that the narrator seems
regularly to espouse racist generalizations about blacks, telling us, for
example, that they're natural servants, perpetually happy, and dog-
like. Interestingly, depressingly, while teaching the novella at Maryland I've had numerous white students voice their agreement, during
this first class, with the basic tenor of the narrator's racist sentiments,
and I've even had some white students eager to don the cap of "authority" to tell us about blacks' relative happiness as slaves. I have to
confess that on occasion, when confronted with such remarks, I solic-
ited the responses of the African American students with the hopes
that they would counter such ignorance, which, of course, only made
matters worse: now the black students in the class, in addition to
trying to learn something about American literature and get a decent
grade, were charged as well with combating racism among Maryland's undergraduates. Some were willing to do this work for me;
others, in the spirit of Babo, preferred to adopt an angry silence. (Or,
after class, in my office, would angrily ask why I was teaching such
a racist text, to which I could only feebly respond, "Wait until you
finish reading the novella before condemning me and Melville.")
What made things especially difficult for the African American students, of course, was that they were a decided minority in the classroom (usually two or three students in a class of thirty). Already self-
conscious about their minority status, they must have been pained to
see that their suspicions of white ignorance of, and even hostility toward, blacks were in some ways justified. And it must then have
been additionally infuriating for them to return to class on the second

day, when we could talk more knowledgeably about Melville's narrative tactics and racial politics, to learn from their Delano-like professor about their complicitous blindness to cultural forms of power.

Arguably, though, I was not so Delano-like, in that I did have a
sense that there was something wrong with the way I was teaching
the novella. Particularly troubling to me was the way I was letting
the novella, or my way of teaching it, reproduce in the classroom
precisely the kinds of racial divisions that the novella was critically
representing and (I quixotically continue to believe) prompting its
readers to overcome. And so in the late 1980s, in the hope of defusing
the potential for racial confrontation in the classroom, I began to reconsider my pedagogical strategies. First, I asked students to read the
novella in its entirety, with the hope that they would see on their
own that Melville's seemingly racist narrator is in fact an ironic narrator who deviously presents Delano's racist perspective as "objective"
truth in order to expose its limitations. To some extent this was a
helpful solution, though far too many students, ill equipped to detect
irony, continued to buy into the narrator's racism, and, more specifically, the authority of the proslavery Spanish deposition, which, after
all, the narrator seemingly presents as the key to the "true history"
of what happened aboard the *San Dominick*.[4] So I tried another tack:
Like the Spanish authorities with regard to Babo, I silenced my students, choosing one semester simply to lecture on the novella—to tell
them what it was all about, how it implicated them, how it educated
them, and so on in an exercise of the worst sort of imperialistic
reader-response criticism.

Not surprisingly, problems remained, for I had not yet come to
terms with the fact that central to my teaching (and reading) of the
novella was an assumption, based on the historical fact of the novella's 1855 publication in *Putnam's,* that Melville's reader was (and always would be) a complicitous, albeit educable, white. To cling to
this assumption while at the same time arguing (as I did in the classroom and in my scholarship) for the transhistorical power of the no-

vella inevitably meant that I would have to elide the politics of identity from a text that, in many respects, is *about* the politics of identity.
In short, my way of reading, dependent on coming to terms with
"blindness" to a black conspiracy without coming to terms with
blindness to issues of racial identity, helped perpetuate the very
blindness that the novella seeks to critique and expose.

These thoughts, I like to think, were in the back of my mind when
I participated, during the summer of 1990, in a University of Maryland faculty seminar, The Curriculum Transformation Project: Thinking about Women. Taught by Professor Deborah Rosenfelt, chair of
women's studies, to approximately fifteen faculty from different departments throughout the university, the seminar focused on the
ways feminist criticism in various disciplinary fields could help us
reconceive our syllabi, our approach to material, our pedagogical
styles, and our critical writing.[5] While I went into the seminar with
the intention of reading as much as I could by and about nineteenth-
century American women writers, I found that "Benito Cereno" remained on my mind as the text I most wanted to learn how to teach
better. As the seminar proceeded, and broadened to consider related
issues of race and class, I became convinced that one of the reasons
"Benito Cereno" posed such a pedagogical problem in my courses
was that it was bearing too much weight as a "representative" text—
which is to say that I was using the novella not only to introduce
students to Melville but also to represent the black experience under
slavery. Leaving aside the large question of whether a white writer
can adequately represent slavery (like Frederick Douglass I think she
can),[6] I came to realize during my summer in the faculty seminar that
my reading list failed to do justice to Melville's knowledge of, indeed
his indebtedness to, African American representations of slavery.
Whatever the specific publishing circumstances of "Benito Cereno,"
the novella came into being and eventually circulated in a complex
discursive field of antislavery writings by whites and blacks alike,
and inevitably would have been interpreted in different ways by dif-

ferent readers. Indeed, it could be argued that the very multiplicity of interpretations the novella was capable of generating was what made it such a powerful and discomfiting text. Some of that discomfiting power, I sensed, could be restored through curricular revision that brought African American texts into my classroom.

Now, I don't want to portray myself as utterly naive, in the summer of 1990, on the issue of canon revision—like many I had read Paul Lauter's essays, Jane Tompkins, the syllabi in *Reconstructing American Literature*, the prospectus of *The Heath Anthology of American Literature*, among other things, and over the years I had added to my reading lists writers like Catharine Sedgwick, Fanny Fern, and of course Frederick Douglass.[7] Still, vis-à-vis "Benito Cereno," much more, I realized, could be done: From the new *Heath Anthology* I could add David Walker's *Appeal to the Colored Citizens of the World* (1829) and Henry Highland Garnet's *Address to the Slaves of the United States* (1843)—two texts published prior to "Benito Cereno," and texts that, more than Douglass's *Narrative*, advocate violent resistance to slavery and represent black rage at enslavers. I could also add T. W. Higginson's account of the Nat Turner rebellion (1861) in order to help students see that not every white writer was paranoid about black revolt; and I could add selections from Harriet Wilson's *Our Nig* (1859) and Harriet Jacobs's *Incidents in the Life of a Slave Girl* (1861), which, at the very least, would work to undermine Delano's stereotypical idealization of black women slaves as "unsophisticated."[8] And so in the fall of 1990 I added these texts to my reading list, and I sensed then, as I continue to sense, a marked improvement in my teaching of "Benito Cereno." Reading these texts in conjunction with "Benito Cereno," students find it much more difficult to accept uncritically the narrator's paternalistic dismissals of the possibility of black intelligence or rage, and they have a speedier and more genuinely sympathetic responsiveness to Babo's artful plottings. Armed with their knowledge of black texts and perspectives, students can also more authoritatively resist or question Melville's representa-

tional strategies, and they feel more confident in resisting and questioning my own admittedly liberal reading of the text. No longer can
white students speak so knowingly of the "benign" nature of slavery;
and no longer must black students feel that the burden is on them to
rebut such ignorance. And of course an added benefit of such curricular revision is that these newly added texts are interesting in and of
themselves, and have helped us address different sorts of issues than
those raised by "Benito Cereno" about the practice and representation
of slavery in America.

Convinced, therefore, that I had made some major strides in reconsidering my teaching of "Benito Cereno," in large part because of my
work in the Curriculum Transformation Project, I was eager to speak
as part of a panel on Teaching about Inequality that Professor Rosenfelt arranged at the University of Maryland. I could offer a glorious
presentation, I thought, on how I had come to "see" what had gone
wrong with my teaching of "Benito Cereno," and I could talk, again
quite gloriously, about how I had skillfully addressed the problem.
However, at our planning session I made a startling discovery that
reminded me once again of my Delano-like perceptual blindnesses:
one of the two African American faculty who had participated in the
summer seminar confessed at this meeting that she had come very
close to dropping out of the seminar, in part because of her perception
of my racial insensitivity. What had happened to generate her response was this: a dean had visited the seminar to talk about the need
for faculty to develop a greater sensitivity to multicultural issues in
the classroom. She showed us a short film, in which a very stupid
English professor, during a class on *Uncle Tom's Cabin,* called on his
one black student to ask what an "Uncle Tom" was. The point was
obvious: the professor, assuming that all blacks would know such
things, had singled out, and thus embarrassed, a student who probably already felt highly uncomfortable with the subject matter. At the
end of the film I launched into a tirade on how exaggerated such a
depiction was, that there was no one on our faculty that obtuse, and

so on. What I hadn't considered at the time was just how similar were my own actions, when teaching "Benito Cereno," of calling on the one or two black students in my class to "refute" the racism of the white students, nor did I know that over the past five years black students had been complaining to people outside the English department about their perception of, and dismay at, racist moments in English classes. Significantly, this dean, against whom I and others in the seminar had so vociferously turned, had been the only African American administrator to visit our summer seminar. Of all the visiting administrators, she had probably made the most helpful presentation. What the two African American participants could see, therefore, in ways that I and many of the white participants could not, was that there was an ugly racial dynamic at work in our protestations of innocence and our subsequently mean-spirited efforts to demean the bearer of bad news. The administrator clearly had hit a nerve, which we sought to mute through intellectual browbeating. The revelation, then, at the planning seminar, of my blindness to such a dynamic took the glitter out of my proposed talk, though it convinced me, if I really needed convincing, of the continuing vitality of "Benito Cereno" as a text that speaks to the difficulty of seeing one's way past such blindness.

All of which leads me to some final remarks on "Benito Cereno," multiculturalism, and the politics of identity. While much of what I've been describing emerges out of my wrestling with the complexities of teaching "Benito Cereno" in a multiracial classroom, and my sense that this sort of wrestling must continue, it's difficult, as a teacher of "Benito Cereno," not to have some doubts about multiculturalism (or "political correctness") as a pedagogical agenda, particularly when it brings with it the smug assurances that I brought into our planning session. After all, one could argue that Captain Amasa Delano himself—blind, naive, loathsome—is a kind of multiculturalist. At the island of St. Maria off the coast of Chile in 1799, a wonderfully multicultural and multiracial setting, Delano must make sense of Spanish, Catholics, and blacks, and he proceeds to do so in ways that,

for his time (and for Melville's), could be called intellectually advanced. Like many Northern advocates of the virtues of "free labor,"
he regards the Spanish suspiciously as a slave power; like these same
"free labor" advocates, and many intelligent Protestants of the time,
he regards Roman Catholicism, hierarchical and imperialistic, as a
vestige of the past.[9] And like some of the seemingly more scientifically
advanced white thinkers of the mid-nineteenth century, he has a
"scientific" view of racial differences—hence his belief that the more
white blood a slave has, the more rebellious he or she will become.
Additionally, with his reference to the explorer John Ledyard, we
learn that Delano has been reading the new texts of African exploration, most likely Mungo Park's 1799 *Travels in the Interior Districts of
Africa* (which refers to Ledyard), in an effort, so such a 1790s "liberal"
might declare, to better understand, and so to think well of, black
people and their cultures.[10] Thus when Delano views the African slave
women with their children, he thinks of them fondly, in terms of the
"anthropological" and "empirical" discourses of the day, not as subjects to be dominated, but as models of maternal devotion: "Unsophisticated as leopardesses; loving as doves. Ah! . . . these, perhaps, are
some of the very women whom Ledyard saw in Africa, and gave such
a noble account of."[11]

Can we draw analogies between Delano's smug "multiculturalism"
of the late eighteenth century and the multiculturalism, particularly of
liberal white male professors, of the late twentieth century? Perhaps.
For I worry about how the desire to be multicultural occasionally can
tempt white professors in particular to adopt toward their minority
students a colonizing perspective disturbingly like Delano's—a perspective in which we feel too confident of our knowledge of where,
say, our African American students are coming from and what they
want out of our classes, too comfortable, in short, that we "know" the
other and thus can teach the other in predetermined ways. Such
confidence, I think, in which group identity takes precedence over
individual identity, will almost always work against good teaching.

Yet it can be difficult, in the current political context, *not* to view individuals in relation to a group identity. I will cite one final personal example. Last year, in a course on Melville, I quickly took note of the fact that there was one African American student in the class; I decided that because he was the only African American student he must feel marginal and uncomfortable. When, in discussing *Typee,* I suggested that Melville's presentation of the French colonization of the Marquesas Islands could be read as an antislavery allegory, I happily concluded that, in powerful ways, I had made the text relevant for the student most likely (I somehow had decided) to find it irrelevant. About halfway through the class, this particular student raised his hand and demanded to know why I had "ruined" the text for him by offering such a predictably "leftist" reading of such an enjoyable and escapist work. His comment, of course, was welcome and it helped initiate a vigorous discussion of Melville's politics in *Typee;* but unbeknownst to my students I was thinking, mortified and ashamed, "Benito Cereno."

Bad identity politics of this sort are not just something that professors do to students. When my black students would complain to me about my choice of teaching what they initially regarded as a racist text, I could sense, among some, that what added to their frustration was their belief that it is ultimately the case that white teachers teach white texts that reflect a "white" point of view. When I added African American texts to my reading list, I sensed additionally that some of my black students associated the white-authored texts (and characters like Delano and Cereno) with me and the black-authored texts with themselves. This was not an entirely unhealthy development, for it helped empower students who might otherwise have remained silent and apathetic. Yet assumptions about the kinship among, say, white authors and white professors and students, or black authors and black professors and students, are based on reified notions of racial identity that pay scant attention to the varied historical experiences of groups and individuals.[12] Recently, in an effort to personalize my reading of the text, and to encourage my black students in particular not to link me historically with Melville's white racists, I've spoken of my family's nineteenth-century history as victims of Russian pogroms. My autobiographical remarks were not meant to equate my family's history under anti-Semitic rule with the family histories of African Americans under slavery. But to float the (admittedly) false analogy is to disrupt totalized assumptions about the persistence of a monolithic whiteness from Melville's time to the present, and to suggest that there is nothing about my whiteness that ineluctably makes "Benito Cereno" *my* text. When I am teaching "Benito Cereno," as when I'm teaching Stowe's *Uncle Tom's Cabin* or Douglass's *Narrative*, I am teaching what I am not. Unless we begin to assign only our own critical writings, literature professors will always be teaching what we are not. Our job is to teach the other (texts) to the other (our students) and in doing so, as Michael Bérubé and Cary Nelson have recently (and bravely) pointed out, "we cannot do otherwise than to speak for others."[13] This essay on reconsidering "Benito Cereno" is an effort to show how one professor has attempted to do just that without presuming to be the other.

Had the monoculturalist polemicists attended any *one* of my classes on Melville over the past ten years, they surely would have had no problem in pointing out, for those who take pleasure in such things, a number of intellectually limited or even ludicrous moments in my teaching. Because they are so unwilling to grant to professors who displease them a self-critical and evolving consciousness about their pedagogical practices, I would imagine that in pointing out these moments they would have presumed, as Kimball and Bernstein seem to presume when describing such moments in their books, that my teaching methods simply reflect the unreflected-upon leftist agenda of a pitiable dupe of current academic fashion. Moreover, I have no doubt that, were monoculturalist polemicists to stumble across this essay, they would type it as just another breast-beating confession of guilt by someone out to win his liberal spurs. Nevertheless, I will continue to worry over the misprisions and gropings so central to my pedagogical experiences, for I remain convinced that the kinds of issues, problems, and questions I've been discussing are *enabled* by multicultural and multiracial approaches to literary study and pedagogical practice, and provide teachers and students with a more capacious knowledge of the cultural engagements and work of literary texts. (I am by no means calling for a return to the "certainties" of my undergraduate reading experiences.) As long as the revisionary multicultural project can help us ask interesting and troubling questions, and can help us be aware of the challenges facing us when teaching different texts in different classroom settings, it's a project worth pursuing and taking seriously. And though I'm not yet convinced of the direct causal influence of what we do in the classroom on what goes on in the world outside the classroom, if multiculturalism can help us make America into a better nation where there's less inequality, less domination, less blindness, then so much the better.

NOTES

A somewhat different version of this essay, "Teaching in the Multicultural Classroom: Reconsidering Melville's 'Benito Cereno,'" first appeared in *MELUS* 19 (spring 1994): 111–20. My thanks to the editors for permission to reprint. I first presented some of the material in the essay at the 1991 meeting of the Modern Language Association in San Francisco. I am grateful to Professor Deborah Rosenfelt for inviting me to speak on her panel on Curriculum Transformation Projects and for her helpful comments on the paper.

1. See Dinesh D'Souza, *Illiberal Education: The Politics of Race and Sex on Campus* (New York: Free Press, 1991), esp. 194–228. And see also Paul Berman, ed., *Debating P.C.: The Controversy over Political Correctness in the Classroom* (New York: Dell, 1992); Roger Kimball, *Tenured Radicals: How Politics Has Corrupted Our Higher Education* (New York: Harper and Row, 1990); and Richard Bernstein, *Dictatorship of Virtue: Multiculturalism, and the Battle for America's Future* (New York: Random House, 1994).

2. See, for example, Sidney Kaplan, "Herman Melville and the American National Sin: The Meaning of *Benito Cereno*," *Journal of Negro History* 41 (October 1956): 311–38; 42 (January 1957): 11–37; H. Bruce Franklin, *The Wake of the*

Gods: Melville's Mythology (Stanford: Stanford University Press, 1963); and Robert Lowell, *"Benito Cereno"* (1964), in *The Old Glory* (New York: Farrar, Strauss, and Giroux, 1968).

3. For a fuller contextualization of this position, see Robert S. Levine, *Conspiracy and Romance: Studies in Brockden Brown, Cooper, Hawthorne, and Melville* (New York: Cambridge University Press, 1989), 165–230.

4. Herman Melville, "Benito Cereno" (1855), in *Billy Budd, Sailor and Other Stories* (New York: Penguin Books, 1970), 288.

5. For a searching discussion of curriculum transformation projects, see Sharon Groves, "A Question of Change," *Arizona Quarterly* 45 (autumn 1989): 97–109.

6. During the 1850s Frederick Douglass defended Harriet Beecher Stowe from attacks by Martin Delany, who thought a white writer could not properly represent the experience of slaves. See Robert S. Levine, "*Uncle Tom's Cabin* in *Frederick Douglass' Paper*: An Analysis of Reception," *American Literature* 64 (March 1992): 71–93.

7. See Paul Lauter, *Canons and Contexts* (New York: Oxford University Press, 1991); Paul Lauter, ed., *Reconstructing American Literature: Courses, Syllabi, Issues* (Old Westbury, NY: Feminist Press, 1983); Paul Lauter et al., eds., *The Heath Anthology of American Literature* (Lexington, MA: D. C. Heath, 1990); and Jane Tompkins, *Sensational Designs: The Cultural Work of American Fiction, 1790–1860* (New York: Oxford University Press, 1985).

8. Melville, "Benito Cereno," 251.

9. For excellent discussions of free labor ideology and rhetoric in the antebellum North, see Eric Foner, *Free Soil, Free Labor, Free Men: The Ideology of the Republican Party before the Civil War* (New York: Oxford University Press, 1970); and David Brion Davis, *The Slave Power Conspiracy and the Paranoid Style: Images of Conspiracy in the Slavery Controversy* (Baton Rouge: Louisiana State University Press, 1969).

10. Of course from our 1990s perspective it's not too difficult to see that Northern liberals like Delano read Mungo Park and others in order to reaffirm their sense of cultural superiority and to justify practices of domination. But the disjunction between Delano's idealizing beliefs and his participation in the social practices of the dominant culture is precisely what Melville wants to convey about self-satisfied white liberal New Englanders, whether they be sea captains of the 1790s, merchants of the 1850s, or even (I'd go so far to say) abolitionists who displayed a paternalistic "love" of black people. On the "scientific" racism of the time, see William Stanton, *The Leopard's Spots: Scientific Attitudes towards Race in America* (Chicago: University of Chicago Press, 1960). For a discussion of racism among antebellum abolitionists, see Leon F.

Litwack, *North of Slavery: The Negro in the Free States, 1790–1860* (Chicago: University of Chicago Press, 1961), esp. 214–46.

11. Melville, "Benito Cereno," 251.

12. Not everyone (perhaps no one) has a "pure" racial identity. As Carla Peterson has argued, it might be more productive to focus on the ways texts, and the reading of texts, can help us construct and deconstruct "ethnic/racial boundaries." "*Borderlands* in the Classroom," *American Quarterly* 45 (June 1993): 298. In my view, no text more profoundly involves, or implicates, the reader in this process than "Benito Cereno."

13. Michael Bérubé and Cary Nelson, eds., *Higher Education Under Fire: Politics, Economics, and the Crisis of the Humanities* (New York: Routledge, 1995), 306.

BIBLIOGRAPHY

Berman, Paul, ed. *Debating P.C.: The Controversy over Political Correctness in the Classroom.* New York: Dell, 1992.

Bernstein, Richard. *Dictatorship of Virtue: Multiculturalism, and the Battle for America's Future.* New York: Random House, 1994.

Bérubé, Michael, and Cary Nelson, eds. *Higher Education under Fire: Politics, Economics, and the Crisis of the Humanities.* New York: Routledge, 1995.

Davis, David Brion. *The Slave Power Conspiracy and the Paranoid Style: Images of Conspiracy in the Slavery Controversy.* Baton Rouge: Louisiana State University Press, 1969.

D'Souza, Dinesh. *Illiberal Education: The Politics of Race and Sex on Campus.* New York: Free Press, 1991.

Foner, Eric. *Free Soil, Free Labor, Free Men: The Ideology of the Republican Party before the Civil War.* New York: Oxford University Press, 1970.

Franklin, H. Bruce. *The Wake of the Gods: Melville's Mythology.* Stanford: Stanford University Press, 1963.

Groves, Sharon. "A Question of Change." *Arizona Quarterly* 45 (autumn 1989): 97–109.

Kaplan, Sidney, "Herman Melville and the American National Sin: The Meaning of *Benito Cereno.*" *Journal of Negro History* 41 (October 1956): 311–38; 42 (January 1957): 11–37.

Kimball, Roger. *Tenured Radicals: How Politics Has Corrupted Our Higher Education.* New York: Harper and Row, 1990.

Lauter, Paul. *Canons and Contexts.* New York: Oxford University Press, 1991.

———, ed. *Reconstructing American Literature: Courses, Syllabi, Issues.* Old Westbury, NY: Feminist Press, 1983.

Lauter, Paul, et al., eds., *The Heath Anthology of American Literature*. Lexington, MA: D. C. Heath, 1990.

Levine, Robert S. *Conspiracy and Romance: Studies in Brockden Brown, Cooper, Hawthorne, and Melville*. New York: Cambridge University Press, 1989.

———."Teaching in the Multiracial Classroom: Reconsidering Melville's 'Benito Cereno.' " *MELUS* 19 (spring 1994): 111–20.

———. "*Uncle Tom's Cabin* in *Frederick Douglass' Paper*: An Analysis of Reception." *American Literature* 64 (March 1992): 71–93.

Litwack, Leon F. *North of Slavery: The Negro in the Free States, 1790–1860*. Chicago: University of Chicago Press, 1961.

Lowell, Robert. "*Benito Cereno*." In *The Old Glory*. New York: Farrar, Strauss, and Giroux, 1968.

Matthiessen, F. O. *American Renaissance: Art and Expression in the Age of Emerson and Whitman*. 1941. Reprint, New York: Oxford University Press, 1974.

Melville, Herman. "Benito Cereno." In *Billy Budd, Sailor and Other Stories*. New York: Penguin Books, 1970.

Peterson, Carla. "*Borderlands* in the Classroom." *American Quarterly* 45 (June 1993): 295–300.

Stanton, William. *The Leopard's Spots: Scientific Attitudes towards Race in America*. Chicago: University of Chicago Press, 1960.

Tompkins, Jane. *Sensational Designs: The Cultural Work of American Fiction, 1790–1860*. New York: Oxford University Press, 1985.

14

"Young Man, Tell Our Stories of How We Made It Over": Beyond the Politics of Identity

GARY L. LEMONS

To Be Black, Male, and Feminist: *Teaching What I Am*

Speaking about the power of the erotic in the lives of women, Audre Lorde has said,

> As women, we have come to distrust that power which rises from our deepest and nonrational knowledge. We have been warned against it all our lives by the male world, which values this depth of feeling enough to keep women around in order to exercise it in the service of men, but which fears this same depth too much to examine the possibilities of it within themselves. (1984, 53–54)

Reflecting on the fear of men who resist movement into the space of "nonrational knowledge" and the dehumanization of women such fear exacts, I have moved to resist the power of the "male world." I have moved to transgress boundaries of patriarchy, manhood, and masculinity to assert a liberatory pedagogical practice that affirms, honors, and respects the mind, body, and soul.

As a black male professor of literature claiming feminism as the primary location from which to perform a pedagogical practice in resistance to racism, sexism, classism, and homophobia, I construct a form of identity politics that moves beyond unitary, monolithic, heterosexist, nationalist, and essentialized race/gender boundaries of who I am, should be, ought to be, might be, can or cannot be in the classroom. My pedagogy is rooted in risk-taking; it merges the "personal" and the "political" to produce an antiracist/feminist approach to teaching literature. My goal is for students to come to consciousness about the interrelated ways racism and sexism affect the gendered, racialized, classed, and sexualized status of their bodies in white supremacist, capitalist, patriarchal culture. This essay examines the methodological imperatives that define, determine, and guide what I represent as a black male feminist approach to teaching African American literary texts. I pose for consideration the notion that education that compels our students to critical consciousness should be liberatory for students as well as teachers.

Articulating a liberatory pedagogy often means putting forth teaching strategies that challenge the "safe" space of professorial authority, move us to rethink our academic training as "field experts," and press us to confront the multicultural, racial, sexual, and ethnic identities of our students. These teaching strategies compel us to transgress disciplinary boundaries, critical perspectives, and the narrow ideology of identity politics that would have us teach only what we "appear" to be.

Teaching beyond identity politics in the classroom necessarily implies border crossing, transgressing notions of fixed categories, constructing transformative pedagogies that resist, work against essentializing representation. In *Teaching to Transgress: Education as the Practice of Freedom*, bell hooks maintains that a liberatory pedagogy is freeing for student and teacher, that education should be about the practice of freedom where

> Progressive professors working to transform the curriculum so that it does not reflect biases or reinforce systems of domination are most often individuals willing to take risks that engaged pedagogy requires and to make their teaching practices sites of resistance. (1994, 21)

As a professor committed to education as a liberatory experience, I interpret hooks to mean that narrow, shortsighted, essentialist ideas of teachers teaching only what they "are" inhibits the learning process and undermines education's humanizing power.

As a feminist professor who is by gender categorization "male" and by racial classification "black," I teach undergraduate and graduate courses ranging from literature to cultural studies in which the organizing perspective is situated within a feminist framework. Clearly, from a standpoint that represents gender/race problematics around the idea of a (black) man teaching feminism, considering the popular misconception that black men are antifeminist, I represent a position that goes against the gender/race script regarding "men in feminism." Counter to popular cultural and black nationalist beliefs, feminism is (1) not for "women only," (2) not the ideological property of white middle-class women, and (3) not man-hating or emasculatory.

Teaching students how to interrogate and critically oppose the capitalist, racist, sexist exploitation of women as a black/male/feminist is not about "teaching what I'm not," *but about teaching what I am*—an advocate of a feminist movement in which women *and men* united across race, class, and sexual preference struggle to end sexual oppression. As a black/male/feminist professor, I am most inclined to think about personal and political intersections, particularly about how to theorize black men's relation to feminism while working a critique of patriarchy and sexual oppression.

(Re)theorizing (Black) Men in Feminism: Toward a Transformative Pedagogical Practice

Exploring pedagogical formulations I have enacted around feminism, blackness, gender, and sexuality, this essay maps the evolution of my feminist consciousness as a "risky" process, laying bare my thoughts on what I choose to call the conundrums of "black/male/feminist

positionality." This represents a standpoint fraught with contradiction, in which the notion of "feminist men" teaching in the academy
raises issues of male exploitation, appropriation, and colonization of
feminism. Can male feminist positionality work as a radically transgressive pedagogical location in which men teach to empower
women *and men* to critically oppose sexism and patriarchy without
replicating patriarchal hegemony in women's liberation struggle? In
Men in Feminism, Stephen Heath addresses this question in his essay
"Male Feminism." He argues that

> Men's relation to feminism is an impossible one. This is not said sadly
> nor angrily (though sadness and anger are both known and common
> reactions) but politically. Men have a necessary relation to feminism—
> the point after all is that it should change them too, that it involves
> learning new ways of being women *and men* against and as an end to
> the reality of women's oppression—and that relation is also necessarily
> one of a certain exclusion—the point after all is that this is a matter for
> women, that it is their voices and actions that must determine the
> change and redefinition. Their voices and actions, not ours: no matter
> how "sincere," "sympathetic" or whatever, we are always also in a male
> position which brings with it all the implications of domination and
> appropriation, everything precisely that is being challenged, that has to
> be altered. (1987, 1)

Without question, feminist movement against patriarchal and sexist
domination must be woman-directed; women must necessarily stand
in subject relation to the struggle against sexual oppression, of which
men are the perpetrators. While Heath says that men cannot relate to
feminism politically, he admits that "men have a necessary relation to
feminism" because they are the object of transformation. Both men
and women (but men especially) must through feminist liberation
reconstruct ways of knowing and relating to each other unencum-
bered by male supremacy. On this point I certainly agree. However,
the suggestion that feminist strategizing to end sexist oppression is
one of "certain [male] exclusion . . . a matter for women" brands
feminism as a separatist ideology that subscribes to *women only* think-

ing. Not only is this idea sexist, it promotes a form of essentialist thought that fails to hold men accountable toward the eradication of sexual domination. Women cannot end sexism without men in comradeship with them in feminist movement. Calling for the inclusion of "men in feminism," bell hooks maintains that the struggle against sexist oppression will be most successfully fought when men undergo feminist transformation, when they are challenged by women to understand that the oppression of women is a form of self-oppression:

> Women can no longer allow feminism to be another arena for the continued expression of antagonism between the sexes. The time has come for women active in feminist movement to develop new strategies for including men in the struggle against sexism. . . . As long as [poor or working-class men are] attacking women and not sexism or capitalism, [they] help to maintain a system that allows [them] few, if any, benefits or privileges. [They are the] oppressor. [They are the] enemy to women. *[They are] also an enemy to [themselves]. [They are] also oppressed.* (1984, 69, italics added)

Women can no longer afford to theorize men on the margin of feminism when women's liberation is a matter of women's *and men's* daily political struggle. That women should exclude men from feminism on the basis of a fear that men will appropriate and subsequently colonize feminism does not stand. By including men in feminism, women end the stigma of feminist movement as a separatist enterprise that alienates men and reinforces forms of sexual oppression feminists seek to eradicate.

No one can argue against the fact that men already/always stand in problematic relation to feminism. Heath suggests that "men's relation to feminism is an impossible one" because male advocacy is *naturally* invested "in a male position which brings with it all the implications of domination and appropriation." Acting out patriarchal benevolent desire to protect women in feminism from the evils of men who desire nothing more than to take it over, Heath argues a position that supports the stance of antifeminist men, who refuse any move to (re)conceptualize manhood and masculinity beyond patriarchy. Moreover, his gender-exclusive "feminism is for women only" standpoint undervalues the potential impact of antisexist men engaged in the politics of feminist transformation. Men must learn how to oppose sexist practice, just as women must be educated in ways to resist it. Are either likely to do so outside the challenge of feminist movement?

Counter to the implications of Heath's assertions, women are not born into feminism. Neither are they *naturally* predisposed to feminist thought and practice. They (like men) can *become* feminists. Feminist thinking leading to critical opposition of male domination is learned. And just as men have learned to practice sexism as a sign of manhood and masculinity, men can unlearn male supremacist thinking. When feminist pedagogues who are men embrace education as the practice of freedom, we construct radical teaching strategies that enable the development of feminist consciousness in the classroom. We show male (and female) students how to formulate feminist critiques of sexism (as well as racism, classism, heterosexism, and homophobia), participating in a liberatory space that promotes an atmosphere of transformation that engenders self-actualization for students as well as professors. When I teach, students come to know that—regardless of the particular subject matter—my pedagogical strategies are linked to the idea of education as a holistic practice where mind, body, and spirit come together to project a vision of social change. Self-actualization as a key piece in the feminist positionality I construct in the classroom means that feminism enables me to move radically against the grain of patriarchal manhood and masculinity to effect an anti–male supremacist stance. Thus, as feminist allies of women in the liberation struggle to end sexism and sexual oppression, men complement "their voices and actions" toward a radical revisioning of gender relations beyond all forms of domination, including heterosexism.

Teaching Black Lesbian Subjectivity: From Homegirls to Sister Outsider *and Back Again*

Teaching courses in which feminist thinking is linked to a liberatory pedagogy, I have employed texts in my syllabi meant to destabilize certain race, gender, and sexual constructs that suggest that these categories in and of themselves exist as natural, nonproblematic locations for the formation of identity politics. In my pedagogical practice, two black feminist texts have become crucial pieces toward (de)mythologizing black sexuality; they have enabled my attempt to displace essentialist ideology, which suggests that "true blackness" obtains only in the framework of heterosexuality. Barbara Smith's *Homegirls: A Black Feminist Anthology* and *Sister Outsider: Essays and Speeches by Audre Lorde* not only challenge heterosexist notions of the (black) feminine, they put forth critical agendas that promote efforts to rethink definitions of womanhood. Moreover, for students critically grappling with and taking apart myths and stereotypes that racially and sexually "other" black women, these texts are enabling tools, empowering students to construct serious feminist critiques of universalized womanhood.

Calling for students to rethink notions of womanhood has to do with my desire to (de)center ideas of the feminine invested in "cult of true womanhood" ideology. Reconsidering the feminine (moving against the grain of white supremacist historical construction of "woman"), I suggest to them that their study of the U.S. construction of female identity necessitates a complex analysis of the interrelation of gender, race, class, and sexuality. I also maintain that a radical revisioning of womanhood that is truly liberatory for all women (and men) cannot take place without the theoretical and critical practice of black feminists. If we are to develop a progressive analysis of gender that resists all forms of domination, it is crucial that black women and women of color theorize the feminine.

For the first time in my teaching career as a college professor, I determined to place at the center of a course an analysis of black lesbian subjectivity. Employing it as a critical location from which to theorize about womanhood, female identity, and sexuality, I recently taught an undergraduate course called Redefining Womanhood: (Re)-writing the Black Female Self, organized around essays, poetry, and short stories in *Homegirls*. Seeking to demystify the black lesbian subject in literature, I began the course with Jewelle Gomez's essay "A Cultural Legacy Denied and Discovered: Black Lesbians in Fiction by Women." Reclaiming the invisible lives of black lesbians in black women's fiction, Gomez provided us with a literary history and tradition from which to begin theorizing new notions of womanhood:

> The shadow of repression has concealed the Black Lesbian in literature in direct proportion to her invisibility in American society.... Not surprisingly, we are the least visible group not only in the fine arts, but also in popular media, where the message conveyed about the Lesbian of color is that she does not even *exist*, let alone use soap, drive cars, drink Coke, go on vacations, or do much of anything else. (1983, 110)

Employing the black lesbian literary text to engage a critique of heterosexist/racist ideas of womanhood, I found in *Sister Outsider* the ideological tools to construct a liberatory (re)reading of the (black) feminine. Never having taught a lesbian text, I had to resist the fear that my reading and representation of it pedagogically would appropriate or exploit the discursive practice of black women for the sake of my own "male-conceived" ideas of how I wanted to destabilize female heterosexuality. Yet I knew that Audre Lorde's essay "Uses of the Erotic: The Erotic as Power" would offer the precise theoretical model to read black lesbian fiction.

In fact, "Uses of the Erotic," as an essay critically engaged in clarifying the personal/spiritual/political dimensions of female power as erotic expression, works in paradigmatic relationship to an autobiographical short story Lorde composed for *Homegirls* entitled

"Tar Beach." The first piece of fiction we chose to read in the anthology, it represented a space of gender and sexual freedom in which to challenge traditional ideas of the feminine while radically reformulating it. If we were going to take on the project of redefining womanhood (from the perspective of the black lesbian writer), it required a radical departure that would not only bring my own race, gender, and sexual identities under scrutiny, but would also push the women in the course to interrogate their own identity locations.

A story about the love and sexual intimacy that evolve between the narrator and a black woman singer named Afrekete (whom we come to know as "Kitty" as the narrative develops), "Tar Beach" illustrates the power of the erotic. Linking its thematic representation of eroticism to Lorde's "Uses of the Erotic," I put forth a critical reading of "Tar Beach" to display its transgressive movement across sexual boundaries aimed to acknowledge, celebrate, and affirm the source of women's power. Calling for women to rethink the order of their lives, Lorde defines and reclaims the erotic as a crucial element in the survival of women:

> As women we need to examine the ways in which our world can be truly different. I am speaking here of the necessity for reassessing the quality of all the aspects of our lives and of our work, and of how we move toward and through them. . . . When I speak of the erotic, then, I speak of it as an assertion of the lifeforce of women; of that creative energy empowered, the knowledge and use of which we are now reclaiming in our language, our history, our dancing, our loving, our work, our lives. (1984, 55)

Situated in the *Homegirls* section titled "Black Lesbians: Who Will Fight for Our Lives but Us?" "Tar Beach" narratively organizes around several thematic strands that anchor its "uses of the erotic" in a focus on the language, history, dance, loving, work, and lives of black lesbians. Set in the New York City in the late 1950s between the Village and Harlem, "Tar Beach" autobiographically unfolds a

woman-identified cultural landscape where Lorde describes/repre-
sents/celebrates butch/femme fashion, nature, goddess myth, the
black female body, and the erotic, functioning in symbiotic relationship converging in "fluid" images of water, sea, tide, and juices.
Lorde's sensual representation of the visual, audial, tactile, palatable,
aromatic emerge from a location of deep feeling within the self where
the sensual comes together with the spiritual and political. Affirming
their connection, Lorde maintains that

> The dichotomy between the spiritual and the political is also false,
> resulting from an incomplete attention to our erotic knowledge. For the
> bridge which connects them is formed by the erotic—the sensual—
> those physical, emotional, and psychic expressions of what is deepest
> and strongest and richest within each of us, being shared: the passions
> of love, in its deepest meanings. (56)

In "Tar Beach," narrative description of lesbian fashion codes sig-
nals the intense interest of the author in projecting a "style" of cloth-
ing, music, and body performance that enhances an aesthetic/sensual
appreciation for lesbian space. Food even becomes a conduit through
which the erotic is signified, as the relationship between the narrator
and Afrekete evolves and deepens. The first powerful employment of
food as substance of developing significance in the narrative works in
the context of a summer's night party in a brick-faced Queens home.
"[T]he downstairs pine-paneled recreation room was alive and puls-
ing with loud music, good food, and beautiful Black women in all
different combinations of dress." As the centerpiece of a table delecta-
bly arranged with a variety of foods, Pet (the evening's host) had
prepared

> a huge platter of succulent and thinly sliced roast beef, set into an
> underpan of cracked ice. Upon the beige platter, each slice of rare meat
> had been lovingly laid out and individually folded up into a vulval
> pattern, with a tiny dab of mayonnaise at the crucial apex. The pink-
> brown folded meat around the pale cream-yellow dot formed sugges-
> tive sculptures that made a great hit with all the women present. (146–
> 47)

As if in preparation for the erotic entrance of Afrekete into the narrator's psychic, spiritual, emotional, and physical space, "The room's particular mix of heat-smells and music [gave] way in [her] mind to the high-cheeked, dark young woman with the silky voice and appraising eyes" (147). Afrekete acts as the living embodiment of women's power. Like Shug Avery in *The Color Purple*, she is a blues woman. Possessed with the power of song, she lives fully, transgressing the narrow boundaries of societal moral dictates. Lorde infuses the physicality, voice, and eyes of "Kitty" (as she wished to be called) with symbolic/trophic stature. Rehearsing their initial meeting, Lorde represents Afrekete in ethereal and earthy terms that register most resonantly in a *smell* of familiarity:

> [She had] collarbones that stood out like brown wings from her long neck. . . . Her hair had been straightened into short feathery curls . . . [similar] to my own. Kitty smelled of soap and Jean Naté, and I kept thinking she was bigger than she actually was, because there was a comfortable smell about her that I always associated with large women. I caught another spicy herb-like odor, that I later identified as a combination of coconut oil and Yardley's lavender hair pomade. Her mouth was full, and her lipstick was dark and shiny. (147)

Their relationship unfolds in a ritual play of music, dance, and rhythm. With the music of Ruth Brown in the background, Afrekete introduces her name to Audre "snapping her fingers in time to the rhythm of it." And it is Kitty's eyes—their "calmly erotic gaze"—that prompts Audre to say, "Let's dance." Moving together in a "basic slow bump and grind . . . the crowded . . . floor left us just enough room to hold each other frankly, arms around neck and waist, and the slow intimate music moved our bodies much more than our feet" (146–48).

From that point on, even though two years transpire between the evening of that dance and the next time they meet, the sensual dimension of "dance" re-enfolds the rhythmic nature of the couple's reunion. In the Page Three, a "gay-girl" bar frequented by Audre, she and Kitty resume their dancing—this time to Frankie Lymon's "Goody, Goody" and calypso music by Harry Belafonte. But on this occasion, Kitty asks Audre to dance. Where Audre's first description of Afrekete only associated her physical stature with "goddess-like" qualities, her second account explicitly conjures up imagery connected to African antiquity contrasted with the modern attire worn by Kitty, clad as a contemporary "black" diva. "[H]er chocolate skin and deep, sculptured mouth reminded me of a Benin bronze. Her hair was still straightened, but shorter, and her black Bermuda shorts and knee socks matched her astonishingly shiny black loafers. A black turtleneck pullover completed her sleek costume." And in the ritual of dance, the image of Afrekete takes on a much deeper significance, meaning, and emotional impact upon Audre's life:

> Dancing with [Kitty] this time, *I felt who I was and where my body was going, and that feeling was more important to me than any lead or follow* . . . as Kitty and I touched our bodies together in dancing, I felt my carapace soften slowly and then finally melt, until I felt myself covered in a warm, almost forgotten, slip of anticipation, that ebbed and flowed at each contact of our moving bodies. (149–50, italics added)

Afrekete *moves* to nurture and replenish the body and soul of Audre from this point on until their final meeting and separation.

As the couple journey toward the fulfillment of a summer romance in Harlem, Lorde constructs the passion of sexual intimacy in the sensual where smell, touch, sound, sight, and taste converge in a celebration of erotic sensation. Anticipating their first sexual encounter together, Audre registers a religiosity of desire in religious terms. On the way to Kitty's uptown apartment, Audre notes that "[t]he smell of [Afrekete's] warm body, mixed with the smell of feathery cologne and lavender pomade, *anointed* the car." On another occasion she observes that "[t]he sound of our bodies meeting is *the prayer of all strangers and sisters*." Remarking on Kitty's maintenance of plants in her apartment, Audre traces the movement of sunlight "through the mass of green plants that Afrekete tended *religiously*." In a moment of passionate intimacy, she observes hers and Afrekete's as *"sacred"* bodies in the moonlight (150–57, italics added).

Almost from the beginning of the narrative to its denouement, the lovers' interaction expresses itself in a "liquid" discourse. Repeatedly images of the sea, ocean, water, fruit, and natural body fluids are invoked. Linked to tropes that signify the feminine as sacred, Audre and Afrekete speak and act through a language bathed in free-flowing movement—against rigidity toward the organic. In keeping with the theme of the erotic as sacred, one may say that liquid substances perform a baptismal function in the narrative. Sea and ocean imagery occur and reoccur in the text: "Her lips moved like surf upon the water's edge"; "dark bodies, sacred as the ocean at high tide"; "crickets keeping time with the pounding of a tar-laden, treacherous, beautiful sea." Reflecting on her first visit to Kitty's apartment, Audre poeticizes its thirty-gallon fish aquarium "that murmured softly, like a quiet jewel, standing on its wrought-iron legs, glowing and mysterious . . . magical" (152–57).

Kitty's apartment, full of green plants, is a world of sight and natural wonder for Audre. Her entrance into its erotic space is marked by typographical shifts in the text in which fantasy, dreams, and reality merge. Passages written in italics represent the power of the erotic on the terrain of explicit sexual desire acted out. Audre imagines Afrekete's body as fertile soil in which "my fingertips tingl[e] to play in her earth." Envisioning her a (West Indian) goddess of fertility, a cultivator of fruit, Lorde recalls,

> And I remember Afrekete, who came out of a dream to me always being hard and real as the fire hairs along the underedge of my navel. She brought me live things from the bush, and from her farm set out in cocyams and cassava—those magical fruit which Kitty bought in the West Indian markets along Lenox Avenue. (153, italics in original)

But both women transform each other's bodies into sites for fertile cultivation via fruit from the islands. The most sensually eroticized passages in the text poetically depict the central place exotic fruit occupies in their lovemaking.

> We bought red delicious pippins, the size of french cashew apples. There were green plantains, which we half-peeled and then planted, fruit-deep, in each other's bodies until the petals of skin lay tendrils of broad green fire upon the curly darkness between our upspread thighs. *There were ripe red finger bananas, stubby and sweet, with which I parted your lips gently, to insert the peeled fruit into your grape-purple flower.* (153–54, italics in original)

Lorde's sexually explicit representation of the power of the erotic in the couple's sexual play works against a reductionist/pornographic reading of the text. Moreover, the more the couple move toward sexual consummation of their love, the more nature commands a crucial presence. Incorporating various fruit in their lovemaking ritual, Audre and Kitty affirm a "natural" interplay between nature and the body: "*I held you, lay between your brown legs, slowly playing my tongue through your familiar forests, slowly licking and swallowing as the deep undulations and tidal motions of your strong body slowly mashed ripe banana into a beige cream that mixed with the juices of your electric flesh*" (154, italics in original). The straightforward account Lorde narrates here attests to her belief and celebration of the notion in "Uses of the Erotic" that sexual expression that affirms, values, and empowers its subject allows for an uninhibited acting out of joyous sexual pleasure:

> The erotic has often been misnamed by men and used against women. It has been made into the confused, the trivial, the psychotic, the plasticized sensation. For this reason, we have often turned away from the exploration and consideration of the erotic as a source of power and information, confusing it with its opposite, the pornographic. But pornography is a direct denial of the power of the erotic, for it represents the suppression of true feeling. Pornography emphasizes sensation without feeling. (54)

Just as sea, ocean, and tide manifest figuratively to define the free-flowing nature of the couple's relationship, so nature conspires with the liquid of fruit and body juices to inform the intensity of erotic pleasure, dream, desire. Sanctioned by the light of a "Midsummer Eve's Moon," Audre and Afrekete "mak[e] moon, honor, love . . . reflected in the shiny mirrors of our sweat-slippery dark bodies." Audre responds, "and I felt the moon's silver light mix with the wet of your tongue on my eyelids" (157).

The most performative illustration of the erotic's creative power occurs when Audre, having made an avocado paste, transforms the body of Afrekete into a goddess of nature. *"The oil and sweat from our bodies kept the fruit liquid, and I massaged it over your thighs and between your breasts until your brownness shone like a light through a veil of the palest green avocado, a mantle of goddess pear that I slowly licked from your skin"* (155, italics in original). Literally and figuratively, Audre receives nourishment from a goddess of nature. As goddess, Afrekete is a teacher of women. Audre proclaims, "Afrekete taught me roots, new definitions of our women's bodies—definitions for which I had only been in training to learn before" (154).

The power of the erotic in the lives of these two women has resonance in the political as well as the sexual realm, and it is its power in the political that can, according to Lorde, empower all women with the capacity to effect change. "Recognizing the power of the erotic within our lives can give us the energy to pursue genuine change within our world." She does not exclude men from its liberatory power, but she calls out men's fear of "examin[ing] the possibilities of it within themselves" as a location that perpetuates their devaluation and reduction of the erotic to the pornographic. Again, I cite her discussion where she distinguishes between pornography and eroticism to focus attention on its political dimension: "There are frequent attempts to equate pornography and eroticism, *two diametrically opposed uses of the sexual.* Because of these attempts, it has become fashionable to separate the spiritual (psychic and emotional) from the political, to see them as contradictory or antithetical" (55–56, italics added).

As a text constructed in autobiographical reflection, first-person

telling steers the narrative movement of "Tar Beach"; the voice we
hear most often is Audre's, pointedly recalling conversations with
Afrekete:

> We talked sometimes about what it meant to love women. . . . Once we
> talked about how Black women had been committed without choice to
> waging our campaigns in the enemies' strongholds, too much and too
> often, and how our psychic landscapes had been plundered and wea-
> ried by those repeated battles and campaigns. (154–55)

And Afrekete, responding to the experience of black lesbians in political struggle of women loving women that Audre characterizes, testi-
fies to its pain but also the resiliency born of it: "And don't I have the
scars to prove it. . . . Makes you tough though, babe, if you don't go
under. And that's what I like about you; you're like me. We're both
going to make it because we're both too tough and crazy not to!" That
the women are both "too tough and crazy" not to survive signifies the
notion of living against the grain, transgressing the boundaries of
heterosexism, "do(ing) that which is female and self-affirming in the
face of a racist, patriarchal, and anti-erotic society" (59). Audre, interpreting her relationship to Afrekete in political terms, articulates the
price "paid for that toughness"—knowing that living in a space of
black lesbian subjectivity necessarily means continual struggle and
negotiation of the idea "that soft and tough had to be one and the
same for either to work at all" (155).

Reflecting on the breadth, depth, and force of the love Audre and
Afrekete shared, appropriately Lorde (as author) registers its chemistry figuratively in a trope on nature: "like elements erupting into an
electric storm, exchanging energy, sharing charge." Intertwined in a
symbiotic relationship, the lovers exist in a kinetic inter(play) among
nature, music, and dance, and the sexual performs a ritual out-work-
ing of erotic power. Acknowledging the depth of the relationship and
the deeply felt presence of "Kitty" in her life, Audre declares at the
core of its meaning, "[Afrekete's] print remains upon [her] life with
the resonance and power of an emotional tattoo" (157–58).

"Teaching (Myself) to Transgress": Putting the Theory of an Engaged Pedagogy into Practice

This section—partly descriptive, analytical, and theoretical—represents the voices of seminar participants in the Redefining Womanhood course speaking about the complexity of its focus on female identity/sexuality in black lesbian literature complicated by the intervention of male feminism and the contested space of identity politics in the classroom.

For me, teaching Audre Lorde's "Tar Beach" was a liberatory process, where I let go of the fear that being a man could only mean necessarily misrepresenting the author, her text, and its meaning. Summoning up courage to transgress internalized sexist ideas that men have no business teaching or writing within a feminist construct—whether about the feminine, womanhood, or women's sexuality—I sought to contest, undermine, and subvert the phallic power men represent by putting my insecurities about teaching feminism out for class discussion. As my students learned to cross borders in Redefining Womanhood, so I came to understand the power of Audre Lorde provoking me toward redefining (black) manhood. Black men must begin interrogating our own sexuality beyond the destructive power of heterosexism and homophobia, which have dominated and impaired our vision of black liberation struggle. Commenting on the impact of *Homegirls* on her, one woman in the course remarked,

> Black feminist consciousness pushes your own boundaries and provides you with the material necessary to push those of others. The short stories in *Homegirls* forced me to redefine my conception of womanhood by giving me greater knowledge and a better understanding of black lesbian identity. They made me realize that though well intentioned in my condemnation of homophobia, my ignorance had led me to hold beliefs that were just as unenlightened as those of the people whom I was opposing. I was defending lesbian identity without knowing exactly what it was. Before reading . . . stories by black lesbians, my only contact with fiction centering around lesbian subjectivity, written by a

lesbian had been through ... a white lesbian writer. I now feel my personal/political views of lesbianism are more firmly grounded. I have works to refer to when discussing black lesbian identity and I no longer have to make uneducated assumptions.

From my perspective as a black male professor advocating feminism, discoursing on and teaching the black lesbian text at the center of "redefining womanhood" represented the critical and pedagogical risks I have decidedly taken to construct an "engaged pedagogy" around an anti–racist/sexist/heterosexist standpoint in my course repertoire. At several points in a course (the first day of class, mid-term, and at the end of the term), I will ask students to respond in writing to the syllabus and the fact that the course is being taught by a black male professor. What difference does it make for a man to teach feminism to a group of women and/or men or both? What does it mean for a *black* man to teach feminism to a class in which white women predominate?

Thinking about these questions and identity problematics in Redefining Womanhood, I had to consider what it meant for me to teach feminism to a group of women in which there were diverse racial, sexual, and class politics. Responding to my location in this mix and the identity politics informing the dynamics of this particular class, one woman student from a multiracial background wrote,

> The different racial, sexual, social, economic and political identities of those in the seminar were highlighted by the Black male professored situation. [His] being a man meant that the class did not have a common gender identity. [His] race meant that some of us could identify with [him] on racial grounds, but most could not. The ties between the group were established through a common identification with and appreciation of black feminist thought and the common desire to redefine womanhood. At times I forgot the existence of those ties and felt alienated from the class because of my own multinational and multiracial standpoint. However, reading the works of international women proved to be what was necessary for me to become refocused on the ties within the group while at the same time taking into account the differences.

They helped me realize that it is possible for us to find unity through difference.
(italics added)

Early on in the course, we addressed certain pedagogical issues having to do with the identity of the professor and what happens to those teachers who do not mirror/represent what they teach. Contesting the rigidity of fixed identities (while problematizing the idea of men teaching feminism), on the first day of class, I placed front and center the question, "Since men are not women, should we teach courses in feminism?" At the same time, I posed other related questions. Should white professors teach black, Native American, Asian, or Chicano/a studies, for example? Should heterosexuals teach gay and/or lesbian studies? Opening on to such complex questions as a means to discussing the politics of identity in the classroom means taking risks, particularly when the teacher's body/identity stands at the center of contestation.

Throughout the term (working from the syllabus, which included a reading list of writings by black women/women of color in and outside the United States), I encouraged women in the course to develop a broader perspective in their class discussion and writing that would challenge essentialist attitudes of sexuality, gender, race, class, and nation. As stated earlier, the seminar's main objective was the destabilization of these categories, prompting each woman to rethink the stability of her own identity formation within them. Moving from reductive thinking toward an acknowledgment of difference, we attempted to confront racist, sexist, classist, heterosexist, and homophobic systems of female oppression in and outside the United States—as well as in the classroom itself.

In Redefining Womanhood we often struggled, working through the polemics of race in the classroom. Yet we battled to resist flat, one-dimensional ideas of the feminine that suggested that there must be mirror correlation between what one represents and what one "is" (as if the sum total of any individual could be reduced to a single identity). At times it appeared that the differences between us were too great to overcome. At other times, we saw clearly the complex relation among race, class, gender, sexual oppression, though the seminar was driven by the intensity of some women's emotional investment in who they represented themselves to be racially, sexually, and ethnically. Pedagogically foregrounding the "differences" the women represented in the seminar, however, I aimed to disrupt the idea that any of us could claim safety in the identities we inhabited.

Class discussions between women of color and white women were complicated by the history of racism in the United States and in the feminist movement. Its long-standing effect resonates in one black woman's comments on the issue of race and who spoke or *chose* not to speak in class:

> The strategy of using silence to gain power or control has been used continually and consistently throughout this course for the "white feminists" to gain power in terms of what has been discussed, what [would] be discussed and what [was] accomplished this semester. . . . I (did) not feel it [was] my responsibility to engage these white feminists in dialogue to produce a useful class. Everyday I have to push myself as a woman of color, poor woman, black woman, oppressed, sometimes privileged woman to speak. . . . I believe that the majority of students used silence to counteract what they were learning.

I too experienced feelings of "outsiderness" and silence. After I shared this in class, one of the women in the seminar reflected on it:

> [He] articulated [his] initial fears related to being a black man teaching a class on feminist theory. . . . [I]t was important that [he] brought [his] problem to the table from day one. It enabled us to discuss the issue as a class, and for me, the discussions helped me to problematize and deal with my own position as a *white* female in a class on black feminist theory. (italics in original)

Yet within the domain of the classroom, I remain conscious of the potential pain transgressive pedagogy may invoke in students when they are asked to unpack the baggage around the identity problematics they bring with them.

I remember distinctly one class session of the Redefining Womanhood course when certain of the women adamantly voiced their opposition to the idea of men as feminists and my feeling of having to defend a personal claim to feminist positionality. The problematics of my being a man in the class and issues of sexism and patriarchy had to do with not only my physical presence as a "black man" (with all its myths and stereotypes in tow) but also the privilege with which my male voice resonated. Questioning the power of my voice in the classroom, another woman student wrote that

> As for the politic of this class being taught by an Afro-American teacher ... I do think it went fairly well. However, what I have to stress again [as she had in her midterm evaluation] is the degree to which [he must] keep struggling with how much [he] dominate[d] class discussion. It [points to] the need to interrogate the role [male] authority plays in the classroom.

The same woman followed the above statement with "every time someone raised their voice or disagreed with me ... they were turning into my Dad."

In light of the very real "differences" gendering the seminar's race politics, one pivotally important way I determined to undermine identity politics of gender and race had to do with the way I privileged sexual difference around black lesbian subjectivity. During the first half of the semester, we read the groundbreaking fiction, poetry, and essays by black lesbian writers in *Homegirls*. Asserting black lesbian subjectivity as a revolutionary liberatory space in which to rethink heterosexist/racist/classist attitudes about womanhood, I privileged this location as a way for all of us to begin a reconsideration of our own gender, race, and sexual politics.

In the second half of the course, we concentrated on writings by black women outside the United States in the "Third World," Europe, and the Caribbean in *Theorizing Black Feminisms,* edited by Stanlie M. James and Abena P. A. Busia, and *Daughters of Africa,* edited by Margaret Busby, texts that located themselves in a diasporic representation of black women/women of color. Many of the essays, stories, poems, and memoirs were by biracial and multiracial/multiethnic women, all in political struggle around women's movement. Discussing and writing about the contested identities these perspectives represented, we had begun a reconsideration of the ways our privileged location in the United States had provided us only one reality of women's lives globally. Reading international feminist texts by black women/women of color, we gained insight into the complex matrix of oppression that determined their lives.

Our understanding took on a much deeper resonance when my colleague M. Jacqui Alexander came to class to discuss one of her essays I had assigned on the status of women in the Caribbean. Having assigned "Not Just (Any) *Body* Can Be a Citizen: The Politics of Law, Sexuality, and Postcoloniality in Trinidad and Tobago and the Bahamas" for class discussion, I knew that the multilayered trajectory of its analysis would challenge us. As a black lesbian, Caribbean feminist, Alexander offered theoretical and critical perspectives that situated the *reality* of her identities and charged the seminar's dynamics in a way I had not witnessed before. Her political and scholarly relationship to the set of imperatives around which she writes coalesced in a powerfully moving way for the women (and myself) in the class session that day.

In Alexander's pedagogical performance, author, text, and teaching practice converged. I observed the thorough way she guided us through the text via chalkboard illustration, which made for a compelling display of "holistic" teaching. She engaged our minds, bodies, and spirit. Without diminishing the crucial importance of U.S. black women's critique of the simultaneity of oppression around race, class, and gender, Alexander strategically demonstrated how the interrelation of domination worked in the lives of Caribbean women at the intersection of sexuality. About the impact of postcolonial nation/state analysis, one woman had this to say:

> One of the most interesting and intense readings we [did] this semester [was] M. Jacqui Alexander's piece. . . . Although I was moved to think about many issues brought to light in this text, this piece really challenged my way of thinking along the lines of state and government . . . [as] expression[s] of ruling class interests . . . adjudicat[ing] on behalf of the ruling class only . . . [that] [t]he idea of consensus is manufactured. . . . This was interesting to me in that I had always thought these things myself, *but never really had a name for it or could locate this way of thinking in an established body of thought.* (italics added)

During that class session, observing Jacqui "acting out" the critical imperatives of her text in the typically self-possessed manner I have come to associate with her teaching style, I experienced the joy of learning from one's comrade.

And in the End, Who Do I Think I Am Anyway? Restating, Reaffirming, Re-imagining Education as a Liberatory Practice

As a feminist black man, over the span of my teaching career, I have developed a transgressive/risk-taking pedagogy. In the process, I have traversed the boundaries of race, gender, and sexuality—to effect an approach to teaching African American literature governed by an ongoing commitment to foregrounding literary representations of black women's struggle against sex and race oppression, patriarchy, and misogyny. At the juncture of race, gender, and sexuality, I have evolved feminist/antiracist teaching strategies in the classroom that clarify my personal and political struggle to build bridges across the contested spaces of the politics of identity, defying racial, sexual, class, and heterosexual mythologies of black women and men toward transformative ideas of gender and sexual relations.

In the context of an integrative model of feminist movement, my collegial, pedagogical, and scholarly relationship to Jacqui Alexander affirms the cross-gender comradeship bell hooks speaks of in *Feminist*

Theory: From Margin to Center, where women and men struggle together in feminist solidarity to end the sexual oppression of women.
Thus, I teach the narratives of black women persecuted, sexually as-
saulted, and even killed because their lives do not fit into colonial,
national, sexist, patriarchal, homophobic, unitary, and/or static ideas
of womanhood—believing that their stories (in and outside of the
United States) must be read and taught without censure. I hear the
voices of these women telling me that their stories must be told, that
I cannot be governed by the dictates of the politics of identity.

We have arrived at a moment of crucial urgency in the academy
for those of us who educate as the practice of freedom. We know that
crossing borders has been a question of life and death. In the stories
of black women/women of color, the voices of the oppressed tell me
that I have a political obligation to teach about them—their struggle,
the battles they wage for liberation. Communicating this imperative
to women represents the challenge of what I call a "border-crossing"
pedagogy. Many women in the Redefining Womanhood course came
to understand this at the end of the term. The same white woman
student who wrote the comment above further stated,

> I wonder sometimes what I [was] doing taking a course on black femi-
> nist theory. I wonder I [was] "culture surfing." I doubt my reasons for
> [having] engag[ed] in such a dialogue. But then I read a text such as
> Jacqui Alexander's or bell hooks', and find myself thinking, "Yeah,
> right," or "I'm so glad I'm not the only one who thought that," or "I
> didn't know that, but now something else makes sense to me," and I
> know it [was] a good choice. Black feminist theory is not all about black
> feminists. If it were, where would it leave Gary [Lemons], as a black
> man? And why, when I can see parallels in my own experiences . . .
> within my own working-class white hometown, shouldn't I use those
> experiences to build bridges between myself and those who are like-
> minded? Does one have to be a black woman to be engaged with black
> feminist theory? Hardly not.

More than simply coming up with "PC"-titled courses neatly cross-
referenced under the rubrics of black, gender, feminist, and women's

studies, I work across academic and political locations, representing a complex pedagogical practice that seeks not only to dislodge essentialist/reductive ideas about black women, but also to call out the patriarchal/sexist/homophobic colonization of black men, manhood, and masculinity. My aim is twofold: (1) to invite students through the study of literature as cultural artifact to examine the universe of the text as one way of reading the "real" world text of human relations, toward a more just and humane society where all life is valued, and (2) to teach holistically, performing a pedagogical practice that honors the integral relationship among mind, body, and spirit. Such a standpoint requires a pedagogical practice located in a commitment to radically revisioning the classroom, where teachers and students effect border crossing as a liberatory strategy for learning. In this transformative space, as bell hooks has said, classrooms become "sites of resistance"—sites of intervention.

NOTE

This essay has been deeply enriched by the insights of women students in Redefining Womanhood: (Re)writing the Black Female Self. I would like to thank personally the following women who shared in this endeavor, Leah Albrecht, Stacy Bowers, Isabelle Elisha, Ann Fuller, Andrea Laramie, Claire Mysko, Shoshana Oxman, Karen Ruiz-Cordell, Rachel Weiss, and Noelle Williams. Also I would like to thank Jacqui Alexander, whose critical perspective on Audre Lorde's notions of the erotic affirmed and deepened my own thinking regarding its power.

BIBLIOGRAPHY

Busby, Margaret, ed. *Daughters of Africa: An International Anthology of Words and Writings by Women of African Descent from the Ancient to the Present.* New York: Pantheon Books, 1992.

Heath, Stephen. "Male Feminism." In *Men in Feminism,* ed. Jardine and Smith. New York: Methuen, 1987.

hooks, bell. *Feminist Theory: From Margin to Center.* Boston: South End Press, 1984.

————. *Teaching to Transgress: Education as the Practice of Freedom.* New York: Routledge, 1994.

James, Stanlie M., and Abena P. A. Busia, eds. *Theorizing Black Feminisms: The Visionary Pragmatism of Black Women.* London: Routledge, 1993.

Jardine, Alice, and Paul Smith, ed. *Men in Feminism.* New York: Methuen, 1987.

Lorde, Audre. *Sister Outsider: Essays and Speeches by Audre Lorde.* Freedom, CA: Crossing Press, 1984.

Smith, Barbara, ed. *Homegirls: A Black Feminist Anthology.* New York: Kitchen Table: Women of Color Press, 1983.

15

Disciplines and Their Discomforts: The Challenges of Study and Service Abroad

GERARD ACHING

By the time *Forrest Gump* received thirteen Academy Award nominations, a discernible distinction had arisen between a "popular" appreciation for the movie's charm, humor, and pathos and a critique that decried the film's oversimplification and parody of social unrest in the sixties. What facilitated this discrepancy was an innovative series of special effects that superimposed Tom Hanks's character on news footage some thirty years old and allowed him to assume a protagonism in which his strategic insertions into American history produced an ambivalent mix of leftist nostalgia and right-wing ridicule. These superimpositions gave the film its controversial edge. Yet, as he moved almost effortlessly against the grain of these temporal and political disjunctures as the simpleton/hero who succeeded by carrying out every order to a T and keeping all his promises, I could not help but wonder about Forrest Gump's notion of his own identity and politics. Gump claimed that he was not a bright man, but in the context of the film's condensed interpretation of U.S. history as well as in the current hostility toward Washington, his briefly stated self-affirmation was brilliant because of its implicit criticism of today's political climate. I was struck by the logic and resonances of Forrest

Gump's retort to anyone who questioned his intelligence: "Stupid is as stupid does!"

Gump's adage does not affirm or deny his intelligence. Possessing no evident subject or object, his statement is neither self-referential nor accusatory. As in the best of maxims, his words comfortably bridge the particular and the universal. At the same time, it is this claim to universality that Gump employs to avoid answering confrontational questions about his intelligence. This strategy permits him to forgo the articulation of an identity or, at least, to defer naming himself until his actions can name him. In short, what I find most provocative about Forrest Gump's retort is not only the way it creates a mutually constitutive relationship between identity and credibility but the fact that the contexts of his response cause the semantic and ideological weight of the affirmation to fall on the side of action and, by implication, activity and activism: one is stupid *only insofar as one acts* stupidly. At the end of the day, actions speak louder than words. And if, as Gump would have it, identity is commensurate with actions, then strategies become the means by which one consciously creates that identity. In *The Practice of Everyday Life,* Michel de Certeau argues that "[a] strategy assumes a place that can be circumscribed as *proper* (*propre*) and thus serve as the basis for generating relations with an exterior distinct from it (competitors, adversaries, 'clientèles,' 'targets,' or 'objects' of research)" (xix). De Certeau's definition posits strategies as diversely situated competitive practices. Gump, however, undercuts any such notion of a differentiated "exterior" by shifting nonchalantly between the "conservative" and "liberal" camps of the cultural politics of the 1960s. In this light, Gump's apparent ingenuousness is not just a humorous take on recent U.S. history, but an ingeniously ambivalent strategy that reconfigures, for instance, the media's coverage of the desegregation of education in the South.

As Gump assumes the role of the simpleton who deftly weaves his protagonism into particular historical episodes, his fatuity *appears to function* as a disclaimer against politicization. Gump, we are led to believe, is such a simpleton that he could not possibly possess a political consciousness. But because his interventions recontextualize these episodes in overtly contradictory ways, his foolishness frames, at first glance, a series of narrative attempts to revisit recent moments in American history when physical confrontations at home revealed and hardened the lines that separated political camps. The strategic ambivalence of Gump's ingenuousness is especially evident, however, when he finds himself in the middle of the confrontation between Governor Wallace and the National Guard that President Kennedy had mobilized to escort a group of black students through the doors of the University of Alabama. In this episode, Gump shuttles between the polarized stances that inform the conflict by (mis)taking the racist slur "coon" (nigger) to mean "raccoon" on the one hand and running after one of the black students to give her the book that she dropped, on the other. His intervention, therefore, is not merely evocative or nostalgic for those who adhere(d) to their respective sides of this confrontation, but also highly provocative in light of today's debates on affirmative action and equal opportunity programs. At the close of this scene, Gump's double-edged strategy loses its duplicity when he follows the black students into the building. Already enrolled in that university, Gump simply walks through the door to enter an institution where his enigmatic presence as the "local idiot" who makes it to college never becomes an issue. The conflation of his stupidity and admissibility ends up mocking the endeavors of the black students who risked their lives to secure an education.

Identity and credibility are also considered mutually constitutive in academia. Hence, I would like to bring my reflections above to bear on the perception that identity issues are politicizing today's scholarship, or, more precisely, that ethnic, sexual, and cultural persuasions have become markers against which credibility in certain academic disciplines is being measured. The supposition here is that who we are determines what and, in particular, how well we do. My goal is to illustrate that this identity-based definition of credibility can be misleading and essentialist in a debilitating and counterproductive manner for scholarship and that there are meaningful albeit uncomfortable ways to go through and beyond the territorial stand-offs that this kind of definition produces. The first section of this essay theorizes "credibility" as an area and range of competitive practices or strategies in which the polite or unspoken refusal to take a side in debates within one's own field amounts to a tangible political stance. The second supplements the first by helping to assuage the discomforts of those who *are* interested in entering unfamiliar areas of scholarship and by showing how professors and students can evaluate and profit from these discomforts in new learning environments. Undoubtedly, the professor's syllabus facilitates modes and degrees of access to knowledge. But the students' preparation, motivation, and uncertainties also provide them with their own agencies. In this second section, I describe a study and service program that seven students and I helped launch in (Puerto) Limón, Costa Rica, in the summer of 1994. Since we were all new to the area, contentions about our status and responsibilities in the community as well as our own troubled self-appraisals emerged and coincided in illuminating ways. I am interested in interrogating what these internal and external pressures reveal about the negotiated relations between identity and credibility.

In this essay, I employ the terms "identity" and "credibility" conjointly in order to elucidate the politics of facilitating or forestalling access to knowledge. I do so to imagine a scholarly activism that would not fall into the trap of classifying "new" scholarship and academic disciplines according to essentialist criteria. It is necessary to explode the widely disseminated myth that the minority scholar, for example, not only is a purveyor of difference but also represents its most competent spokesperson. Such a purview fails to account for the fact that not all minority scholars are interested in investigating "minority issues." This kind of institutional discrimination is harmful because it exerts pressures on these scholars to "produce" gendered, racialized, or orientalized discourses that are locked into embattled positions within academia. This strategic segregation directly impinges on the minority scholar's right to academic freedom. For Aijaz Ahmad, the task of the "practitioner of academic radicalism" today is equally formidable because he or she occupies "so beleaguered a space that any critical engagement with the *limitations* of one's own intellectual and political formation becomes difficult" (65, emphasis added). My interest in coupling "identity" and "credibility" is also motivated by a desire to steer clear of the trap at the other end of the essentialist paradigm: the tendency on the part of some poststructuralists to valorize both sides of an argument for the sake of a supposedly objective lucidity. Herein lies the ingenious activism that Gump practiced. This coupling, therefore, is my way of insisting that providing ourselves and our students with credibility or access to knowledge occurs in contexts that are always already politicized and that our interventions there are determined by the limitations that we and/or others place on our engagements.

However, before I examine the play between identity politics and the creation of professional and institutional borders for "new" epistemologies, I should explain why it is necessary to recognize that the identity/credibility "problem" is to a certain degree a perceived one. It is useful to keep the word "perception" in mind for two reasons. The first is historical and methodological: there still exists in some quarters of academia the false assumption that ethnicity, for example, is the sole interest of ethnic and area studies and that this concept played a less political role in "traditional" European and American literatures and criticism. "Ethnicity" is now more consciously invoked to help illuminate literary texts. But it does not require a great stretch of the imagination to see that in the nineteenth century, for instance, certain conceptualizations of whiteness constituted the unmarked subjectivity in this country's Manifest Destiny, or in Ernest Renan's "What is a Nation?" (a speech he delivered at the Sorbonne in 1882), and in literatures also informed by such notions of community, nationhood, and citizenship. Such an assessment, of course, is mostly available through critical hindsight. Nevertheless, that it is possible to argue today that ethnicity is not the domain of colored people only attests to the success and challenges of a powerful combination of traditional exegeses and deconstructive practices that literary critics in gender, ethnic, and postcolonial studies had begun exploring widely in the late 1980s. Their research on the formation of "peripheral" identities consistently interrogated the structures that produce marginalization, and it is this engagement with the "centers" of power that offers fresh (but not necessarily new) opportunities for scholarship. The second reason for noting the "perception" that identity issues are politicizing scholarship is rhetorical and thus open to further debate. To a large extent, the accusation is a distorted way of acknowledging that real changes are taking place in the academic interests of those students who want to keep abreast of the globalization of cultures and who, consequently, request and sometimes demand the inclusion of nontraditional epistemologies in the university's course offerings. The distortion often occurs when these demands get refracted through various levels of administrative funding and hiring practices.

Credentials and Credibility

My interest in identity/credibility distinctions emerges not from the imposition of essentialisms by either side of the debate but from the unspoken or sometimes polite, professional refusal to cross disciplinary lines. Examining how the idea of theory as conversation sometimes passes itself off as Bakhtinian dialogism, Ahmad associates such "politeness, accommodation and clubby gentlemanliness" with "a peculiarly American kind of pluralism" (70). How often have we uttered or heard, for instance, "I don't do feminism" or, with respect to other current critical approaches, "that is not my field"? There is no denying that our academic freedom gives us the right to proffer such statements. Understandably, it is also difficult to keep abreast of new developments in every related field of inquiry. But the ready claim to ignorance and to a lack of credibility in "politicized" approaches to one's own field becomes suspicious when it is not accompanied by further commentary, unfriendly or otherwise. After all, is it not precisely these encounters with the limits of our knowledge that turn us into perpetual students? If I am overstating my case, it is because I want to suggest that there lies an area of silent discomfort between the "I do this" and the "I don't do that" that sometimes gets conveniently confused with respectful equanimity. In an intriguing comparison between political correctness and critical disinterest, Larry Scanlon points out that Matthew Arnold defined criticism (in the latter's own words) as a "disinterested endeavor to learn" and that for the Victorian critic "to be disinterested was to resist the assumptions of his culture's dominant ideology. It was less a matter of being apolitical than of being oppositional in exactly the way postmodern theory understands the term" (13). According to these definitions of criticism—ones Scanlon values because of their attention to process and continuous reassessment—it makes a great deal of sense to encourage the transgression of methodological and disciplinary boundaries.

As it stands, however, my assertion is idealistic. It does not take into consideration that credibility is not only expertise in an academic field—that is, not only the approaches to knowledge, for example, that de Certeau's "expert" and "philosopher" practice (6–7)—but also an economy in which knowledge gets quantified as intellectual capital and professional investments. In this scenario, identity politics in academia are not just limited to debates about essentialisms and their relationship to epistemologies but include an intense competition to create and promote reputations. Kimberly W. Benston argues that "[t]he self of reputation commodifies identity, readying it for exchange in the public commerce of social power. But it is successfully launched into circulation only when etherealized as the 'something' of a nonreciprocal private self-enrichment" (439). If it is certain that identities can be commodified in this manner, then the inverse—disenfranchisement or the loss of that " 'something' of a nonreciprocal private self-enrichment"—must also play a defining role in this economy of access to knowledge and reputation. Within the notion of credibility, in other words, we should take note of the diverse ways we work toward keeping our credentials current and distinguish those methods from our attitudes toward unfamiliar areas of inquiry. Through this awareness of the political economy of professional access to knowledge, it would be easier to see how ethnicity, culture, gender, and sexuality are not "new" epistemologies to be delegated spaces of their own but innovative and, yes, politicized engagements with "traditional" disciplines.

Let us briefly look at one way engagement through methodological or disciplinary "transgressions" has enriched scholarship. We have access to radical approaches in which modernity, to name a well-researched and highly competitive area of scholarly work, may be defined in a revolutionary manner. Think, for instance, of the rich challenge to European historiography, self-definitions, and cultural ideologies that C. L. R. James presented in 1938 when he wrote in *The Black Jacobins* about the French and Haitian Revolutions, indicating that "[t]he blacks were taking their part in the destruction of European feudalism begun by the French Revolution, and liberty and equality, the slogans of the revolution, meant far more to them than to any Frenchman" (198). Similarly, there are profound implications for the study of American literature when Toni Morrison in *Playing in the Dark* turns the table to investigate "the impact of racism on those who perpetuate it" (11) and claims authoritatively, "My project is an effort to avert the critical gaze from the racial object to the racial subject; from the described and imagined to the describers and imaginers; from the serving to the served" (90). And, finally, imagine the possibilities for scholarship when Paul Gilroy argues that slavery was "*internal* to the structure of western civilisation" (9) and posits the

Black Atlantic as a "counterculture of modernity." These approaches all engage with ongoing debates on modernity and utilize discourses on oppression not to separate identities but to elucidate how historically they have been inextricably bound in various forms and degrees of social antagonism. This antagonism has not disappeared. And in academia, as I have already mentioned, it gets played out in combinations of academic and professional strategies and decision-making processes.

Yet even if we all admit that this antagonism persists, we must still find a way to address and critique one another constructively. Toward this goal, I agree with Satya Mohanty when he makes the following point in a special issue of *PMLA* on colonialism and the postcolonial condition. His words apply equally well to our focus on identity and credibility:

> For we can learn from others only if we take them seriously enough to imagine situations in which they may in fact be wrong about some things in the ways that we can specify and understand. The version of multiculturalism that demands that we suspend judgment on purely a priori grounds offers at best a weak pluralist scenario of noninterference and peaceful coexistence that is based on the abstract notion that everything about the other culture is (equally) valuable. Given the lack of understanding or knowledge of the other, however, the ascription of value (and of equality among cultures) is either meaningless or patronizing. Genuine respect depends on a judgment based on understanding, arrived at through difficult epistemic and ethical negotiations. (113)

What Mohanty calls "difficult epistemic and ethical negotiations" will occupy my attention in the rest of this essay. For it is precisely through these negotiations that the essentialist identity/credibility formulation may be resemanticized not to establish difference as an autonomous category of knowledge but to comprehend this relationship between identity and competence as self-knowledge that is a priori and asymmetrically constituted by difference.

The personal and intellectual discomforts I describe in the following section illustrate some of the ways self-knowledge is constantly being pressured either to respect, assimilate, or ignore difference. In Costa Rica, my students were responsible for some language instruction, and I observed them as they contended with the difficulties of comprehending their own place and function in this program. Their efforts are instructive for two reasons. The first is empirical: because my students expressed themselves orally and in writing in varying degrees of candor, their discomforts provide ample proof of "difficult epistemic and ethical negotiations." The second is pedagogical. It is crucial to emphasize that what we communicate to our students is not simply an enumeration and assembly of "facts" but the means by which they in turn can enjoy access to privileged cultural literacies. Knowledge is, after all, what knowledge does.

The Discomforts of Outsiders

> The fight between my idea of the glamour of the travel-writer and the rawness of my nerves as a colonial traveling among colonials made for difficult writing.
> —V. S. Naipaul, *The Enigma of Arrival*

In *Imperial Eyes,* Mary Louise Pratt employs the term "contact zones" to refer to "social spaces where disparate cultures meet, clash, and grapple with each other, often in highly asymmetrical relations of domination and subordination—like colonialism, slavery, or their aftermaths as they are lived out across the globe today" (4). Besides taking her cue from Fernando Ortiz, the Cuban ethnologist who invented the term "transculturation" in order to avoid the imperialist overtones of the word "acculturation" and to imagine and account for the competing subjectivities of colonials, Pratt also develops an analysis that incorporates the kinds of deconstructive practices I pointed out earlier in the works of James, Morrison, and Gilroy.[1] In

Limón, Costa Rica, my students and I were not only observers but participants in ongoing cultural changes. And because we had entered unfamiliar intellectual territory—our "contact zone"—accompanied in varying degrees by what Naipaul in the epigraph above calls the "rawness" of nerves that "made for difficult writing," I propose for further interrogation the terms "areas or zones of disciplinary discomfort." I employ them to describe our activities in Limón as well as to address at a wider, symbolic level some of the contingencies and consequences of entering unfamiliar fields of critical inquiry.

After successful team efforts by members of the university administration and faculty to launch the course, seven students and I undertook and completed the first Summer Study and Service in Costa Rica Program.[2] The six-credit course incorporates interdisciplinary research and education abroad (four credits) and service to the community (two credits). The 1994 summer catalogue described the course as follows:

> This eight-week course combines interdisciplinary study of the history and culture of the Afro-Caribbean and Latin American town of Limón in Costa Rica, with on-site interaction with the populace through community service placement at St. Mark's School (kindergarten through ninth grade), where students will assist teachers with English language instruction. Knowledge of Spanish is helpful but not necessary.
>
> The presence of the English-speaking community, whose members immigrated around the turn of the century to Central America from former British West Indian colonies, encourages an interrogation and investigation of several issues, among them: the history and status of African diaspora populations in the region and in transnational culture; the continuities and differences between immigration to Costa Rica, and to the United States; the role of the artist as historian/critic/commentator; the transactions between British imperial policies and North American economic expansion into the region; the status of English as both the *lingua franca* of global economics and as Limón's "native tongue"; and the implications of the student's own volunteerism.
>
> This program is unique at Rutgers in combining study abroad with volunteer service. Participants will work closely with Limón's English-

speaking community at their invitation. In return for the exceptional
responsibility that students undertake, they will experience a deeper
and more informative contact with this community than is typical of
study-abroad programs.

The program is not housed in any one academic department, so that
syllabi will vary according to the field, interests, and methodology of
the professor in charge. I work in a language and literature department, and my syllabus focused on three interrelated areas of research:
(1) the reading and discussion of texts on colonial Caribbean experiences (three times a week)—particularly ones in which protagonists
describe their coming of age under colonialism; (2) a weekly discussion about the pedagogical practices of English instruction at St.
Mark's; and (3) comparative analyses between the students' personal
experiences of education in the United States and what they observed
as teacher's aides in their classrooms. Our texts included *West Indian
Folktales*, edited by P. Sherlock; Shakespeare's *Tempest*; Alejo Carpentier, *The Kingdom of This World*; George Lamming, *In the Castle of My
Skin*; Jamaica Kincaid, *Annie John*; and *Green Cane and Juicy Flotsam*, an
anthology of short stories by Caribbean women writers edited by
Carmen Esteves and Lizabeth Paravisini-Gebert. Because they were
also responsible for keeping journals, the anthropological/autobio-
graphical facet of our approach provided students with the greatest
interdisciplinary flexibility and, consequently, presented me with the
most unknowns, since the approach to what they observed around
them would ultimately be theirs. With respect to the final paper, my
only formal stipulation was that the students find ways to incorporate
all three aspects of the course into their writing. They were to present
me with their proposals for consultation before returning to the
United States, where they would complete the final draft.

The service aspect of the course is consistent with other programs
the university has developed with its surrounding communities. This
time, though, we would be extending the notion of community beyond national borders. Before leaving for Costa Rica, I had intended

to develop and evaluate a theory and practice of citizenship that would emphasize the interconnectedness of our activities as individuals, students, academics, and members of national and international communities. Toward delineating a feasible scope of empirical activities for citizenship participation in this course, I juxtaposed for analysis—and for reasons that will become evident later—U.S. proposals to extend its economy across national borders through the North American Free Trade Agreement (NAFTA) and local efforts by communities here and abroad to contribute to the self-sufficiency and vitality of their neighborhoods and regions. Current affairs, in my opinion, oblige us to explore, propose, and critique more comprehensive and at the same time accessible notions of citizenship that would link a constructive critique of these transnational initiatives with academic preparation for a "less bordered" world. However, even though my theorizing and their ethical underpinnings seemed worthwhile, they proved more suited to a comprehensive curriculum debate than to an eight-week summer program. The reality and limits of what we could accomplish in the course soon whittled the loftiness of my ideals to manageable expectations and to a critical evaluation of the benefits of "partial success," especially since we were only the first contingent of what we hoped would be an annual program with long-term goals. I will return to this issue later.

Before discussing the nature and contexts of my students' discomforts, and for the sake of my argument that this disquietude is not unique to a single identity but concomitant with the vulnerabilities we risk exposing when we "acquire" knowledge of another culture, I should briefly describe the diversity of the students who took the course. Of the seven students, two were male. Six were undergraduates majoring in pre-med, English/Africana studies, sociology, political science, history/Puerto Rican and Hispanic Caribbean studies, and English respectively; the graduate student was pursuing a master's in labor relations. All were U.S. citizens or residents, and their national/ cultural backgrounds included Afro-Panamanian, Bermudan, Puerto

Rican/Dominican, Irish-American, Indo-Trinidadian, Jewish-American, and Honduran/Salvadoran. Their socioeconomic backgrounds varied from working- to upper-middle-class.

Although some of us felt at home in the diversity of this West Indian/Central American environment, all the students expressed nervousness and insecurities about the responsibilities they would be assuming as teacher's aides. Some of these anxieties stemmed from their lack of teaching experience, a condition that time would in part remedy. But it was the cultural implications of their volunteerism that brought equally complex issues into focus. The course's service component meant that they would have to not only observe but also participate in the socialization of St. Mark's students to become responsible Costa Rican citizens. As if this situation were not riddled enough with culturally specific internal contradictions (such as some St. Mark's students' disproportionate allegiances to both a West Indian heritage and the Costa Rican state), the Rutgers students also had to face the prospect of positioning themselves in an environment they did not fully comprehend even though it physically surrounded them. As complicated and dissimilar as my students' private negotiations about these matters might have been—for as they taught they also had reason to reflect on their own upbringing and education in the United States and elsewhere—there was a general consensus concerning the need to investigate further an important area of disciplinary discomfort. Although I managed to anticipate this area in my syllabus, I was surprised by the unexpected, even dramatic ways opinions about language acquisition became a source of contention among us (my students and myself), among members of the school's faculty, and also on occasion between both groups. Meanwhile, it was the analysis of a certain passage from Lamming's *In the Castle of My Skin* in our own class that brought these issues to the fore, obliging us to evaluate our place in St. Mark's curriculum.

The students and I discovered that teaching English at St. Mark's was no inconsequential affair. The most immediate and resolvable difficulties were logistical. By the beginning of our second week, however, the students began voicing their doubts about the purposes and usefulness of their presence in the school and community. As I observed them, their uncertainties paralleled my gradual awareness that the assimilation of cultural knowledge is not reducible to absolute qualifiers like success or failure and that epistemologies are also knowable by and at the *limits* of their claims. My students were beginning to realize that most of their students would not be proficient in English by the time they were ready to return to the United States. These feelings of inadequacy were further compounded by the ways the curiosity and affection of the St. Mark's student body had touched us. My students could not help but wonder what good they would accomplish in eight weeks.

Even though my students were trying to ascertain the consequences of their presence and activities, it did not occur to them then that it was their very presence with all its intellectual discomforts that would make a difference in the long run. To a large extent, their frustrations exposed a restricted conceptualization of language acquisition and proficiency in which language functioned as a portable, transferable tool. While they readily acknowledged that a language was insepara-ble from the culture that breathed life into it, they were beginning to perceive the extent to which resistance to St. Mark's instruction of English *as a foreign language* to meet Costa Rica's educational require-ments also informed their students' outlook.[3] (This issue also held great significance for those Rutgers students who had studied and/or undergone formal and informal ESL training in the United States.) This resistance has historical roots in Limón, where most of Costa Rica's English is spoken, and maintains its vibrancy in the attitudes that some St. Mark's students expressed toward their English curricu-lum. According to Trevor Purcell's detailed study of the region and to some of the St. Mark's teachers who remember, West Indians in Limón province adamantly refused to educate their children in Costa Rican schools for several generations, preferring instead to teach them in their own denominational schools. Today, the official language of instruction is Spanish, and most of the student body speaks Spanish better and more frequently than English. Compounding this situation is the fact that the new generations show signs of impatience with the older generation's preoccupation that the loss of English also means the loss of a West Indian heritage. In the midst of these generational shifts, our presence as a diverse group of English-speakers from the United States was truly enigmatic. Our limited credibility—for I was the only one formally trained in language instruction—was not in question. It was our presence and the attitude toward English in and outside the school's classrooms that we communicated directly and indirectly to St. Mark's students that made our intervention worthwhile.

The assertion that our presence was beneficial might sound inexcusably "political," but the position of English in Limón province and in the rest of Costa Rica was already politicized when we arrived. In order to appreciate this context and how we entered it, we must delve further into the history of English in Limón. In the 1870s, because of the incorporation of British West Indian blacks in British and U.S. commercial ventures such as railway construction and the establishment of United Fruit Company in Central America, the most recent English-speaking populations took root on Costa Rica's Atlantic coast. Trevor Purcell reports that a combination of high unemployment in the British West Indies and "cultural and nationalistic ties with their colonizer" made the option to migrate desirable and that "[a]ccording to the account of some first-generation migrants, American labor recruiters operating in Jamaica at the time spoke from church pulpits, explaining to prospective workers that if they went to work for the United Fruit Company they would be serving Her Majesty's cause" (29).[4] Costa Ricans worked on the highland portion of the railway from San José to the Atlantic coast, but as working conditions grew worse and casualties increased, mostly due to disease and the difficult terrain, the government withdrew its own laborers, and American contractors brought in workers from nearby British colonies. The advantage of West Indian laborers for American contractors was that they spoke English, and it was this preference for English-speaking employees and the linguistic and cultural politics that informed it that divided West Indians and Hispanics in Costa Rica, even when the latter began their strike against United Fruit in 1934. Marcus Garvey, who founded one of the still-active branches of the Universal Negro Improvement Association in Limón, and his pursuit of the rights of West Indian laborers separate from the province's Hispanic workers contributed to a "wedge against class alliance" (37). In any case, because these contractors valued West Indian workers over their Hispanic counterparts, a division between the two groups developed and to some extent can still be perceived in the mutual suspicions and cultural politics that exist in Costa Rica today.

The North American Free Trade Agreement helps define the place of English in our transnational modernity. Because Costa Rica plans to enter the trading bloc, fluency in English has become a matter of economic competitiveness once again. This situation and the fact that the training of English teachers and curriculum development are being centralized in the capital, two and a half hours away by road, affect the pressures placed on language acquisition and proficiency at St. Mark's and other schools in Limón province at various levels. Costa Rica is the stablest and one of the most well-off countries in Latin America. Its disbanded military, free market policies, environmental conservation, and ecotourism have created the long-standing friendship and presence of American business executives, tourists, researchers, and retirees that the country now enjoys. Of all the countries in Central America, Costa Rica is best poised to enter the free trade agreement. At one level, our presence in Limón did not differ from the host of researchers and visitors to whom the community had opened itself in the past. That we were a diverse group of English speakers from the United States added a complexity to the presence of mostly white tourists who help "to retard the encroachment of

Spanish while simultaneously slowing the sagging prestige of English" (Purcell 114). Because "[w]hite is a legitimizing color" (114) in the history and cultural politics of English in the region, our multiracial appearance for some of the school's students must have been puzzling, but no more puzzling than the already complicated perception of English-speakers in the region. Purcell reports that a British woman teaching English in Limón found that children usually spoke to her in Spanish and that one four-year-old liked her because—and the child said this in Spanish—"although she is white, she is really Black for she speaks English" (120). At another level, we were not typical visitors. We would be preparing the school's students in tangible ways to compete in the marketplace; we would be helping them gain access to certain kinds of knowledge.

Consciously facilitating their students' access to knowledge became my students' concern. This issue surfaced obliquely in one of our readings. When we were discussing Lamming's novel about a group of adolescent friends growing up under British colonialism in the West Indies, we came across a curious reference to language as a "passport." The narrator-protagonist uses the word to try to account for a dangerous alienation in which the language skills of British colonial subjects gave them access to a realm of social privileges in which they still could not express their desires. (One of my students had a similar experience with ESL education in the United States and wrote about it.) The novel's narrator asserted that

> [l]anguage was a kind of passport. You could go where you like if you had a clean record. You could say what you like if you know how to say it. It didn't matter whether you felt everything you said. You had language, good, big words to make up for what you didn't feel. And if you were really educated, and you could command the language like a captain on a ship, if you could make the language do what you wanted it to do, say what you wanted it to say, then you didn't have to feel at all. You could do away with feeling. That's why everybody wanted to be educated. You didn't have to feel. You learnt this and you learnt that, and you knew a Jack for a Jack and an Ace for an Ace. You were alright.

Nothing would ever go pop, pop, pop in your head. You had language to safeguard you. (154)

This "pop, pop, pop" refers to the manner in which certain characters in the novel suddenly became overwhelmed by their inability to express and fulfill personal desires. In any case, our discussion focused on the nature of the "passport" we were helping to provide for St. Mark's students. This question inspired my students to tackle in their papers subjects including the politics of teaching "standard," North American English in Limón at the same time that it was necessary to acknowledge the historical and cultural significance of the Limonense-Jamaican English; the intricacies of gearing students at St. Mark's to become Costa Rican citizens when Costa Rica, as it prepares itself for participation in NAFTA, is making demands on all its young nationals to attain fluency in English; and a few comparative and frequently moving analyses of the cultural contexts in which they and their students at St. Mark's were disciplined in the United States and Limón respectively. By the end of our stay, it had become obvious that we had entered a situation in which a linguistic and cultural passport was still in the process of being prepared. We feared that we could not determine nor minimize the degree of alienation the children's passport would contain; that is, the extent to which the English curriculum ignored the gap between their West Indian heritage and Costa Rica's educational plans. This dilemma, one that has as much to do with a need to find a practical, pedagogical solution as with the Costa Rican government's policy on English programs in Limón, intensified our discomfort, because we realized that we had arrived at the limits of our usefulness and service to the community. We had seen that some St. Mark's students were more acquainted with English and tended to be more fluent in it than others. For the most part, this "imbalance" could be attributed not to ancestry, grade level, or any such categorization of identity, but to the degree to which their parents and grandparents encouraged them to speak English at home. Some students, therefore, required English as a foreign language and others needed it to be taught as a second language. This situation cannot be resolved unless St. Mark's also begins to make autonomous decisions about its own English curriculum. Despite our good intentions and differences of opinion about them, these decisions were not and could not be ours to make.

One final observation. Every St. Mark's student is responsible for a booklet that contains such things as the school's guidelines on comportment, civic virtues, and respect for the environment. It also has sections for keeping track of grades and attendance and blank pages specially designated for a continuous communication flow between parents and teachers on any subject pertaining to the student's progress. Imagine our surprise when we found out that the booklet was not only a condition for classroom admissibility but was commonly called the student's "pasaporte"!

Conclusion

My students' efforts and disquietudes represent contextualized negotiations between how they perceived themselves and what they proposed to accomplish in our program. These negotiations took place in two areas of disciplinary discomfort that we should distinguish in order to appreciate the modes and means of access to knowledge available to those who are interested in actively contributing to current debates about scholarship. The first deals with real or empirical limitations. Analogous to professors whose work constitutes only a fraction of the intellectual production in their fields, my students acted within structures over which they could not exert control. They participated in activities whether or not they fully agreed with St. Mark's pedagogical practices, Costa Rica's education policies, and NAFTA's implicit linguistic requirements for admission to the regional trading bloc. Faced with these overwhelming complexities, it was no surprise that they doubted the goals and efficacy of their volunteerism. But this inability to visualize the whole should not hamper their and our interest in critiquing institutional and other forms of official knowledge. Our presence as English-speakers from the United States affected the nature of our work even before we began teaching at St. Mark's. Critical pedagogical practices do not take place in political vacuums. Rather, they provide fresh opportunities for "difficult epistemic and ethical negotiations."

The second area of disciplinary discomfort proved more challenging. The students found that their aspirations and good will were not sufficient to eliminate or even assuage their doubts, anxieties, and hesitations. Some of them assumed that their U.S. citizenship or residence with all its stereotypical privileges hindered their effectiveness as teacher's aides. Others felt that being more experienced or accomplished teachers might help them cope better with their culture shock—that is, they expected that their competence would provide them with the means by which they could mitigate their outsidedness. Both sets of assumptions posit authority in individual modulations of the identity/credibility relationship that we have been examining in this essay. However, when my students came to the troubling realization from our discussions of Lamming's novel that expertise in a language could also be used as a strategy not to clarify but to obfuscate cultural locations, they began to interrogate more productively the nature and consequences of their role in equipping their students with particular cultural "passports."

The most satisfying experience for me was to witness how my students attempted to meet the challenges of their environment and to make use of their experiences of family life, American education systems, and American citizenship training in order to pose questions and possible solutions concerning their students' development and future. In this scenario, the varying degrees of success that my students enjoyed in our program emerged from the gradual acknowledgment of the limitations placed on their endeavors. Moreover, unlike Forrest Gump and his facile poststructuralist activism, my students exhibited their gumption, if you permit me this pun, when they began to imagine and appreciate the frontiers of their own self-understanding.

NOTES

I would like to thank Professors Cecelia Lawless and Judylyn Ryan for their critiques of an earlier version of this essay.

1. See Fernando Ortiz, *Contrapunteo cubano del tabaco y el azúcar* (Havana: Jesús Montero, 1940), 137–42.

2. Originally, nine students had enrolled in the course. I suspect that the two who dropped the course in the first week did so because of some of the physical discomforts and culture shock that we all experienced.

3. Language is a complex matter in Limón. Trevor Purcell reports that there are three main languages used in Limón province today: Spanish and a continuum extending from standard English to Limón Creole in which most speakers occupied a restricted area of competence. At the same time, because of U.S. tourism and culture industries, North American English is also entering the parlance of the young. See Trevor Purcell, *Banana Fallout: Class, Color, and Culture among West Indians in Costa Rica* (Los Angeles: University of California Press, 1993), 106–7. The way these languages were spoken was also determined by generation, education, and race (Purcell 111).

4. In 1871, a contract was signed between the Costa Rican government and Henry Meiggs, a North American, to build the railway linking the Meseta Central and the Atlantic coast. Meiggs's nephew, Minor C. Keith, later took over the contract and became one of the founders of the United Fruit Company and its representative in Costa Rica (Purcell 25).

BIBLIOGRAPHY

Ahmad, Aijaz. *In Theory: Classes, Nations, Literatures.* London: Verso, 1992.

Benston, Kimberly W. "Being There: Performance as Mise-en-Scène, Abscene, Obscene, and Other Scene." *PMLA* 107 (1992): 434–49.

de Certeau, Michel. *The Practice of Everyday Life,* trans. Steven Rendall. Berkeley: University of California Press, 1988.

Gilroy, Paul. *The Black Atlantic: Modernity and Double Consciousness.* Cambridge: Harvard University Press, 1993.

James, C. L. R. *The Black Jacobins: Toussaint L'Ouverture and the San Domingo Revolution.* 2nd ed. New York: Vintage Books, 1989.

Lamming, George. *In the Castle of My Skin.* Ann Arbor: University of Michigan Press, 1991.

Mohanty, Satya P. "Colonial Legacies, Multicultural Futures: Objectivity, and the Challenge of Otherness." *PMLA* 110 (1995): 108–18.

Morrison, Toni. *Playing in the Dark: Whiteness and the Literary Imagination.* New York: Vintage Books, 1993.

Pratt, Mary Louise. *Imperial Eyes: Travel Writing and Transculturation.* London: Routledge, 1992.

Purcell, Trevor W. *Banana Fallout: Class, Color, and Culture among West Indians in Costa Rica.* Los Angeles: University of California Press, 1993.

Scanlon, Larry, and Elizabeth Fox-Genovese. "Debating Political Correctness." *Academe* 81 (1995): 8–15.

16

Scratching Heads: The Importance of Sensitivity in an Analysis of "Others"

DONNA J. WATSON

One discussion currently taking place in the literary community is the question of whether or not racial or sexual identity as it applies to academic writers should be considered an influential factor that enables or assists one's ability to critically analyze a text. Clearly, it is to the advantage of some that the rift currently existing between colored and white women increase; to harness the energy of female intellect is deconstructive, I would argue, to certain spheres of academia. With this in mind, it occurred to me that a black woman's examination of her own writing might begin to explain the implications of insensitivity and exclusion consciously or unconsciously demonstrated by white academics, whether in organizing conference panels or in writing or teaching about texts by minorities.

I offer that examination in these pages; but first, let me make some straightforward observations about the issue. Clearly, black women bring an invaluable cultural familiarity to the interpretation of black texts that is important, indeed essential, to the discussion, interpretation, and analysis of works by black women writers for scholars and students alike. Not only are we able to code switch at will, but we also have the advantage of comprehending and interpreting the language of these texts—black English and its oral traditions, including idioms such as the verbal "girl" and "chile" and the nonverbal rolling of eyes, and *sth* (sucking of teeth). I personally would be upset listening to an interpretation of a novel by Toni Morrison, for example, that lacked the rich flavor that comes naturally to black language—written, spoken, physical, academic, anecdotal, or analytical. It would be like meat without gravy, cornbread without greens, black-eye peas without rice, and wings without hot sauce for most black women writers/readers.

When approaching black literature, scholars of color or ethnicity are armed with a fine-tooth analytical comb. Positioning the text between our legs like sisters often do when scratching heads, our mental thighs embrace it, enabling us to steady the pain as we dig deeper into the textual hair; sensitively we scratch the sickness out of and conduct further analysis into what hides beneath and within the scalp of the subtext; as it begins to breathe it exhales the hidden messages encoded within the narrator's voice.

This is not meant to deny the value of white female scholars' interpretation of a black woman writer's work. But it is critical that we seek researchers and critics who bring special cultural memory to literature by black writers.

But the issue takes in far more than this. "What is Black?" I wonder. The transatlantic slave trade forced Africans to migrate to Europe, the West Indies, and South and North America, and their descendants adopted, creolized, mixed with, and assimilated the dominant cultures' behavior particular to geographic locale, often at the cost of their own beliefs and customs. Once transported west, members of strong religious cultures such as those found among the West Africans could no longer freely practice their beliefs in ancestor veneration or the continuum of life after death (opening the way for the establishment of control through the fear of death). Although we were dispersed and altered, our cultural memory remained intact as many groups diversified and developed into what is commonly referred to as "black people." Moreover, there are threads connecting the African within us: underlying philosophical trusses, a central cosmology, or controlling ideal bind us together as "black" and make us unique, rather than opposite to white North Americans. Our "blackness," therefore, is exhibited in various forms of expression encompassing unique and vastly different experiences.

All of us—black, white, red, yellow, brown—feel, think, see, and write in order to communicate. But often, the purpose of writing for those who live on the margins has been to keep at bay feelings of impending madness generated by the perpetual contradictions that motivate society. The notion of writer as chronicler, recorder, promulgating the oddities, absurdities, and ironies of human existence and behavior, struggling to coexist with nature and society, is familiar territory. For black women-artists-writers, the struggle to maintain sanity, balancing the mundane with the world of our imaginations, is profoundly challenging.

Like the characters in Toni Morrison's *Beloved*, black women writers often have one foot in this world and one in the next in order to cope with the deafening silence and blinding invisibility suffered under the yoke of colonization. Our sanity and survival have depended on our ability to express artistry through work—in cooking, quilting, tending gardens, and telling stories to our children. What makes one stew tastier, one quilt more comforting, one garden more appealing to the eye, or one story better or more valuable than another is the writer's innate ability to "story tell." What one has been through and how one expresses her experience is commonly known as *flava'* (flavor or flair) in our communities.

We are people of the Nommo (word), keepers—rather than owners—of the word, whose cultures dictate sharing and passing on, through verbal, visual, or written expression, the knowledge of the circle of life and death. We process our experiences, understand and transmit knowledge through the power of words. Originally the oral tradition was the main form of expression used to accomplish tribal socialization. Our sojourn in America, however, resulted in the repression of our languages and denial of access to the written English tradition; the knowledge of books that relate ideas, communicate, educate, and inform was the legacy of the white privileged class and forbidden to the slave.

Still, we found the words to tell our stories, listening to them evolve as we relied on the cultural memories of our African past, living now within the context of slavery: Congo square, sugar cane, full moon, Jim Crow, sharecropping, and the blues are some things that reshaped our narrations, metamorphosed native tongues into Creole languages as a way of communicating. Teeth sucking, soft moaning, low grunting, eye rolling, head shaking, "Chile...," nonverbal codes, and what we did not say were highly important subtexts flavoring the dullness of servitude.

It follows then that as we write, even though it is not always our intention, the gift of narrative voice unconsciously engages an unknown audience's ear as if they were sitting down with us by the fireside resting their weary bones. To fiercely engage the mind from beginning to end, to suck it into the whirlwind of a novel from which one surfaces only for necessary breath or tears is the accomplishment of black women writers such as Toni Morrison.

But whether the writer is known or unknown, her storytelling captures our imaginations, transporting us through doorways. The creation of different, colored, unfamiliar realms is as necessary as life-breath itself; it is what fills our emptiness, what satisfies our intellectual hunger, what keeps our very essence from flying apart, what grounds us in this world, what allows us to let go of the pain of rememory. We are writing a missing ingredient of literature: the story of the strong and powerful black female voice.

Since the time the system of patriarchy began colonizing the jungles of the world, man has conquered other people, uprooting them, imposing laws, standards, customs, and institutions, including politics, language, and education, on the subjugated in order to maintain control. At first the master has a direct hand in the metamorphosis from a free thinking-acting people to the altered state of slave, usually by inciting the fear of death through cultural and racial annihilation, as in the case of Nazi Germany. But later, the master controls indirectly through enforcers elected from the lower classes: the Roman guard, the slave catcher, and the police are examples of those anxious to release their frustrations on the powerless because of their own condition of diminished social or economic power. Next, the master further removes himself while still maintaining control through a select group of puppeteers; delegates chosen from the ranks of the colonized, including overseers, house slaves, religious leaders, and educators, enforce his will. The last and most complex level of colonization occurs when the slave, caught in a world bereft of color and voice, polices herself.

Not until the slave is psychologically free can she be truly free. A unique form of self-hatred develops from the condition of voiceless invisibility; we fly apart as we become desensitized, accepting the conditions of servitude. Although we are not grounded within the framework of dominance, we do not flee, because we are not willing to risk the consequences of capture; hand in hand we lead our daughters to the master's special cabin in the slave quarter in exchange for a blanket or petticoat, and piece by piece, like scraps of quilting, we unravel at the seams of our true essence as our voices slowly disappear. We commit acts of self-genocide such as drive-by shootings and gang warfare because we cannot let go of self-hatred steeped in the pain of rememory.

Eventually, we begin to ignore our condition, having been taught that we are less than perfect, or less than animal. With downcast eyes we turn our heads when children are sold away from mothers, husbands are sold away from wives. We block out screams in the night of slaves being tortured by the lash, or burned at the stake like Morrison's Sixo as the master fumes, incapable of understanding his dying song as his spirit transcends the flesh.

It becomes, therefore, necessary for black women writers like Morrison to assist us in understanding and transcending the pain this world has inflicted on itself. To name the fears that help us perceive the ghosts, invisible to others yet clearly visible within the voices of our narrations, is the black woman writer's primary task; using words, she sculpts our experience, claiming it, creating doorways through which the stench of blistering flesh cannot intrude. As she scratches the sickness of dehumanization onto paper, the writer transmutes the experience into powerful Nommo, defining, protecting, releasing the spirit necessary for transformation and survival in a world that does not include our voice.

Some may argue that times and attitudes fostered by four centuries of institutionalized racism, sexism, and prejudice have changed in this country since slavery was abolished, or even within the last twenty years, since the civil rights movement and the antiwar movement of the 1970s. I, for one, believe that not much has changed except the scenery (else why are we discussing this matter?). Yet I do believe that the potential for change, though invisible, still remains.

If we are to embrace the dawn of a new era together, although we may not fully understand each other, we must insist on and actively practice sensitivity. Sensitivity—simple acts of human kindness—is called for, and indeed necessary, if the pursuit of scholarly study is truly about developing a clearer understanding of ourselves and where we stand in relation to textual analysis of the literature of "marginal" cultures. White scholars writing about black literature, and white professors teaching it, must at the least be sensitive to the history of heinous crimes committed during and after slavery, to the rape, terrorism, torture, maiming, and killing of a people, which arrested its development and continue to haunt and sicken our society today. The tree carved by the white boys on Sethe's back while the schoolteacher looked on from the tower of icy objectivity is scarred onto our cultural memories. That tree must not be reinscribed on us by an insensitive, icily objective scholarly pen. Our writing is our hope; it must not be the object of further exploitation.

Although we are not enemies, still we fear. But what is it that we fear? Perhaps by naming it, by scratching heads, by identifying and exchanging our views, whatever our race, our sex, our class, we do what is sorely needed to ease the pain of rememory. We fear the madness of Miss Anne's kitchen; we fear the touch of the master's (her husband's) hand on our behind, whispering in our ear that he will be at the cabin after supper tonight; we fear that instead of voicing her anger at his licentiousness she will instead turn a deaf ear to her own heart, and inflict her pain, grief, and inner turmoil on the slave woman out of a growing sense of powerlessness to act against inhumane behavior.

To look at our fear, at the ghost babies transfigured and different from ourselves, to hear the invisible voices whisperscreaming what was not said, what was never allowed to be spoken or written, is the only way we can transcend the underlying fear that breeds a lack of trust and an ever growing chasm between Miss Anne and Beulah, between black and white, between white feminist literary critic and Colored humanist reader/writer. We must put a stop to this fear and this estrangement if we are sensitive, strong, and spiritual enough.

17

Who Holds the Mirror? Creating "the Consciousness of the Others"

MARY ELIZABETH LANSER

I want to teach what I am not. In fact, I feel that I am uniquely and appropriately equipped to teach what I am not. I want to teach in a vibrant and reflective and self-consciously interdisciplinary black studies department. I want to teach the foundations of black education as history. I want to be a builder of interracial intellectual bridges. I want to build community. I want to see many black students in my classes. I want to work with a variety of African and African American colleagues, among others, to produce successful students, sound scholarship, and ways to move the messages off campus and onto the streets.

I am a white, female Ph.D. candidate in a department of education theory and policy studies. Currently I am working to complete a thesis on the origins and growth of black studies as an academic discipline. Due to a quirk in the structure of my disciplinary home and perhaps in my own personality as well, I am specifically and predominantly trained in West African and African American history. I am more adept in the historiography of nineteenth- and twentieth-century black nationalism and emigrationism than I am in the pedagogy and current curriculum status of whole language teaching and learning, or the latest word on outcomes based education. Ask me to talk about vouchers, or community control of education, and I will likely begin my discussion with nineteenth-century African Free Schools. I may then leap the Atlantic to talk about African nationalism and African education, discussing significant regional differences that defy neatly packaged and imported paradigms of change and development, while making comparisons with conditions and aspirations for community control vis-à-vis integrated schools here in the United States.[1]

My training defies simplistic categories. My knowledge base is interdisciplinary, and in one important sense, I am what I want to teach—a new creation, solidly rooted and trained in the American educational experience—if that experience is read as a study in black and white. In my choice of disciplinary homes, I gambled that the academy would be ready for what I intended to become—a knowledgeable and passionate participant/observer of the interracial interaction that occurs along the shadowed concourses of the color line.

My formal departmental home, education policy studies, was conceived as a way to expand and rejuvenate a flagging department of education foundations. Education foundations is a synthetic discipline designed to apply the social sciences and humanities to problems in education, to inform policy makers at the state and national levels, and to contextualize the process and products of schooling at all levels. The parent disciplines for the foundations of education are sociology, history, and philosophy. Comparative and international studies in education also became an important part of education policy and foundations as the United States began to market American educational models around the globe. More than a few of the significant faculty who supervised my training were trained themselves through the dispensation of national defense funds in the form of institutional or student aid.

I began my studies in comparative and international education, focusing on development projects implemented in Africa through official development assistance. The interaction between national policy, administrative regulations, ideology, and local needs and conditions was fascinating to me. I wanted to know how much we control our institutions and how much we are controlled by them, and planned to do a takeoff on the title of Michael Kammen's cultural history of the U.S. Constitution, *A Machine That Would Go of Itself.* I wanted to illustrate how even the best of intentions by international donors could be subverted by slavish adherence to institutional regulations and policy, in spite of what was indicated by local circumstance in the host countries. Whether one acts on the local, national, institutional, or individual level, it is always important to be able to locate the sites of conflict and creativity.

I can document every good intention of pursuing a career in international education in some capacity, but I permitted family to get in the way of that goal. Changing direction to suit unanticipated demands in raising my son brought me face to face with another connection between what I want to teach and what I am and am not.

That connection is a son and a daughter. All biases accounted for, Barrett and Jennifer are gentle, lovely young people. They are African American children, at least by this year's census categories. Jennifer's father, who has been dead nearly seventeen years, was raised in Boston. Barrett's father was raised on the family farm in eastern Nigeria.

What started out as a moderately directed drift in a social and political direction became a studied effort to rationalize my own multiplying identities and to assist my children in seeing beyond what Ayi Kwei Armah calls the "veils" that float between levels of lived, dreamed, and believed realities. I am reminded of my sister-in-law urging me to "leave the black world and return to my own." What in heaven's name possessed her to think that I had gone anywhere in the first place? What made her think that I was accepted into the "black world" or that I had any real "place" to return from?

Certainly there was no place where the complexities of my choices and my natality were automatically recognized. I was never accepted automatically in the black community, and I was no longer unconditionally accepted as part of "my own" white world either. In some cases, I was rejected outright. More often the rejection simply came in the form of nonrecognition.

I have spent many years on the margins, socially and economically, and I am continually reminded on all sides that I am neither one thing nor another. There were attendant cultural and psychological shifts that were internal to my development, but they are still something of a puzzle to be worked out as I go along. About the time that I was realizing that I needed to act in my life, to give name and voice to myself and my children, the academic lexicon was beginning to fill with the words of voices from the social, economic, and political margins.

Most of the voices were those of women of color, but something in their stories resonated inside my own experiences, and I longed to reach out to them and holler, "Here I am! Can I come and work there with you?" But I was afraid that they would look right through this ghostly figure, misty, defying comfortable definition. Besides, their positions in the academy and in the media seemed to be arranged by special dispensation in many cases. They never seemed, in real life, to be in positions to make decisions.

I was never able to find a niche for myself on my own campus in women's studies or in black studies, and my home department, though not restrictive, declined to advocate on my behalf at critical moments. A combination of severely limited financial resources, the demands of unsettled family ties, and the desire to move beyond the conventional in my studies did not inspire nurturing responses as I sought to examine the questions that bloomed from the grafting of learning and experience.

But there is more to this question of what I am and what I want to teach. There are many cultural issues, economic considerations, political exigencies, individual preferences, and institutional mandates to which individual knowing is frequently subordinated. The collection of experiences and what I have formalized as research and writing are important, but they are not cut from whole cloth, fully formed or perfect in their reflection of the world. Achieving a place and an audience for my work demands constant vigilance and an endless energy for explaining who I am and why I do what I do—how I think the pieces fit and where. It also requires that I listen faithfully for my own preconceived notions of the world.

I am reminded of a chance meeting on the steps of the library one spring afternoon. There in the massive entry, I was engaged in conversation by a visiting professor from Korea in need of directions to somewhere on campus. In the course of that meeting I learned two things. I learned that he was a scholar of English language and literature with a specialization in the literature of William Faulkner. Simultaneously, I discovered a bias that I never knew I harbored until that moment. If I could not fathom entirely the South of William Faulkner or Tennessee Williams, how could this stranger, this "pretender-to-the-chair" claim to shed light on a genuinely American mystery?

I told him my thoughts and we talked for an hour; not directly about my reaction, but about his struggle to learn an alien language and culture and his awareness of the different levels that one achieves in the process of learning and teaching, in the interchange of intellect and experience. We left unanswered the speculation of how well he might fare if he tried to sell his expertise to a U.S. university. I had seen the limitations of creative marketing in the academy, having had close secondhand experience of the difficulties encountered by Africans trying to obtain work in U.S. universities.

My acquaintance from Korea had no need or reason to try to test the boundaries of those limitations. I now think that may be our loss. What he brought to the study of Faulkner was a passion for learning, a self-critical eye, and a mirror through which we-subject are able to see us-object. It is a rare perspective among academics, who tend to prefer holding their own mirrors—much as I prefer taking out my own splinters. For some scholars, criticism is a matter of perspective—detached, analytical, and dispassionate. For others it is a matter of survival at many levels.

The freedom to perform critical analysis is the most highly touted function of the academy. And if freedom is the very soul of inquiry, then objectivity is the flesh and bones. I have often wondered, not so much at the putative power of the intellect over the sensate, but that the two means of knowing are often presented as an either-or proposition, while the spiritual has been removed from the formula entirely. Academic perspective is either internal or external; it is never both simultaneously; it rarely reflects the motion of life. Detachment is sufficient validation for a proposed "truth," while subjective commitment to a lived reality many times remains unfunded and often unemployed.

In terms of learning and teaching the history and lived experiences of Africans and their descendants, there has been an inordinate emphasis placed on perspective. There was a time not long ago when black scholars were not permitted to teach white students about the black experience. Jim Crow had something to do with it in the South, but in the premier Northern bastions of critical inquiry and knowledge production, the shunning of the Negro scholar was explained as a matter of "perspective." How could "they" ever be sufficiently objective to critically examine and interpret the black experience? Predominantly white universities were closed to them from the time that Alain Locke and W. E. B. Du Bois, Charles S. Johnson and Carter Woodson challenged the gatekeepers with competitive credentials in philosophy, sociology, and history, and were denied.

Perspective in black studies has always been a hotly contested issue. Who will hold the mirror? Until the last twenty to twenty-five years, there were few black scholars in historically white universities at all. Black history was either ignored by mainstream scholarship or appropriated by it. Although W. E. B. Du Bois, with his *Philadelphia*

Negro, was one of the earliest pioneers in American sociology, the Carnegie Corporation looked to Sweden for a social scientist to review the conditions of race in America in the late 1930s. John Stanfield's *Philanthropy and Jim Crow in American Social Science* and August Meier's *Black History and the Historical Profession 1915–1980* are useful texts covering critical years in the development of black scholarship, but these texts still fall short of the full picture. Even today, the contributions of Southern black scholars and historians, the torchbearers of the story of Africans in America in the impenetrable evil of Jim Crow, are not systematically or analytically documented. Since these scholars often lacked the professional passport to American intellectual-land, they have been ignored.

A corollary to perspective is characterization. Whose animation of the black experience is the most authentic? Is it possible to speak of authenticity in the academy, or does objective analysis demand a "Gunnar Myrdal," an external adjudicator of the claims of black people against a system designed to oppress systematically? Is there room in the academy for multiple biases?

My mentor and teacher was an Africanist, a historian, trained at Michigan State University in the 1960s. He told two stories that remain with me as guides. The first concerned the time he was told that he could never be objective about the black experience in America, could not gain sufficient distance to be objective. The second described how he was challenged to display his credentials for teaching American history, for fear that he might tell only the "black" side of the story.

Frequently, interracial objectivity has been unidirectional—white scholars get to hold all the mirrors. The dominant culture's insensitivity and challenge to perspective and characterization of the black experience as recorded by black people has created an intellectual moat around black studies that is most difficult to bridge. White scholars who scoff at the defensiveness of black scholars and black students or the assertion of "natural" right to self-representation in the academy sound irrationally argumentative to me, and serve only to solidify the antagonism and distrust.

On the other hand, not all efforts by white scholars to engage issues in black American life are insensitive or contentious. In the course of my dissertation research I came upon a book called *The Way of the Black Messiah,* by Theo Witvilet, a lecturer in the theological faculty of Amsterdam University. On the back jacket it is noted that the book "should be read particularly by those who think that black theology is in fact a mirror image of the white theology it attacks and is inherently racist [inverse racism], or those who think that black theology is inherently an American phenomenon."

There are faults in the story he tells. For example, the nineteenth-century American roots of black theology are elided, except in a bibliographic essay, so that the focus is nearly exclusively on the Black Power movement beginning in 1966 with Willie Ricks and Stokely Carmichael on the "Meredith march" through Mississippi. But it is in the bibliographic essay and in the narrative itself that one finds black voices telling the story of the black experience.

Rather than examining the secondary analysis of white scholars of that period or the annals of periodicals and the popular press, Witvilet trusts the voices of black people themselves to tell the story of the struggle against systematic racism and the part played by black Christian theology. The synthesis is more than useful.

Witvilet holds a mirror that reflects not only his perspective as a scholar external to the American experience, but also a range of critical perspectives emerging from black scholarship that challenge the conventional wisdom concerning black theology that has emerged from the work of white American scholars. There is a scarcity of such inclusive scholarship. Many white scholars specializing in various aspects of the black experience have a tendency to de-emphasize the texts of black analysts and scholars of African American life.

Witvilet is important, in more general terms, because he represents a growing interest by European scholars in black studies. In Europe, black American social, political, and economic issues and cultural products are offered as part of American studies rather than in specialized departments of black or Africana studies. White scholars are the dominant European scholars teaching black culture. Given the fact that there is a historic African, Afro-Caribbean, and African American presence in European countries, it will be interesting to see how they figure into this European interest in African American culture.

It will be equally interesting to see how black studies scholars in the United States make efforts to impact the research and teaching on black culture in European universities. At a conference held on Tenerife Island in the Spanish Canaries, Henry Louis Gates cohosted many European and American scholars in conjunction with the Collegium for African American Research, a new association of European scholars. Not all black studies scholars will be as sanguine about the efforts of white European scholars to hold the mirror for black studies.

Objectivity alone, of course, does not constitute disingenuous or bad scholarship. But often alternative perspectives, available from the texts of black people themselves, are ignored, misread, or devalued as merely idiosyncratic or not representative of the "black experience," however that may be defined. Only those broadly familiar with the original texts themselves would begin to understand how misreading and oversight on the part of mainstream researchers have resulted in a tendency by some members of the black intellectual community to separate from the dominant culture.

Also important are the kinds of research questions pursued by both black and white scholars. What might be perceived as an issue of purely impersonal and passing academic or policy interest to a white scholar could be of a very personal and immediate interest to a black scholar who sees the potential for harm or good to the black community, as he or she defines "community." Black scholar-activists often challenge accepted orthodoxy in any number of disciplines in the social sciences and the humanities, creating serious professional and personal challenges not only to the system but to their own, often itinerant, careers.

Another area of concern in the development of black studies in white universities is the notion of a common set of objectives among black people and a common place and/or state of mind called "community." In the early years of the demand for black studies, many black scholars and students were challenged by the defenders of the academic and political status quo to define what was meant by the black "community."

Many scholars have denied the existence of a common community of culture among black people that is unique to all black people in America. Africans and West Indians are separated out; Southern black people are separated from Northern; urban black people separated from rural black people. The contention was and remains that the black community is an illusion and a contrivance. The idea that black people are united monolithically against a monolithic and systematic racism is still a deeply contested part of black political and intellectual life. There is a conversation about community that occurs within and one that occurs outside the black community. To date, the two "voices" still do not communicate particularly well, regardless of color.

During the late 1960s, black culture, the black experience, and the black community were all potential spaces for dialogue and intraracial as well as interracial communication on university campuses. What developed instead looked more like a Roman circus. The patricians watched as their agents drew blood, but they rarely lost any themselves. University administrators and other governing officials, however threatened, were rarely hospitalized. In the quest for "community," students were hospitalized frequently; some were maimed; others died.

Vital to understanding the issues of perspective and characterization in the teaching of black history and culture, and other disciplines important to black people, is an understanding of the roots of black studies as both an intellectual pursuit and a way of life. Without that it is virtually impossible to comprehend the territoriality that has developed among black scholars in black studies. As a discipline, black studies emerged with the explicit aim of redressing grievances registered by both black students and black scholars. Many of those grievances were connected to issues of perspective, characterization, authenticity of voice, truthfulness of content, fullness of representation, and definitions of what constitutes the black experience and the black community.

Black studies programs proliferated, almost as the final salvo, at the end of one of the many intense and sustained thrusts for racial liberation in U.S. history. More than that, the demand was for an independent institutional home in predominantly white universities that were still recovering from the democratizing effects of GIs on campus from World War II, the war in Korea, and the war in Vietnam. The addition of a conflicting political agenda like that of black studies was difficult for university administrations to embrace with sustained seriousness.

Further, market demands for an educated workforce combined with the GI Bill to force elite centers of arts and science to become far more vocational in their missions and philosophies in order to fill a burgeoning corporate managerial structure. These conditions also required a realignment of admissions and retention standards that initially affected more young white males than any other group. In the 1950s and 1960s U.S. universities were already undergoing a major internal crisis in terms of identity and purpose. Nevertheless, black studies became a major tributary in the crosscurrents of a larger educational, social, and economic transformation.

Understandably, the temptation is to see the black studies movement as something bold and new. Many discussions of black studies began in the late 1960s with the inauguration of the first black studies department at San Francisco State University, or even later with the first black studies department to offer a Ph.D. at Temple University under the auspices of Professor Molefi Kete Asante. However, both Black Power and Afrocentricity are simply branches of the same tree that took root the instant black people began to seek public venues for recording their own New World history, in both written and oral form. As ideas or ideals, Black Nationalism, Pan-Africanism, Black Power, and Afrocentricity contain inherent instances of paradox, and reflect both interracial and intraracial interaction.

However, the messages of nineteenth-century writers and orators inform black studies of the culturally congruent production of African American people and their various responses to racialized oppression that have shaped their historical and contemporary existence in the United States for several hundred years. Much of the nineteenth-century public and private discourse on issues black and white has been preserved, with all its paradox and power to explain intact. History helps us identify parallels in current conditions, which in turn help us to identify concepts of lasting value that are often confused with intellectual or political fads and fashion, for lack of historical perspective. The ensuing texts, culled from the record, mirror much of what we would understand today as the politics of identity.

Though the following words were spoken by Maria Stewart more than 160 years ago and 135 years before the inauguration of the first black studies department at San Francisco State University, they resonate with the promise and paradox of education-for-liberation, in terms that reflect much of the current public debate concerning black/Africana studies. As her words indicate, black liberation was contingent on self-help, self-determination, and self-knowledge through education. That education was to supersede the intellectual production of the majority culture—an intellectual production that registered Africans as one step removed from "brute creation."[2]

Education for self-knowledge and self-determination was more than a matter of disproving the social Darwinists. Stewart emphasizes that the temporal focus for black liberation must be on the past and the present, the continental United States and the continent of Africa. Values and ethics play a major role in racial uplift, and she anticipates that Africans in America will one day multiply the power of their backs with the power of their brains. Their political voices will resonate in the "house" of their oppressors—which, by dint of labor if not always of citizenship, is their own house as well.

In a lecture given at the African Masonic Hall in Boston in 1833, Maria Stewart said,

> History informs us that we were sprung from one of the most learned nations of the whole earth; from the seat if not the parent of science. Yes, poor despised Africa was once the resort of sages and legislators of other nations, was esteemed the school for learning, and the most illustrious men in Greece flocked thither for instruction. But it was our gross sins and abominations that provoked the Almighty to frown thus heavily upon us, and give our glory unto others. . . . [I]t is of no use for us to boast that we sprung from this learned and enlightened nation, for this day a moral gloom hangs over millions of our race. . . . O ye *sons of Africa* when will your voices be heard in our legislative halls in defiance of your enemies contending for equal rights and liberty. . . . Let our money, instead of being thrown away as heretofore, be appropriated for schools and seminars of learning for our children and youth. . . . The rays of light and knowledge have been hid from our view; we have been taught to consider ourselves as scarce superior to the brute creation; and have performed the most part of American drudgery. Had we as a people received one-half the early advantages the whites have received, I would defy the government of these United States to deprive us any longer of our rights. . . . They would drive us to a strange land. But before I go, the bayonet shall pierce me through. African rights and liberty is a subject that ought to fire the breast of every free man of color in these United States.[3]

Note her use of "African" with reference to black people and the liberation struggle. Prior to the 1830s, the term "African" was used to denote all people of African descent. "African" was replaced in the freed black community, in the early decades of the nineteenth century, with the phrase "men of color" in recognition of the perceived and real distance between Africans who had attained a degree of freedom, education, and entry into American society and Africans who were still arriving directly from the continent as slaves, the generations of slave men and women still in bondage, and the black poor who were neither slave nor free. In 1833, the term "colored" indicated varying degrees of mixed racial inheritance; it connoted a general optimism concerning the potential for increased participation by the freedmen in the civil life of the young nation. Seventeen years later the Fugitive Slave Act would put a dent in that unreasonable optimism — unreasonable given the continual erosion of the rights of freedmen in the Northern states from the late 1700s on.

The modern connection between biology and ideology is peculiar to black/white race relations in both Europe and America. Stewart's speech contains fragments of that connection. For example, "O ye sons of Africa" were the men seated before her in the assembly hall. They were also the "men of color" or "freedmen" in her closing statements. "Africans" were the enslaved, though it is not difficult to contend that she was also referring to those freedmen and women caught in the chains of poverty and ignorance.

One thing is most clear from Stewart's use of the naming convention that was current for those times. The black race in America or the United States was not monolithic. Its members did not always share the same circumstance or ideology. They did share, however, the same easily recognizable condition as sons and daughters of Africa.

The notion of a coherent black identity, particularly as expressed in the ideology of common experience and community central to black studies, poses a particularly important paradox in the development of black studies. It is sometimes as difficult for some black people to reconcile as it is for the majority of white people. The reality of unity-in-blackness and the reality of differences in the black experience do not emerge in obvious patterns of cause and result. White scholars and policy makers frequently stress the differences among black people who are influenced by geographic location, location in the labor force, and other material conditions of black people across the United States. That the two realities exist side by side is often ignored.

Whatever the diversity within the black community, one thing is fairly certain. Black studies was firmly grounded in black urban culture—primarily in the Northern and Western United States. Houston A. Baker recently noted that "since Black Studies was founded as a social, scholarly and pedagogical enterprise to deal with black culture, I would have to account for the relationship of such studies to black urban culture. Black urban culture, I believe, provided much of the impetus for Black Studies' founding, and surely in our own era, it is the locus of quite extraordinary transnational creative energy."[4]

The critics of black studies made much of the fact that students and activists were frequently children of the black working class and black bourgeoisie whose "culture" was removed from impoverished Southern black culture, whose members still suffered the effects of generations of Jim Crow and the lack of employment and education. They were also distanced from impoverished Northern urban black people, who seemed to be the off-campus focus of the young activists. Recent autobiographies such as Brent Staples's *Parallel Time* demonstrate clearly that these presumed "cultural" differences, based on assumptions of the determining power of class, were quite artificial.

To those who equated black urban life with black pathology, the Northern urban black poor were an anathema on American faith in individual achievement and opportunity. They were the internal immigrants who never seemed quite capable of moving out of the ghettos as had generations of European immigrants before them. The "culture" that held them in the chains of poverty never has been deemed worthy of preservation by the dominant culture.

In order to put this notion of unity and diversity in perspective, let us return to yet another nineteenth-century example that still is instructive for the present. Consider for a moment a comparison of perspectives from Sojourner Truth and Frances Ellen Watkins Harper on the subject of universal suffrage. Neither woman supported universal suffrage solely on the basis of race alone. Each had her own specific recommendation for extending the vote. Both clearly rejected the equation of Africanness with ignorance.

Frances Harper was raised a literate black woman in Baltimore's free black community, and Sojourner Truth, in her own words, came "from another field, the country of the slave."[5] Education and its relationship to the political participation of black people clearly meant different things to these women. To one it was the education of life and letters. To the other, it was life's lessons engraved across the back as well as the mind.

To Harper, injustice and ignorance existed in both black and white people, and she favored a restricted suffrage that would meet the test of universal truth and justice. To Sojourner Truth, universal suffrage was to be, as its name implied, full political participation and representation for all. Harper sustained a position that advocated education for social change. For Sojourner Truth also, it is clear that the right to vote, even when enforced and exercised, does not always bring full representation or the satisfaction of particular needs. For both women, courage and intelligence were necessary in the fight against injustice. To make a case for the difference in political ideologies between the women does not in any way imply that either one was less aware of their collective status as black women in a dominant culture that did nothing but diminish their humanity.

It is absolutely critical for all teachers in black studies to understand the history of black intellectual production that led to its emergence as a discipline in university curricula. It is necessary to see that African-centered thought is historically much more than myth-making a feel-good curriculum. It is the crux of much of the paradox of black history and black culture and it is the source of its uniqueness and strength. The focus on Africa and the defining dialogues of community must be seen as explanatory elements in black studies that are even more important than "race."

It seems to me, more often than not, that a solid case can be made for the territoriality among black scholars when it comes to black studies. The stresses and pressures of personal bigotry and institutionalized racism are currently creating a palpable rage among black people that is only further inflamed by the currently fashionable denial of racism and race. As I am frequently reminded, the smarmy maunderings of self-appointed "good guys"-in-white are not welcome among angry black people.

There is also the issue of numbers. Ray Winbush, the Benjamin Hooks Professor of Social Justice at Fisk University, says that considerations of individual privacy make it difficult for the National Council on Black Studies to get accurate numbers of black faculty in black studies programs. He estimates an average of seven black faculty in state universities and ten in private universities. David McBride, chairman of the African and African American studies department at Pennsylvania State University, estimates the percentage of black studies faculty at between 1 and 2 percent of all liberal arts faculty in most large universities, which is probably very close to Winbush's estimate. The numbers of black faculty are minuscule, and the proportions of black faculty to white faculty don't change much when we look at the total faculty at major universities.

Rest assured that I am not suggesting that all black Ph.D.'s want to or ought to teach in black studies. However, the simple truth is that the advent of black studies brought the largest number of black faculty into white universities in the entire history of higher education. Although I would prefer to argue for expanded budgets for black studies programs and departments than to argue the color line for black studies faculty, I realize that the present gains have been long in coming, and difficult in the making. So, what is it exactly that I think I am doing?

I am looking for a specific place to exercise a combination of historical record and lived experience to ground the act of teaching black intellectual history to men and women in university classrooms. In doing so, I dare to hold the mirror for the "other," recognizing that the face reflecting back at me will most likely be my own. I do not approach that task as either a right or a privilege. It is, as I noted earlier, something closer to a total commitment for which I have prepared myself over many years, and with a full understanding of the difficulties and high hopes for the opportunities.

Thirty years ago I would never have been compelled to write this essay. I would have simply carved out a data set or a series of documents and gone to work in a discipline where my color or the color of my "subjects" was incidental to the precepts of the discipline in which I would research and teach. At least I would have been trained to believe that disciplinary inquiry and professional methods superseded any question of culturally or racially contested identity. But times have changed.

It is, I believe, a change for the better. Experience tells me that even the least astute student can spot a phony or someone who has no direct experience with the subject matter. In *Beyond the Culture Wars*, Gerald Graff calls academic conflict a revitalization of American education. He makes friends with the conflict that comes with the inclusion of previously excluded groups. Of those who refuse he says, "I suspect that the teachers who have reacted [to criticisms] by canceling their courses and offering themselves to the media as helpless victims of political correctness would have done better to stay and argue the issues with their students."[6] I hope to take that critical, crisis-driven spirit of inquiry into my own classroom and let it guide and permeate my research.

My last thought is that I have always hoped to be able to forge interracial bridges to critical thinking and humane action by teaching and writing what I live. There is in me an old yearning that I have followed to this place and time, and I have not been alone in recognizing that tugging against the grain. bell hooks says, "Yearning is the word that best describes a common psychological state shared by many of us, cutting across boundaries of race, class, gender, and sexual practices.... the yearning that wells in the hearts and minds of those whom [master] narratives have silenced is the longing for critical voice."[7] I believe that I have found the voice; now what I seek is a place and an audience.

NOTES

The title of this essay is taken from the last few lines of *The Fire Next Time*. In those lines, James Baldwin leaves with us his own individual vision of American redemption: "If we—and now I mean the relatively conscious whites and the relatively conscious blacks, who must, like lovers, insist on, or create, the consciousness of the others—do not falter in our duty now, we may be able, handful that we are, to end the racial nightmare, and achieve our country, and change the history of the world."

1. Mary E. Lanser, "From Piggeries to Beggaries: West African Education from the Bo School to Structural Adjustments—1890's to 1990's" (paper presented to the twelfth annual Pan-African Studies Conference, hosted by the Midwest Association for Pan-African Studies and the African and African American Studies Department, Pennsylvania State University, April 1994).

2. The recent publication of *The Bell Curve* is but one in a long line of nationally recognized and acclaimed reminders that the days of social Darwinism have not ended, and thus the aggressively defensive posture of many black people may not be as overstated as some of us might wish to believe.

3. "A lecture on African rights and liberty" delivered at the African Masonic Hall in Boston, February 27, 1833, in *Maria W. Stewart: America's First Black Woman Political Writer: Essays and Speeches*, ed. Marilyn Richardson (Bloomington: Indiana University Press, 1987), 59.

4. Houston A. Baker, Jr., *Black Studies, Rap and the Academy* (Chicago: University of Chicago Press, 1993), 2.

5. Bert James Loewenberg and Ruth Bogin, eds., *Black Women in Nineteenth Century American Life: Their Words, Their Thoughts, Their Feelings* (University Park: Pennsylvania State University Press, 1976), 238.

6. Gerald Graff, *Beyond the Culture Wars: How Teaching the Conflict Can Revitalize American Education* (New York: W. W. Norton, 1992), 9.

7. bell hooks, *Yearning: Race, Gender, and Cultural Politics* (Boston: South End Press, 1990), 27.

BIBLIOGRAPHY

Armah, Ayi Kwei. *Fragments*. Boston: Houghton Mifflin, 1970.

Baker, Houston A., Jr. *Black Studies, Rap and the Academy*. Chicago: University of Chicago Press, 1993.

Baldwin, James. *The Fire Next Time*. New York: Dial Press, 1963.

Du Bois, W. E. B. *The Philadelphia Negro: A Social Study*. Philadelphia: University of Pennsylvania Press, 1899.

Kammen, Michael. *A Machine That Would Go of Itself: The Constitution in American Culture*. New York: Knopf, 1986.

Loewenberg, Bert James, and Ruth Bogin, eds. *Black Women in Nineteenth Century American Life: Their Words, Their Thoughts, Their Feelings*. University Park: Pennsylvania State University Press, 1976.

Meier, August, and Elliot Rudwick. *Black History and the Historical Profession, 1915–1980*. Urbana: University of Illinois Press, 1986.

Richardson, Marilyn, ed. *Maria W. Stewart: America's First Black Woman Political Writer: Essays and Speeches*. Bloomington: Indiana University Press, 1987.

Stanfield, John H. *Philanthropy and Jim Crow in American Social Science*. Westport, CT: Greenwood Press, 1985.

Staples, Brent. *Parallel Time: Growing Up in Black and White*. New York: Avon Books, 1994.

Witvlet, Theo. *The Way of the Black Messiah: The Hermeneutical Challenge of Black Theology as Theology of Liberation*. London: SCM Press, 1987.

18

Daughters of the Dust, *the White Woman Viewer, and the Unborn Child*

RENÉE R. CURRY

The first feature-length film in theatrical distribution made by an African American woman, *Daughters of the Dust* (1992), resounds with various discourses of journeying. Director Julie Dash sets this film in the remote Sea Islands along the coast of Georgia. The history of the slave trade involving these Sea Islands intersects with Dash's concern for African American journeys toward origins. This intersection provides the setting for both a personal and a metaphoric guide to rendering and reading African American women's lives:

> The genesis of the idea came from always hearing my father being called a Gee-chee and then wanting to do something on Gee-chee culture, which is also called Gullah. . . . I also collected stories from relatives who came from the area. I included some of [my mother's] recollections of folklore . . . I included lots of my father's stories, and my grandmother's on my father's side, and my aunts. Things that they used to say, I used as dialogue.[1]

In this way, the journey of making the film names the personal as catalyst for researching and embracing the historical.

The discourses used to speak this particular history reflect what feminist literary critic Deborah E. McDowell refers to as a recurrent motif of the journey in black women's literature.[2] Preparation for journeying floods the on-screen imagery in *Daughters of the Dust*, and discussions about journeying abound as the Gullah peoples living on the Sea Islands along the coast of Georgia make arrangements for their emigration to the North.

When asked in an interview to provide a synopsis of the film, Dash replied,

> It's about a family that's preparing to migrate North and the great grandmother is trying to get them to remain on the island. The story is concerned with conflict and struggle as the family prepares to migrate North at the turn of the century. That's not a great synopsis. It's such a dense script. . . . There are so many subplots that it's hard to say that it is any one thing. To really make it simple, it's about a family of women who carry their cultural traditions into the future. These women carried scraps of memories from the past, and, then, they carry these same scraps of memory into the future.[3]

The film opens with fragmented images of blue-stained hands, a boat landing, and a fully dressed woman rising out of the water. The camera then concentrates lingering, medium-shot gazes on three different women. Yellow Mary and her companion Trula travel in a boat that stops to pick up Viola. Trula and Viola, cousins, travel back to the Sea Islands in order to witness the passage of the family's migration North as well as to facilitate the staying behind of the great-grandmother, Nana Peazant. Although much traveling and many journeys permeate the narrative construction of this film, I wish to discuss a different journey as regards *Daughters of the Dust:* the journeying eye of the white woman viewer as it surveys the first feature film made by an African American woman. This journey entails discussion of theoretical issues such as positionality as well as white women's personal/political issues such as fear, resistance, mastery, and psychological safety.

The preceding description of the film's opening accurately highlights the women pictured in *Daughters of the Dust,* the camera techniques, the remote setting that instigates the journey, the action, and the movement of the plot. However, Toni Cade Bambara's description of the film's opening reminds me to transcend the general accuracies

of my "privileged" white gaze. She immediately situates more complex axes of journeys defined by political action and a particular
historical moment:

> We meet the Peazants in a defining moment—a family council. Demo-
> cratic decision-making, a right ripped from them by slavery and re-
> gained through emancipation, hallmarks the moment. The Peazants and
> guests gather on the island at Ibo Landing for a picnic at a critical
> juncture in history—they are one generation away from the Garvey and
> the New Negro movements, a decade short of the Niagara/NAACP
> merger. They are in the midst of rapid changes; black people are on the
> move North, West, and back to Africa (the Oklahoma project, for in-
> stance). Setting the story amid oak groves, salt marshes, and a glorious
> beach is not for the purpose of presenting a nostalgic community in a
> pastoral setting. They are an imperiled group.[4]

Bambara reads the often untold and ever accumulating history of
enslavement and its consequences in the mere setting of *Daughters of
the Dust,* where I had read mostly visual details of the scene.

Historian Margaret Washington Creel points out that the predominantly African-born slaves brought to these Sea Islands originated
from the same parts of Africa: the Kongo-Angola region, the Liberian
Hinterland, the Windward Coast, and perhaps Upper Guinea.[5] Viewing this film as a white woman requires grappling with the particularities of slavery and origins offered by Bambara and Creel. Viewing this
film as a white woman requires grappling with assumptions about
definitions of United States involvement in the enslavement of black
peoples, about where slavery occurred in the United States, and about
generalizations regarding slavery. Viewing this film studiously requires replacing assumptions and generalizations with an immersion
into particular historical and representational details only recently
uncovered and made available by historians, anthropologists, lin-
guists, literary critics, and film scholars working on the history of
enslavement and its consequences in the United States.

The viewing becomes even more complicated for a white woman,
because while trying to study the accuracies of history, while trying to

shift the weight of whiteness so that I can see and attempt to under-
stand new particulars regarding slavery, I must also remain aware of
Julie Dash's role as practitioner of cinematic artistry. *Daughters of the
Dust* is not a documentary; it is a fiction. bell hooks reminds us that

> one of the major problems facing black filmmakers is the way both
> spectators and, often, the dominant culture want to reduce us to some
> narrow notion of "real" or "accurate." And it seems to me that one of
> the groudbreaking aspects of *Daughters of the Dust*, because it truly is
> a groundbreaking film, is its insistence on a movement away from
> dependence on "reality," "accuracy," "authenticity," into a realm of the
> imaginative.[6]

All viewers of African American film must work to separate fiction
from history, but white viewers must first care to know that a particular history, albeit one to be separated from fiction, exists.

When accounting for such discrepancies in viewing between white
women and black women viewers, Alile Sharon Larkin faults Holly-
wood's control of the black image as well as white women's participation in reaping "the benefits of white supremacy," a white supremacy
that allows and encourages an "ahistorical approach towards Black
women."[7] My white woman's eye travels Julie Dash's film with a lens
that differs from Toni Cade Bambara's, and this essay sets out to
explore the differences of this journeying white eye and the implications of these differences.

Journeying and traveling prove distinctly apropos tropes when
discussing the Sea Island peoples, because these peoples associated
the concept of traveling with spiritual transformation:

> The most important indication of spiritual transformation was the vi-
> sion or *travel* as interpreted by the spiritual parent. "This word *travel*,"
> wrote one Methodist missionary, "is one of the most significant in their
> language, and comprehends all those exercises, spiritual, visionary and
> imaginative which make up an 'experience.' "[8]

The eye of the white woman viewer certainly must undertake a spiritual as well as an intellectual and emotional transformation in order

to experience this film with any sense of the integrity with which Julie Dash made it.

The motif of the spiritual transformation provides a theme common to black women writers. Deborah McDowell describes the black female's journey as "part of an evolutionary spiral, moving from victimization to consciousness."[9] However, Dash revises this explanation of the African American woman's journey by eradicating the victimization: "Specifically, I focus on intragroup relationships, rather than on images of Black women as victims of the outside world that's impacting on them."[10] By emphasizing the variations of choices made by individual women in the film, *Daughters of the Dust* expands and problematizes the journey as motif in black literature and film.

As journeys differ, so do viewing experiences. In her book *The Making of the Daughters of the Dust,* Dash privileges three audiences for the film: "black women first, then the black community and white women."[11] Privileged by invitation, my viewing journey also flaunts the so-called privilege afforded me by my whiteness. This "privilege" has as its foremost consequence my blindness to the particulars occurring in black women's lives and in their art.

As I made my journey toward an accurate and responsible viewing of the film, it became clear that content as well as historical and theoretical context required further research, because my position as a white woman researcher of black art itself needed study. Ironically, African Americans have written the accumulating, but still minute, body of work regarding the white woman as reader and viewer of the black text. Barbara Smith rails against that specialized "lack of knowing" practiced by the white woman and suggests that she read with a sense of her privilege, not as a favor to black women, but as a favor to herself.[12] When white critic Minrose Gwin suggests that white women learn to read ourselves in black women's texts as white other,[13] Barbara Christian quickly says no—read as a white *woman*. Why turn into "otherness" the strongest connection we have?[14] And Toni Morrison suggests that along with the continued study of racism's impact on

African Americans, we should study "the impact of racism on those who perpetuate it."[15] The varied messages to white women have a clear theme: read with an eye to personal and institutionalized privilege and with an awareness of personal blind spots.

White women must read black texts to learn—if not to fully understand—what whiteness means to black people and to learn that whiteness exists. And yet, another task exists—that of discovering what whiteness means to white people. White, as racial nomenclature, has constituted a given, an entity never to undergo scrutiny; white has been equated with the state of being human. Reading with an eye to one's own whiteness means penetrating that blinding aura of years of racial ignorance. Judith Levine writes that

> Whiteness is the most obscure difference of all—because it is not considered a difference. Even to radical white American thinkers, whiteness has long assumed the status of normalcy; like heterosexuality, it is the center around which everything else moves, the standard against which the other is inferior, deviant, exotic, or simply noteworthy.[16]

She notes further that once we name whiteness and witness it in ourselves and others, we can begin to participate differently in conversations about race relations. "Race" then will constitute more than "just something that happens to someone else, the people with 'race.' "[17]

Levine ultimately deems it necessary for white people to reject whiteness, to unload it like a burdensome, yet unnamed, knapsack. I aggressively veer away from this viewpoint because I do not believe that a rejection of whiteness is necessary, possible, or desirable. White people subjecting ourselves to self-hatred and/or incapacitating guilt furthers no conversation. But recognizing the burdens and the freedoms of the knapsack called whiteness, and doing something different with this burden/privilege—shifting the way we carry the burden and sharing the freedoms it contains—provoke new conversations and new arguments.

This task seems to belong to all white people, but for white women who want more than a rhetorical connection with all women, the task becomes more immediate. White women do not have to wait for their oppression by white men to be lifted in order to practice carrying our whiteness differently. We do not have to prioritize our work in this way. It is important to remember that "Black women do not necessarily see the Black male as patriarchal antagonist but feel instead that their racial oppression is 'shared' with men."[18] What white women need to understand is that "Where we have foregrounded one antagonism in our analysis, we have misunderstood another, and this is most dramatically illustrated in the applications of the notion of patriarchy."[19] The white woman's position has not always been a compatible one or a safe one for black women to share.

What Dash tries to capture on screen is a space safe from whiteness/normalcy. "Black women's efforts to find a voice have occurred in at least three safe spaces. One location involves Black women's relationships with one another. . . . in Black churches . . . or in Black women's organizations."[20] Never before has cinematic space been depicted as safe space for African American black women to gather. "Institutions controlled by the dominant group such as schools, the media, literature, and popular culture are the initial source of externally defined, controlling images."[21] Dash breaks this tradition by usurping media space for the safe expression of black women. She removes them from whiteness, or rather she neither recognizes, situates, nor comments on any totally non-black women. She centers black women's experiences, arguments, laughter, ethics, and behavior as the sole motivation for the film and its narrative. The only whiteness present on screen belongs to Trula, a light-skinned, red-haired African American whose entire site invites interrogation: Is she lesbian? Is she white? The only whiteness present serves to provoke questions about its position, its look, its nature, its definition, and its fixity.

The mere act of centering the speaking black women in her film, complicated by the act of having them speak Gullah, is a radical departure from the way black women have traditionally been portrayed on screen.

> Usually non-white or female others are positioned as visibly and unalterably different and as silenced, excluded from language. Unheard, these others are seen as weaker and more primitive, yet as threatening and powerful as well. In these cases where the racial, colonial, or national other is actually heard in mainstream films, her or his speech is usually an incomprehensible babel, part of the background, a block of sound. Because we cannot understand her or him, we are sure that s/he is relatively unimportant. Only to the degree that s/he adopts the language of the dominant culture is s/he granted "the status of speech as an individual property right."[22]

Dash moves both the physical presence of the black woman as well as this issue of language to the forefront of the film. The language these women in *Daughters of the Dust* speak is not babel; rather, it constitutes a language in need of preservation, a language that fully expresses a particular culture, a particular historical moment. These women do not speak background noise. Dash foregrounds the issue of language and the people attached to it by using this film as the historical monument raised to honor the Gullah women.

The white viewer immediately recognizes that Gullah is not babel. And, although this language might at first seem designed to marginalize white people, in fact, during the nineteenth century, such a critical mass of black peoples spoke Gullah in the Sea Island area that white people also learned it, making Gullah the dominant form of language in this area:

> In the lopsided demographic circumstances of the lowcountry nearly all whites necessarily had much contact with blacks, but many blacks had only limited contact with whites. The Waccamaw planters by and large learned to talk like their slaves rather than expecting their slaves to talk like them. . . . Northern and English visitors rarely failed to note the extent to which the planters, outnumbered nine to one by their slaves, absorbed elements of Gullah.[23]

Julie Dash approximates the position experienced by the white colonizer of the nineteenth century for her white audience by demanding
that such audiences negotiate an understanding of the Gullah language.

By "position," I mean what Homi Bhabha means when he describes
the "reinforcing and contradictory effects 'class, gender, ideology,
different social formations, varied systems of colonization, etc.' have
on people."[24] According to Bhabha, these reinforcements and contradictions support the way power makes itself known in discourse
both through oppositions between "black" and "white" discourse and
through interconnections experienced by the colonizer and the colonized.[25] In other words, Dash re-creates Gullah as a site of interconnectedness between colonizers and colonized. She positions the language, not only as that language most like African languages, but also
as that language once and still shared by peoples, black and white, of
the Sea Islands.

Along with Gullah, which serves as an overt articulator of the
journey, Julie Dash provides an encoded language system that also
speaks of the women's journeys: the language of hair. A substantive
instance of viewing like a white woman from a so-called privileged
position is watching *Daughters of the Dust* with the assumption that all
women's attire in film matters to the degree that it cinematically
denotes class, sexual attitude, locale, personal taste, time period, or
self-esteem. Viewers have been trained to decode the costumes of
cinematic characters in order to quickly ascertain the types of people
involved in the plot. Dash writes that she particularly wanted to make
a film from an Afrocentric point of view right down to the costuming.
When pressed for particulars, she says,

> Like the "doo-rag" on the hair and how it's tied.... The way we
> approached it was to do as your mother did—and as did her mother
> before her. So, it would be tied in a much different way than what
> popular American culture would allow us to see it. The manners in

which African women tie their heads with scarves has different meanings.[26]

I did not notice the intricacies of the doo-rags either the first or the
second time I watched the film. My position as a white woman rendered me not only unknowing, but also unaware of my lack. In
researching the meaning of these "doo-rags," I listened to Dash tell
bell hooks that she designed the doo-rags "as your mother did." The
"your" does not refer to my mother, and Dash thereby renders me
motherless, without birthright to this information. The details only
become discernible once I choose to break the aura of blind white
privilege with a genuine sense of curiosity. Upon studying the small-
est element of the costuming, I realize that I have not viewed this film
with much clarity. Having to be told by someone else to look at the
invisible, in the form of quite visible doo-rags, triggers the need and
the creation of an entire new context.

The question comes up at this point whether certain black members
of the audience might also lack the experience to recognize the semiotic resonances of the doo-rags in *Daughters of the Dust*. The answer is
yes, of course, and this answer reveals the problematic that white
positioning transcends the notion of white-skinned and instead becomes occupiable thinking space. Certain areas of white lack may be
traversed by all peoples of color. Further, certain areas of white fulfillment may be traversed by all peoples of color. White skin signifies
only the likelihood of lack, not its inevitability. And since this space,
like any "position," merely constitutes thinking space that may be
occupied, this position may be shed or moved through.

Although seemingly a minor detail of the film, more suited to a
discussion of the development of a period piece than as a political or
semiotic challenge, the doo-rag and the "politics of the hairdo"[27]
speak volumes about the image of blacks in this country. In his essay
"In the Kitchen," Gates remarks that "the most important thing about
our gas-equipped kitchen was that Mama used to do hair there."[28] He
describes in detail the process that women went through in his Ma-

ma's kitchen in order to get their hair straightened. He provides the history of straightening black hair and names Madame C. J. Walker, "the woman who invented the process of straightening kinky hair."[29] He also provides all the names embedded in black culture for these products, products not sold to white people in this country. Gates says,

> I used all the greases, from sea-blue Bergamot and creamy vanilla Duke (in its clear jar with the orange-white-and-green label) to the godfather of grease, the formidable Murray's. Now, Murray's was some *serious* grease. Whereas Bergamot was like oily jello, and Duke was viscous and sickly sweet, Murray's was light brown and *hard*. Hard as lard and twice as greasy, Daddy used to say. Murray's came in a orange can with a press-on top. It was so hard that some people would put a match to the can, just to soften the stuff and make it more manageable. Then, in the late sixties, when Afros came into style, I used Afro Sheen. From Murray's to Duke to Afro Sheen: that was my progression in black consciousness.[30]

These products are not simply products; rather, they represent cultural consciousness in a capitalistic society. These products are what the culture sold its peoples, or certain of its peoples, in order to make them presentable, in order to "straighten" them out.

Gates goes on to discuss "rags" and "do-rags." (Dash and Gates spell "do(o)-rags" differently). He says people also wore " 'rags'— cloths or handkerchiefs—around their heads when they slept or played basketball. Do-rags, they were called. But the result was straight hair, with just a hint of wave. No curl."[31] The history of the signification of doo-rags, first worn by early slaves and still worn by contemporary basketball players, marks a complex and evolving attitude toward "straightening." A white person, or any person occupying a white position, most likely would not recognize this doo-rag as a signifier of whitening; he or she sees the doo-rag, if at all, as unremarkable adornment.

Patricia Hill Collins discusses the issue of hair and hair rituals among women in the African American community. She cites an excerpt from historian Elsa Barkley Brown's work to point out the storytelling and the rituals associated with the doing of hair in the black community:

> Except for special occasions mama came home from work early on Saturdays. She spent six days a week mopping, waxing and dusting other women's houses and keeping out of reach of other women's husbands. Saturday nights were reserved for "taking care of them girls" hair and the telling of stories. Some of which included a recitation of what she had endured and how she had triumphed over "folks that were lower than dirt" and "no-good snakes in the grass." She combed, patted, twisted and talked, saying things which would have embarrassed or shamed her at other times.[32]

Julie Dash refers to a scene that did not make it into the film, a scene about hair: "And another scene that we didn't get a chance to shoot was the family hairbraider braiding the map of their journey north, in the hair design, on a woman's head."[33]

The white woman viewer must look through a different lens for the history of the African American woman, a lens capable of framing both historical and semiotic particularities. Dash offers the metaphor of Gullah as an overt example of the many languages, visual and aural, that speak this history. She provides the sign of the doo-rag as an encoded semiotic chronicler of black women's journeys. Finally, Dash also offers an intriguing visual and aural cinematic site as the political space most in need of negotiation among feminist women— that of the Unborn Child.

Giving voice and cinematic substance to an Unborn Child in a film about women and directed by a woman comes treacherously close to the feminist issue that, according to bell hooks, never yielded the same currency to white and black women—the issue of abortion. hooks claims that for white women, abortion stands out as *the* reproductive rights issue, overshadowing issues of sterilization, race, and class in the women's movement.[34] Dash gives voice to the Unborn Child as a way of sounding this volatile site of discourse. The site houses an intersection among the beliefs of the African ancestors about the power of the Unborn, the beliefs of white feminists regarding reproductive rights, and the current needs and aspirations of African American women artists.

The site of the Unborn Child makes me personally uncomfortable for the exact reasons that Dash wants to make me, a white woman feminist, uncomfortable. The Unborn Child resurrects numerous fears associated with the politics of abortion, reproduction, and women's primacy as mothers: the fear that the "pro-life" movement could and would use this material as an affirmation of life at all stages in the womb; the fear of the potential of any and all abortion politics to divide women one from another; the fear that women are indeed more different from one another than they are similar and that the desire to bear children provides the differing mark; the fear that the various heritages to which women pledge allegiance may, in fact, bear a stronger pull on women than do their contemporary women peers; and, ultimately, that any show of divisiveness among women regarding abortion rights might bring down all the gains that feminists (of all races and genders) have accomplished in this area over the past few decades. Julie Dash's Unborn Child bears the burden of these fears, and it is to Dash's credit that she flaunts the fears before all women, but particularly white women, so that we name, define, and begin to negotiate this fear before it overwhelms us.

The narrating discourse of the journeying Unborn Child, while it provides a representation of fear for some viewers, also provides another link in Julie Dash's concern with the journey toward origins as both a personal and a metaphoric guide to the film. Nana Peazant calls on the Unborn Child being carried by Eula to help her and the family members with the departure. The film's director responds cinematically to this call by using the voice of the Unborn Child as narrator for parts of the film, thereby introducing a discourse of the journeying unborn: "A remember de call of my grea grandmudda.... A remember de journey home ... A remember de long walk ta de family graveyard, ta de house that A would be born in, . . . ta de picnic site. A remember an A recall."[35]

This discourse is a particularly intimate and autobiographical one for Dash herself. In the preproduction days of the film she found herself pregnant:

> I had to quickly make a decision as to what I was going to do. I had two choices—to put off the production for at least another year or to have an abortion. I made my decision to go forward with the filming of *Daughters*. I flew back to Atlanta to have the abortion. This was a painful decision many women have had to face, especially women who must rely on their physical as well as mental stamina to perform professionally. Unfortunately, many women do not have the same options that I had. At least I could still make a choice. *Daughters* would become the child that I would bear that year.[36]

The discourse of the Unborn Child, then, while often central to the structure and the narration of the film, also serves as political and autobiographical journeying for Dash herself through the making of a film.

The form and content of the making of this film coalesce in the narrative design of the Unborn Child. As the site of Dash's personal and political decision to abort her own child, the film simultaneously provides an admission that the Unborn Child has a voice. As such, this site defers to the rituals and religions of Dash's African ancestors. Aborting the child does not mean silencing the belief that the child had a voice; indeed, she gives it a voice in her film. Aborting the child does not mean buying into white culture's—particularly feminist culture's—fear that giving voice to an unborn child would accord the child status as a viable life, thereby constituting admission to murder. But this site is not a contradictory place for Dash. It is a unifying place, a place where life structures meet and interact—a place that gives birth to art.

According to Patricia Hill Collins, "White feminist work on motherhood has failed to produce an effective critique of elite white male analyses of Black motherhood."[37] White women have colluded in allowing the stereotypes of the mammy, the welfare mother, and the matriarch to stand strong. But many other types of motherhood have occurred in the African American community. "Bloodmothers" and "othermothers" provide whatever care the community children need. "Grandmothers, sisters, aunts, or cousins act as othermothers by taking on child-care responsibilities for one another's children."[38] Thus, in Dash's film, the strong bonds between the Unborn Child and the grandmother speak a truth about othermothers and the nonreification of the biological mother. The biological father in *Daughters of the Dust*, Eli, has concerns about his connection to the Unborn Child, given that Eula, his wife, was raped. However, Nana tries to dissuade him from these concerns:

> *Nana:* The ancestors and the womb are one. Call on your ancestors, Eli. Let them guide you. You need their strength. Eli, I need you to make the family strong again, like we used to be.
> *Eli:* How can you understand me and the way I feel? This happened to my wife. My wife! I don't feel like she's mine anymore. When I look at her, I feel I don't want her anymore.
> *Nana:* You can't give back what you never owned. Eula never belonged to you, she married you.

Nana Peazant refuses to participate in Eli's confusion about possession, ownership, and fatherhood.

Joan Raphael-Leff tells us in *The Psychological Processes of Childbearing* that African men view their children as achievements.[39] She goes on to provide information that elucidates Nana Peazant's beliefs about the womb and the ancestors being unified:

> In some cultures, conception is believed to be the result of spirit entry, magical impregnation, ancestor intervention or reincarnation necessitating various rituals and observances to ensure conception, and the safety of the pregnancy, the woman, her baby and/or the community at large.[40]

Such perceptions about the fetus or unborn child are not peculiar to African-related communities. Many cultures have varying beliefs regarding conception and the fetus:

> The Eastern Ojibwa mother of Perry Island, Canada believes her child learns in the womb from the mother talking and teaching its soul and shadow such information as the habits of animals it would encounter as it grew up. . . . The Arapesh of New Guinea believe the baby sleeps in the womb until ready for birth, then dives out. The Iatmul head-hunters of the Great Sepik river believe an unborn child can hurry or delay and chooses its own time of birth. A Jewish folkloric belief holds that unborn babies know "everything" but as the time of birth approaches, each is touched above the upper lip by the Angel Gabriel, whereupon s/he forgets all previous knowledge but retains forever the imprint of his finger.[41]

In her work regarding patriarchal images of the maternal voice in film, Kaja Silverman asserts that the unborn and the newborn child have often been portrayed as trapped inside a dangerous enclosure created by the maternal voice.[42] Interestingly, Dash breaks form with this imagery by having the Unborn Child speak from the womb in narrative voice-overs. The technology of film also allows Dash to create the spirit of the unborn child visually. She looks about five years old. She runs through people's bodies in the film, and she runs along the beach with the wind. Dash's Unborn Child as portrayed in *Daughters of the Dust* is neither trapped nor in danger. She has a voice of her own, a voice strong enough for the grandmother to hear.

The first time we hear the voice of Eula's Unborn Child, she tells us a story. As a raconteur, she is positioned as a recollector even though she has not yet been born:

> My story begins on the eve of my family's migration North. My story begins before I was born. My great great grandmother, Nana Peazant, saw her family coming apart. Her flowers to bloom in a distant frontier.

The Unborn Child speaks the story as her own, as the story she has already been born into. She is possessive about the story, evidenced

by the plethora of "my's": "my family," "my story," "my great grandmother." This is her story. She has a story as an Unborn Child.
Interestingly, the first specific relationship she discusses is that with
her great grandmother, which supports her awareness of this significant othermother.

The second time the Unborn Child speaks, she tells us that "Nana
prayed and the old souls guided me into the New World." She knows
exactly how she got here. But the "New World" she refers to remains
ambiguous: the "New World" could refer to America (as learned from
the ancestors), or it could be that she already exists in a world and
that birth provides her a New World to exist in differently.

The womb is a place in this film from where the Unborn Child can
see faces and can smell odors and fragrances. She has her senses, and
her mother's body does not block her view at all, nor does it contain
her. Her spirit leaves the mother's body at will (or whim). She says, "I
can still see their faces, smell the oil in the wicker lamps." The womb
houses the new and the old, and the womb is, simultaneously, vessel,
place, and spirit. It is not the organic, biological construct of science
and medicine.

This spirit can also be seen by others. Nana Peazant "sees" the
Unborn Child, but she sees her more with her intuition than with her
eyes. Mr. Snead, the photographer, sees the Unborn Child through his
camera lens, which proves an interesting gesture on Julie Dash's
part—employing the camera as sonographic instrument. In this gesture, she lets us know that the camera can serve as a lens into space
that we might not otherwise see.

The Unborn Child that we see is not all serious, wise, and bearer of
terrific weight. She can be quite childlike and playful. She admits,
"I was traveling on a spiritual mission, but sometimes I would get
distracted." In the film, she becomes childishly distracted by a catalog
picture of a stuffed toy bear.

The end of the film represents the Unborn Child's journey as the
most memorable, as the highlight of the movie. She traipses along the

beach alone, one with the sand, with the dust of the beach, and she stands alone along the horizon, emblem of all that is past, present, and future, here and distant. The Unborn Child is of her parents, but also of the world. She represents the eternally Unborn, the untouchable. And Dash makes her sturdy. Dash does not make her an emblem of the political right-to-life. It is not that type of life to which Dash's Unborn Child refers. She is, rather, emblem of the spirit that cannot be touched, harmed, or forgotten; the spirit that cannot be removed ever from the past; the spirit that passes in and out of this world by choice. She serves as an emblem of that which cannot be destroyed, of the African human spirit, of that which simultaneously remains behind, but which also grows "older, wiser, stronger."

Julie Dash sounds the struggles of emigrating peoples in order to revitalize and prolong the memory of journeying, because her life experience tells her that the journeys might soon be suppressed:

> when I probed my relatives for information about the family history in South Carolina, or about our migration north to New York, they were often reluctant to discuss it. When things got too personal, too close to memories they didn't want to reveal, they would close up, push me away, tell me to ask someone else.[43]

Daughters of the Dust invites viewers, some white, some black, to keep the journeying alive so that we too may eternally remain in the Unborn position of growing older, wiser, and stronger through our interconnected pasts, presents, and futures.

In order to respond justly to the invitation to view *Daughters of the Dust* that Julie Dash offers white women, we must view differently than we have viewed all other previous films. We must admit that this film provides a first, a one-of-a-kind opportunity to start anew, to see with fresh eyes. Part of this admission means "reading" the film with an eye toward historical and aesthetic particularities pertinent to the study of various African Americans. It means doing research and returning again to the film. Admitting the need to read (and view) anew and to read (and view) again means that the white woman viewer must problematize the relationship between the many African Americans and the many U.S. landscapes, must problematize the relationship between the many whites and the many U.S. landscapes. It means shifting the focus of racial study toward a scrutiny of whiteness and lack or a scrutiny of whiteness and privilege, and away from the sole study of blackness and oppression.

Viewing anew also means a release of mastery for the white woman viewer. The white woman viewer, as well as many other peoples occupying a similar position, has never seen such a film to date, and must leave behind certain skills mastered in the viewing of previous films. Any white woman journeying toward teaching this film must consider her position as white woman in order to provide ample access to the film for her students. Teaching Dash's *Daughters of the Dust* provides a singular occasion to raise issues of alterity, positionality, mastery, and whiteness in the classroom, an occasion well worth the personal and political effort.

NOTES

1. Zeinabu Irene Davis, "An Interview with Julie Dash," *Wide-Angle: A Quarterly Journal of Film, History, Theory, Criticism and Practice* 13, nos. 3–4 (1991): 11–13.

2. Deborah E. McDowell, "New Directions for Black Feminist Criticism," in *The New Feminist Criticism: Essays on Women, Literature and Theory,* ed. Elaine Showalter (New York: Pantheon, 1985), 195.

3. Davis, 112.

4. Toni Cade Bambara, "Reading the Signs, Empowering the Eye: *Daughters of the Dust* and the Black Independent Cinema Movement," in *Black American Cinema,* ed. Manthia Diawara (New York: Routledge, 1993), 122.

5. Margaret Washington Creel, *"A Peculiar People": Slave Religion and Community Culture among the Gullahs* (New York: New York University Press, 1988), 15–17, 32.

6. Julie Dash, with Toni Cade Bambara and bell hooks, *Daughters of the Dust: The Making of an African-American Woman's Film* (New York: New Press, 1992), 31.

7. Alile Sharon Larkin, "Black Women Film-Makers Defining Ourselves:

Feminism in Our Own Voice," in *Female Spectators: Looking at Film and Television*, ed. E. Deidre Pribram (New York: Verso, 1988), 157.

8. Joseph E. Holloway, ed., *Africanism in American Culture* (Bloomington: Indiana University Press, 1990), 80.

9. McDowell, 195.

10. Davis, 11.

11. Dash, 66.

12. Smith, 168.

13. Minrose C. Gwin, "A Theory of Black Women's Texts and White Women's Readings, or . . . The Necessity of Being Other," *NWSA Journal* 1, no. 1 (1988): 22.

14. Barbara T. Christian, "Response to 'Black Women's Texts,' " *NWSA Journal* 1, no. 1 (1988): 49.

15. Toni Morrison, *Playing in the Dark: Whiteness and the Literary Imagination* (Cambridge: Harvard University Press, 1992), 11.

16. Judith Levine, "The Heart of Whiteness: Dismantling the Master's House," *Voice Literary Supplement*, September 1994, 11.

17. Levine, 16.

18. Jane Gaines, "White Privilege and Looking Relations: Race and Gender in Feminist Film Theory," *Cultural Critique* 4 (fall 1986): 66.

19. Gaines, 67.

20. Patricia Hill Collins, *Black Feminist Thought: Knowledge, Consciousness, and the Politics of Empowerment* (New York: Routledge, 1991), 96.

21. Collins, 95.

22. Christine Anne Holmlund, "Displacing Limits of Difference: Gender, Race, and Colonialism in Edward Said and Homi Bhabha's Theoretical Models and Marguerite Duras's Experimental Films," in *QRVF: Quarterly Review of Film and Video* 13, nos. 1–3 (1991): 3.

23. Charles Joyner, *Down by the Riverside: A South Carolina Slave Community* (Chicago: University of Illinois Press, 1984), 208.

24. Holmlund, 6.

25. Holmlund, 6.

26. Davis, 116.

27. Henry Louis Gates, Jr., "In the Kitchen," *New Yorker*, April 18, 1994, 82.

28. Gates, 82.

29. Gates, 84.

30. Gates, 84.

31. Gates, 85.

32. Collins, 25.

33. Dash, 53.

34. bell hooks, Gloria Steinem, Urvashi Vaid, and Naomi Wolf, "Let's Get

Real about Feminism: The Backlash, the Myths, the Movement," *Ms.* 4, no. 2 (1993): 38.

35. Dash, 167.

36. Dash, 9–10.

37. Collins, 116.

38. Collins, 119–20.

39. Joan Raphael-Leff, *Psychological Processes of Childbearing* (New York: Chapman and Hall, 1991). Mark A. Reid, "Dialogic Modes of Representing Africa(s): Womanist Film," *Black American Literature Forum* 25, no. 2 (summer 1991): 25.

40. Raphael-Leff, 56.

41. Raphael-Leff, 119.

42. Kaja Silverman, *The Acoustic Mirror: The Female Voice in Psychoanalysis and Cinema* (Bloomington: Indiana University Press, 1988).

43. Dash, 5.

BIBLIOGRAPHY

Bambara, Toni Cade. "Reading the Signs, Empowering the Eye: *Daughters of the Dust* and the Black Independent Cinema Movement." In *Black American Cinema*, ed. Manthia Diawara.

Christian, Barbara T. "Response to 'Black Women's Texts.'" *NWSA Journal* 1, no. 1 (1988).

Collins, Patricia Hill. *Black Feminist Thought: Knowledge, Consciousness, and the Politics of Empowerment.* New York: Routledge, 1991.

Creel, Margaret Washington. *"A Peculiar People": Slave Religion and Community Culture among the Gullahs.* New York: New York University Press, 1988.

Dash, Julie, with Toni Cade Bambara and bell hooks. *Daughters of the Dust: The Making of an African-American Woman's Film.* New York: New Press, 1992.

Davis, Zeinabu Irene. "An Interview with Julie Dash." *Wide-Angle: A Quarterly Journal of Film, History, Theory, Criticism and Practice* 13, nos. 3–4 (1991).

Diawara, Manthia, ed. *Black American Cinema.* New York: Routledge, 1993.

Gaines, Jane. "White Privilege and Looking Relations: Race and Gender in Feminist Film Theory." *Cultural Critique* 4 (fall 1986).

Gates, Henry Louis, Jr. "In the Kitchen." *New Yorker*, April 18, 1994.

Gwin, Minrose C. "A Theory of Black Women's Texts and White Women's Readings, or ... The Necessity of Being Other." *NWSA Journal* 1, no. 1 (1988).

Holloway, Joseph E., ed. *Africanism in American Culture.* Bloomington: Indiana University Press, 1990.

Holmlund, Christine Anne. "Displacing Limits of Difference: Gender, Race, and Colonialism in Edward Said and Homi Bhabha's Theoretical Models and Marguerite Duras's Experimental Films." *QRVF: Quarterly Review of Film and Video* 13 (1–3). 1991.

hooks, bell. Gloria Steinem, Urvashi Vaid, and Naomi Wolf. "Let's Get Real about Feminism: The Backlash, the Myths, the Movement." *Ms.* 4, no. 2 (1993).

Joyner, Charles. *Down by the Riverside: A South Carolina Slave Community.* Chicago: University of Illinois Press, 1984.

Larkin, Alile Sharon. "Black Women Film-Makers Defining Ourselves: Feminism in Our Own Voice." In *Female Spectators: Looking at Film and Television,* ed. E. Deidre Pribram. New York: Verso, 1988.

Levine, Judith. "The Heart of Whiteness: Dismantling the Master's House." *Voice Literary Supplement,* September 1994.

McDowell, Deborah E. "New Directions for Black Feminist Criticism." In ed. Elaine Showalter.

Morrison, Toni. *Playing in the Dark: Whiteness and the Literary Imagination.* Cambridge: Harvard University Press, 1992.

Raphael-Leff, Joan. *Psychological Processes of Childbearing.* New York: Chapman and Hall, 1991.

Reid, Mark A. "Dialogic Modes of Representing Africa(s): Womanist Film." *Black American Literature Forum* 25, no. 2 (summer 1991).

Showalter, Elaine, ed. *The New Feminist Criticism: Essays on Women, Literature and Theory.* New York: Pantheon, 1985.

Silverman, Kaja. *The Acoustic Mirror: The Female Voice in Psychoanalysis and Cinema.* Bloomington: Indiana University Press, 1988.

Smith, Barbara. "Toward a Black Feminist Criticism." In ed. Elaine Showalter.

Contributors

GERARD ACHING is Assistant Professor of Spanish and Portuguese at Rutgers University in New Brunswick, New Jersey. He has written on Spanish American *modernismo* and on nineteenth- and twentieth-century Caribbean literatures. His most recent book is *Discourses of Engagement: The Politics of Spanish American Modernismo* (forthcoming). He is currently working on a book, entitled *Nostalgia for Carnival,* on the contemporary cultural politics of Caribbean carnivals.

CELESTE M. CONDIT is Professor of Speech Communication at the University of Georgia. She is the author of *Decoding Abortion Rhetoric: Communicating Social Change* (University of Illinois, 1990), and coauthor with John Louis Lucaites of *Crafting Equality: America's Anglo-African Word* (University of Chicago Press, 1993). She has just coedited *Evaluating Women's Health Messages: A Resource Book* with Roxanne Louiselle Parrott (Sage, forthcoming), and is working on research in the discourse of medical genetics.

RENÉE R. CURRY is Associate Professor of Literature and Writing at California State University San Marcos. She has edited *Perspectives on Woody Allen* (G.K. Hall/Macmillan, 1996), and has coedited *States of Rage: Emotional Eruption, Violence, and Social Change* (New York University Press, 1996). She is currently at work on a book, *White Women Writing White,* which discusses the positionality and authorship of twentieth-century white women poets in the United States.

BARBARA DIBERNARD is Director of Women's Studies and Associate Professor of English at the University of Nebraska-Lincoln. Her most recent publications include *"Zami:* A Portrait of an Artist as a Black Lesbian," in *Kenyon Review;* and "Being an I-Witness: My Life as a Lesbian Teacher," in *Private Voices, Public Lives: Women Speak on the Literary Life,* ed. Nancy Owen Nelson (University of North Texas Press, 1995).

CHRISTIE FARNHAM, formerly Director of Women's Studies and member of the Afro-American Studies Department at Indiana University, is presently Associate Professor of History at Iowa State University. She is founding editor of the *Journal of Women's History* and has edited *The Impact of Feminist Research in the Academy* (Indiana University Press, 1987). She is author of *The Education of the Southern Belle* (New York University Press, 1994) and articles on African American history. Currently, she is working on a history of African American women from the seventeenth century to the present.

CRAIG W. HELLER is a lecturer in the Women's Studies Program at Pennsylvania State University. His research is on feminist pedagogy and the effects of gender on student socialization in higher education. For the 1995–96 academic year, he is Visiting Lecturer in the Institute of African Studies at the University of Nairobi.

J. SCOTT JOHNSON is Assistant Professor of Political Science at Saint John's University in Collegeville, Minnesota. He has previously published in the *American Political Science Review* on Nietzsche and Foucault. He is presently working on an essay concerning two intentional fallacies and a monograph on Shakespeare and political theory.

JACQUELINE JONES is Truman Professor of American Civilization at Brandeis University. She is the author of *The Dispossessed:*

America's Underclasses from the Civil War to the Present (Basic Books, 1992); *Labor of Love, Labor of Sorrow: Black Women, Work, and the Family from Slavery to the Present* (Basic Books, 1986, winner of the Bancroft Prize in American History and finalist for the Pulitzer Prize in American History); and *Soldiers of Light and Love: Northern Teachers and Georgia Blacks, 1965–1873* (University of North Carolina Press, 1980; 1992). Her essays on gender, race, and class have appeared in numerous anthologies and historical journals. Jones is currently at work on a book titled *American Work: A Social History.*

INDIRA KARAMCHETI is Assistant Professor at Wesleyan University in Middletown, Connecticut. She is completing a book on the formation of postcolonial studies as a discipline in United States academia.

JENNIFER KELLEN is a senior political science major at the College of Saint Benedict in Saint Joseph, Minnesota. She is writing an honors thesis on welfare reform and will attend graduate school in public policy a year after graduation.

MARY ELIZABETH LANSER is a doctoral student in educational theory and policy studies in the College of Education at Pennsylvania State University. She is currently writing a dissertation tentatively entitled "Legitimacy and Empowerment: Twin Issues in Conflict for Black Studies."

GARY L. LEMONS is Director of the Literature program at Eugene Lang College, the liberal arts undergraduate division of the New School for Social Research in New York City. He teaches courses in African American literature, race, gender, and feminist studies. He is also a faculty member of the New School's graduate program in gender studies and feminist theory.

ROBERT S. LEVINE is Associate Professor of English at the University of Maryland, College Park. He is the author of *Conspiracy and Romance: Studies in Brockden Brown, Cooper, Hawthorne, and Melville* (Cambridge University Press, 1989), and the editor of the forthcoming *Cambridge Companion to Herman Melville.* He recently completed a book manuscript on the intersecting careers of Martin Delany and Frederick Douglass.

KATHERINE J. MAYBERRY is Professor of Language and Literature at the Rochester Institute of Technology. She is the author of *Christina Rossetti: The Poetry of Discovery* (Louisiana State University Press, 1989), and, with Robert E. Golden, *For Argument's Sake* (HarperCollins, 1990 and 1996). She has published numerous essays on Victorian literature, Toni Morrison, and Alice Munro. Currently, she is finishing a book titled *The Paradox of Narrative: Subversive Strategies from Charlotte Brontë to Alice Munro.*

NANCY J. PETERSON is Assistant Professor of English at Purdue University-West Lafayette and also serves on the American studies and women's studies program committees at Purdue. She is the assistant editor of *Modern Fiction Studies* and is currently working on a book about the writing of alternative histories in literary texts by marginalized women, *Refiguring the Wounds of History.* A recent essay on Louise Erdrich's *Tracks* appeared in *PMLA* (1994).

JANET M. POWERS has been teaching at Gettysburg College since 1963. A specialist in South Asian literature, she also teaches courses in the civilization of India and women's studies. She has published articles in *World Literature Today, Literature East and West, CEA Critic, Journal of Modern Literature, Journal of South Asian Literature, World Literature Written in English,* and *South Asian Review.* Eleven entries in the Encyclopedia of World Literature in the Twentieth Century bear her name.

GREG SEIBERT is a senior political science major at Saint John's University in Collegeville, Minnesota. He is writing an honors thesis on the libertarian communitarian debate over the family. He expects to volunteer for a year after graduation before pursuing a career in teaching.

LAVINA DHINGRA SHANKAR is completing her Ph.D. in English at Tufts University, where she has taught freshman composition and literature for five years. She is coediting a forthcoming anthology of critical essays titled *Closing the Gap: South Asian Americans in Asian America.* Her publications include an article on the portrayal of women's education in British Victorian fiction in *Studies in Popular Culture,* a forthcoming essay in *Multiculturalism and Representations,* and another on the conflict between First and Third World feminisms in Bharati Mukherjee's fiction.

CELIA SHAUGHNESSY is a senior political science major at the College of Saint Benedict. She is writing an honors thesis on music in Plato and Aristotle. She will attend graduate school in public policy after graduation.

DONNA J. WATSON is a poet, playwright, and storyteller. Her work has been published in *Catalyst* magazine, *Pacific Review,* and *West Side Story.* Her work also appears under the names d. j. Watson and Dahome Darran. She learned the art of storytelling from her father, Chapman C. Johnson. She currently resides in southern California with her son Raqim, healing spirits.

BARBARA SCOTT WINKLER is Visiting Assistant Professor in Women's Studies. She has written on the history of women's studies programs and on feminist pedagogy. Her article, "'It Gave Me Courage': What Students Say about Women's Studies," was published by *NWSA Perspectives.* She is currently working on a history of the relationship between feminist pedagogy and feminist theory.

Index

Able-bodied, 132–51
Ableism, 136, 139; anti-, 144
Abortion: politics of, 345–48
Academic freedom, 289, 290
Aching, Gerard, 14, 285–307, 357
Affirmative action: challenges to, 5, 40, 41n; and faculty hiring, 203; and minority student enrollment, 1
Africa, 119–20; free schools of, 316; history of, 109
African: as term, 327–28
African American: film, 335–39; history, 10, 107, 108, 177–89; literature, 26, 28, 32, 70–71, 253, 260, 265–81; studies, 18, 108, 183; women, 81–82; women's history, 12, 177–87; women's literature, 25, 308–14, 335; See also Black; Minority
Africology, 120
Afrocentrism, 10, 39, 117–22, 128n; critique of, 121–25; development of, 326
Ahmad, Aijaz, 289, 290
AIDS, 55
Akbar, Ak'im, 127n
Alabama, University of, 287
Albrecht, Lisa, 51
Alcoff, Linda, 30–31
Alexander, M. Jacqui: "Not Just (Any) Body Can Be a Citizen," 280–81
Allen, Dennis, 67n
Althusser, Louis, 201, 211
American Historical Association, 127n
American literature: study of, 292; teaching, 8, 28–40, 243, 246
American studies, 51–52
Amsterdam University, 322
Angelou, Maya: *I Know Why the Caged Bird Sings*, 184, 185

Anti-Defamation League of B'nai B'rith, 128n
Anti-Semitism, 112, 118, 123
Anzaldúa, Gloria: *Borderlands/La Frontera: The New Mestiza*, 26–28
Appropriation, 114; of feminism, 262–63; *See also* Imperialism
Apthekar, Bettina, 29
Ariel, 223, 225
Aristotle, 165
Armah, Ayi Kwei, 317
Arnold, Matthew, 291
Asante, Molefi, 118–22, 326
Asia: literature of, 71–72
Assimilation, 126n
Austen, Jane, 202, 206
Austen, Ralph, 121–22
Authenticity, 71, 78, 108, 185–86, 224–25; in the academy, 107, 321; genetic, 221. *See also* Authority; Credibility; Expertise
Authority, 48, 107, 203; challenges to, 12, 157–62, 260; in the classroom, 63–64, 70–80, 96–97, 108, 112, 197–98, 209n, 210n, 216–26, 230–35; definition of, 51; disciplinary, 10; problematizing, 216; professor's, 3; resistance to, 224. *See also* Authenticity; Credibility; Expertise; Power

Baker, Houston A., Jr., 329
Bakhtin, Mikhail, 79, 290
Baldwin, James: *The Fire Next Time*, 333n
Bambara, Toni Cade, 336–38
Barbados, 200
Belafonte, Harry, 270
Bellarmine College, 41

Bell-Scott, Patricia, 25
Bensonhurst, 39
Benston, Kimberly W., 291–92
Berman, Paul: *Debating P.C.*, 242
Bernstein, Richard, 254; *Dictatorship of Virtue*, 242
Bérubé, Michael, 254
Bhabha, Homi, 73–74, 79, 343
Biology: class, 220
Bisexual, Gay and Lesbian Mountaineers (BIGLM), 52–60
Black: aesthetic, 121; lesbian literature, 265–75, 309
Black Nationalism, 326
Black Power movement, 322, 326
Black Student Association: at Iowa State University, 123–24
Black studies, 2, 15, 112–15, 119–22, 315, 320, 325–31; and African American students, 114; appointments in, 108; commitment to social justice, 120; legitimation of, 119–20; movement, 121, 128n. *See also* African American, studies
Black, Sunshine, 152
Blackness, 25–26, 34, 309–10, 353
Bloom, Harold, 201
Brandeis University, 184, 187
Brent, Linda: *Incidents in the Life of a Slave Girl*, 142. *See also* Jacobs, Harriet
Brewer, Rose M., 51
Brontë, Charlotte, 202, 206
Brown, Elsa Barkley, 28–29, 346
Brown, Ruth, 269
Browning, Robert, 204
Brown University, 184
Buffington, Nancy, 231
Burke, Edmund, 98
Busia, Abena P.A.: *Theorizing Black Feminisms*, 279–80. *See also* James, Stanlie M.
Busby, Margaret: *Daughters of Africa*, 279–80

Caliban, 215, 221–26
California, University of, 41n; Santa Barbara, 217
Canon, 28; expansion, 203; literary, 38, 200, 205, 212n; political theory, 98–100; revision of, 41n, 208–9n

Caribbean: colonial, 296; women in the, 280–81; women writers, 296
Carmichael, Stokely, 322
Carnegie Corporation, 321
Carpentier, Alejo: *The Kingdom of This World*, 296
Cather, Willa, 210n
Census Bureau, 110
Central Park jogger, 39
Cesaire, Aime: *A Tempest*, 223
Chicago, University of, 9
Chicano/a: sexuality, 57, 62
Childers, Mary, 31
Chinese Exclusion Acts, 198
Chopin, Kate, 41
Christian, Barbara, 339
Chronicle of Higher Education, 18–19
Chrystos, 152; "Ceremony for Completing a Poetry Reading," 152
Civil Rights movement, 1, 313
Civil War, 178, 189, 241
Clarke, John Henrik, 127n
Clifford, James, 71, 76–79
Coalition building, 48–51
Coleridge, Samuel Taylor, 207n
College of Saint Benedict, 86, 93
Collegium for African American Research, 323
Collins, Patricia Hill, 36, 345–46, 348–49; "The Social Construction of Black Feminist Thought," 81–82
Colonialism, 293; British, 302
Colonization, 73, 75, 312, 343
Color, 328
Columbia University, 243
Comer, James P., 190
Comer, Maggie: *Maggie's American Dream*, 190
Communication: discipline of, 163, 166–67, 171; person-centered, 171, 173n
Community: black, 324–25
Composition: courses in, 117, 217–20
Comrades in Arms, 60
Condit, Celeste, M., 11, 155–74, 357
Connors, Debra, 135–36
Conrad, Joseph, 207n; *Lord Jim*, 243
Conservatism, 16, 24, 39, 108, 111; course content, 160; cultural, 40; and education, 16; educational, 4; sexual, 56

"Contact zones," 294–95
Control: by male students, 157–62; through enrollment, 167
Cook, Timothy, 137
Credibility, 217, 290–93; challenges to, 17–18, 94; definition of, 18; identity-based, 3–7, 14, 18, 286–88, 305; instructor's, 156. *See also* Authenticity; Authority; Expertise
Creel, Margaret Washington, 337
Curriculum: development, 52; revisions of, 40, 249–50, 256n, 260
Curry, Renée, R., 15–16, 335–56, 357

Dante Alighieri, 207n
Dash, Julie: *Daughters of the Dust*, 15, 335–52; *The Making of the Daughters of the Dust*, 339, 343–44, 346, 348
Davis, Angela, 186
Davis, Barbara Hillyer, 63
Deadmon, Professor, 162
de Certeau, Michel: *The Practice of Everyday Life*, 286, 291
Delany, Martin, 256n
Derrida, Jacques, 197, 201
Dewey, John, 113
DiBernard, Barbara, 10, 131–54, 358
Dickens, Charles, 206, 242; *David Copperfield*, 202; *Oliver Twist*, 202
Dickinson, Emily, 41
Difference, 25, 73, 139; bridging, 28, 33–34, 82; celebrating, 39; cultural, 35, 71; gender, 101; negotiating, 59; racial, 39, 340; recognition of, 48; visible, 216. *See also* Multiculturalism
Dill, Bonnie Thornton, 49
Disability: identity through, 133–38; literature by women with, 11, 131–52; rights, 136, 138, 150; and standpoint epistemology, 138–39; women with, 131–52
Disability Rag, 138–39
Diversity, 25; student, 1. *See also* Multiculturalism
Doonesbury, 162
Doo-rag, 343–46
Douglass, Frederick, 184, 248–49, 256n; *Narrative of the Life of Frederick Douglass*, 254
Drive-by shootings, 120

Drugs, 120
D'Souza, Dinesh: *Illiberal Education*, 241–42
Du Bois, W. E. B., 320; *Philadelphia Negro*, 320–21n *Souls of Black Folk*, 184
duCille, Ann, 18
Dworkin, Andrea, 159–60

Egypt, 118–20, 122
Eisenstein, Hester, 135
Eliot, George, 206
Ellison, Ralph: *The Invisible Man*, 36
Ellsworth, Elizabeth, 50, 63
English: classes, 117, 195, 197–207, 219, 251; language, 217, 219, 300–302; language instruction, 296–303; *See also* Literature
Erdrich, Louise, 210n; *Love Medicine*, 198
Escoffier, Jeff, 43
ESL, 299, 302
Essentialism, 23, 57, 61–63, 110, 170, 228; challenges to, 11, 14, 17, 49, 122, 141, 260–63, 265, 277; debates about, 291
Esteves, Carmen, 296
Estrich, Susan: *Real Rape*, 86
Ethnography, 9, 71, 73, 75–80
Eurocentrism, 119, 124
Evans, Sara, 49
Expertise, 12, 17, 37; disciplinary, 114, 291; student, 37, 62–63. *See also* Authenticity; Authority; Credibility

Family, 92
Fanon, Franz: *Black Skin, White Masks*, 202
Far, Sui Sin, 210n
Farnham, Christie Pope, 10, 107–38, 358
Farrakhan, Louis, 128n.
Faulkner, William, 29, 38, 319; *As I Lay Dying*, 29
Federal Writers Project, 184, 185
Feminism, 14, 100; definition of, 89–90, 98; history of, 116; international, 196; men's relation to, 261–64; organizing, 49, 51; postcolonial, 197, 201; racism in, 278; white, 24–25, 29–31, 35, 314. *See also* Pedagogy, Women's studies
Feminist: black theory, 265–81; classroom, 47–48; pedagogy, 47, 63; political the

Feminist (*Continued*)
　ory, 85–103; standpoint epistemology,
　138–39; theory, 9
Fern, Fanny, 249
Fields, Karen: *Lemon Swamp and Other*
　Places, 184. *See also* Fields, Mamie
　Garvin
Fields, Mamie Garvin: *Lemon Swamp and*
　Other Places, 184. *See also* Fields, Karen
Filmer, Sir Robert, 98
Fine, Michelle, 134–36
Finger, Anne, 148–49; *Past Due: A Story of*
　Disability, Pregnancy and Birth, 142, 147
First world, 196
Flava', 310
Forrest Gump, 285–87, 289, 305
Forster, E.M., 202, 207n
Foucault, Michel, 125, 166, 201, 211; criti-
　cism of, 196, 208n
Freire, Paulo, 37, 211n, 230
Freud, Sigmund, 86, 197
Fuss, Diana, 207n, 209n

Gallagher, Tess, 145
Garcia, Mario T., 28
Garnet, Henry Highland: *Address to the*
　Slaves of the United States, 249
Garvey, Marcus, 108, 301, 337
Gates, Henry Louis, Jr., 128n, 195, 207n,
　323; "In the Kitchen," 344–45
Gays: and the military, 60
Gender: instructor's, 229–35; politics, 11;
　studies, 93; *See also* Identity; Lesbigay;
　Subject position
Georgia, University of, 157, 159, 163
GI Bill, 1, 325
Giddings, Paula, 36
Gilligan, Carol: *A Different Voice*, 86
Gilroy, Paul, 292–93, 294
Giroux, Henry, 36
Gomez, Jewelle: "A Cultural Legacy De-
　nied and Discovered: Black Lesbians in
　Fiction by Women," 266
Grades, 163
Graff, Gerald: *Beyond the Culture Wars*,
　332; *Professing Literature: An Institutional*
　History, 207n
Gramsci, Antonio, 168, 173n, 211n; *Selec-*
　tions from the Prison Notebooks, 195, 210n

Greece: classical, 119, 122
Gullah: language, 342–43, 346; people, 335
Guthrie, Tyrone, 9, 95
Gwin, Minrose, 339

Hammond, James Henry, 189
Handicap, 135, 151–52. *See also* Disability
Hansen, Kim, 151
Hardy, Thomas, 206; *Mayor of Cast-*
　erbridge, 202; *Tess of the D'Urbervilles*,
　202
Harper, Frances, 210n, 330
Hawkins, Yusef, 39
Heald, Susan, 230–31
Heath Anthology of American Literature, 249
Heath, Stephen: *Men in Feminism*, 262, 264
Heller, Craig, 13, 228–37, 358
Hemingway, Ernest, 41
Herrnstein, Richard: *The Bell Curve*, 180.
　See also Murray, Charles
Heterosexism, 33, 53
Heterosexuality; as norm, 53; teaching
　from a position of, 32–33, 58
Higginson, T. W., 249
Hilliard, Asa, 127n
Hine, Darlene Clark, 121
Historicism, 243
Historiography, 10, 123, 190
History: American, 118, 188–94; discipline
　of, 115–17, 181–84, 194; feminist, 116;
　method, 125; and postmodernism,
　126n. *See also* African American
Hobbes, Thomas, 97, 98
Holocaust, 115
Homophobia, 33, 275–77
hooks, bell, 7, 23–26, 31, 35, 36, 128n, 231,
　282–83, 333, 338, 344, 346; *Feminist The-*
　ory: From Margin to Center, 281–82;
　Teaching to Transgress, 23–25, 260–61
House of Representatives, 5
Howe, Irving, 212n
Huggins, Nathan, 114–15
Hughes, Langston, 29, 32
Hull, Gloria, 25
Hurston, Zora Neale: *Dust Tracks on a*
　Road, 195

Identity, 54, 97, 132–40; black, 328; black
　male, 275–79; in the classroom, 209n;

complexity of, 26–27, 49, 68n, 151, 180, 196–207; contested, 332; and credibility, 3–7, 15, 287–93; definition of, 2, 17, 133–34; female, 265; gender and sexual, 47, 53–57, 61–62, 68, 92, 101–2, 133; group, 252–53; postcolonial, 12; professor's, 3, 11, 23–40, 53–54, 58, 102–3, 207, 259–65, 275–79; racial, 12, 57, 68, 248, 253, 257n; as relational, 58; student, 24, 32–38, 54–57, 80, 112, 244–46, 260. *See also* Minority; Subject position
Identity politics, 2, 19, 107, 241, 244, 248, 251, 253, 259, 291, 326; challenges to, 27, 110, 132–34, 150, 206, 279, 282; in the classroom, 8, 276–77; complexity of, 196; debate about, 5, 24–25; and faculty credibility, 3–4; and pedagogy, 6, 7–9, 38, 141; and poststructuralism, 2–3; and separatism, 24; rise of, in higher education, 2–7
Imperialism: cultural, 202; discursive, 30. *See also* Appropriation
India, 202; civilization and literature of, 70–72; ethnicity, 219
Iowa State University, 107
Islam, Nation of, 123, 128n

Jackson, Jesse, 39
Jacobs, Harriet: *Incidents in the Life of a Slave Girl*, 184, 249. *See also* Brent, Linda
James, C. L. R.: *The Black Jacobins*, 292, 294
James, Stanlie M.: *Theorizing Black Feminisms*, 279–80; *See also* Busia, Abena P. A.
Jim Crow, 109, 178, 185, 320, 321, 329
Johnson, Charles S., 320
Johnson, Christy, 152
Johnson, J. Scott, 9, 85–101, 358
Jones, Jacqueline, 12, 36, 177–94, 358; *The Dispossessed*, 179, 187; *Labor of Love, Labor of Sorrow*, 177–80, 186
Journal: student writing, 143–44, 147–48, 150–52

Kaahumanu, Lani, 57
Kammen, Michael: *A Machine That Would Go of Itself*, 317
Kampf, Louis, 235
Karamcheti, Indira, 12–13, 215–27, 359

Karenga, Maulana, 127n
Karmazin, Michelle, 151
Keith, Minor C., 306
Kellen, Jennifer, 85–101, 359
Kendrick, Deborah: "For Tess Gallagher," 145–46
Kennedy, John F., 287, 317
Kimball, Roger, 254; *Tenured Radicals*, 242
Kincaid, Jamaica: *Annie John*, 296; *Green Cane and Juicy Flotsam*, 296
King, Martin Luther, Jr., 76, 186
King, Rodney, 188
Kingston, Maxine Hong, 210n; *China Men*, 198; "No Name Woman," 142; *Woman Warrior*, 198
Korea, 319
Kramer, Hilton, 39
Kristeva, Julia: *Strangers to Ourselves*, 195
Kumin, Maxine: "Making the Jam without You," 142

Lacan, Jacques, 201, 210n
Lamb, Charles, 202
Lamming, George: *In the Castle of My Skin*, 296, 298, 302
Lanser, Mary Elizabeth, 15, 315–34, 359
Larkin, Alile Sharon, 338
Larsen, Nella, 210n
Lather, Patti, 62
Lauter, Paul, 249
Ledyard, John, 252
Lee, Spike, 38
LeMaistre, JoAnn, 142
Lemons, Gary L., 14, 259–84, 359
Lesbianism: black, 266–74; class discussions of, 32–33
Lesbigay: literature, 7–8, 32–33; scholarship, 43; studies, 48, 52–64; transsexuality, 66. *See also* Gays; Lesbianism; Queer
LeSueur, Meridel: "Annunciation," 142
Levine, Judith, 340
Levine, Robert S., 13, 17, 241–58, 360
Lewis, Jerry, 149: telethon, 148
Lewis, Magda Gere, 231–32
Limon, Costa Rica, 294–306
"Linguistic turn," 125
Literature: classroom, 224; evaluation of, 140–41; study of, 222; teaching, 260. *See also* American; African American; Asia;

Literature (*Continued*)
  English; Multicultural; Native American; Women's studies
Locke, Alain, 320
Locke, John, 98
Lorde, Audre, 25, 259, 265–75; "The Master's Tools Will Never Dismantle the Master's House," 81–82; "Now That I Am Forever with Child," 142; *Sister Outsider: Essays and Speeches by Audre Lorde*, 265–66; "Tar Beach," 14, 267–75; "Uses of the Erotic: The Erotic as Power," 266–68, 272–73
Lugones, Maria, 80–82
Lusted, David, 62
Lymon, Frankie, 270

MacKinnon, Catharine, 96
Mair, Nancy: "Shape," 146
Malcolm X, 111
Marshall, Paule, 210n; *Brown Girl, Brownstones*, 200
Martin, Tony, 128n
Marx, Karl, 197
Marxism, 121
Maryland, University of, 13, 245–50
Matthews, Gwyneth Ferguson, 142
Matthiessen, F. O., 243
Maugham, Somerset, 206
Mayberry, Katherine, 1–19, 41n, 360
McBride, David, 331
McDowell, Deborah E., 335, 339
Meier, August: *Black History and the Historical Profession 1915–1980*, 321
Meiggs, Henry, 306
Melanin, 119
Melville, Herman: "Benito Cereno," 13, 241–56; *Moby Dick*, 242; *Typee*, 253
Mena, Maria Christina, 210n
Men's studies, 101
"Meredith march," 322
Mexican: sexuality, 57, 62
Michigan State University, 321
Michigan, University of, 53
Michigan Womyn's Music Festival, 131
Military: gays in, 58, 59–60
Minh-Ha, Trinh T., 72–73, 75, 82, 197
Minority: teacher, 216–26, 226n. *See also* African American; Black; Disability;

Gays; Identity; Lesbigay; Native American; Women's studies
Mirikitani, Janice, 210n
Miscegenation, 109–10
Mohanty, Chandra, 35
Mohanty, Satya, 293
Moody, Anne: *Coming of Age in Mississippi*, 184
Morrison, Toni, 8, 41n, 210n, 294, 309, 311, 339; *Beloved*, 35, 38, 177, 198, 310, 312; *The Bluest Eye*, 36, 73; *Playing in the Dark*, 26, 292; *Song of Solomon*, 35; *Sula*, 35, 38; teaching, 34–38
Mostern, Kenneth, 37
Muhammad, Khalid, 128n
Mukherjee, Bharati, *Wife*, 73
Multicultural: body, 225; education, 9, 201; issues, 250; literature, 80, 199, 206, 228–29; pedagogy, 7; revolution, 4; teacher, 207; theory, 80
Multiculturalism 6, 16, 38–40, 42n, 212n, 241–55, 293; American, 203; criticism of, 40; debates on, 244; impact of, 42; support of, 39–40. *See also* Difference, Diversity
Multilingualism, 202
Murray, Charles: *The Bell Curve*, 180, 333n. *See also* Herrnstein, Richard
Muslim, 123

NAACP, 337
Naipaul, V. S.: *The Enigma of Arrival*, 294–95
National Council of Black Studies, 121, 331
National Endowment for the Arts, 5
National Endowment for the Humanities, 5
National Gay and Lesbian Task Force, 59
Native American: gender roles in, 55; literature, 28, 29, 110, 210n; and sexuality, 57, 78
Naylor, Gloria: *Bailey's Cafe*, 78
Nazi Germany, 312
Nelson, Cary, 254
New Criterion, 39
New Criticism, 243
New Negro movement, 337
Ng, Faye Myenne: *Bone*, 79

N'gugi wa Thiong'o: *Decolonising the Mind*, 211
Nietzsche, Friedrich, 197
Nile valley, 119, 121
Nobles, Wade, 127n
Nommo, 310, 313
North American Free Trade Agreement (NAFTA), 297, 301, 303–4

Ohmann, Dick, 235
Oklahoma project, 337
Olmsted, Frederick Law, 189, 190
Olsen, Tillie, 141; *Silences*, 140
"One drop rule," 109–10
Orner, Mimi, 50–51, 63
Ortiz, Fernando, 294
Osterud, Nancy Grey, 64
Other, 2, 70–82. *See also* Difference

Palo Alto, 244–45
Pan-Africanism, 326
Panopticon, 166, 172n
Panzarino, Connie, 139, 151, 152; *The Me in the Mirror*, 142–43, 151
Paravisini-Gebert, Lizabeth, 296
Park, Mungo, 256n; *Travels in the Interior Districts of Africa*, 252
Pascoe, Peggy, 42
Pataki, George, 5
Patriarchy, 96, 235, 259–64, 311, 341
Pedagogy, 62; active audience, 166–67; active learning, 113–14; audience of one, 95–97; "border-crossing," 282–83; building bridges, 28–34; cooperative, 97; critical, 65n; discussion method, 113–14; feminist, 47–51, 63, 95–96, 210n, 228–36; Foucauldian, 166; free writing, 144–45; group work, 232; and identity politics, 7–9; information processing, 167–68, 171; interpretation, 77–78; lecture method, 113–14, 247; liberatory, 259; participant observation, 76–79; performance of race, 225–26; performance/reading, 146; polyphonic mode, 79–80; progressive, 7, 11; round-robins, 142–43, 147–48; shifting subjectivities, 34; silence, 233–35; and student particularities, 163–65; teaching as an ally, 48–65; transforming, 35–40. *See also* Teaching

Penley, Constance, 210n
Peterson, Carla, 257n
Peterson, Nancy J., 8, 23–46, 360
Pigmentation, 109
Plato, 86, 97, 98
Platt, Mary Frances, 139
Political correctness, 5, 38–39, 73, 251; language, 143, 145; and teaching, 198
Pope, Christie, 10, 107. *See also* Farnham, Christie Pope
Pornography, 55, 58, 272–73; class presentation on, 59
Positionality, 13–14, 32, 343–46
Positive Images: Portraits of Women with Disabilities, 136, 141
Postcolonial: condition, 293; faculty, 205, 223; identity, 12, 206; literature, 220–21; theory, 73
Postmodernism, 125; and history, 115, 126n; theory, 291. *See also* Poststructuralism
Poststructuralism, 2–3, 210n, 224. *See also* Postmodernism
Poverty, 179–80, 200–201; feminization of, 120
Power: cultural, 244, 247; teacher's, 231–36. *See also* Authority
Powers, Janet M., 8, 70–84, 360
Pratt, Mary Louise: *Imperial Eyes*, 294
Prejudice, 217–18; in class, 67n
Presentism, 116
Progressive: teaching, 166–69, 171–72
Prospero, 215, 221–25
Purcell, Trevor, 299–300

Queer, 56; as term, 66n, 67n

Race: concept of, 209n
Racism, 112, 119, 122, 126n, 186, 199; classroom discussions of, 12, 25, 34, 39; history of, 278; impact of, 292; opposing, 35, 246, 322; "scientific," 256n; sentimental, 187
Rainbow coalition, 39
Rape, 92
Raphael-Leff, Joan: *The Psychological Processes of Childbearing*, 349–50
Reader response theory, 79, 247
Reagon, Bernice Johnson, 49

Reconstructing American Literature, 249
Renan, Ernest, 289
Representation, 76, 226; politics of, 36–37
Reproduction: rights, 55
Resistance, 225; narrative of, 221–22
Rich, Adrienne, 29, 32, 132–33; "Compul-
     sory Heterosexuality and Lesbian Exis-
     tence," 33, 86
Ricks, Willie, 322
Rome: classical, 119, 122
Rosenfelt, Deborah, 248, 250, 255n
Rousseau, Jean Jacques, 86, 97, 98
Russ, Joanna: *How to Suppress Women's
     Writing,* 140
Rutgers University, 295, 298–99

Sa, Zitkala, 29, 210n
Said, Edward, 195, 208n, 211n
Saint John's University, 86, 93
Sandoval, Chela, 34
San Francisco State University, 2, 120, 326
Sarton, May: *Journal of a Solitude,* 140
Scanlon, Larry, 291
Scapp, Ron, 31
Schilb, John, 49, 231
Schlesinger, Arthur M., Jr., 44
Schreiner, Kelly, 152
Scott, Joan W., 40, 114
Sea Islands, 336–38
Secret Relationship between Blacks and Jews,
     123
Sedgwick, Catharine, 249
Sedgwick, Eve Kosofsky, 43n
Segregation, 113
Seibert, Greg, 85–101, 361
Separatism, 24; ethnic, 40; racial, 26
Sewall, Samuel: "The Selling of Joseph,"
     189
Sexism, 39, 63, 112, 230
Sexuality: history of, 53–55
Shakespeare, William, 206; *As You Like It,*
     202; *Hamlet,* 202; *Macbeth,* 202; *The Mer-
     chant of Venice,* 202; *A Midsummer
     Night's Dream,* 202; *The Tempest,* 221–23,
     296
Shankar, Lavina Dhingra, 12–13, 195–214,
     361
Shankar, Rajiv, 211n
Shapiro, Joseph, 133–34; *No Pity,* 137

Shaughnessy, Celia, 85–101, 361
Shelley, Percy Bysshe, 204
Sherlock, P.: *West Indian Folktales,* 296
Shrewsbury, Caroline, 47
Silko, Leslie Marmon, 41, 210n; *Storyteller,*
     78
Silverman, Kaja, 350
Simpson, O. J., 36, 188
Slave narratives, 184, 185
Slavery, 107, 109–11, 115, 127, 190, 230,
     243, 292, 311–14; and the Gullah people,
     337–38; history of, 245; representation
     of, 248; resistance to, 249
Slotkin, Richard, 199
Smith, Barbara, 25, 339; *Homegirls: A Black
     Feminist Anthology,* 265–66, 275, 279
Social construction, 61–63, 110, 135–37,
     140, 150; and race, 110
South, 185, 189
Spanish: classes, 219
Spivak, Gayatri, 31, 43n, 195–206, 207n,
     211; "Draupadi," 208n; and identity pol-
     itics, 199, 205; *In Other Worlds,* 196
Standpoint theory, 125
Stanfield, John: *Philanthropy and Jim Crow
     in American Social Science,* 321
Stanford University, 93, 244–45
Staples, Brent: *Parallel Time,* 329
Staples, Robert, 127n
Stendhal, 242
Stereotype, 74, 79 81, 150, 230, 232; racial,
     108–9
Stewart, Maria, 326–28
Stowe, Harriet Beecher, 256n; *Uncle Tom's
     Cabin,* 250, 254
Student: as audience, 163; black graduate,
     182; conservative, 28; female graduate,
     160–61; first-year, 188–94; goals, 163–65.
     See also Identity
Subaltern, 31, 199
Subject position, 230–36
Suffrage: universal, 330
Sycorax, 221

Teaching: and critical common sense,
     169–72; definition of good, 161; evalua-
     tions, 159–61, 167; feminist, 159–61; im-
     proving, 122, 126n; and theory, 155–57
     165–71; what you are not, 7–9, 14–15,

31, 124–25, 132–33, 150, 165, 180, 195–96, 192–93, 204–5, 261, 315. *See also* Pedagogy
Teaching What You're Not, 133
Tempest, A, 223. *See also* Cesaire, Aime
Theology: black and white, 322–23
Third world, 43, 111; identity, 196, 201
Tolstoy, Leo, 242
Tompkins, Jane, 196, 208n, 249
Trail of Tears, 198
Transsexuality, 66n
Truth, Sojourner, 330
Turner, Nat, 108, 249
Twain, Mark, 38

"Unhandicapping Our Language," 146
United Fruit Company, 300–1, 306
Universal Negro Improvement Association, 301

Viewers: black women, 338, 344; white women, 16, 337–39, 343–44, 346, 352–53
Voices from the Shadows: Women with Disabilities Speak Out, 141

Walker, Alice, 25; *The Color Purple*, 184, 269; "Everyday Use," 142; "In Search of Our Mothers' Gardens," 140
Walker, Clarence, 128n
Walker, David: *Appeal to the Colored Citizens of the World*, 249
Walker, Madame C. J., 345
Wallace, George, 287
Wallace, Michele, 39–40
Wall Street Journal, 242
Walther, Malin LaVon, 41n
Washington, Booker T.: *Up from Slavery*, 184–85
Watson, Donna J., 15, 308–14, 361
Wellesley College, 177, 179, 184

West, Cornel, 31, 36, 38, 43, 128n; *Race Matters*, 191
West Virginia, University of, 48, 51; Council on Sexual Orientation, 66; Provost's Multicultural Committee, 68; student population at, 57
Wharton, Edith, 210n
Whiteness, 16, 25–26, 35, 132, 254, 289, 340–42, 353
Williams, Tennessee, 319
Wilson, Harriet: *Our Nig*, 249
Winbush, Ray, 331
Winkler, Barbara Scott, 8, 47–69, 361
With the Power of Each Breath: A Disabled Women's Anthology, 131, 134, 140–41
With Wings: An Anthology of Literature by and about Women with Disabilities, 141
Witvilet, *The Way of the Black Messiah*, 322
Wolf, Naomi, 86
Wollstonecraft, Mary, 98
Women's movement, 25, 63, 99. *See also* Feminism
Women's studies, 13, 18, 48, 71, 72, 101; classrooms, 63, 112, 228–36; commitment to social justice, 120; faculty, 85–86; literature, 10, 133; minor, 93; teaching, 32, 47, 49, 80, 228. *See also* Feminism
Woodson, Carter, 320
Woodward, C. Vann, 44
Woolf, Virginia, 141, 207n; *Life As We Have Known It, Memoirs of the Working Women's Guild*, 140; *A Room of One's Own*, 140
Wordsworth, William, 204, 206, 207n
Workers: American, 188–94

Yamamoto, Hisaye, 210n
Yeats, William Butler, 207n